Sport in the Iberian Peninsula

This is the first book in English to offer an overview of the development of the sport industry in Spain and Portugal, examining the social, economic, cultural, and political impact sport has had in this region and on world sport more broadly.

Drawing on sources in Spanish and Portuguese, the book presents important new perspectives and empirical material not previously available to English-speaking audiences. With a strong focus on management, development, economics, governance, and law, set in a broader historical and socio-cultural context, the book explains the unique characteristics of the sport industry in the Iberian Peninsula. It takes a deep dive into Spanish and Portuguese football—in many ways the centre of gravity of Iberian sport—and into sport tourism, a hugely significant component of the broader economy of the region. The book also considers important emerging themes in Iberian sport, from the development of women's sport to the global profile of Cristiano Ronaldo and Rafael Nadal, and considers the wider influence of Iberian sport across the wider Hispanic diaspora.

This is fascinating and illuminating reading for anybody with an interest in sport business and management, global sporting cultures, international business, or Hispanic or Latin American studies.

Jerónimo García-Fernández is an associate professor of sports science in the department of physical education and sport at the Universidad de Sevilla, Spain. His research focuses on the management of fitness centres, customer loyalty, consumer perception, digital transformation, customer satisfaction, and analysis of professional profiles linked to the sport and fitness sector. In 2016, he was President of the Ibero-American Congress on Sports Economics that took place in Spain, and in 2020 and 2021 was President of the International Conference on Technology in Physical Activity and Sport. He is the CRDO (Chief Research and Development Officer) of Fitbe Spin-off, a university startup focused on consumer management in fitness centres.

Moisés Grimaldi-Puyana is an associate professor of sports science in the department of physical education and sport at the Universidad de Sevilla, Spain. His research examines the management of sport organisations, and particularly the perceived satisfaction and customer loyalty of clients in sport organisations.

Moreover, he has studied the management and recreation of sport organisations, and conducted professional profiles linked to the sports sector. He has led multiple projects related to sport with agencies in both the public and private sectors. Many of these projects have focused on the transfer of researcher findings to the needs of these sports organisations.

Gonzalo A. Bravo is a professor of sport management in the College of Applied Human Sciences at West Virginia University, USA. He teaches undergraduate and graduate courses in sport governance, international sport, research methods, and the socio-cultural and ethical dimensions of sport. His research examines issues on organisational behaviour and the policy and governance of sport. He has given more than 100 presentations in sport management and sport sociology at conferences hosted all over the world, and been invited to give keynote addresses in universities in Brazil, Canada, Chile, China, Macao, Japan, Korea, Mexico, the United States, Spain, Venezuela, and Zimbabwe.

Routledge Research in Sport Business and Management

Embedded Multi-Level Leadership in Elite Sport
Edited by Svein S. Andersen, Per Øystein Hansen and Barrie Houlihan

Good Governance in Sport
Critical Reflections
Edited by Arnout Geeraert and Frank van Eekeren

Stakeholder Analysis and Sport Organisations
Edited by Anna-Maria Strittmatter, Josef Fahlén and Barrie Houlihan

Sport and Brexit
Regulatory Challenges and Legacies
Edited by Jacob Kornbeck

Sport Management Education
Global Perspectives and Implications for Practice
Edited by Mike Rayner and Tom Webb

Digital Business Models in Sport
Edited by Mateusz Tomanek, Wojciech Cieśliński and Michał Polasik

Sport Management, Innovation and the COVID-19 Crisis
Edited by Gözde Ersöz and Meltem Ince Yenilmez

Sport in the Iberian Peninsula
Management, Economics and Policy
Edited by Jerónimo García-Fernández, Moisés Grimaldi-Puyana and Gonzalo A. Bravo

For more information about this series, please visit www.routledge.com/Routledge-Research-in-Sport-Business-and-Management/book-series/RRSBM

Sport in the Iberian Peninsula

Management, Economics and Policy

Edited by Jerónimo García-Fernández, Moisés Grimaldi-Puyana and Gonzalo A. Bravo

LONDON AND NEW YORK

First published 2023
by Routledge
4 Park Square, Milton Park, Abingdon, Oxon OX14 4RN

and by Routledge
605 Third Avenue, New York, NY 10158

Routledge is an imprint of the Taylor & Francis Group, an informa business

© 2023 selection and editorial matter, Jerónimo García-Fernández, Moisés Grimaldi-Puyana and Gonzalo A. Bravo; individual chapters, the contributors

The right of Jerónimo García-Fernández, Moisés Grimaldi-Puyana and Gonzalo A. Bravo to be identified as the authors of the editorial material, and of the authors for their individual chapters, has been asserted in accordance with sections 77 and 78 of the Copyright, Designs and Patents Act 1988.

All rights reserved. No part of this book may be reprinted or reproduced or utilised in any form or by any electronic, mechanical, or other means, now known or hereafter invented, including photocopying and recording, or in any information storage or retrieval system, without permission in writing from the publishers.

Trademark notice: Product or corporate names may be trademarks or registered trademarks, and are used only for identification and explanation without intent to infringe.

British Library Cataloguing-in-Publication Data
A catalogue record for this book is available from the British Library

Library of Congress Cataloging-in-Publication Data
Names: García-Fernández, Jerónimo, editor. | Grimaldi-Puyana, Moisés, editor. | Bravo, Gonzalo A., 1959– editor.
Title: Sport in the Iberian peninsula : management, economics and policy / edited by Jerónimo García-Fernández, Moisés Grimaldi-Puyana and Gonzalo A. Bravo.
Description: Abingdon, Oxon ; New York, NY : Routledge, 2023. | Series: Routledge research in sport business and management | Includes bibliographical references and index.
Summary: "This is the first book in English to offer an overview of the development of the sport industry in Spain and Portugal, examining the social, economic, cultural, and political impact sport has had in this region and on world sport more broadly. Drawing on sources in Spanish and Portuguese, the book presents important new perspectives and empirical material not previously available to English-speaking audiences. With a strong focus on management, development, economics, governance and law, set in a broader historical and socio-cultural context, the book explains the unique characteristics of the sport industry in the Iberian Peninsula. It takes a deep dive into Spanish and Portuguese football – in many ways the centre of gravity of Iberian sport – and into sport tourism, a hugely significant component of the broader economy of the region. The book also considers important emerging themes in Iberian sport, from the development of women's sport to the global profile of Cristiano Ronaldo and Rafael Nadal, and considers the wider influence of Iberian sport across the wider Hispanic diaspora. This is fascinating and illuminating reading for anybody with an interest in sport business and management, global sporting cultures, international business, or Hispanic or Latin American studies"— Provided by publisher.
Identifiers: LCCN 2022025248 | ISBN 9781032018904 (hardback) | ISBN 9781032053158 (paperback) | ISBN 9781003197003 (ebook)
Subjects: LCSH: Sports administration—Spain. | Sports administration—Portugal. | Sports—Economic aspects—Spain. | Sports—Economic aspects—Portugal.
Classification: LCC GV713 .S67723 2023 | DDC 796.06/9—dc23/eng/20220630
LC record available at https://lccn.loc.gov/2022025248

ISBN: 978-1-032-01890-4 (hbk)
ISBN: 978-1-032-05315-8 (pbk)
ISBN: 978-1-003-19700-3 (ebk)

DOI: 10.4324/9781003197003

Typeset in Goudy
by Apex CoVantage, LLC

Contents

List of Contributors	x
Preface	xvii
Acknowledgements	xxiii

1 Sport in the Iberian Peninsula: an introduction   1
JERÓNIMO GARCÍA-FERNÁNDEZ, MOISÉS GRIMALDI-PUYANA,
AND GONZALO A. BRAVO

2 Socio-cultural and historical background of sport in Spain
and Portugal   14
DAVID MOSCOSO-SÁNCHEZ, FRANCISCO PINHEIRO,
AND XAVIER PUJADAS

3 The European Union and sport: economy, public policy and
legislation   24
PILAR APARICIO-CHUECA, AMAL ELASRI-EJJABERI, XAVIER
TRIADÓ-IVERN, AND MARC BLANCH CASADESÚS

4 The sport systems in Spain and Portugal   34
MARIA JOSÉ CARVALHO, MARÍA JOSEFA GARCÍA-CIRAC,
AND MARISA SOUSA

5 The legal framework of the sports industry in Spain and Portugal   46
VICENTE JAVALOYES SANCHIS AND RICARDO FERNANDES CARDOSO

6 Public policies and sport participation in Spain and Portugal   56
FERNANDO LERA-LÓPEZ, ANTONIO G. GÓMEZ-PLANA,
AND ANTÓNIO DE ARAÚJO BARROS MAIA

7	From buildings and equipment to 'spaces' for sports in Spain JUAN MANUEL MURUA	70
8	Sports gambling in Spain PLÁCIDO RODRÍGUEZ AND LEVI PÉREZ	85
9	The Iberian fitness industry: experiences from Portugal and Spain PABLO GÁLVEZ-RUIZ, JERÓNIMO GARCÍA-FERNÁNDEZ, CELINA GONÇALVES, AND VIRGINIA ALCARAZ-RODRÍGUEZ	98
10	Economic and social effects of sporting events and organisations in Spain and the Iberian Peninsula FERRAN CALABUIG MORENO, DAVID PARRA-CAMACHO, AND JOSEP CRESPO-HERVÁS	109
11	Sports entrepreneurship and intrapreneurship in the Iberian Peninsula: a bibliometric analysis ALEJANDRO LARA-BOCANEGRA, PALOMA ESCAMILLA-FAJARDO, MARÍA HUERTAS GONZÁLEZ-SERRANO, MARÍA DEL ROCÍO BOHÓRQUEZ, AND MOISÉS GRIMALDI-PUYANA	123
12	The Spanish football league and the foreign players GABRIEL CHAVES, JAUME GARCÍA, DANIEL ORTÍN, AND FEDERICO TODESCHINI	140
13	The Portuguese football league 'Liga Portugal' THIAGO SANTOS, PEDRO FATELA, LUÍS VILAR, AND BERNARDO GONÇALVES	154
14	La Roja, Real Madrid, and Barça: a Historic Perspective CARLES MURILLO FORT AND FRANCISCO PUIG	164
15	Spanish women's leagues and the push towards professionalisation JOSÉ MANUEL SÁNCHEZ-SANTOS AND MARY ELENA SÁNCHEZ-GABARRE	177
16	La Vuelta: impact on Local Communities JOSÉ MIGUEL VEGARA-FERRI, JOSÉ MARÍA LÓPEZ-GULLÓN, ARTURO DÍAZ-SUÁREZ, AND SALVADOR ANGOSTO	188

17	Traditional games and sports of the Iberian Peninsula as tourist attractions GONZALO RAMÍREZ-MACÍAS, AUGUSTO REMBRANDT RODRÍGUEZ-SÁNCHEZ, AND Mª JOSÉ LASAGA-RODRÍGUEZ	199
18	Nautical sports in Spain ISRAEL CARABALLO VIDAL AND JOSÉ V. GUTIERREZ-MANZANEDO	209
19	Global brands from the Iberian Peninsula: Nadal, Gasol, Cristiano, and Mourinho LEONOR GALLARDO AND JORGE GARCÍA-UNANUE	222
20	Sport governance in Portugal LUIZ HAAS AND TIAGO RIBEIRO	232
21	Evaluating the performance of Spanish sport federations: a multiple goal approach PATRICIO SÁNCHEZ-FERNÁNDEZ, LUIS CARLOS SÁNCHEZ, AND ANGEL BARAJAS	245
	Index	257

Contributors

Virginia Alcaraz-Rodríguez is a faculty member in the Department of Human Motor Skills and Sport Performance at the University of Seville, Spain, where she teaches courses in the Sport and Exercise Sciences program. She is a member of the research group Management and Innovation in Sports Services, Leisure, Recreation, and Social Action at the same university. Her research focuses on inclusivity in physical activity, sport and fitness organisations, event management, and the social influence of sport.

Salvador Angosto is a researcher affiliated with the University of Murcia, Spain. His main research lines focus on sport events, sport volunteering, and sport technologies. He has experience in sport event and volunteering management.

Pilar Aparicio-Chueca is Associate Professor in the Department of Business at the University of Barcelona, Spain. She is also the director of the master's degree in sport business management at the University of Barcelona, Spain. Her research focuses on health economy, sport management and innovation, and education research.

Angel Barajas is Professor and Head of the Department of Finance at the Saint Petersburg School of Economics of Management (NRU Higher School of Economics), in Russia. He is also the academic supervisor of the ID Lab at the same institution. He is a researcher for the Spanish Economic Observatory of Sport program in Sport at the University of Vigo, Spain. His research interests include investment valuation, intellectual capital, and finance of sports.

Israel Caraballo Vidal is Professor in the Physical Activity and Sport Sciences program at the University of Cádiz, Spain.

Ricardo Fernandes Cardoso graduated from Lusíada University of Oporto, Portugal, has a postgraduate degree in corporate law from the School of Law of the University de Coimbra, a master's in international sports law from the University of Lleida, Spain, is a doctoral student in law at the University of Lleida, and is a lawyer.

Maria José Carvalho is Professor at the Faculty of Sport at the University of Porto, Portugal. She holds several positions in academic and professional sport organisations, including member of the Centre of Research, Education, Innovation, and Intervention in Sport, and vice president of the disciplinary board of the Portuguese Football Association. Her research focuses on sport management, sport law, sport public policies, and gender and sport.

Marc Blanch Casadesús is a predoctoral researcher in the business department at the University of Barcelona, Spain. His research areas include sport business, management, and policy.

Gabriel Chaves holds a master's degree in economics from the Barcelona Graduate School of Economics and Universitat Pompeu Fabra, Spain. He is a doctoral student at the Queen Mary University of London, UK. His research interest is in labour economics and applied microeconomics with a focus on unemployment, immigration, and public policy.

Josep Crespo-Hervás is an associate professor at the University of Valencia, Spain. He has led the planning and organisation of different international sporting events in the Valencian Hockey Federation. His research focuses on sport consumers' behaviour and sporting events.

António de Araújo Barros Maia holds a bachelor's degree in sport science from the University of Beira Interior-Covilhã, Portugal. He is currently pursuing a master's degree in high-performance sport coaching at the School of Human Kinetics at the University of Lisbon, Portugal.

Arturo Díaz-Suárez is Professor in Sport Management at the University of Murcia, Spain. Currently, he leads several funded research projects that focus on sport, physical activity, and health promotion.

Amal Elasri-Ejjaberi is Professor of Business at the Universitat Oberta de Catalunya (UOC), Spain. She teaches strategy and change management courses in the Faculty of Economics and Business. Her research interest is in sport management, customer satisfaction, and e-learning.

Paloma Escamilla-Fajardo is a member of the Sport Management & Innovation Research Group of the University of Valencia, Spain. Her research examines the role of entrepreneurship and its influence on sport economics. She also studies the social impact of sport organisations.

Pedro Fatela is Professor in the Sport Sciences program in the Faculty of Human Kinetics at Universidade de Lisboa, Portugal. His research focuses on strength training, fatigue, and neuromuscular functions in exercise. He is a certified football coach and a sport commentator for the *Sociedade Independente de Comunicação* in Portugal.

Leonor Gallardo is Professor at the University of Castilla-La Mancha (UCLM) in Spain. She is also the Director of IGOID (Research in the Management of Sport Organisations and Facilities) and IGOID-SPORTEC, a spin-off of the University of Castilla-La Mancha.

Pablo Gálvez-Ruiz is an associate professor and researcher at the Valencian International University, Spain. He is also the Club Manager of BeOne Fitness & Sport. His research interest is in sport management and sport marketing, specifically the examination of the business models and the organisational culture and engagement of fitness centres.

Jaume García is Professor of Applied Economics in the Department of Economics and Business at Universitat Pompeu Fabra, Spain. He was previously President of the Spanish Statistics Office and member of the European Statistical Governance Advisory Board. His research interests are in microeconometrics, labour economics, health economics, housing economics, and sports economics.

María Josefa García-Cirac is Professor in the Law School at the University of Salamanca, Spain. In the past, she was Minister of Culture and Tourism of Castilla and León and President of the Legislative Assembly of Castilla y León. Her research focuses on administrative law, sports law, human rights, and the environment.

Jorge García-Unanue is an associate professor at the University of Castilla-La Mancha (UCLM), Spain. His research focuses on sport management, facilities, policies and digitalisation. He is a member of IGOID Research Group and founder of IGOID-SPORTEC, a spin-off at the UCLM.

Antonio G. Gómez-Plana is an associate professor in the Department of Economics at the Public University of Navarra, Spain, and Senior Researcher at the Institute for Advanced Research in Business and Economics. His research focuses on the evaluation of public policies at national and international levels.

Bernardo Gonçalves is Coordinator at Casa Pia Atlético Clube. His research interest is in the management of football. He has been involved in different managerial capacities with Sporting Clube de Portugal and the Skating Federation of Portugal.

Celina Gonçalves is Professor and Sport Management Coordinator at Maia University, Portugal. She is also member of the Research Centre in Sport Sciences, Health, and Human Development (CIDESD).

María Huertas González-Serrano is an associate professor at the University of Valencia, Spain. Her main research lines are sports entrepreneurship and intrapreneurship. She has published on sports entrepreneurship, intrapreneurship, sustainable entrepreneurship, lifestyle entrepreneurship and entrepreneurial ecosystems in scientific journals.

José V. Gutierrez-Manzanedo is an associate professor in the sport sciences program at the University of Cádiz, Spain. His research focuses on physical activity, health, and performance in nautical sports.

Luiz Haas is a doctoral student in sport management and a lecturer in the Faculty of Human Motricity at the University of Lisbon, Portugal. He was the former president of the Brazilian Association for Sport Management. His research focuses on the management and governance of sport organisations.

Alejandro Lara-Bocanegra is an instructor in the Department of Physical Education and Sport at the University of Seville, Spain. He teaches undergraduate courses in sport and exercise sciences. He has worked for more than 15 years with athletes in training and high-performance sports. His line of research is in sport entrepreneurship and intrapreneurship.

María José Lasaga-Rodríguez is an associate professor in the Department of Physical Education and Sport at the University of Seville, Spain. Her research interests are physical education, early childhood education and outdoor education.

Fernando Lera-López is a professor in the Department of Economics at the Public University of Navarra, Spain. His research focuses on sport participation and the economic, social, and health impact of sport and physical activity.

José María López-Gullón is Sport Manager and Researcher at the University of Murcia, Spain. He has more than 20 years of professional and academic experience in sport management, sport sciences, and sport performance.

Ferran Calabuig Moreno is an associate professor at the University of Valencia, Spain. His research focuses on sport consumer behaviour, sport marketing, sport entrepreneurship, and the social impact of sport. He regularly publishes in the area of sport management, marketing, and entrepreneurship in prestigious international journals.

David Moscoso-Sánchez is an assistant professor at the University of Cordova, Spain. He is the former President of the Sports Sociology Research Committee of the Spanish Federation of Sociology and the Scientific Director of the International Sociological Sport Observatory (ISSO) in Barcelona. He is also the editor of *Sociologia del Deporte*.

Carles Murillo Fort is Emeritus Professor of Applied Economics at the Universitat Pompeu Fabra (UPF) in Barcelona, Spain. He is a Distinguished Professor and Director of the master's degree in Sport Management at the UPF Barcelona School of Management, President of the Spanish Society of Sports Economics, and member of the Board of the Sport Industry in Catalonia.

Juan Manuel Murua is an economist and independent consultant in city management who specialises in policies for the promotion of physical activity and health. In working as a consultant, he has managed and supported the design and initiation of different projects related to sport and city management, sustainable and healthy cities, and local development plans supported by sport.

Daniel Ortín holds degrees in economics and journalism from Universitat Pompeu Fabra, Spain. In the past, he interned at *Mundo Deportivo*, a sport newspaper in Barcelona, where he was a web reporter covering FC Barcelona news. His research interest is on applied microeconomics and the sport economics of football.

David Parra-Camacho is Assistant Professor at the University of Valencia, Spain. His line of research focuses on the social and economic impact of sport events.

Levi Pérez is an associate professor of economics in the Department of Economics at the University of Oviedo, Spain.

Francisco Pinheiro is a researcher at the University of Coimbra, Portugal. He is also the coordinator of the Portuguese Group for History and Sport.

Francisco Puig is Professor of Business Strategy at the University of Valencia, Spain and Coordinator of the research group GESTOR (Organisational Geostrategy: Clusters and Competitiveness). His research focuses on the intersection between location-strategy-performance.

Xavier Pujadas is Senior Lecturer in Sport History at the Department of Physical Activity and Sports Sciences at the Universitat Ramon Llull, Barcelona, Spain. He is also the Director of the Research & Innovation Group on Sport and Society and Coordinator of the Research Network on Women's History and Sport in Spain.

Gonzalo Ramírez-Macías is an associate professor and research fellow of physical education and sport history in the Department of Physical Education and Sport at the University of Seville, Spain. His research interests are in the history of contemporary physical education.

Plácido Rodríguez is a professor in the Department of Economics at the University of Oviedo, Spain. He is the current director of *Fundación Observatorio Económico del Deporte* and the former president of the International Sport Economics Association. In 2018, he was awarded the Lawrence H. Hadley Distinguished Service Award for contributions to sport economics.

Augusto Rembrandt Rodríguez-Sánchez is an associate professor in the Department of Physical Education and Sport at the University of Seville, Spain. His research topics include physical education, martial arts, and combat sports, as well as the social aspects of sport.

María del Rocío Bohórquez is a professor in the Department of Social Psychology at the University of Seville, Spain, where she teaches bachelor's and master's level courses in sport and exercise sciences. She is President of the Andalusian Association of Sport and Exercise Psychology. Her research topics are interpersonal relationships in sports, team building, and improvement strategies.

Tiago Ribeiro is an assistant professor of sport management in the Faculty of Human Kinetics at the University of Lisbon, Portugal. His research focuses on sport mega-events, and the social impact of sport and the Olympic legacies. He was the research manager at Sport Evolution Alliance in Portugal, and a research fellow at the *Fundação de Amparo à Pesquisa* in Rio de Janeiro (FAPERJ) and the Olympic Studies Centre.

Luis Carlos Sánchez is a lecturer in the Department of Economics at the University of Oviedo, Spain. He is also a credit risk analyst in a public financial institution. His research focuses on sport economics and corporate governance.

Patricio Sánchez-Fernández is an associate professor in the Department of Finance and Accounting at the University of Vigo, Spain. He is also Vice Managing Director of the governance and economics research network at the University of Vigo and Director of the MBA program in sport at the same institution.

Mary Elena Sánchez-Gabarre is a doctoral student in Economics. She holds a master's degree in banking and finance at the Faculty of Economics and Business at the Universidade da Coruña, Spain. She served on the organising committee of the XI Ibero-American Congress on Sports Economics.

José Manuel Sánchez-Santos is an associate professor at the Faculty of Economics and Business at the Universidade da Coruña, in Spain. His research focuses on sport economics. He is a member of the Spanish Society of Sport Economics (SEED) and the International Association of Sport Economists (IASE).

Vicente Javaloyes Sanchis is a professor at the INEFC Lleida, Spain. He is also a member of the Jurisdictional Committee of the Royal Spanish Football Federation.

Thiago Santos is a professor and coordinator in the sport management program at the Universidade Europeia in Lisbon, Portugal. His research interests include sport management, sport marketing, and consumer behaviour in sport. He is the former vice president of the Brazilian Association for Sport Management.

Marisa Sousa is a doctoral student in sport management in the Faculty of Sport at the University of Porto, Portugal. She holds a master's degree in sport management and high-performance training. She is the manager of the aquatic activities in the UPFit Programme at the University of Porto. She is also a swimming coach at the Leixões Sport Club. Her research focuses on sport management and sport marketing.

Federico Todeschini is Principal Data Analyst at Pepsico in Barcelona, Spain. He was previously Senior Analyst at the Catalan Institute of Public Policy, Advisor to the Deputy Chief of Staff in Argentina and a consultant at the Inter-American Development Bank. His research interests are in program evaluation, particularly in welfare, education, health, and labour activation programs as well as sport economics.

Xavier Triadó-Ivern is an associate professor at the University of Barcelona, Spain. He is vice-rector for Digital Transformation at the University of Barcelona.

He is also a member of the Research Group in Business at the University of Barcelona.

José Miguel Vegara-Ferri is a doctoral student at the University of Murcia, Spain. He has worked and collaborated with the organisation of many sport events in Spain, including road races, national championships, and multi-sport events. His research interest is in the social evaluation and tourist impact of sport events.

Luís Vilar is Pro-Rector of Innovation and Technology at the Universidade Europeia in Lisbon, Portugal. His research focuses on management, leadership, and communication in sport.

Preface

Carles Murillo Fort
President of the Spanish Society of Sports Economics (SEED)

The interrelation between political, economic and sports management aspects is a phenomenon that is present in the daily activities of the main stakeholders of the sports system. The concretion to a certain territorial area does not detract from its validity but, on the contrary, allows delving into closer and surely daily aspects. This approach has been the one that has presided over the very successful proposal by the publishers of the book. The work of Jerónimo García-Fernández, Moisés Grimaldi-Puyana and Gonzalo A. Bravo deserves sincere applause for the magnificent power of resolution of the initial idea and its concretion to the sports phenomenon in Spain and Portugal.

The Spanish Society of Sports Economics (SEED; www.seed-deporte.es) is not alien to the perspective developed in this work, neither regarding to thematic aspects nor to the territorial specification. Not in vain, the statutes of the SEED indicate that

> the areas of interest are, among others, research in sports economics, the management of sports entities, the analysis of sports policies, the evaluation of activities and sports events, as well as the analysis of the functioning of sports services, promoting a multidisciplinary and international approach.

On the other hand, it should be remembered that CIED, SEED's annual congress, owes its acronym to the original title that refers to America (Ibero-American Congress of Sports Economics). Our partners and participants in the activities of the SEED scientific society are academics and professionals from economics and sports management, but also from sociology, the governance of sports entities and related sectors and, ultimately, interested in public policies related to sport.

There is a third aspect that deserves a special comment from SEED. Many of the authors of the works in this book make up the great family that has been configured around the activities promoted and organised by said scientific society. The book and the SEED share diversity and plurality in the origin of its members, in their areas of thematic specialty and in the points of view of the analysis and the proposal of solutions. The sports system is experiencing important moments of change due to both technological innovation and the consequences of the severe blow received because of the health crisis as of 2020. The responses of the main agents in the sector have, in general, been praiseworthy for its resilience and for its ability to overcome from the incorporation of new ideas and perspectives. A large part of these changes will mark the future agenda of sports policy and the strategies of sports entities. The articles that make up the different parts of the book constitute elements of great documentary and analytical wealth to guide future actions.

To the editors and the authors of the works we must recognise their merit, effort and success in the development of the works that are part of this book. From now on, the book is a must-see reference for all those interested in the economic, social, political and cultural aspects of sport in Spain and Portugal and, by extension, in any other corner of the world geography where there are elements for transfer the methodological approach and the results of the work.

José Carlos Reis
President of Portugal Activo/AGAP

This work has a very special meaning for sport in our countries, Portugal and Spain. The proximity of the two countries in terms of language and even culture, has allowed a parallel path, despite the differences in size and investment capacity. The analysis carried out on Peninsular sport, in its different dimensions: financial, political, and legal, gives us an outlook of what sport was in these countries in the past, what is currently happening and its future perspectives.

It is, undoubtedly, an important contribution to study and mainly to define guidelines for the development of our sport. In this book there is a concern, of the authors and the topics covered, to provide the greatest number of tools possible so that we can all have a more in-depth knowledge of this area.

Sports management is a matrix present throughout the various articles, allowing a deepen knowledge of the best practices of sports management in the Iberian Peninsula and enabling its knowledge at a world level. It should also be noted that, throughout the book, great importance is given to the value of sport, as a factor of development and as an aggregator of society, reaffirming his decisive role in the entire economy and culture of Portugal and Spain.

As the representative Association of Fitness in Portugal, we welcome the high contribution that this work brings to study, reflection, and future perspective of sport and, concomitantly, of fitness. There is a parallel or similarity between sport and fitness because both contribute to a more active and healthy society. Said that, much of what the authors discuss in this book has a direct transfer to our specific activity of fitness. In conclusion, we intend to reaffirm the relevance of this work for the knowledge of sport in the Iberian Peninsula and congratulate all the authors for the high technical and literary quality of the themes presented.

We wish your publication to be a success and we will do everything to promote its dissemination in our country and beyond.

Fernando París Roche
President of Federation of Sports Management Associations of Spain (FAGDE)

The book you have in your hands will undoubtedly represent a qualitative leap in publications and academic studies on the organisation and management of sport in Spain and Portugal. On the one hand, because of its ambition in terms of its agenda and because of the cast of 50 authors and collaborators who contribute their academic and technical work to the publication; and on the other, because of the singularity of doing it not around a country but around a geographical territory: the Iberian Peninsula, shared by two sister countries.

In the first case, the book incorporates a set of chapters around different facets of sports organisation, management, economy, public policies, industry, or legislation, history, etc. representing a diversity of views of the phenomenon and the sports system from different disciplines and different angles that enrich the text. This diversity of views reinforce and consolidate the set of subsystems and realities that underlie the word or the inclusive concept of 'sport'. We talk about show sports, professional figures, but we also talk about the practice of the citizen, the economic impact of events, the fitness industry or sports tourism. An interesting miscellany, which gives solidity and reinforces the sports sector.

In the second case, the treatment that the editors give to the two countries that make up the Iberian Peninsula is important; brother countries, which share centuries of history, of neighbourliness, but which have lived—until a few years ago, and in my personal opinion—with their backs turned on each other. Only in the last two or three decades have the two countries—and the people who live in them—increased tourist, cultural, academic, economic and personal relations. This publication, and the relations generated, will also help to strengthen ties in the world academic and management and to strengthen, if possible, the already excellent relations that exist between the sports managers of both countries.

And the most important aspect of the publication is the objective of transferring the experience in the management and organisation of sport, its promotion policies or its economic impact outside of our countries, of our geographical environment. As the editors point out in their introduction, it is about filling the gap that exists in the academic literature in English on the realities of the Iberian Peninsula, an 'area that does not receive the same attention as other regions of the continent'. Because although there is already an academic, technical or scientific literature in our countries on many of the issues addressed in this publication, these literatures have a very local path, a very specific scope, very small, without projection abroad.

This book is therefore a very valuable instrument from the point of view of our public policies in sport and foreign action, for Spain and Portugal.

My best wishes for success to the editors, my thanks to all the collaborators and the hope that this publication will serve both to help us get to know ourselves better abroad, as well as to get to know ourselves better.

Manel Valcarce
CEO Valgo Consulting

After two decades, the European Charter for Sport has been reviewed by the Council of Europe, emphasising the importance and benefits of sport in European society and urging governments to get involved in its development and promotion. Some benefits act transversally on citizens in areas as relevant as health, inclusion, education or sustainability, and the European Union lays the foundations for the principle of 'right to sport', where everyone must be able to access and practice.

Without a doubt, this is an essential proposal that is motivated by the facts and evidence that sports practice has shown for years and that has grown progressively improving people's physical condition and quality of life. It is especially important in the Iberian Peninsula, where Spain and Portugal have experienced an increase in statistics in all areas represented by the sports sector.

In fact, this progress and evolution has allowed these countries to take various approaches apart from the traditional concept of sport, as evidenced by various documents published by the WHO, the UN, or the Helsinki and Vocasport reports. The dimensions of sport not only cover the federative and competitive sphere but also the promotion of physical activity and health, both in the public and private sectors: educational sport at school and university, sport as an element of social integration, or in the recreational field and promotion of leisure, tourism and of course the economy.

Favoured by the sporting achievements of both Spain and Portugal in numerous competitions and their great organisational capacity to host high-level sport events, in addition to the growing interest of the population in physical activity as a habit of life, the current context allows us to visualise a brighter future for the development of the sports industry which will allow this sector to become a key element for the improvement and progress of Iberian societies.

Despite the magnitude of and increase in development of sport, there is still a vast amount of work to be done, and there is a large segment of the potential population to whom we must offer an adequate service adapted to their needs. Collaboration between countries, administrations, companies and entities will be key to achieving optimal levels of sports practice in society as well as greater expansion and recognition of sport as an essential service and activity for citizens.

In our actions and decisions, we have the great challenge of improving and professionalising a sector that requires proper management of both its processes, products, services and equipment, as well as human relations with both our teams and our users. Having the necessary knowledge and tools to achieve excellence in sports policies, governance—the management of the organisations of the countries that make up the Iberian Peninsula—becomes an obligatory requirement that we cannot postpone.

The sport of all and for all is also a matter of state, both in Spain and Portugal, and as such, governments must be aware by approving old claims in their legislation, making sports practice effective and real as an essential service, reducing VAT, promoting tax incentives, regulating and ordering professionals, updating the sports law and promoting their integration and collaboration in the health system.

We have in our hands a book comprising 21 chapters developed by a large number of experts, academics and scholars of sport in its different dimensions, which gives us a unique opportunity to learn and improve professionally, through practical, useful content, based on study and experience, which we will be able to transfer to our projects and facilities, to our entities and organisations, to our teams, and above all to improve the development of sport and its value in our environment, taking the experience of clients and users to promote excellence and the real benefits that its practice means.

As Mireia Belmonte, Spanish Olympic swimmer, used to say, the 'elevator to success is out of order; you have to climb the stairs little by little'.

Let's take advantage of this great work that will surely exceed our expectations.

Vera Pedragosa
Research Centre in Business and Economics (CICEE). Universidade Autónoma de Lisboa

This book represents an important milestone in the evolution of literacy in management, economics and policy matters. It bases its study objective on different scientific areas such as law, economics, public policy, management, marketing, sociology, history and tourism. The different scientific areas are relevant and justify the presented theme: the management, economics and policy of sport in the Iberian Peninsula.

In Europe, the free movement of money, people and products has always had an added value in attracting and gaining the loyalty of Olympic athletes, professional players, tourists, students, academics, researchers, sport and non-sport organisations who consider Europe as a safe haven for their businesses, lives, families, physical activity, exercise and sport.

Historically, the relationship between Spain and Portugal, including the Iberian Peninsula with Gibraltar and Andorra, has always been inseparable, in which the common denominator 'sport' has provided high local, regional, national and cross-border economic impacts. Thus, this book, from a historical perspective, will seek to analyse not only the economic impact but also the cultural and political impact that sport has across Spain and Portugal, without neglecting the Iberian Peninsula. It will also analyse the impact that sport has beyond these countries, from a migratory perspective of sport professionals in the territory. The migration of football athletes, male and female, also creates a basis for the development of the countries and related areas with impact on the society. Moreover, the innovation of new businesses, promoted by entrepreneurship, is not neglected in its relationship with tourism and the economy. Between Spain and Portugal alone, for numerous reasons linked to sports (e.g. Rafael Nadal, Pau Gasol, José Mourinho and Cristiano Ronaldo) every year, these countries attract the attention of millions of people all over the world, physically or virtually. The sport involvement is not indifferent to the vision of other organisations that approach the phenomenon of the sports industry for the purpose of synergy and scale economy.

For all these aspects, the book adds value to the sports industry, through the division into five parts with 21 thematic chapters (e.g. Public Policy; Management, and Sport Economics; Spanish Women's Leagues; Portuguese Football League; Entrepreneurial Sport; Sports Events; Sports Gambling; Building and Equipment; Local Communities; Traditional Games and Tourism Attractions; Nautical Sports; Brand Sports Celebrities; Governance of Sports Federations) that complement and interconnect with each other, adding knowledge to sport in a global perspective, with high multidisciplinarity, seeking to fill a market gap in terms of knowledge and in the language in which the book is written (English).

This book will allow students, academics and others interested in the subject to reflect on the good sporting practices that exist in the Iberian Peninsula and compare them with the good sporting practices that also exist outside the Iberian Peninsula. The scientific growth of the sports industry is visible through this book, written by renowned researchers. The scientific researchers who author this book are specialists in the most diverse areas of sport between Spain and Portugal and the Iberian Peninsula. They are all to be congratulated for the excellence of the texts that they have offered to the service of society. This book is highly recommended.

Acknowledgements

We would like to thank all the authors who have participated in this project. A project of this scope and nature requires involving those who not only have studied and examined the sport phenomena in the Iberian Peninsula, but also those who over the years have come to be recognised as leading scholars in their respective fields. To each and every one of them, we extend our most sincere thanks. Likewise, we appreciate the support of different organisations that have not only endorsed this project but have also served as model organisations in promoting and advancing the sport industry in the region, especially the Spanish Society of Sport Economics, *Portugal Activo*-AGAP, Federation of Sport Management Associations of Spain, Valgo Consulting and Universidade Autónoma de Lisboa. We would also like to extend our sincere thanks to the editorial staff at Routledge, particularly to Simon Whitmore for believing in our idea and encouraging us to pursue this project. Finally, we extend our gratitude and love to the members of our family for their constant support and encouragement: Elisa Márquez González, María García Márquez, Alba García Márquez, Patricia Ferrer Cano, Lucía Grimaldi Ferrer, Mara Grimaldi Ferrer, Gretchen Peterec, Sebastian Bravo-Peterec and Sara Bravo-Peterec. The weight of this type of project is typically endured by those who are closest to us. Without their support, this project would have never reached the finish line.

Chapter 1

Sport in the Iberian Peninsula
An introduction

Jerónimo García-Fernández, Moisés Grimaldi-Puyana, and Gonzalo A. Bravo

Introduction

The Iberian Peninsula is connected to the rest of Europe by the southern Pyrenees. Geographically, the peninsula is in the southwest of the European continent and surrounded mostly by the Mediterranean Sea and the Atlantic Ocean and its southern tip is narrowly separated from Northern Africa. The name of *Iberia* has its origin in the ancient inhabitants who first arrived in this area. The Greeks called all of those who lived beyond the Ebro River *Iberos* as a result of the natural boundary separation this river had from the rest of the European continent (Payne, 1973). The peninsula has undergone different names such as *Hispania* by the Romans and *Al-Andalus* during the Muslim rule from 771 to 1492 (Hervás & Abengoechea, 2020; Núñez, 2011).

The Iberian Peninsula is a territory that has hosted different cultures for more than 3,000 years, as evidenced by the number of civilisations (i.e., Tartessians, Celts, Phoenicians, Carthaginians, Greeks, Romans, Visigoths, and Muslims) that have left their mark in terms of culture, history, language, and miscegenation (Hervás & Abengoechea, 2020; Payne, 1973). Currently, the Iberian Peninsula is made up of Spain and Portugal, two countries with a long history and mainly responsible for one of the biggest world explorations of the 14th through 16th centuries. During that time, several Spanish and Portuguese explorers took the colossal task to explore the New World under the orders of the crown of their respective kingdoms (del Valle et al., 2020). Among these is Christopher Columbus,[1],[2] who in 1492 landed in what today is the Americas, giving rise to several other explorations across the Atlantic. Equally important in the saga of exploring the New World are Portuguese explorers such as Bartolomeu Dias, João Fernandes, Fernão de Magalhães, Vasco de Gama, and Pedro Alvarez Cabral, navigators who reached almost every corner of the world (Rubiés, 2011). All of them were inspired by Prince Henrique de Portugal, later known as Henry the Navigator, who is credited for being the man who sparked maritime explorations in the Atlantic and across the world (Elbl, 2001). Rubiés (2011) noted that explorations from the 14th century onwards were motivated not only to increase trade but also to pursue strategic and religious goals.

DOI: 10.4324/9781003197003-1

In the Iberian Peninsula, there are also two additional territories, Andorra, a sovereign state located in the Pyrenees between Spain and France, and the British territory of Gibraltar, which is in the southwest part of the Peninsula. Portugal—or the Portuguese Republic, which is in the extreme west part of the Peninsula—occupies about 15.2% of the territory (92,226 km2) with a population of 10.3 million people. Portugal is a democratic state, whose capital is Lisbon (European Union, n.d.) On the other hand, Spain—or the Kingdom of Spain, with a population of 47.4 million people—occupies the entire north, centre, and east of the peninsula, equivalent to 85% of the territory (505,944 km2). Spain is a social and democratic state whose form of government is a parliamentary monarchy, and its capital is Madrid (European Union, n.d.)

Since the 19th century, the political systems of Spain and Portugal have had a similar evolution, with a tendency towards homogeneity and even synchrony in time (Payne, 2011). The simultaneous processes of democratisation and Europeanisation are the best reflections of this convergence in the form of government and the functioning of political life, a pattern of parallel development which has enabled strong bilateral relations.

Sport in Spain and Portugal plays a significant role not only in enhancing people's regional and national identities but also in being part of many other public policies, such as health, education, culture, youth, and tourism (Fernandes et al., 2011; Puig et al., 2010). Sport is as well an activity with a significant economic impact at the local and regional levels, which are demonstrated to have been better shielded—compared to other industries—during the economic crisis of the late 2000s and also during the middle of the COVID-19 pandemic in 2020 (2Playbook, 2021). In Spain, for example, and despite the high levels of unemployment reached during that time, the sport industry showed not only great resilience and stability (Grimaldi-Puyana et al., 2016) but also many teams and athletes reached unprecedented success at the international level (Rioja, 2020).

Sport that takes place in Spain and Portugal attracts the attention of millions of people worldwide, particularly those who follow and watch one of the most intense football leagues in the world. Sport in the Iberian Peninsula is also important for people outside Europe, particularly as a port of entry for professional players, Olympic athletes, and scholars from Latin America and parts of Africa who are in search of a career in sports or are looking for better training and educational opportunities in sports (Jansen & Engbersen, 2017; Poli et al., 2015). The significance of sport in this region is best illustrated by the impact of renowned Spanish athletes like Rafael Nadal, Paul Gasol, Raul, Sergio Ramos, Fernando Alonso, Miguel Induráin or Portuguese footballers like Eusebio, Cristiano Ronaldo, Luis Figo, and Paulo Futre, who not only gained global recognition and established themselves as unique global brands but also contributed to elevating the country brand of their respective nations (Carter, 2020; Nicolau & Santa-María, 2017). Similarly, football clubs like Real Madrid, Barcelona, Atletico Madrid or Sevilla in Spain, and Porto and Benfica in Portugal have reached regional and global appeal, putting their teams on the map of global sports (Saharoy, 2020). But sport in the

Iberian Peninsula is not just football. Sport also plays a crucial role in the broader tourist industry (Law, 2018), whether this is by attracting millions of people to be active participants in golf, hiking, skiing, running, or aquatic sports or just by attending world-class sports events such as La Liga football matches, the ATP tennis tour, *La Vuelta a España* and the Tour of Portugal (*Volta a Portugal*) in cycling, the Formula One Grand Prix of Spain in Barcelona, PGA and LPGA golf events, or motorcycling races or by witnessing traditional folk games like *traineras* in the Basque Country, *bolos serranos* in Andalusia, or *malha* in Portugal.

Purpose of this book

One of the goals of this book was to bridge the gap between the knowledge produced and published on sport economics, sport policy, and management in Spain and Portugal, published in English, and similar literature that has been published in Spanish and/or Portuguese. Arguably, these two sets of literature vary significantly. The second group not only outnumbers the first in terms of quantity of publications and authors but also is less known within the English-speaking audience. Providing a platform of visibility to a select group of Spanish and Portuguese scholars in sport management, sport economics, and sport law to the English-speaking audience is an important task. Previous research has shown that the impact in which a message is transmitted varies significantly based on the position of the language in the global language network (Ronen et al., 2014). This means the message is perceived to be more or less influential depending on the language used. Thus, publishing in English becomes more influential when conveying scientific ideas. Although in this work, several of the authors are well known within the scientific community worldwide, others are less known within the English-speaking circles. In this anthology, a second goal was to provide a platform for academics from Spain and Portugal to communicate their research on sport management, sport economics, and sport law to those outside of the Iberian Peninsula.

This book provides an overview of the development of the sport industry in the Iberian Peninsula, analysing the social, economic, cultural, and political impact sport has had in this region. Contributors in this book examine the sport phenomena using different frameworks of analysis including law, economics, public policy, management, marketing, sociology, history, and tourism. Each chapter describes and analyses an array of issues related to sport that affect not only the course of sports organisations but also their impact on the local and regional communities across the Iberian Peninsula.

This book intends to reach an academic audience worldwide interested in the broad field of sport management, sport economics, and sport policy. This book also aims to serve as a resource for policymakers and public administrators interested to understand and know more about the role sport plays in the peninsula. We have invited to be part of this anthology a group of selected scholars with different backgrounds and expertise in matters related to sport in Spain and Portugal.

Organisation of the book

This book is the result of a collaborative effort of 58 scholars from universities in Spain, Portugal, and the United States. The book is organised into five parts. In each part, authors have discussed and provided unique perspectives of themes that relate to a broader theme that represent different aspects of the sport sector across the Iberian Peninsula. These broader themes were titled as (a) the context of Iberian sports; (b) public policies, management, and sport economics; (c) the football industry; (d) events and sport tourism; (e) and branding, governance, and sport federations. In the next section, we provide a summary of the main ideas and findings described in each chapter of the book.

The context of Iberian sports

Understanding the evolution and the impact political processes have upon countries becomes essential for an understanding of modern societies. In Chapter 2, Moscoso-Sánchez, Pinheiro and Pujadas take a socio-historical look at the impact of the socio-cultural, political, and economic transformations Spain and Portugal experienced during the 1970s. These authors use secondary data extracted from different public authorities in Spain and Portugal, as well as data from municipalities and sporting associations, to examine how the educational system and municipal sports policies have all contributed, mostly through clubs and sport federations, to open the access to sport in both Spanish and Portuguese societies. They also examine the changes that occurred in both countries' sporting systems, focusing on the historical, legislative, and political occurrences. Moscoso-Sánchez et al. also examined how the popularity of sport has influenced the rise of popular culture in these countries and how a hegemonic sporting paradigm has emerged due to the influence of global marketing forces, specifically the so-called 'sporting spectacles' and their accompanying 'sports heroes'.

In addition to discussing the factors that shape the course of sport at a macro level, the authors in this section also discuss how regulatory frameworks, particularly the role of the European Union and the sports legislation in each country, have influenced the sport systems in Spain and Portugal. In Chapter 3, Aparicio-Chueca, Elasri-Ejjaberi, Triadó-Ivern, and Blanch Casadesús discuss the role the European Union has had in the promotion of sport in the region. They note how sport has contributed to boosting the European Union's (EU) economy, as well as creating an impact on people's lives across Europe. To contextualise their analysis, Aparicio-Chueca et al. provide an overview of the regulatory framework that governs most EU sports policies, including the impact of some of the EU's projects and programs in sport, such as the Erasmus + program, the European Week of Sport, and some of the sport policies related to immigration and integration. Since 2009, the EU has worked on several sport policies among its members. The authors use the Euro Barometer poll to assess the impact some of these projects have had across the region. These initiatives not only have provided funding to members countries of the Union but also have facilitated sport-related collaboration with many international organisations. To advance some of its sport-related policies, the EU has used soft policy tools, including guidelines, suggestions, and subsidies.

In Chapter 4, Carvalho, García-Cirac, and Sousa argue that the ties that exist between Spain and Portugal are not only geographical, but, they contend, that over the years both countries have developed similar structures and governance practices within their respective sport systems. Portugal and Spain are countries that, in the past, and due to the Treaty of Tordesillas in 1494, shared the world as the two major powers. In this regard, these two kingdoms were not only important drivers but also pioneers of globalisation and intercontinental communications thanks to the explorations conducted during the Age of Discoveries.[3] In terms of sport, these authors argue that Portugal and Spanish not only have a lot in common in terms of their sport systems but also the influence and success of their athletes have had in other countries across continents, making them global icons of the 21st century. The authors contend that understanding the similarities and differences within the political, organisational, and legal domain of sport in Spain and Portugal, as well as how sport practices have been disseminated in international contexts, become critical to value the contribution these two nations have bestowed to the world.

Following with the background provided in the first three chapters of Part I of the book, the authors of Chapter 5 direct their analysis to the laws that rule sport in Spain and Portugal. Here Javaloyes Sanchis and Cardoso provide an interesting discussion about the ever-revolving frictions that exist between sport regulations and the body of laws, something that scholars have called 'conflict of laws' (Snyder, 2003). In this chapter, the authors examine the legal framework that defines the playing field in Spain and Portugal and explain how these legislations impact the sport organisations that are part of the sport system in these countries. They note that an industry cannot exist without a set of standards that regulate its practice and development, but due to the existence of its own *lex sportiva* and the application of unique ways to resolve endogenous problems, sport and the organisations that are part of the sport system have typically claimed an *island* status. However, in the sport legal framework, state requirements coexist with standards set by sports organisations. Consequently, the authors argue that many stakeholders part of the sport system in Spain and Portugal have learned to coexist on shaky grounds, where the uniqueness of sport typically collides with the public protection of fundamental rights.

Public policy, management and sport economics

In Part 2, the authors discuss issues related to the public policies, management, and economics of sport in the Iberian Peninsula. In Chapter 6, Lera-López, Gómez-Plana, and de Araújo Barros discuss the different sport policies developed in both countries and the laws that regulate this activity. Their analysis focuses on explaining the impact different levels of public administration have on sport participation. They examine the evolution of sport participation by identifying similarities and differences and how specific public policies in sport influence sport participation. They also examine how public funding of sport, done through various levels of government, impact sport participation. In Chapter 7, Murua also discusses the impact of public policies in Spain but he focuses his analysis on public spending in sport facilities. The author argues that during the mid-1970s the transition to democracy in Spain and the passage of the European Charter on Sport had a significant influence on the growth of public investment in sport facilities. However, Murua points out that although more facilities were built during this time, the demand for sport did not grow accordingly. On the other hand, the unique positions of the autonomous regions and the uneven power of many institutions that also participate in the promotion of sport has significantly increased the challenges of effective planning and decision making. As a result, a considerable portion of this obligation at the local level has fallen now to City Halls. The author concluded that in Spain, policies and programs have completely changed the demand for sports. With the popularity of outdoor sports on the rise, the main challenge now is deciding which policies to implement in this large network of sport facilities, many of which are not only outdated but also do not serve the demands and preferences of users.

In Chapter 8, Rodríguez and Levi Pérez move away from the policy discussion to concentrate on the economic impact of sport betting in Spain. In their analysis, they describe the evolution and current state of the Spanish sports betting sector. According to the authors, in 2018, sport betting generated more than €9,300 million which represents 39% of the entire gambling industry, which in Spain accounts for close to 0.9% of the country's GDP. The authors note that although in Spain legal gambling in sports have existed for decades, it has been restricted mostly to the outcome of football matches through football pools, which in Spain are known as *La Quiniela*. The economic and social impacts of these pools has been significant as a portion of these funds have supported charities and sport organisations, including the 1982 FIFA World Cup and the 1992 Olympic Games, both events that were hosted in Spain. It was not until 2008 when bookmakers were granted the first licenses to handle sports betting in several Spanish provinces, despite there not being any regulation for sport gambling. In 2011, the Spanish government took steps to regulate and legalise sports gambling in all its forms including football pools, fixed-odds sports betting, and sports betting exchanges both offline and online.

In Chapter 9, Gálvez-Ruiz, García-Fernández, Gonçalves, and Alcaraz-Rodríguez address the evolution of the fitness industry in Portugal and Spain, focusing on the challenges, opportunities, and the strategies used by operators to keep this sector profitable. As the fitness industry keeps growing over the world, the number of facilities, users, and total income generated has been particularly noticeable in Spain and Portugal. Data from this industry place these two countries on the top of the list internationally, promising a blooming future for owners, investors, and operators in the field. According to the authors, most fitness centres in Spain and Portugal have built successful business models that could be marketed to other countries, allowing them to replicate, modify and/or improve upon the successful experience achieved in the Iberian Peninsula. Gálvez-Ruiz et al. contend that many fitness-related sport products and services offered in the Iberian region are characterised by a having high level of innovation. The new forms of sports and exercises offered integrate new technologies which align well with the evolving demand of the fitness services and types of customers. Examining and understanding the supply and demand for services, style of management, consumer profiles, as well as the communication strategies used in the demanding Spanish and Portuguese market could eventually result in a guide or model of best practices for other countries where this industry is still in its early stages of development.

In Chapter 10, Calabuig Moreno, Parra-Camacho, and Crespo-Hervás discuss the social and economic impact of sport events in the Iberian Peninsula. The authors note that in the Iberian region, particularly in Spain, the economic impact of most sport events have been characterised by using the input-output methods as well as cost-benefit analysis. The social impact of sporting events also has been assessed using quantitative techniques through the analysis of the host community's perception of the effects of these events in the community. The authors conclude that while the economic impact of sport events can be quantified, the social impact is more difficult to quantify and measure objectively. They also note that while assessing the impact of sport events is not a new endeavour for the social scientist in the region, many more studies and more geographic diversification of these studies are needed. Currently, many of these studies tend to be led by two research centres, one in the region of Valencia and the other in the region of Asturias.

Finally, in Chapter 11, Lara-Bocanegra, Escamilla-Fajardo, González-Serrano, Bohórquez, and Grimaldi-Puyana argue that the economic crisis of the 2000s hit severely Portugal and Spain with higher rates of unemployment. As a result of this, governments in these countries began promoting entrepreneurship to stimulate growth and job creation. Lara-Bocanegra et al. contend that because of the wide array of business opportunities the sport sector has to offer, this area seems ideal to develop entrepreneurship and entrepreneurship opportunities. In Spain, in recent years there has been an increase in the number of organisations in the sports sector dedicated to the management of facilities and/or activities of sport clubs or gyms, suggesting that the number of sport entrepreneurs has increased. The authors in this chapter conducted a bibliometric analysis to find out the state of the research on entrepreneurship and intrapreneurship in sport in the Iberian Peninsula. Findings of the thematic analysis revealed that studies on sport entrepreneurship and intrapreneurship in Spain and Portugal can be grouped in five main areas: entrepreneurship education and entrepreneurial intentions in sport science students; entrepreneurial orientation and innovation as an antecedent or consequence in sports organisations; social entrepreneurship in sport; sustainable sport entrepreneurship; and sustainable economics and its relation to entrepreneurship in sport.

The football industry

The authors of this section provide different analyses of topics that relate to the football industry in Spain and Portugal. In their analyses, the authors examine factors that influence the arrival of players from Latin America to play in Spain; the evolution and professionalisation of the Portuguese Football league; the success factors of Real Madrid and FC Barcelona, and the relationship with the performance of the Spanish Men's National Team; and the challenges of developing a women's professional football league in Spain.

In Chapter 12, Chaves, García, Ortín, and Todeschini use an econometric model to examine the evolution of the Latin American footballers in the Spanish league by analysing how factors such as players' characteristics, type of clubs, and the structure of the football industry could explain the type of players who arrive to play in Spain. Among the players' characteristics, the authors examine nationality, position in the field, number of times a player was nominated to play in the national team, and the player's former clubs before joining a Spanish team. In terms of the team's characteristics, they examine the team's standing in the league and budget. Regarding the structure of the football industry, the authors consider the economic importance of the league from where these players were previously recruited and the international dimension of the league they played before arriving in Spain. The authors concluded that for the sample of their study more than 50% of the Latin American players who arrived to play in the Spanish League had not previously played for their national team. However, 29.3% of them played at least one game for the national team afterward. They also noted that certain institutional restrictions that occurred in the early 1970s and mid-1990s affected equally the arrival of players from Latin America and Europe. The authors concluded that the numbers of the Latin American footballers who arrive today are higher compared to those who arrived in the early 1970s, but today's players do not show the same quality on average when compared to players that arrived in the past because today there are less institutional constraints.

Meanwhile, in Chapter 13, Santos, Fatela, and Vilar provide an overview of the development and challenges faced by professional football in Portugal, particularly with the creation of the Portuguese Professional Football League, also known as *Liga Portugal*. The Portuguese League of Football Clubs was originally founded in 1978 but in 1991, changed its name to Portuguese Professional Football League. The authors contend that the emergence of *Liga Portugal* was directly influenced not only as a response to the demands of the Players Union but also to broader political changes that occurred in the Portuguese society during the mid-1970s. The authors note that despite *Liga Portugal* being considered a strong football league it does not resemble other stronger leagues in Europe. However, they state that *La Liga* has significantly contributed to the export of talent to European football and also serves as a gateway to the European football market. The authors argue that *Liga Portugal* needs a better competitive balance and a more equal distribution of revenue from television rights, which will give smaller clubs a greater chance of competing with the larger ones. In this regard, they note that significant progress must be made for the League to achieve better and more sustainable economic and sport success.

In the case of the professional football competition in Spain, *La Liga*, the authors of Chapter 14 Murillo and Puig note that a great part of the success of this league can be explained by the growth and professionalisation of the football industry in Spain, which they note has grown at a faster pace when compared to *Liga Portugal*. In Chapter 13, Murillo and Puig discuss the factors that have contributed to the success of the two historically most accomplished teams of *La Liga* -Real Madrid and FC Barcelona- to explain the extent these two teams have influenced the success of the Men's National Football team, also known as *La Roja*. The authors noted that the presence of Real Madrid and FC Barcelona in *La Roja* is evidenced by the number of players these two teams historically have contributed to the Men's National Football squad. Moreover, these two teams also concentrate the largest number of followers within Spanish football. The historical rivalry between these two teams has triggered not only better competition but has forced them to implement successful business and managerial strategies to stay on top of the demands of the business of football. As a result, they have positioned themselves as undisputed clubs in global football. Real Madrid and FC Barcelona have created a positive effect favouring not only the performance of *La Roja* but also the development of Spanish football.

Although Spain has one of the strongest and most attractive professional football leagues in the world, that does not include women's football. The process of professionalisation of women's sports in Spain significantly lags behind other professional sports in the Iberian Peninsula. In Chapter 15, Sánchez-Santos and Sánchez-Gabarre examine the evolution and expansion of women's sport in Spain with a focus on women's football. Albeit a first division competition in women's football exists since the 1990s, throughout this time that league has functioned only as semi-professional. The authors note how, among other reasons, existing laws have prevented the advancement and professionalisation of women's football. Only recently has professional women's football league gained momentum to finally achieve professional status. The authors note that one of the main implications of the professionalisation of women's football is the impact it could have on other women's sports to decide to turn professional as well.

Events and sport tourism

The geographical location, climate, gastronomy, and safety of the Iberian Peninsula have made it an ideal destination for tourists to visit for leisure (Leitão et al., 2021) or to participate in or attend a sport event (Law, 2018; Melo et al., 2021). In part 3 of the book, the authors provide analyses of three different issues all related to sport tourism. In Chapter 16, Vegara-Ferri, López-Gullón, Díaz-Suárez, and Angosto examine the social and economic impact of *La Vuelta España*, an annual cycling road race event with multiple stages all over the country that has become the largest and most important sport event in the Iberian Peninsula. According to the authors, what makes *La Vuelta* such an important event is not only the high media coverage and popularity but also is its capacity to reach small communities where larger sports events cannot be hosted due to the lack of infrastructure. In 75 years of *La Vuelta*, more than 500 communities have hosted the start and/or finish lines of this event. Each stage in this event generates significant tourist interest by attracting people from all over Spain and Europe. Fans of *La Vuelta* visit local towns to see not only the cycling race but also to participate in many other cultural and leisure activities that are organised before and during the day of the race.

Furthermore, in Chapter 17, Ramírez-Macías, Rodríguez-Sánchez, and Lasaga-Rodríguez describe how several traditional games and sports in the Iberian Peninsula represent important tourist attractions for many communities in the region. The authors argue that traditional sports represent a form of heritage where traditions and customs are passed from one generation to the next. In their analysis, they distinguish between active and passive traditional sports tourism. The popular pilgrimage walk *Camino de Santiago* is discussed as a form of active sport tourism. Although for some this activity might not represent a sporting activity in the traditional sense, the authors noted that walking and hiking in the outdoors does represent a form of exercise that according to the European Sports Charter falls in the category of a sporting activity. The authors also discuss activities in which a tourist can opt to take an active or passive role. That is the case of *Basque Pelota*, a traditional sport popular in the Basque country, or *Valencian Pilota*, a traditional street game that is played in the region of Valencia. The authors argue that traditional games and sports in Spain and Portugal are not only relevant for the cultural heritage of the region and the country but also have become important tourist attractions with a direct impact on the local economy.

Then, in Chapter 18, Caraballo Vidal and Gutierrez-Manzanedo look at how tourism and sport interact in the development of naval stations in Spain. They argue that in many instances the growth of a region may be determined by the presence of nautical stations which, among other things, contribute to job creation. In Spain, the growth of nautical sports began in 1960, when the Spanish government decided to boost tourism and real estate. The authors note within the business of nautical sports marinas represent the most important type of infrastructure. Today in Spain, there are 292 marinas with 131,100 berths with 68% of them located on the Mediterranean coast. Where there is a marina, many other services can be offered and developed. Boat mooring, nautical sports excursions, and nautical sports events are some of the main services that are part of nautical sports tourism. But despite the booming effect that nautical sports can have on the local economy, the authors note that this activity also presents numerous challenges, particularly in terms of sustainability and the impact the indiscriminate growth of nautical facilities will create on the environment.

Branding, Governance, and Sport Federations

In the fifth and last section of this book, we include three chapters that at a first sight they are only loosely related, but in the larger picture, they describe the conditions needed for the business of sport to operate effectively. Authors Gallardo and García-Unanue discuss some of the attributes and accomplishments of the most valuable sports figures in the Iberian Peninsula and how they have turned into global brands. Haas and Ribeiro explain the conditions that have restrained and fostered the governance of sport in Portugal. Finally, Sánchez-Fernández, Sánchez, and Barajas discuss the importance of evaluating the sport federations in Spain.

In Chapter 19, Gallardo and García-Unanue make the argument that talent is not enough to succeed in sport. Athletes need to also understand the world that surrounds them and pay attention to what matters to people. Most importantly, successful athletes must behave according to the values they stand for. In their analysis, the authors describe the business success of tennis player Rafael Nadal, former basketball player Pau Gasol, footballer Cristiano Ronaldo, and manager Jose Mourinho. Arguably, these individuals represent the most recognisable examples of what sport in the Iberian Peninsula has offered to the rest of the world in the last two decades. Gallardo and García-Unanue content that their brand represents their *value promise* to those that follow them. These athletes have successfully translated their athletic talent to the outside of the field of play which has made them not only rich and famous but also beloved celebrities. As a result of their leadership and communication style, their socially responsible attitude, their entrepreneurship spirit, and their savvy way of managing social media, Nadal, Gasol, Ronaldo, and Mourinho have all turned into global brands.

In Chapter 20, Haas and Ribeiro look at the structural changes in the governance of sport in Portugal since the first law of the sport was passed in 1990. The authors use a three-prong approach developed by Henry and Lee (2004) to analyse how the governance of sport has evolved in Portugal. Haas and Ribeiro note that sport in Portugal has been significantly influenced by the presence of the State, to what they refer to as 'state interventionism', a practice that is common where the government exerts a great deal of influence on defining the way the entire sport system and its multiple stakeholders interact. The authors contend that this interventionist role of the state is positive as it provides a direction (through the passage of policies and regulations) on how organisations should navigate the broader system. However, they argue that an interventionist role is not enough to change the culture and dynamics of how sport organisations work. An aspect that is particularly relevant when organisations need to create changes in the way they operate to advance and reach good governance practices such as transparency, accountability, democracy, equity, and social responsibility.

Lastly, in Chapter 21, Sánchez-Fernández, Sánchez, and Barajas argue on the importance of conducting evaluations of the performance of sport federations. In Spain, like in most countries, sport federations are private entities but also, they are treated as institutions of public utility. As a result, sport federations are granted to receive public funding from the government. Developing a control system that evaluates the performance of organisations is critical in public administration not only as a tool to assess the economic and financial objectives but also as a mechanism by which the government can conduct a fair distribution of resources based on clear performance criteria. Therefore, in this chapter Sánchez-Fernández et al. developed a set of performance indicators to evaluate sport federations in the areas of financial management and sustainability, which means the extent the federation operates with enough resources to survive. The second area pertains to success in international competitions, which means the numbers of medals and/or cups achieved in international competitions. Then is the area of sport development which involves the extent to which a given federation is expanding and has enough of base of athletes at the grassroots level. Results revealed that most federations are in good standing regarding financial sustainability, which according to the authors it means federations show economic responsibility. In terms of international success, the sample shows a great dispersion of results, and regarding sport development, it shows relatively low scores for this area.

Notes

1 Although Cristopher Columbus was Italian, his expedition was supported by Isabel I Queen of Castile and Fernando II King of Aragon, who were the Spanish Catholic monarchs during Columbus's exploration to the New World.
2 For centuries Columbus was considered to be the first European to land in the Americas until archeological excavations conducted in 1960 found evidence of a Viking settlement in Newfoundland, Canada, that dates back to 960–1060 AD (Kuitems et al., 2022).
3 The 'age of discovery' or 'age of exploration' goes from the mid-15th century to the mid-16th century where several maritime explorations, lead mostly by Portuguese and Spaniards explorers, were launched in search for new routes to increase trade as well as to pursue strategic and ideological goals (Mitchell, 2020.)

References

2Playbook. (2021, May 21). *La industria del deporte en España: 15.788 millones de negocio, 37.231 empresas y 195.133 empleados*. www.2playbook.com/macro/radiografia-macro-deporte-en-espana/industria-deporte-en-espana-15788-millones-negocio-37231-empresas-19513 3-empleados_3814_102.html

Carter, H. (2020, October 13). Nadal, Spain's real king! *Majorca Daily Bulletin*. www.majorcadailybulletin.com/news/comment/2020/10/13/73311/nadal-the-real-spanish-king.html

del Valle, I., More, A., & O'Toole, R. S. (Eds.). (2020). *Iberian empires and the roots of globalization*. Vanderbilt University Press.

Elbl, I. (2001). Henry 'the navigator'. *Journal of Medieval History*, 27(1), 79–99.

European Union. (n.d.). *Country profiles*. https://european-union.europa.eu/principles-countries-history/country-profiles_en

Fernandes, A. J. S., Tenreiro, F. J. D. S., Quaresma, L. F. E. S., & de Oliveira Maçãs, V. M. (2011). Sport policy in Portugal. *International Journal of Sport Policy and Politics*, 3(1), 133–141.

Grimaldi-Puyana, M., García-Fernández, J., Gómez-Chacón, R., & Bravo, G. (2016). Las organizaciones medianas de gestión de instalaciones deportivas son las más rentables en período de crisis. In P. Gálvez Ruiz et al. (Eds.), *Economía, gestión y deporte. Una visión actual de la investigación* (pp. 343–346). Thompson Reuters/Arazandi.

Henry, I., & Lee, P. C. (2004). Governance and ethics in sport. In J. Beech & S. Chadwick (Eds.), *The business of sport management* (pp. 25–42). Prentice Hall.

Hervás, J. M. R., & Abengoechea, J. J. S. (2020). *Hispania: La península ibérica en la Antigüedad* (Vol. 91). Ediciones Universidad de Salamanca.

Jansen, J., & Engbersen, G. (2017). Have the Olympic Games become more migratory? A comparative historical perspective. *Comparative Migration Studies, 5*(1), 1–15.

Kuitems, M., Wallace, B. L., Lindsay, C., Scifo, A., Doeve, P., Jenkins, K., . . . Dee, M. W. (2022). Evidence for European presence in the Americas in ad 1021. *Nature, 601*(7893), 388–391.

Law, W. (2018, February 5). Sports tourism scores in Spain. *Tourism Review News.* www.tourism-review.com/sports-tourism-revenue-growing-in-spain-news10466

Leitão, J., Ratten, V., & Braga, V. (2021). *Tourism innovation in Spain and Portugal.* Springer Nature.

Melo, R., Andrade, C. S., Rheenen, D. V., & Sobry, C. (2021). Portugal: Small scale sport tourism events and local sustainable development. The case of the III Running Wonders Coimbra. In R. Melo, C. Sobry, & D. Van Rheenen (Eds.), *Small scale sport tourism events and local sustainable development* (pp. 173–190). Springer.

Mitchell, J. B. (2020). European exploration. *Encyclopedia Britannica, 29.* www.britannica.com/topic/European-exploration

Nicolau, J. L., & Santa-María, M. J. (2017). Sports results creating tourism value: Rafael Nadal's tennis match points worth €12,000,000. *Tourism Economics, 23*(3), 697–701.

Núñez, M. A. M. (2011). ¿Por qué llegaron los árabes a la Península Ibérica?: Las causas de la conquista musulmana del 711. *AWRAQ: Estudios sobre el mundo árabe e islámico contemporáneo* (3), 21–36.

Payne, S. G. (1973). *A history of Spain and Portugal* (Vol. 1). University of Wisconsin Press. https://libro.uca.edu/payne1/spainport1.htm

Payne, S. G. (2011). Spain and Portugal. In S. G. Payne (Eds.), *Spain: A unique history* (pp. 111–127). University of Wisconsin Press.

Poli, R., Ravenel, L., & Besson, R. (2015). Exporting countries in world football. *CIES Football Observatory Monthly Report, 8*, 1–10.

Puig, N., Martínez, J., & García, B. (2010). Sport policy in Spain. *International Journal of Sport Policy and Politics, 2*(3), 381–390.

Rioja, R. (2020, November 25). El inicio del siglo XXI: la edad de oro del deporte español. *20minutos.* www.20minutos.es/deportes/noticia/4485569/0/deporte-espanol-edad-oro-siglo-xxi/

Ronen, S., Gonçalves, B., Hu, K. Z., Vespignani, A., Pinker, S., & Hidalgo, C. A. (2014). Links that speak: The global language network and its association with global fame. *Proceedings of the National Academy of Sciences, 111*(52), E5616–E5622.

Rubiés, J. P. (2011). The worlds of Europeans, Africans, and Americans, c. 1490. In N. Canny & P. Morgan (Eds.), *The Oxford handbook of the atlantic world:1450–1850* (pp. 21–37). Oxford University Press.

Saharoy, S. (2020, August 3). Real Madrid and FC Barcelona are world football's most valuable brands. *The Times of India.* http://timesofindia.indiatimes.com/articleshow/77325479.cms?utm_source=contentofinterest&utm_medium=text&utm_campaign=cppst

Snyder, D. L. (2003). International sports law. In D. J. Cotten & J. T. Wolohan (Eds.), *Law for recreation and sport managers* (3rd ed., pp. 34–43). Kendall Hunt.

Chapter 2

Socio-cultural and historical background of sport in Spain and Portugal*

David Moscoso-Sánchez, Francisco Pinheiro, and Xavier Pujadas

Introduction

This chapter examines, from a socio-historical perspective, the influence of social, cultural, political, and economic changes on the development of the sport phenomenon in Spain and Portugal since the second half of the 20th century.

Bearing in mind the nature and specific characteristics of the dictatorships in both countries, it analyses the ups and downs of the sport system and the emergence of important contradictions in its final stages. After a long period in which sport was just a mere vehicle of nationalist fascist propaganda—with football being almost the only protagonist—, during the stage closest to the democratic transition and the start thereof the sport system was marked by a contradiction, that is, sports practice increased among the urban population, new sports realities came to the fore, and the regime found it impossible to universalise sports practice due to a vertical and inefficient structure.

In view of this, the democratisation process of sport in the two transitions (Spanish and Portuguese) was initially unclear and was based on slow structural changes and on sport policies that would progressively incorporate increased social participation, as they would be decentralised to local councils and popular sport was promoted from an initial phase until the 1990s. This period addresses the process of expansion of sport in the Spanish and Portuguese societies. This work also critically analyses the changes taking place in the sport system of both countries, given some historical, legislative, and political events, and looks at how the sport phenomenon influenced popular culture. Finally, the work addresses the consolidation of a hegemonic sport model, characterised by the global commodification of the so-called 'spectator sport' to the detriment of popular sport or sport for all.

Sport and politics at the end of the Spanish and Portuguese dictatorships

Despite the geographical and political proximity between these two countries, the sporting dynamics in Spain and Portugal ended up showing their own specific characteristics throughout the dictator regimes of both countries. In the Portuguese case, when the dictator regime came to power in May 1926 sport was in a process of consolidation and popularisation. The sport reality during the Portuguese dictatorship (1926–1974) was challenging, dominated by football, cycling, and roller hockey, and by a romantic vision of amateurism that delayed professional sport.

In the early 1930s, there was a sign of rapprochement between sport and fascism when the sporting milieu organised, for the first time, a Congress of Sports Clubs in Lisbon in December 1933. A Committee was then set up that put forward its core demands to the newly appointed head of government, António de Oliveira Salazar, who recognised the importance of 'physical culture discipline' for the 'benefit of Portugal' and the 'resurgence of the homeland' (Botto, 1955). Salazar promised to build a National Stadium in Lisbon—the first 'ambition' of Portuguese sport—and was supported by all. In the following years, the dictatorial regime set up the main sport structures, of a political-ideological nature, which lasted strong until the 1970s. Sport in a work context followed the guidelines issued by FNAT—*Fundação Nacional para a Alegria no Trabalho* [the National Foundation for Joy at Work], created in 1935. Youth organisations dedicated to sport and physical activity were then created for men (*Mocidade Portuguesa*—Portuguese Male Youth Organisation, in 1936) and for women (*Mocidade Portuguesa Feminina*—Portuguese Female Youth Organisation, in 1937). The INEF—Instituto Nacional de Educação Física [National Institute of Physical Education] was set up in 1940 for training teachers, and in 1942 the *Direcção-Geral de Educação Física, Desportos e Saúde Escolar* [Directorate General for Physical Education, Sport, and School Health] was created to supervise all Portuguese sport in the fascist period.

To complement this process, over the next decades the Portuguese dictatorial regime followed the example of the 'spectacularization politics' (Vassort, 2002) of the 1930s European fascist regimes, with the 'aim of showing the symbiosis between the two ideologies: the ideology of fascism and the ideology of sport' (Ibid., p. 176). With the start of the so-called concrete phase (Pinheiro, 2012, p. 67), particularly in football, many stadiums were built able to accommodate large crowds, of which the National Stadium, inaugurated in 1944, is a fitting example.

The overseas policy of the Portuguese fascist regime benefitted the most from this dynamic. The idea of 'nation' and the interpretation of the 'interest' of the Portuguese empire was at the centre of the political and ideological discourse (Pinto, 2004, p. 60), placing sport at the service of this idea. Football clubs from Mainland Portugal often visited the Portuguese African colonies (especially Angola and Mozambique), stressing the idea that the nation and the Empire stood united, with other sports following suit. Football turned out to be the greatest expression of that idea of a nation, based on the victories of SL Benfica in the European Champion Clubs' Cup in 1961 and 1962, Sporting CP in the Cup Winners' Cup in 1964, and the triumphant campaign of the national team in the 1966 World Cup (3rd place). Sport was also mediatised in Portuguese society with the arrival of television in the 1950s, speeding up a process that until then had been bolstered by the radio and the press. Nevertheless, a new phase began after the outbreak of the Colonial War, student protests in the 1960s, and the wearing down of the regime, with inconsistencies in the relationship between sport and fascism, culminating in a desire for renewal after the 1974 democratic revolution.

In the case of the Spanish sport system, the 1960s also marked a shift in direction. While the Francoist state progressively moved away from the harsh postulates of the post-war period—influenced by Falangism and the leaders involved in the Civil War—the official discourse on sport evolved to a 'public need', in line with what was happening in European democracies (Santacana, 2011, p. 226). When the head of the National Sports Delegation, General Moscardó, passed away in 1956, he was succeeded by the more moderate José Antonio Elola Olaso. The National Sports Delegation changed its name to 'National Delegation of Physical Education and Sports' (DNEFyD—Delegación Nacional de Educación Física y Deportes), with the approach to sport being more formative and less militaristic, as 'it is a comprehensive educational instrument, not only in physical terms but also in intellectual and moral terms, being integrally human' (Boletín de la DNEFyD, 1959, p. 4).

Along with the shift in discourse, from the 1960s onwards sports clubs were allowed to choose some of their board members. The new vision of the dictatorship challenged for an increasing presence of sport in Spanish society, which should be promoted through the construction of sports facilities and by making people aware of the benefits of physical activity.

Against the background of the economic development of the 1960s, this process of sporting openness was consolidated with the adoption of the Physical Education Law [Ley de Educación Física] in 1961, which made it possible to increase the DNEFyD's revenue, thanks to the stake in the profits of the sports betting services. According to this law, 'the State recognises and guarantees the rights of Spaniards to physical education and practice' and 'physical education is a public need and will therefore receive the protection and assistance of the State'. This legal recognition brought, for the first time, Franco's discourse on sport and physical education closer to the idea of sport as a tool to promote health, as advocated by other European states.

In the same vein, the new legislation created the National Institute of Physical Education (INEF—Instituto Nacional de Educación Física) 'for the training and retraining of physical education teachers and sports coaches' (Article 15). The regulation also officially established the 'full sovereignty' of the Spanish Olympic Committee and promoted a plan for the construction of sports facilities.

Nevertheless, the effectiveness of these legal provisions and the renewed sport-related discourse was limited. Some novel initiatives such as the creation of the Madrid INEF came to fruition (1967), as did the advertising campaigns for the practice of sport, for example, *'Contamos contigo'* [We count on you], or the 'operation 100,000' for the procurement of basketball players (Solar, 2020, p. 89). However, these initiatives proved to be ineffective when it came to the construction of facilities, due to the limited and inefficient investment plan and the historical lack of infrastructures. The reality is that there was a remarkable growth in the situation in the early 1960s, but woefully inadequate by European standards at the time.

The number of federated players in Spain nevertheless multiplied five-fold in ten years, from 106,453 in 1960 to 524,091 in 1970. The most significant increase occurred in the 1970s, reflecting a change in mindset, external influence, modernisation in citizens' habits, and economic growth. Thus, at the end of the Franco dictatorship in 1974, there were 1,340,803 federated athletes (Pujadas & Santacana, 1995, p. 192). The campaigns to boost the sporting activity and the cultural and socio-economic changes in the 1960s revealed a paradox in the last decade of the dictatorship: an increase in citizens' awareness of sport and, at the same time, the regime's limited capacity to make it possible for them to practice sport. According to a survey in 1975, 22% of citizens practised some type of sport, while at the same time stating that the greatest obstacle to practice was the lack of facilities and 'the lack of interest of the bodies responsible for such matters' (Abadía & Pujadas, 2010, p. 36).

Towards a democratic sport system

The democratisation of the state's structures in Spain did not begin immediately after Franco's death. The Spanish transition model, known as 'change without rupture', involved a slow road to the democratisation of the sport system but without a real transformation in the first years and against a background of political, social, and economic uncertainty and instability (Pujadas & Abadía, 2020). Indeed, Franco's National Sports Delegation and the 1961 Physical Education Law remained in force until 1977 and 1980, respectively (BOE, 1961). The promotion of municipal policies on the social expansion of sport (Abadía, 2007) and the shifts towards 'sport for all' with the 1978 Constitution can be considered as the key elements to understand the actual start of the democratisation of sport. García and Lagardera (1998) argue that the democratic transition and in particular the 1978 Spanish Constitution played a decisive role in the dissemination of sport in Spain, by allowing this activity to not be regarded as a privilege of a minority. As stated in Chapter Three of Section I of the Spanish Constitution (Article 43.3) 'the public authorities shall promote health education, physical education, and sport'.

The democratic process was a salutary shock in many social fields, including sport, which was no stranger to this climate of change and demands. According to some authors (*Ibid.*, p. 37), 'the aim was to broaden the bases of popular sport, allow the greatest possible number of people to practice sport in adequate facilities, universalise the teaching and practice of physical education and sport at school, viewing sport as a citizen's right, a public service'. The sporting situation in Spain normalised from this moment on. The Spanish Constitution provided the political and administrative institutions with basic legislation to achieve this objective. Article 1 of Law 13/1980 on Physical Culture and Sport was aimed at 'the promotion, guidance, and coordination of physical education and sport, as essential factors in the training and integral development of the person'. The implementation of this law meant, in practice, that all educational establishments had to provide sufficient sports infrastructures for the teaching of physical education. Moreover, it supported the construction of other sports facilities and spaces for the promotion of sport.

The number of sports facilities in those years in Spain increased from 19,418 in 1975 to 48,723 in 1986 (a 60% increase). According to data from the National Census of Sports Facilities (Consejo Superior de Deportes, 2021a), in the latter year, 32% of educational centres already had some of these facilities.

In this context, several measures enshrined in the 1975 *European Sport for All Charter* were implemented. Following the Charter, the Spanish Administration should promote sport activity and the construction of sports facilities through city councils and schools. This resulted in an 11% increase in the number of athletes between 1980 and 1985, that is, 25% and 34%, respectively.

This upward trend in the number of athletes and facilities continued until the mid-1990s, so much so that in 1995 the number of Spanish athletes was close to 39%, according to data from the *Survey of Sports Habits in Spain* (Centro de Investigaciones Sociológicas, 1995), and the number of sports facilities totalled 66,670 in 1997, according to the *National Census of Sports Facilities* (Consejo Superior de Deportes, 2021a), an increase of 27% compared to 1986.

By the early 1990s, sport had become so important among the Spanish population that it is difficult to understand today's society without seeing sport as an essential part of its culture. As Lagardera (1992, p. 16) put it, 'the men and women of today have learned to live by running after a ball, watching the Olympic finals on television, betting money or using tracksuits and sports shoes as their usual sportswear for their physical activity or weekend breaks'.

The conquering of the cultural imaginary by sport also extended to the Portuguese case, as a process of continuity, but also of acceleration, as from the 1974 democratic revolution. As part of the 'renovation' effort, Decree-law 408/71 was published on September 27, 1971, introducing the new Organic Law of the Ministry of National Education, which regulated the youth and sports sector. This latter domain included the Directorate General for Physical Education and Sports and the Sports Development Fund, the former having to 'supervise' all Portuguese sport and the latter to 'provide support' and 'financial aid' to 'private sporting initiatives'. Two years later the government took action to reorganise this Directorate General (Decree-law 82/73), changing the ideology based on elitism to 'creating mass sporting habits in the country', as stated in the Preamble to the 1973 Decree-law.

This concern was strengthened after the establishment of democracy in 1974 with the start of the 'period of 'sport for all'' (Rosário, 1996, p. 283) and sport as a 'right of the people' (Carvalho, 1977). Political and social efforts were made to replace the fascist structure set up in the 1930s, the legislation was amended, informative documents were produced, and meetings and training activities were organised, notably, the National Sports Meeting (ENDO) in March 1975 on the topics of 'Sport is Culture' and 'Rethinking Sport'. An ideological characterisation of the Estado Novo also emerged, based on the concept of the '3 Fs' (a trilogy formed by Fátima, Football, and Fado), to explain the fascist process of social numbness through religion, sport and music.

At the institutional level, the following developments were made: the INEF became ISEF—Higher Institute of Physical Education (part of the Technical University of Lisbon); definition of the new articles of incorporation of the Directorate General for Sports (DGD) and FNAT, converted into INATEL—National Institute of Portugal for the Use of Workers' Leisure Time; the Schools for Physical Education Instructors, clearly ideological in nature, were extinguished. In the following years, a vast body of legislation on sport was adopted, which would lead to the definitive publication of the Sport System Act (LBSD) in 1990 (Law 1/90), which attempted to cover all areas of Portuguese sport and promote gender equality—data from 1978 to 1979 show that out of 27,948 sports players in Portugal, 90% were men and only 10% were women. Following the new concerns of the DGD, other initiatives were put in place related to sports for the disabled and the elderly. However, the 1980s were marked by asymmetries between regions in terms of the number of participants and the distribution of sports facilities, evident in the National Sports Charter published in 1984.

The Portuguese sport panorama was radically changed in the early 1990s with the publication of the aforementioned LBSD and a vast body of legislation that reflected the political will to remodel the sports sector. The DGD and the Sports Development Fund were extinguished in 1993, and the Sports Institute was created. The opening of new courses was promoted to endure the academic training of physical education and sports graduates. The 'post-revolutionary' idea of 'sport is culture' gradually began to fade away, while (professional) sport as a commodity and spectacle, garnering large audiences, and based on the popularity of football picked up momentum.

The consolidation of the logic of trade versus popular logic: the hegemony of competitive sport and spectator sport

As in Portugal, the encouraging trend that had marked the democratisation of sport in Spain during the first democratic phase dissipated gradually over time. First, the percentage of athletes only increased by 1% between 1995 and 2014 (39% and 40%, respectively), in contrast with the 11% growth between 1980 and 1995. Secondly, the growth in the number of sports facilities built fell considerably between 1996 and 2020: while in 1996 the ratio of sports facilities per 1,000 inhabitants was 1.73, this ratio now dropped to 1.67, according to the latest data from the National Census of Sports Facilities (Consejo Superior de Deportes, 2021a).

This translates as meaning that the low participation in sport in Spain is related to a change in sports policy, which began to put professional sport and spectator sport before sport for all. In fact, this was influenced by the change in the legislation regulating sport in this country in 1990 and the holding of the Barcelona '92 Olympic Games. As regards the former, Law 13/1980 on Physical Culture and

Sport was repealed by a new legal framework, Law 10/1990 on Sport. The new law was a turning point in Spanish sport policy, as its priorities were the professional regulation of sport and the consolidation of top-level competition. The place of popular sport is not very clear in this law. Thus, while at the beginning of Spanish democracy sport emerged alongside the concept of citizenship, with the maturity reached after the enactment of Law 10/1990 on Sport citizenship is pushed to the background, behind sports organisations and professional sport.

It is no accident that this law was created two years before the Barcelona 92' Olympic Games, and that since then public funding for competitive sport has increased, one of which was the Support Plan for Olympic Sport (ADO), created in 1989 by the Spanish government to support high-performance athletes. The programme financed the full-time training and preparation of top-level Olympic athletes. Moreover, an ambitious project was developed for the construction of high-performance and sports development centres, aimed at achieving excellence in sports performance.

Public funding for competitive sports has increased since then at the expense of funding for physical education and popular sport. According to INE data, most of the government budget in Spain for sport—which is barely 0.01% of national GDP (€3.3 inhabitant/year)—is allocated to federated sport and competitive sport. In 2010, it had already accounted for 92% (€156 M) of this budget, compared to 100% in 2018 (€175 M) (Consejo Superior de Deportes, 2021b).

The fact that the funds allocated to the promotion of sport for all in Spain have dropped significantly since the 1990s to this day, in contrast to those for competitive sport, maybe that the responsibility to promote popular sport was gradually transferred from the state administration to the regional governments, and from these to the city councils, with public intervention in sport being diminished and limited. For example, while the general state administration devoted 0.06% of its budget in 2018 to sports-related items (€3.7 inhab./year), the regional governments allocated 0.19% (€7.7 inhab./year) and city councils allocated 3.23% (€50.2 inhab./year) to these items (Consejo Superior de Deportes, 2021b). This situation is a handicap for small municipalities, which are left with no budget to promote sport.

Following the 2008 economic crisis, this situation has tended to worsen, with many Spanish city councils privatising municipal sports services, justifying this on the grounds of the need to rationalise public spending. Similarly, the Spanish National Government cabinet with responsibility for sport reached the point of not dedicating any budget allocation to school sport and sport promotion since 2018. This situation could be explained, among other reasons, by the gradual interest of the mass media in sporting events, the marketing generated around the world of sport, and the change in values in Spanish society over the last three decades.

Meanwhile, to this day in Spain there is still an unacceptable percentage of the population without access to sport, especially women, the elderly, and the lower classes—a clear continuation of chronic social inequalities (or 'sporting divide') that have persisted since the pre-democratic period. Inequalities in access to sport are not only due to socio-demographic and socio-economic factors, but also to territorial factors, as there are clear differences in the number of athletes between autonomous communities, and between cities and towns.

As a consequence of the coronavirus pandemic crisis, the current situation is already daunting, as some of the measures adopted are aimed at the consolidation of this sporting reality. The Royal Decree of 21 April on additional urgent measures to support the economy and employment was adopted in April 2020, Article 26 of which creates the Spanish Global Sport Foundation (Fundación España Deporte Global). This measure points to the continuation of a model of high sports industry in Spain and sustains football as a monopoly sport. The measure represents the formula 'more football, more competition, more show', overlooking the fact that it is in the general interest of the country to prioritise the 20 million or so people who play sport in this country.

In the Portuguese case, amidst a pandemic (2020–2021), there were no additional measures in terms of support to the sport system. The government set the value of effective expenditure for sport at around €40 M, along the lines of what was done in 2019 in the pre-COVID period. Although most would agree that sport was still 'neglected' and 'a postponed priority' (Silva, 2019), the government's ambition in 2021 was to 'put Portugal in the group of 15 countries with the most active physical and sports activity in the European Union by 2030'.

In percentage terms, total Portuguese public expenditure with sport was about 0.04% in this period, which is quite low when compared to the European average (1% of public expenditure). Despite the low level of government investment, data released in 2010–2012 by the National Statistics Institute (INE) showed that Portuguese sport represented, on average, 1.2% of the Gross Added Value and 1.4% of the full-time equivalent of the Portuguese economy, similar to the metalworking, computer or clothing industries.

There have been successive changes in recent decades in Portugal involving a total of 19 ministers responsible for sport between 1976 and 2007, with marked structural changes in 1993, 1997, 2003, and 2007. The lack of a 'mobilising instrument' with a 'vision of the future for the development of sport in Portugal' is felt by all (Silva, 2009, p. 84). This organisational and legislative instability—more than 60 diplomas on sport were published between 1960 and 2007—hurt the indicators on the sport participation rate, which did not substantially improve over the decades. In 1998, for example, the sports participation rate of Portuguese people between the age of 15 and 74 was 23%, a rate almost identical to that recorded ten years earlier, in 1988 (Marivoet, 2001). And in 2004, as part of a survey undertaken by Eurobarometer on 'The Citizens of the European Union and Sport', the Portuguese society registered a result of 22%, corresponding to Portuguese people over the age of 15 who said they practised sport at least once a week. Worryingly, 73% of Portuguese said that they did not do any sport—the worst in the European Union. These indicators remained almost unchanged over the following decade. However, the number of federated athletes increased from 265,588 in 1996 to

667,715 in 2018, largely due to a greater representation of women in sport, with the number of federated female athletes increasing overall from 70,051 in 2003 to 203,189 in 2018.

Football continued to be the most representative sporting discipline receiving media attention. Its two organisational structures—the Portuguese Football Federation and the Portuguese Professional Football League—have become professional, and a mega-worldwide event was organised in Portugal in 2004—the European Football Championship (Euro), representing a national financial input of more than one billion euros and a debt payable until 2049. Euro-2004 proved to be Portugal's claim on modernity, 30 years after it had come out of the longest fascist regime in Europe, with football becoming a world-level factory for Portuguese celebrities. But while professional football went global, leveraged by players such as Figo, Cristiano Ronaldo, or Mourinho—and their worldwide projection boosted by the social media—, amateur football still lacked organisation and infrastructures to be played by all, just like other sports disciplines. This is a very similar situation to that of Spain, where football also lies at the heart of public action.

Conclusions

The history of sport in the Iberian Peninsula shows a common path. Both Spain and Portugal experienced forty years of dictatorial regimes in the 20th century, which gave rise to a sporting system marked by political instrumentalisation, the prominence of football, and a poor sport structure.

The dictatorships in both countries promoted a sport structure limited to the formal organisation of sport, hindering access to sport to the majority of the population until the 1990s, although today sport participation is still lower than in other countries with a greater democratic sporting tradition. The majority of the population still does not play any sport and there is still a gap that keeps the majority of women, adults, older people, and the lower and lower-middle classes away from this activity. Moreover, there is a blatant territorial imbalance in the supply of sporting facilities, equipment, and activities between large cities and rural areas, and between regions, which is more striking in Portugal than in Spain.

This context is also influenced by the historical territorial imbalances in both countries compared to regions in central and northern Europe, which continue to affect the life chances of the population, not only in terms of access to sport, but also in general in the access to education, employment, and housing. However, other factors also come into play, such as the important political and social weight of football, a sport that 'monopolises' financial resources and institutional attention at the expense of other sports, and the triumph of the logic of trade, which is expressed in the dominance of spectator and competitive sport over popular sport.

Note

* Translation to English funded by national funds through the FCT—Foundation for Science and Technology, I.P. within the scope of the project UIDB/00460/2020.

References

Abadía, S. (2007). The irruption of the sport for all in the city of Barcelona (1975–1982). *Local Sport in Europe. 4th Conference of EASS, 43*(4).

Abadía, S., & Pujadas, X. (2010). The initial post-authoritarian period in Portugal (1974–82) and Spain (1975–82): A suitable framework for a sports democratization process of shared similarities and characteristics. *International Journal of Iberian Studies, 23*(1), 23–37.

Boletín de la DNEFyD. (1959), *190*, 4.

Boletín Oficial del Estado (BOE). (1961). Ley 77/1961 de 23 de diciembre sobre Educación Física.

Botto, J. A. (1955). *Salazar e o desporto*. Policopiada.

Carvalho, M. (1977). Desporto, Direito do Povo. *Revista Vértice, 37*, 402–403.

Centro de Investigaciones Sociológicas. (1995). *Encuesta de hábitos deportivos en España* (1188). www.cis.es/cis/opencm/ES/1_encuestas/estudios/ver.jsp?estudio=1188

Consejo Superior de Deportes. (2021a). *Censo Nacional de Instalaciones Deportivas*. www.csd.gob.es/es/csd/instalaciones/censo-nacional-de-instalaciones-deportivas

Consejo Superior de Deportes. (2021b). *Gasto Público Vinculado al Deporte*. www.culturaydeporte.gob.es/servicios-al-ciudadano/estadisticas/cultura/mc/deportedata/gasto-publico-deportes/gasto-publico-resultados.html

García, M., & Lagardera, F. (1998). La perspectiva sociológica del deporte. In M. García, N. Puig, & F. Lagardera (Eds.), *Sociología del deporte* (pp. 13–40). Alianza Editorial.

Lagardera, F. (1992). El deporte moderno visto desde la sociología histórica. In *Actas del I Encuentro UNISPORT sobre sociología del deporte* (pp. 1–38). UNISPORT.

Marivoet, S. (2001). *Hábitos desportivos da população portuguesa*. CEFD.

Pinheiro, F. (2012). Futebol e política na ditadura. In N. Tiesler & N. Domingos (Eds.), *Futebol português* (pp. 47–82). Afrontamento.

Pinto, A. C. (Ed.). (2004). *Portugal contemporâneo*. Dom Quixote.

Pujadas, X., & Abadía, S. (2020). Deporte, democratización y construcción ciudadana en España. Los límites de un proceso deslumbrante (1975–2020). In N. Puig & A. Camps (Eds.), *Diálogos sobre el deporte (1975–2020)* (pp. 49–62). INDE.

Pujadas, X., & Santacana, C. (1995). *Història il·lustrada de l'esport a Catalunya*. Columna.

Rosário, A. T. (1996). *O desporto em Portugal*. Piaget.

Santacana, C. (2011). Espejo de un régimen. Transformación de las estructuras deportivas y su uso político y propagandístico (1939–1961). In X. Pujadas (Ed.), *Atletas y ciudadanos. Historia social del deporte en España (1870–2010)* (pp. 205–232). Alianza Editorial.

Silva, A. (2009). O Estado, os governos e a administração pública desportiva. In J. Bento & J. M. Constantino (Eds.), *O Desporto e o Estado* (pp. 67–84). Afrontamento.

Silva, J. A. (2019). Desporto a prioridade adiada . . .: orçamento de estado 2019. *Diário de Notícias*. www.dn.pt/opiniao/opiniao-dn/convidados/desporto-a-prioridade-adiada-e-outros-equivocos-orcamento-de-estado-2019-10501453.html

Solar, L. V. (2020). Las políticas deportivas en el proceso de descentralización. In N. Puig & A. Camps (Eds.), *Diálogos sobre el deporte (1975–2020)* (pp. 86–102). INDE.

Vassort, P. (2002). *Football et politique*. L'Harmattan.

Chapter 3

The European Union and sport

Economy, public policy and legislation

Pilar Aparicio-Chueca, Amal Elasri-Ejjaberi, Xavier Triadó-Ivern, and Marc Blanch Casadesús

The regulatory framework of EU policies in the area of sport

Responsibility for sport was assigned to the European Union in December 2009 with the entry into force of the Treaty of Lisbon. The EU is responsible for developing policies based on comparative data and for promoting cooperation and managing initiatives to promote physical activity and sport in Europe.

The data show the decisive role played by sport not only in people's health and physical fitness, but also as an element that helps shape and bind society, improving general well-being and helping to resolve social problems such as racism, social exclusion, and gender inequality. Furthermore, sport is an invaluable tool in the EU's foreign relations.

More than 7 million people are employed in jobs related to sport (the equivalent of 3.5% of total employment in the EU), and goods and services related to sport stand at €294 million, representing 3% of the total gross value of the UE. Sport can also, directly and indirectly, affect the development and cohesion of the regions and can be a very valuable way of relating to different social groups (Bosch et al., 2019).

The Council of Europe was the first intergovernmental organisation to invest in sport in the broader sense, as part of the 1953 European Cultural Agreement. In 1963, the Committee of Ministers of the Council of Europe introduced the 'European sport certificate', aimed at promoting youth participation in the sporting activity by instilling the values of European solidarity. The Council of Europe also formulated the notion of 'sport for all' in 1966 (Dimitrov et al., 2006).

Briefly reviewing the historical background, while the word 'sport' was absent from both the Treaty of Rome in 1957 and the Treat of Maastricht in 1992, it was taken up by the Council of Europe as part of the European Cultural Convention, adopted in 1954. The Council of Europe and the CEE affirmed interest in sport from the end of the 1950s onwards, doing so from different perspectives.

The 'European Sport for All Charter' can be considered as the document that formalised and set the groundwork for European sport nowadays. It started to circulate as the European model and could serve as the basis for member states' government policies (European Comission, 2007, 2015). It was validated by the Parliamentary Assembly in 1972, and later in 1975 passed by the European ministers for sport. Its main objectives were to reiterate the importance of sport in our civilisation, endow it with a structure of cooperation in the headquarters of the Council of Europe itself, and to set out the terms of a recommendation on the European Sport for All Charter.

In 1985, the regulatory framework of sport was incorporated into the Recommendations of the Council of Milan, in which sport was included as one of citizens' special rights (Parrish, 2003a; Gasparini, 2020). And in the 1990s, the EU institutions' interest in promoting sport became further apparent in the issuance of directives and recommendations and the organisation of European sporting events, culminating in the first Directive from the Commission with its guidelines for community sports policies and leading to the First European Sports Forum in 1991. Nonetheless, sport remained without a legal basis incorporated into the foundational treaties, giving the EU no authority in sporting matters.

With the 1992 approval of the European Sports Charter, sport was defined in its social and educational dimensions. In 1995, the Court of Justice of the European Union ruled on the Bosman affair, sustaining that as a professional activity sport was submitted to European rules on the free movement of labour and fair competition. And later, in 1997, an Appendix Declaration on Sport was included in the Treaty of Amsterdam (1997). These were the first significant political signs that the EU member states considered sport and its associated values as important matters. The Declaration highlighted the social dimension of sport and encouraged the European institutions to consult sports organisations in matters of importance in the sporting sphere. It also recommends that particular attention be paid to amateur sport.

In accordance with the social and educational dimension of sport, the First European Conference on Sports was held in Athens in 1999 to debate matters such as the European sports model, the relationships between TV and sport, and the problem of doping. In December of the same year, the European Commission drafted the Helsinki report on sport, which defined the educational and social functions of sport not only in the sense of construction but also in terms of the challenges, barriers, and obstacles it faced, including doping, commercialisation, protection of young athletes, dual careers, and so on.

Parallel to the legal and regulatory construction process and drafting of the Foundational Treaties of the EU, the European Council of Niza in 2000 defined a European model of sport based on respect for cultural diversity and with a clear social dimension. This document underlined the fact that the European Community had only indirect competency over sport, and it also reminded each member state of the need to consider sport in their respective national policies.

At a meeting of the EU Ministers of Education, Culture, and Youth in May 2003, the Council published a declaration about 'the special value of sport for youth', highlighting the function of sport in terms of social cohesion, tolerance and respect, and its contribution to the fight against racism, sexism, and discrimination in general.

The Constitutional Treaty signed in Rome in October 2004 included sport in its Article III, respecting the principle of subsidiarity and the definition of supporting competencies. To this effect, the then European Community equipped itself with tools to implement Europe-wide actions to promote the values associated with sport through social, educational, and cultural initiatives, and/or initiatives aimed at youth and other groups.

With the entry into force of the Treaty of Lisbon in December 2009, for the first time, the European Union acquired a specific competence in sporting matters. Article 6, letter e) of the Treaty on the Functioning of the European Union grants the UE the competence to carry out actions to support and complement the actions of member states in the area of sport, while Article 165 (1) details a sporting policy, providing that '*the Union shall contribute to the promotion of European sporting issues, while taking into account the specific nature of sport, its structures based on voluntary activity and its social and educational functioning*'. Article 165 (2) continues that '*Union action shall be aimed at developing the European dimension in sport, by promoting fairness and openness in sporting competitions, promoting cooperation between bodies responsible for sport, and protecting the physical and moral integrity of sportsmen and sportswomen, especially the youngest sportsmen and sportswomen*'. From now onwards, sport for the EU was no longer transversal in other EU policies but it had its own framework of action and funding that enabled it to launch actions, projects, and initiatives in three main areas: freedom of movement, competencies, and audio-visual and other community policies, especially concerning education, training, and youth. The new competence meant that the EU could intervene in sport and now had a legal basis for supporting this sector structurally via a spending programme funded by the EU budget. Furthermore, it could now speak with a single voice in international fora and third countries. The EU ministers of sport also attend the meetings of the Council of Education, Youth, Culture, and Sports.

During 2014 to 2020, for the first time, a specific budgetary line in the Erasmus+ programme framework was established to support projects and networks in sport, the details of which we will return to in the second part of this chapter.

Furthermore, the EU's competencies in the area of the single market have also had a considerable impact on sport. For example, the Court of Justice of the European Communities has developed important case law with profound implications for the sporting sphere, in the same way as did the Bosman Law. In parallel, the EU has exercised its 'indicative law' powers in closely related areas such as education, health, and social inclusion, through their respective financing programmes.

Globalisation and the high volume and frequency of visitors to Europe indicated that major sporting events could be huge attractions for tourists and an excellent opportunity to accelerate performance, values, and the benefits of both national and international sport. In May 2016, the Council of Europe presented its conclusions about improving integrity, transparency, and good governance in terms of large sporting events. In this document, the Council invited member states to incorporate integrity and transparency in future work concerning sport at the European level, to support the implementation of criteria and procedures related to good governance, and to identify and develop public-private collaboration models and exchange good practices related to this cooperation.

In its session dedicated to sport on 23 May 2017, the Council of Europe, Youth, Culture and Sport adopted the EU's new plan of work for sport (2017–2020), which differentiates between key topics including the integrity in sport (with a focus on good governance, the protection of minors, the fight against match-fixing, doping and corruption), the economic dimension (with a focus on innovation in sport and the single digital market), and sport and society (with a focus on social inclusion, coaches, the media, the environment, health, education, and sports diplomacy).

On December 1, 2020, the Council of European Sports Ministers adopted the fourth EU Working Plan for Sport (2021–2024). Physical activity plays a major role in the plan, which establishes investment in sport and physical activity that is beneficial for health, including the creation of sporting opportunities for all generations, as key priorities.

The plan also proposes 'strengthening the recovery of the sports sector and its resilience to the crisis during the COVID-19 pandemic and aftermath' (European Comission, 2021). Other key areas of action include prioritising capacities and qualifications in sport by exchanging best practices and developing knowledge, protecting integrity and values, and through the socioeconomic and environmental dimensions of sport and the promotion of gender equality. The European Union also aspires to increase the proportion of women in management and coaching posts, promoting equal conditions for all sportspersons, and improving media coverage of women in sport.

Regarding the EU's ecological transition, 'ecological sport' also features as a priority since the plan proposes the development of a common framework with shared commitments that take the European Pact for the Climate into account. Special emphasis is placed on innovation and digitalisation in all the areas of the sports sector.

In response to the COVID-19 pandemic, on 22 June 2020, the Council adopted its *Conclusions on the impact of the COVID-19 pandemic on the sports sector*, proposing different measures for its recovery. The document confirmed that the entire sector had been seriously affected by COVID-19, including economically, and that the pandemic had had devastating consequences for all levels of sport (European Comission, 2021). The Council underlined the need for local, national, regional, and EU strategies to support the sports sector and to ensure that it continued to make an important contribution to the well-being of the citizens of the Union. Among other items, the Council encouraged EU institutions to complement national efforts by channelling financial assistance to the sector through the available EU programmes and funds such as Erasmus+, the European Solidarity Body, the political cohesion funds, and the Investment Initiatives in Response to Coronavirus (IIRC, IIRC+). Furthermore, the Council highlighted the need to promote dialogue between the member states and the pertinent interested parties to debate strategies to allow sporting activities to re-start in a safe and, where possible, coordinated way, and to prevent future crises, to increase the resilience of the EU's sports sector.

On 1 December 2020, the EU's Ministers of Sport held a conference about the current challenges facing the organisation in terms of international sporting incidents. The COVID-19 pandemic has hampered the freedom of movement of sportspeople, made complicated by the different national rules and in constant evolution in terms of PCR tests, quarantine, and other health-related issues. The debate has highlighted the need to increase exchange and cooperation in the sports sector on an EU scale.

On 10 February 2021, the Parliament approved a Resolution that highlighted the need to provide EU member countries with financial, strategic, and practical support to prevent the pandemic from having any lasting effects on youth and sport. The Resolution stressed that financial assistance should not be limited to major sporting incidents with spectators and that base-level sport should be given the maximum importance in the recovery measures. Furthermore, it asked the commission to develop a European approach to address the negative effects of the pandemic in the sports sector.

Impact and actions of EU initiatives in sport

In 1966, the Council of Europe formulated the concept of 'sport for all', designed to raise society's awareness of the universal possibility of doing sport and the importance of access to sport for everyone regardless of age, sex, and ethnicity. The main objective was to defend some common principles and to combat certain phenomena considered contrary to the 'values of Europe' (doping, spectator violence, discrimination in sport, and homophobia). Since then, the EU has implemented different initiatives, programmes, and specific actions related to sport (European Commission, 2019; Fernández, 2017).

With regards to some of the European projects in sport, in 1994 the EOSE[1] (European Observatory of Sport and Employment) was created as an informal group and later officially registered in 2002 as the European Observatory of Sport and Employment (EOSE) (Parrish, 2003b). It is responsible for promoting courses of study and projects related to the area of sporting professions. Its most well-known project on sports education and training in Europe was called 'Vocaesport', which lead to the development of the QEQ (European Qualifications Chart in the sports sector) project, the objective of which was to design a European structure of activities and professions in the sports sector with descriptions of the related competencies based on the levels identified in the QEQ.

In 1973, the Eurobarometer was created as an official statistics body within the 'Public Opinion' section of the European Commission's general organisation areas. The Eurobarometer keeps a regular check of the situation of sport and physical activity in Europe.

The COMPASS project, created in 1998, is an initiative funded jointly by CONI, UK Sport and Sport England, into which other European countries have progressively incorporated. The objective is to examine the existing systems to gather and analyse data on sports participation in European countries to identify the methodologies and merge them.

In 2010, the European Commission published the report 'Strategic Choices for the Implementation of the New EU Competence in the Field of Sport', which measured the results of the public consultation procedure and highlighted the need for EU action to support the social, educational, and health functions of sporting activity.

Regarding the initiatives in sport, one of the first was the designation of the *European Year of Education through Sport* in 2004. This decision coincided with two world-level sports events held in Europe: football's Europa Cup in Portugal and the Olympic Games in Athens. With a budget of €11.5 million, celebrating the European Year served to promote the educational and social values linked to sport in this context of high impact and media coverage and to support the organisation of sporting events from one's own territory and using specific schools, federations, and sports club actions.

In 2006, the European Commission published the first data on the wider economic impact of sport. The results showed that in 2004 sport generated an added value of €407,000 million, or in other words 3.7% of the EU's GDP, and it created jobs for 15 million people, representing 5.4% of the labour force. In 2007, the European Commission set out the provisions of an EU policy for sport in the White Book on sport and the Pierre de Coubertin plan of action (European Comission, 2007). The White Book[2] on sport is the first global initiative in the EU, proposing a series of actions that must be implemented in three areas:

The social role of sport: improving public health through physical activity, the fight against doping, reinforcing the role of sport in education, volunteering activities, social inclusion, the fight against racism, and sport in general as a tool for development.

The economic dimension of sport: collecting comparable data.

The organisation of sport: the specific nature of sport, free movement, player transfers, the protection of minors, corruption and money laundering, the system of licenses for clubs, and audio-visual rights.

These areas are featured in the 'Pierre de Coubertin Action Plan', which details 53 specific proposals for future EU action in these areas. The activities proposed range from supporting an EU physical activity network to launching a study to evaluate the contribution of the sector in the 'Lisbon Agenda for growth and employment in the EU' (Fernández, 2017).

Another European initiative in which sport plays an integral part is the Erasmus+ programme, the hugely consolidated EU project for education, training, youth, and sport for 2014–2020, with more than 40 projects funded in 2015 alone (Figure 3.1).

In the economic area, 1.8% of the annual budget allocated to sport was used in the Erasmus+ program, to support European non-profit collaborative associations

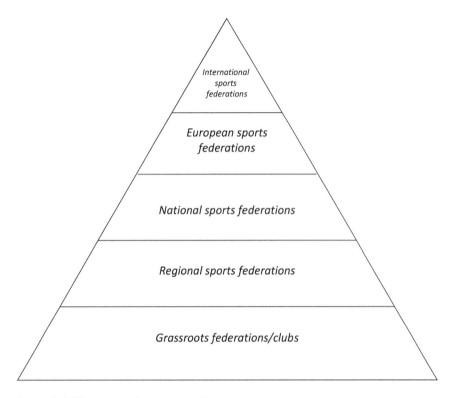

Figure 3.1 The pyramid structure of sport
Source: Adapted from EU White Paper on sport, 2007

and sports events. The programme has also contributed to strengthening the empirical base to formulate policies, or in other words financial studies. Last, the programme has supported dialogue between the pertinent European parties. Since it started, the EU has contributed 266 million euros, with the total amount increasing annually. On May 30, 2018, the Commission published a proposal for regulations to establish the future Erasmus+ programme (2021–2027), wherein the quota for sport remained stable at 1.8% of the total budget, which included the key actions of mobility for learning and support for the development of policies and cooperation. The proposal was later modified and approved in the European parliament in March 2019.

While the Erasmus+ programme impacted directly on the youngest section of society, an initiative with a wider reach among the European population was needed to help combat physical inactivity in the territory. In 2012, the European Week of Sport was launched to encourage European citizens to do physical activity. This action is comprised of a set of initiatives proposed in the European Parliament resolution of the same year, which support the EU via the Erasmus+ programme. It emerged after the Eurobarometer survey showed that 59% of Europeans never or hardly ever exercise or do sport, which impacts not only people's health and well-being but also on the economy in the form of some negative collateral effects such as increased health care costs, productivity loss in the workplace, and reduced employability. Within the framework of this week of sport, the UE has extended the initiative at the local, regional, and national levels using high-level athletes who act as ambassadors during iconic events to promote the week.

Thanks to these sporting proposals, the European population has benefitted from different activities that promote and facilitate sporting involvement on the continent. Although the problem of sedentarism and physical inactivity is being mitigated, social inclusion continues to be one of the EU's priorities for the role of sport in society. Because it brings people together, builds communities, and helps fight racism and xenophobia, sport has the potential to make a decisive contribution to the integration of immigrants in the EU. The use of sport as a diplomatic tool has also been a key driver of EU policies. A high-level group, created to evaluate the potential of sport in terms of EU diplomacy, has examined the positive impact that sports projects can have on strengthening international relations, considering matters like education, the economy, culture, health, and employment. As a result of this work, in 2016 the EU sports ministers drew conclusions about sport diplomacy, confirming the growing status of sport in international relations.

Football plays a key role in social inclusion through the participation of football players' unions (like in the *Show Racism the Red Card* project) and governing bodies like UEFA, which has helped the EU to map out the activities of its member states in support of the social inclusion of refugees.

In 2018, the UE launched the #BeInclusive sports awards to recognise the achievements of the organisations that have successfully developed sports projects geared towards the social inclusion of ethnic minorities, refugees, people with disabilities, and any other group that face challenging social circumstances. The campaign has been gaining momentum since its launch, managing to impact 40 million Europeans in the week the initiative is celebrated via more than 100,000 events in 38 countries. This sports initiative is currently financed with the largest public funding in the world, and its popularity is still growing.

As part of the effort to combat gender stereotypes and to promote women's access to decision-making roles in sport, the Commission is looking to ensure that 30% of decision-making positions are occupied by women in 2020.

The Commission's plans and ambitions to expand and consolidate the role of sport are gathering force in parallel to the growth of the popularity of this initiative. With a budget of 28,000 million euros, the new Erasmus+ programme, which covers the period 2021 to 2027, will fund mobility and cross-border cooperation projects related to learning in the areas of education, training, youth, and sport.

Initiatives with an economic dimension and the relationship between sport and society

In March 2018, the European Union presented the last edition of the Special Eurobarometer public opinion survey on sport and physical activity, the fourth in a series that started in 2002 (Eurobarometer, 2019). For the survey, a total of 28,031 citizens in the EU's 28 member states from different social categories and with different demographics were interviewed face to face in their mother tongue. This tool reveals the dimension of sport in European society and how it behaves in relation to healthy sporting habits. It also analyses the frequency and levels of participation in sport and other physical activities, for example, the time people spend doing vigorous or moderate physical activity, and the amount of time spent walking and sitting down. The survey also focuses on the places where those surveyed do sport and other physical activities, be it in a club or informally in the open air, or even walking to work. Last, it analyses the reasons why people do sport and other physical activities, the obstacles to doing sport more regularly, what type of opportunities or local authority support they can obtain in their area, and participation as volunteers in these activities.

According to the Eurobarometer results, almost half of Europeans never exercise or do sport, and this proportion has been increasing gradually over the last years. Two out of five Europeans (40%) exercise or do sport at least once a week, including the 7% who do so regularly (at least five times a week). However, almost half of those surveyed (46%) never exercise or do sport. Levels of participation have not changed substantially since 2013, although the proportion of those who do not exercise or do sport has gone from 42% to 46%, a rising trend since 2009.

In the EU in general, men exercise or do sport or other physical activities more than women. This disparity is greatest in the 15- to 24-year age group. The amount of regular exercise a person does tends to diminish with age. Participation in sport and physical activity is also less frequent among people with the lowest educational levels and those with the least financial resources.

By country, the greatest proportion of people who exercise or do sport regularly or with some regularities are found in Finland (69%), Sweden (67%), and Denmark (63%). Of those surveyed, people from Bulgaria, Greece, and Portugal were least likely to exercise or do sport, with 68% of people in each of these countries never doing any exercise or sport. The main motives for doing sport or exercising are improved health and fitness, and the main obstacle is lack of time. In general, the most common reasons to take part in sports and physical activities are to improve health (54%) and to improve physical fitness (47%). Other reasons include to relax (38%), to have fun (30%), and to improve physical performance (28%).

Doing sport in more formal environments is less popular than doing so informally in parks and the open air in general, at home, and on the journey from home to school or work. Most Europeans believe that there are opportunities available at the local level to do physical activity, but many of them also think that the local authority does not do enough, with 6% of those surveyed doing voluntary work to support sporting activities.

Conclusions

The European Union plays a leading role in promoting cooperation and the management of initiatives in sport across Europe. There have been several treaties and agreements in favour of giving special attention to the sporting dimension, which found their highest point with the Treat of Lisbon (2009) where the EU acquires for the first time a specific competence in sports matters. Specific initiatives, programmes and actions include the Compass project, the Pierre de Coubertin plan of action, the Erasmus+ programme and the European Week of Sport, among others.

All these initiatives have allowed the European population to benefit from the different activities and promote their sport involvement, with social inclusion being one of the EU's priorities for the role of sport in society.

Notes

1 http://eose.org/.
2 www.planamasd.es/sites/default/files/recursos/libro-blanco-sobre-el-deporte-de-la-ue.pdf.

References

Bosch, J., Murillo, C., & Raya, J. M. (2019). La importancia económica del sector deportivo y el impacto económico de los eventos deportivos. *Papeles de Economía Española* (159), 261–274.
Dimitrov, D., Helmensteia, C., Leissner, A., Moser, B., & Scindler, J. (2006). *Die makroökonomischen Effekt des Sports in Europa*. Studies des Bundeskanzleramts, Sektion Sport.
Eurobarometer. (2019). *Eurobarometer. Public opinion in the European Union*. http://ec.europa.eu/commfrontoffice/publicopinion/index.cfm/Survey/getSurveyDetail/instruments/special/yearFrom/2012/yearTo/2019/surveyKy/2164p
European Comission. (2007). *White paper on sport*. https://eur-lex.europa.eu/legal-content/EN/TXT/PDF/?uri=CELEX:52007DC0391&from=EN#page=14
European Comission. (2015). *Sport in the European Union*. https://ec.europa.eu/assets/eac/sport/library/documents/eu-sport-factsheet_en.pdf
European Comission. (2021). *Facts sheets of the European Union: Sport*. www.europarl.europa.eu/factsheets/en/sheet/143/sport
European Union. (2019). *EU sports policy: Going faster, aiming higher, reaching further*. www.europarl.europa.eu/RegData/etudes/BRIE/2019/640168/EPRS_BRI(2019)640168_EN.pdf
Fernández, I. (2017). Las políticas de la Unión Europea en el ámbito del sport. *Educación Social. Revista de Intervención Socioeducativa*, 65, 57–74.
Gasparini, W. (2020). El Consejo de Europa y el sport: origen y circulación de un modelo deportivo europeo. *Encyclopédie pour une histoire numérique de l'Europe*. https://ehne.fr/en/node/12231
Parrish, R. (2003a). *Sports law and policy in the European Union*. Manchester University Press. https://library.oapen.org/bitstream/handle/20.500.12657/35019/341375.pdf;jsessionid=ED8277AD7D0BBE1471B79A0FB0F99D4A?sequence=1
Parrish, R. (2003b). The politics of sports regulation in the European Union. *Journal of European Public Policy*, 10(2), 246–262.

Chapter 4

The sport systems in Spain and Portugal

Maria José Carvalho, María Josefa García-Cirac, and Marisa Sousa

Introduction

In the southwest part of Europe are Portugal and Spain, two countries that once shared the world as the two major powers. On June 7, 1494, they signed the *Treaty of Tordesilhas*, agreeing on a boundary set at 370 leagues west of the Cape Verde Islands. The lands to the west of that line would be for the crown of Spain, and those to the east would be for the crown of Portugal. Any land already claimed by one side in the other's area of dominance would be handed over to the other country (Page, 2002). Indeed, through the 'Discoveries', these two nations became two key drivers of globalisation and intercontinental communications. Signs of this globalisation today are not only the use of Portuguese and Castilian languages but also their cultures across the world.

Portugal and Spain have similar sport systems, and their influence is felt in other countries across the world. Recognising the similarities and differences between the political, structural, and managerial sport practices in both countries is of paramount importance not only for athletes and administrators in the Iberian Peninsula but also for those interested in advancing scholarship regarding the impact sport in these two countries can offer to the rest of world. The purpose of this chapter is to describe the overall structure of the sport systems in Portugal and Spain, putting special attention on how different stakeholders interact and cooperate to make sport what it is today in these two countries.

Globalisation, sport success, and sport systems

The process of globalisation has been a matter of intense debate in the fields of business and social science (Sage, 2015). Although the concept of globalisation was first advanced in 1983 by Theodore Levitt (Nagel & Southall, 2015), the literature is not in agreement regarding this concept (Sage, 2015). The idea of globalisation as the consolidation of the world into a 'global community' proposed by Robertson (1992) seems appropriate. Here, there is an implied awareness that globalisation has spread across the world economies, political relations, people, and popular culture all over the planet. Therefore, the process of globalisation has

DOI: 10.4324/9781003197003-4

been viewed as a progressive phenomenon that boosts greater human dialogue and friendship (Maguire, 2011).

In Portugal, the men's national football teams have significantly spread the popularity of different forms of football, including association football (or soccer), futsal, and beach soccer, which places Portugal on the world map as a successful country in these sport modalities along with developing important geopolitical influence in international sport. Portuguese teams have achieved several World and European championships in these three modalities. In football, Portugal was the European Champion in 2016; in beach football, it was the European champion in 2019, 2020, and 2021. It was also the World champion in 2019. Finally, in futsal, Portugal won the European Championship in 2018 and the World Championship in 2021.

Similarly, football clubs, such as *Futebol Clube do Porto* or *Sport Lisboa e Benfica*, have been not only two of the most renowned and successful football clubs in the history of Portuguese football but also these clubs had achieved major international trophies. *Futebol Clube do Porto* has won seven major international titles including the European Cup in 1986–1987; UEFA Super Cup in 1987; Intercontinental Cup in 1987; UEFA Cup in 2002–2003; UEFA Champions League in 2003–2004; the Intercontinental Cup in 2004; and UEFA Europa League in 2010–2011 (FC Porto, n.d.). All these international successes make Portuguese football recognised internationally, attracting hundreds of football players from different parts of the world, especially from Latin America, who primarily choose to play in Portuguese clubs (Poli et al., 2019, 2021).

At the individual level, many footballers and coaches from Portugal have chosen to play and work outside Portugal in the main European leagues. Over the last decade, the names of José Mourinho and Cristiano Ronaldo have received not only the largest media coverage, but both have achieved great international success. José Mourinho, known by the nickname 'special one', is currently one of the most successful football coaches of all time, having won competitions in major European leagues and having been voted in 2011 as the best coach in the world by FIFA. Cristiano Ronaldo, considered one of the best footballers of all time, has played in the top European clubs such as Real Madrid, Manchester United, and Juventus. He was also selected several times as the best player in the world by FIFA and has won the *Ballon d'Or* four times.

Likewise, Spanish sport has reached significant attention worldwide. While it is always difficult to single out the most successful athlete, the tennis player Rafael Nadal is perhaps one of the best-known Spanish athletes today. Rafael Nadal, with twenty Grand Slams, five Davis Cups, and two Olympic golds, is today not only the best ranking player in the world but perhaps is one of the most recognised Spanish faces outside Spain. Another popular name among Spanish athletes is basketball player Pau Gasol, an outstanding player who made a successful career in the National Basketball Association (NBA) in the United States, with two gold rings, among many other achievements. There is also Marc Márquez in the sport of motorcycling with six MotoGP titles. Fernando Alonso in Formula I and

Alberto Contador in Cycling are also two important names who have achieved successful careers in their respective sports but also have gained significant global media attention.

But undoubtedly, and just like Portugal, Spain is also known for being the hub of one of the most competitive football leagues in the world. The victory of the Spanish Men's Football team in the 2010 World Cup is a clear example of the relevance football has in Spain. The Spanish Football League *La Liga* is one of the championships with the most number of followers internationally. In Spain, basketball is also a sport that had achieved great success internationally. The Spanish Men's Basketball team has won two golds in the FIBA World Championships; three gold, six silver, and four bronze medals in the European Championships, and three silver and one bronze in the Olympics Games. Also important, and perhaps one of the greatest moments in the history of Spanish sport are the Olympic Games that were hosted in Barcelona in 1992. This event represented an important milestone for Spanish sport that also carried a significant impact on the development of sport in the decades that followed.

Arguably, Spain and Portugal are two countries that have contributed to spread the popularity of sport, and, to a certain extent, to globalised sport through their athletes' achievements, sport teams, and the millions of followers they have all over the world. But regardless of these successes, it is important to note that achieving world status in sport does not happen by chance or can be attributed to as an act of randomness. Instead, for Portugal and Spain, the growth, development, and further success in sport, have been the result of the work of a complex network of collaborations of public and private organisations that have existed for years and have acted at different levels in these two countries.

Over the years, Portugal and Spain have both adopted a sports model and an interventionist legislative model. This means, the public sector and the government at each of its different levels have taken a central role in structuring and developing the foundations of a sport system which is critical for sport organisations to grow. According to Infopedia, the word *system* refers to 'the set of principles that form a doctrine body; form of government; set of dependent parts on each other; set of laws or principles that regulate a certain order of phenomena' (Infopédia, n.d.). Thus, when applying this definition to the question of what is a sport system, we define it as the set of interdependent elements that aim to develop physical activity and sport in a given area. Here, the interdependent elements refer to both public and private organisations as well as other critical stakeholders that play an important role in shaping sport in both Portugal and Spain. These independent elements which create a network of collaborations is what we call a sport system. In the next section, we describe the structure of the sport systems in these two countries.

The sport system in Portugal

The Portuguese sport system has its own dynamics resulting from the interaction between public and private organisations, with specific characteristics and purposes, and experienced by different *sport agents*[1] creating an impact on different entities, communities, and individuals. To understand the impact of a sport system it is important to identify and characterise the type of sport organisations in which the different sport agents operate.

After the political transition that occurred in Portugal during the mid-1970s from a dictatorship regime to a democratic regime, sport found its first reference in the 1976 Constitution of the Portuguese Republic (CRP).[2] Through these constitutional provisions, sport is included as a fundamental right, and it is also through these precepts that the State is entrusted per article 79, of the title Physical Culture and Sport:

> Everyone has the right to physical culture and sport. It is incumbent upon the State, in collaboration with schools and associations, to promote, stimulate, guide and support the practice and dissemination of physical culture and sport, as well as to prevent violence in sport.

In this constitutional norm, the universal right to sport is expressly safeguarded and guaranteed, and the State (including central, regional, and local administrations) is bestowed with a special obligation to enforce this right, including in collaboration with schools and associations (Carvalho, 2009).

When interpreting these constitutional precepts with explicit and implicit reference to sport,[3] it is possible to note that this law encompasses a holistic concept of sport. The law includes and integrates recreational, participatory, and high competition sport with the purpose to improve the health and well-being of the citizens, as well as to improve the performance and development of professional sports. However, this law does not distinguish the different forms of sport practice and calls on schools and sport associations to become effective when pursuing sport development (Meirim, 2002).

Because sport is explicitly addressed in the Constitution of the Portuguese Republic, Carvalho and Mazzei (2019) noted that the framework of a national sport in Portugal is significantly influenced by the State. In this regard, they commented:

> It is true that the intervention of States in Sport is different from one another, with more liberal or more interventionist policies depending on their systems and regimes. Portugal fits into an interventionist model,[4] mainly due to the legislative work in this field, and to the close relationship it establishes with sports federations, especially those that hold the public sport utility status and for financing the construction and requalification of sports facilities.
> (Carvalho & Mazzei, 2019, p. 86)

Regarding *Private Sport Organisations*, in the Portuguese Sport System, we can categorise two types of these organisations: (a) private non-profit organisations, and (b) private for-profit organisations.

Private non-profit organisations are legal entities of an associative nature, whose profits obtained during their annual economic cycle must be reverted to the main activities of the organisation and not to its associates. Within the private non-profit sport category, there are several types of organisations, including sport federations, sport leagues, regional base associations, the Portuguese Confederation of Culture and Recreation Associations, the Sport Foundation, the Sport Confederation of Portugal, and the Olympic and Paralympic Committees of Portugal.

Sport federations[5] are the State's main partners for the implementation of sport policies, representing the governing bodies that are at the top of each sport. In professional sports, which in the case of Portugal refers to League 1 and League 2 in professional football, it is mandatory to have a specific entity for its management. Hence, the existence of the Portuguese Professional Football League. Closely related to the sport federations are the regional associations of which sport clubs of the same modality must be part of. The regional association is of paramount importance because the growth of any given sport depends directly on these associations.

The Portuguese Confederation of Culture and Recreation Associations are entities made of sport clubs that show a more holistic social and political representation. There is also the Sport Foundation, whose purpose is to support the promotion and development of high-performance sports as well as to coordinate the management of the National Network of High-performance Centres. Finally is the Sport Confederation of Portugal whose members are the sport federations, the Olympic Committee of Portugal, and National Paralympic Committee of Portugal, with the exclusive mission of preparing the Portuguese delegations for the Olympic and Paralympic Games.

In terms of private for-profit organisations, these are legal entities of a corporate nature in which their annual profits can be reverted to their partners. Here we find two types of these organisations, sport societies and commercial companies. Sport societies are legal entities that are created exclusively for sport, such as the sport limited companies and single-member sport companies, whose legal standing is established in Law 10/2013. Regarding commercial sport companies, they exist for the practice of a certain economic activity, such as sport event organisations, or those that provide services such as gyms. Within this group, private limited companies are the most common type of commercial sport entities.

In terms of *Public Sport Organisations*, they act at three levels of administration: central, regional, and local. Regarding the central administration, it is important to highlight that these are political entities that are part of the national administration of the country. In the XXII Constitutional Government (República Portuguesa, n.d.), which refers to the XXII Portuguese administration that went from 2019 until 2022, sport in the central government is represented by the Minister of Education, which is responsible to oversee all of the public sport entities related to sport in Portugal. The Minister oversees the Secretary of State for Youth and Sport. For the effective execution of sports policies, there is the Sport Institute of Portugal (IPDJ, n.d) which includes regional delegations all over the country.

Next to the political power, there are two entities, the National Sports Council and the Anti-Doping Authority of Portugal (ADoP, n.d.). Decree-Law no. 315/2007 states that the National Sports Council organisation has the mission of 'elaborating, within the scope of the implementation of the policies defined for physical activity and sport, recommendations that are requested, ensuring the observance of the principles of sports ethics, and exercising the competencies that are committed law'.[6] Then there is the National Anti-Doping Organisation whose main function is the control and fight against doping in sport. This is the entity responsible for adopting rules to conduct, implement, or apply any phase of the doping control procedures.

Regarding the regional public administration, there are two entities with responsibility for sport, one in the Autonomous Region of Madeira and the other in the Autonomous Region of the Azores. In Madeira, it is the Regional Secretariat for Education, Science, and Technology that supervises sport through the Regional Directorate for Sport. In the Azores, these functions fall in the Regional Secretariat for Health and Sport together with the Regional Directorates for Sport in each of its islands.

Concerning public local entities that are part of the Portuguese sport system, these include municipalities, parish councils, and municipal companies. However, it is important to consider that sport organisations that exist in the 308 municipalities are very diverse. Therefore, the way sport is organised at this level depends on the realities of each locality. This includes demographics, population, and the political desire for sport. On many occasions, there exists the possibility to organise municipal companies to manage local sport. Table 4.1 summarises the organisation of the Portuguese sport system.

The sport system in Spain

Similar to what we discussed with the sport system in Portugal, the Spanish sport system also involves a constitutional text with an active participation of several public and private structures. The Spanish Constitution of 1978 refers to sport in article 43.3. Specifically, this article states that 'public authorities will promote health education, physical education, and sport. They will also facilitate the proper use of leisure'. Although the Spanish Constitution does not include sport as a right, it mandates public authorities to promote sport, with the understanding that the term 'promotion' cannot be interpreted just as a simple stimulus. Instead, sport must be understood as a framework that brings administrative and organisational benefits.[7]

The Spanish State is organised territorially in municipalities, provinces, and autonomous communities. Following Article 137 of the Spanish Constitution, all of the public entities that participate in each of these levels have autonomy for the management of their respective interests. Spain has 17 autonomous communities and two autonomous cities.

Table 4.1 The structure of the Portuguese sport system

National Sport System of Portugal	
Private Sport Organisations	Public Sector Organisations

Private non-profit organisations
• Sports Federations
  ○ Club Leagues
• Regional Associations
• Sports Clubs
• Practitioners' Clubs
• Sports Promotion Associations
• Portuguese Confederation of Culture and Recreation Associations
• Sports Foundation
• Sport Confederation of Portugal
• Olympic Committee of Portugal
• National Paralympic Committee of Portugal
	Private non-profit organisations
	• Sports Federations
	  ○ Club Leagues
	• Regional Associations
	• Sports Clubs
	• Practitioners' Clubs
	• Sports Promotion Associations
	• Portuguese Confederation of Culture and Recreation Associations
	• Sports Foundation
	• Sport Confederation of Portugal
	• Olympic Committee of Portugal
	• National Paralympic Committee of Portugal

Private for-profit organisations • Sports societies (SAD and SDUQ) • Commercial companies	**Regional public administration** • Autonomous Region of Madeira • Autonomous Region of the Azores
	Local public administration • Municipalities • Parish councils • Municipal companies

Among the many powers given to the autonomous communities is the promotion of sport and leisure. It should be noted that various articles within the Constitution that relate to or make explicit reference to the 'sport activity', but these articles pertain to the administration of the State, for example, the commercial legislation (art. 149.1.6), the labour legislation (art. 149.1.7), the civil legislation (art. 149.1.8), public safety legislation (art. 149.1.29), and the regulation of conditions for obtaining academic and professional qualifications (art. 149.1.30). Thus, when addressing the role of public sport organisations in Spain, this role must always consider the competencies of the sport activities at the state, regional, and local levels.

The administrative functions of the State with sport are carried out by the *Consejo Superior de Deportes* (CSD) or Higher Sports Council. This autonomous administrative body is established in the Law of Sport 10/1990. In accordance with the Royal Decree 355/2018 of June 6th, it is the responsibility of the Ministry of Culture and Sport, through the CSD, to propose and implement any government sport policies. As a result of this, the CSD assumes, among others, the following roles: (a) authorise, revoke, and approve the constitutional statutes and regulations of the Spanish sports federations; (b) sanction official professional competitions; (c) promote measures to prevent, control, and suppress the use of prohibited substances; (d) act in coordination with the autonomous communities to coordinate the development of the competences outlined in their statutes; (e) authorise the registration of the Spanish sport federations in the corresponding international sport federations; and finally, (f) collaborate with public agencies and sport federations in caring for the environment.

Since 1980, two State laws related to sport have been issued: Law 13/1980, of March 31, known as 'General Law of Physical Culture and Sport',[8] and Law 10/1990, of October 15, on Sport,[9] also referred to as 'Law of Sport'. This law, which is the law that regulates sport and physical activity today, seeks to: (a) promote the practice of sport and govern its operation when occurs beyond the regional level; (b) recognise and facilitate the practice of sport that is organised through associative structures; and (c) regulate spectator and commercial sports.

Within the CSD is the General Assembly of Sport,[10] which is the advisory body of the President of the CSD. The assembly is made of representatives of the State administration, the autonomous communities, local entities, Spanish sport federations, and several other organisations related to sport.

Another entity of the public sector is the Administrative Court of Sport.[11] This is a collegiate state-level body, and while related to the CSD, it acts independently of it. Its main functions are to hear and rule on disputes and breaches related to doping and discipline, and to ensure the legality of the electoral processes of Spanish sport federations.[12] Finally, there is the State Commission against Violence, Racism, Xenophobia, and Intolerance in sport,[13] and the Spanish Agency for the Protection of Health in Sport.[14]

At the regional level, autonomous communities promote the practice of sport and leisure through their own statutes. Thus, each autonomous community enacts its own sport laws and rules that only apply within the jurisdiction of each community. Moreover, and following the guidelines from the Ministry of Culture and Sport, autonomous communities develop administrative structures with the purpose to achieve the broader goals outlined in the Law. That is the case of the General Directorate of Sport, on which various services depend such as the training and the sport activities services. The more specific roles of these administrative structures vary from community to community, but they all focus on the promotion of sport. In addition, autonomous communities have advisory committees and sport courts.

Although the Spanish Constitution does not assign powers to local entities (municipalities and provinces) in the field of sport, all the sport rules and legislations of the autonomous communities establish specific actions related to sport that apply at the local level. These actions focus on issues related to the practice and promotion of sports within the local community and include among others the planning, construction, maintenance, and management of sports facilities, and the collaboration with the regional government and public and private entities for the promotion sport. Local entities also promote the work sport associations do within the community. They also organise and collaborate with different sport entities when hosting tournaments and sport events. Moreover, local communities promote sport within the school system, whether this by supporting activities related to sport coaching and school competitions, or just by promoting the practice of sport for boys and girls (Carrascosa et al., 2020).

To implement some of the actions described earlier, local communities used a variety of strategies and tools, including direct and indirect management. Direct management is used when an autonomous agency within the local community executes these responsibilities. Indirect management occurs when the local community outsources the job to an external organisation. The collaboration of private and public entities is a strategy that allows local communities not only to manage more effectively the delivery and implementation of these services but also to reach out larger audiences. Table 4.2 summarises the organisation of the Spanish sport system.

In terms of the place and role of the private organisation of sport within the larger scope of the sport system in Spain, the Law of Sport of 1990 regulates the role of sport associations. Moreover, these associations are classified as clubs, professional leagues, Spanish sport federations, and sport promotion entities.

Table 4.2 The structure of the Spanish sport system

National Sport System of Spain	
Private Sport Organisations	Public Sector Organisations
Private non-profit organisations • Spanish Sport Federations • Professional Leagues • Sport Clubs • Sport Promotion Entities • Olympic Committee of Spain • National Paralympic Committee of Spain	**Central public administration** • Minister of Culture and Sport • Higher Sports Council (CSD) • General Assembly of sport • Administrative Court of sport • State Commission against Violence, Racism, Xenophobia, and Intolerance in Sport • Spanish Agency for the Protection of Health in Sport
Private for-profit organisations • Sports Corporations (SAD) • Commercial Companies	**Regional public administration** Each of the 17 autonomous community has a department with competence in the field of sport, with its corresponding administrative organisation.
	Local public administration Spanish local authorities (municipalities and provinces) develop sports competencies, through city councils and provincial areas.

In terms of clubs, the Law of 1990 defines sports clubs as 'private associations, who have as their object the promotion of one or more sports modalities within their members, as well as promoting their participation in sport activities and competitions.[15] Regarding professional teams participating in official professional competitions, these take the legal form of a Sport Limited Company.

As for sport federations, in Spain these organisations are private and have their own legal status. Because they are considered a collaborating body of the public administration, they exercise public functions by delegation. As a result, the State through its administration exercises control over these federations. The scope of action and jurisdiction of the Spanish sports federations extends throughout the State, and are made of regional sport federations, sport clubs, athletes, coaches, judges, referees, professional leagues, and other interested groups that promote or contribute to the development of the sport.[16]

Professional leagues are associations of clubs that are constituted, exclusively and obligatorily, when they are part of an official professional competition. Under Article 41 of the Law of Sport, professional leagues are made up of all clubs participating in that competition, and are subject to the following functions: (a) organisation of their competitions, in coordination with the respective Spanish sports federation following the criteria mandated by the CSD, which also goes with the regulations and agreements that exist with other national and/or international regulations; (b) performance, with respect to its members, the functions of guardianship, control, and supervision; and (c) disciplinary power.

Professional Leagues are second-degree associations that possess autonomy in their internal organisation and operations with respect to the Spanish sport federation of which they are part. In Spain, there are two professional leagues: The Association of Basketball Clubs and the National Professional Football League. As professional competitions, these are only found in the first and second division in football, and the first division in basketball.

Finally, two very important sport organisations that are part of the private sector, are the Spanish Olympic Committee[17] and the Spanish Paralympic Committee.[18] The Spanish Olympic Committee was established in 1912 as a private association governed by its own statutes and regulations following the principles and standards of the International Olympic Committee. The Spanish Olympic Committee (COE) is also considered an entity of public utility. Regarding the Spanish Paralympic Committee, it was established in 1995 and has similar functions as the COE, but in the context of athletes with disabilities. The Spanish Paralympic Committee, in collaboration with the Higher Sports Council, also acts as the hub that coordinates all the initiatives related to sport for people with disabilities in Spain.

Concluding Remarks

The way the sport systems in Portugal and Spain are organised shows a great degree of similarities as opposed to differences. Although both countries operate in their own socio-sporting realities, this context shows similarities reflecting their inclusion in Western Europe, considered one of the most advanced sport contexts in the world. As described throughout the chapter, Portugal and Spain present interventionist sport systems where public and private structures collaborate but in which the central government, through legislation, plays a critical role in shaping the entire structure of the system. One difference that is found in the administration of sport in Portugal and Spain deals with the geopolitical and administrative organisations that exist in these two countries. Specifically, in Spain there are autonomous communities which allow each region of the country the capacity to manage its own interests, whereas in Portugal such a public administrative sphere does not exist. Thus, Portugal shows a more centralistic approach when compared to Spain, since it is only organised at the state and local level, while the autonomous level is only characteristic of the Spanish system.

Notes

1 We refer to a *sport agent* to all those primary stakeholders including clubs, associations, leagues, athletes, etc. that primarily benefit from the actions, policies, laws and regulations that resulted from the entities that govern and/or had a direct impact in the sport system.
2 The Constitution of the Portuguese Republic of April 2, 1976, as amended by Constitutional Laws 1/82, of September 30, 1/89, of July 8, 1/92, of November 25, 1/97, of September 20, 1/2001, of December 12, 1/2004, of July 24, and finally 1/2005 of August 12 (7th constitutional review).
3 A combined reading of articles 79, 64 and 70 of the CRP indicate that the funding priority should go to support policies aimed at young people and health promotion. However, other constitutional precepts indicate rights related to sport, namely articles 59, 65, 66, paragraph 1, 69, 71, paragraph 2, 73, paragraphs 1 and 2.
4 For detailed information, see Chaker (1999) and the study of national sport legislations in Europe.
5 The legal regime for sport federations and their public sport utility status is regulated by Decree-Law no. 248-B/2008, of 31 December, already amended by article 4, paragraph c), of Law no. 74/2013, of 6 September (Creates the Arbitral Tribunal for Sport and approves the respective law) and by articles 2 and 4 Decree-Law no. 93/2014, of 23 June.
6 Article 2 of Decree-Law no. 315/2007, of 18 September, establishes the powers, composition and functioning of this Council.
7 In this regard, the Constitutional Court was already ruling, at STC 90/1992, of June 11.
8 Official Gazette of State No. 84 of April 12, 1980.
9 Official Gazette of State No. 249 of October 17, 1990.
10 Official Gazette of State No. 249 of October 17, 1990.
11 www.csd.gob.es/es/csd/tribunal-administrativo-del-deporte.
12 www.csd.gob.es/es/csd/tribunal-administrativo-del-deporte.
13 www.csd.gob.es/es/csd/organos-colegiados/comision-estatal-contra-la-violencia-el-racismo-la-xenofobia-y-la-intolerancia-en-el-deporte.
14 https://aepsad.culturaydeporte.gob.es/agencia.html.
15 Art. 13 Law 10/1990 of October 10, of Sport. Official Gazette of State No. 249 of October 17, 1990.
16 All this is as required by Article 30 of Law 10/1990 of October 15 on sport.
17 www.coe.es/.
18 www.paralimpicos.es/.

References

ADoP. (n.d.). *Autoridade Antidopagem de Portugal* [Anti-doping authority of Portugal]. www.adop.pt/adop/instituicao.aspx

Carrascosa, J. H., Sancho, J. A. M., & Delgado, F. O. (2020). *Municipal promotion of federated sport*. Editorial Reus.

Carvalho, M. J. (2009). *Elementos estruturantes do regime jurídico do desporto profissional em Portugal*. Coimbra Editora.

Carvalho, M. J., & Mazzei, L. (2019). Estado: Intervenção no desporto. In A. Correia & R. Biscaia (Eds.), *Gestão do desporto. Compreender para gerir* (pp. 83–99). Faculdade de Motricidade Humana.

Chaker, A. N. (1999). *Etude des législations nationales relatives au sport en europe*: Council of Europe Publishing.

FC Porto. (n.d.). *Trophies*. www.fcporto.pt/en/club/honours

Infopédia. (n.d.). *Dictionary of Porto Editora*. www.infopedia.pt/dicionarios/lingua-portuguesa/sistema

IPDJ. (n.d.). *Instituto Português do Desporto e Juventude* [Sport Institute of Portugal]. https://ipdj.gov.pt/

Maguire, J. (2011). Globalization and sport: Beyond the boundaries? *Sociology, 45*(5), 923–929.

Meirim, J. M. (2002). *A federação desportiva como sujeito público do sistema desportivo*. Coimbra Editora.

Nagel, M. S., & Southall, R. M. (2015). Do you really want to work in the sport industry? In M. S. Nagel & R. M. Southall (Eds.), *Introduction to sport management: Theory and practice* (2nd ed.). Kendall Hunt Publishing Company.

Page, M. (2002). *The first global village. How Portugal changed the word*. Editorial Notícias.

Poli, R., Ravenel, L., & Besson, R. (2019). The demographics of football in the European labour market. *CIES Football Observatory Monthly Report, 49*.

Poli, R., Ravenel, L., & Besson, R. (2021). Expatriate footballers worldwide: Global 2021 study. *CIES Football Observatory Monthly Report, 65*.

Robertson, R. (1992). *Globalization: Social theory and global culture*. Sage Publications Ltd.

República Portuguesa. (n.d.). *Composição do Governo* [Composition of the government]. www.portugal.gov.pt/pt/gc22/governo/composicao

Sage, G. H. (2015). *Globalizing sport: How organizations, corporations, media, and politics are changing sport*. Routledge.

Chapter 5

The legal framework of the sports industry in Spain and Portugal

Vicente Javaloyes Sanchis and Ricardo Fernandes Cardoso

Context

Sport is today a fast-growing sector, with a relevant economic impact in Europe and a repercussion on national economies comparable to the whole agriculture, forestry and fisheries sector, representing more than 2% of the global GDP of the European Union (EU) and 3.5% of total employment in the EU, with solid incorporation of technology, innovation and development, and a growth rate considerably higher than the average of the European economy.

In Spain, the sports industry generated 2018 an economic activity of 39,117 million euros, equivalent to 3.3% of the gross domestic product (GDP), which creates 414,000 jobs; this is equivalent to 2.1% of the country's employed population. Every million euros that this industry makes in Spain generates 12.4 absolute jobs, 30% more than the average for the rest of the sectors. Furthermore, the industry has an indirect impact of more than 16,432 million euros and an induced impact of 6,917 million euros.

In Portugal, according to data from the National Institute for Statistics, for the year 2019, the 13,624 companies in the sports sector (+3.5% than in 2018) generated 2.1 billion euros in turnover (+14.0%) and 546.1 million euros in remuneration (+12.1%). They brought about 862.6 million euros in gross value added (GVA), 9.6% more than the previous year.

The sports industry is a broad business that ranges from selling food and sports merchandising to selling broadcasting rights and sponsorship agreements. Many subsectors can be identified, from professional sports to fitness, including sports events.

One cannot understand any industry without the set of standards that have a decisive impact on its configuration and development. The sports industry is not removed from this reality. Sport has claimed its qualification as an 'island' due to the existence of its own set of standards (*lex sportiva*) and the application of mechanisms for solving endogenous conflicts. However, the sports legal system coexists with rules that emanate from States, with regulations approved by their own sports organisations. Stakeholders walk on challenging terrain, where the specificity of sport sometimes collides with mandatory public guardianship of fundamental rights.

This chapter aims to approach the legal framework that configures and delimits the sport's scope to understand better the organisations it manages in two sister countries, Spain and Portugal.

Sport and law

The principle establishes that 'lack of knowledge of the law does not exempt one from compliance and that' cannot go unnoticed. And every professional must work to prevent (know and comply with the regulations) rather than remedy (avoid legal consequences). Because the truth is that nothing will happen . . . until it does. And when it does, the results may be irreversible. Admitting the opposite, excusing ignorance of the law, would be equivalent to leaving compliance with them to the willingness of each citizen. This principle of general application does not go unnoticed by all those who work in the sphere of sport. The challenge is finding the relationship between Sport and Law and knowing its reach. Sport as a social phenomenon of extraordinary magnitude cannot be linked to other branches of scientific knowledge that form a global whole. (Cazorla-Prieto, 2013) Indeed, there is no sport without rules, standards, and laws.

Modern sport, mainly based on natural associative structures, cannot exist without developing standards and rules. Rules and standards are part of the definition of competitive sport. Someone establishes that football is played in a field of specific dimensions, with gates and a ball, with the participation of teams of 11 players. But it could also have been agreed that players are 12 or even that one should play with two balls. The regulation gives a sense to sport, configuring it as such.

But it is not easy to define what is 'sport'. The sport includes a very heterogeneous set of activities that have differentiated functioning and structure. Consequently, a legal regime is equally different depending on whether it is professional or for leisure or health purposes, and whether its practice is spontaneous or organised.

The specificity of sport

The autonomy of a branch of Law is acknowledged when the following circumstances apply:

- a differentiated social environment on which to project the standards of order.
- standards that specifically regulate this social phenomenon and constitute an order.
- own or specific principles whence emanate particular standards or regulations.

In this sense, one can affirm that sports law is projected on a differentiated social scope or reality; there are standards, public and private, that govern it specifically, such as the laws or bylaws of sports; one can also identify particular principles applicable to competitive sport.

The specificity of sport was ratified by the Lisbon Treaty of 2007, incorporating the community norm. As such, article 165 of the Treaty on the Functioning of the European Union states: '*The Union shall contribute to the promotion of European sporting issues while taking account of the specific nature of the sport, its structures based on voluntary activity and its social and educational function*'.

The existence of a dense legal-public order of sport with numerous laws and regulations, together with a broad legal-private order of sport made up of federative and club provisions, has been mirrored in the publication of codes of sports law and repertoires of sports case-law that show the importance of sports for the different legislators.

This normative framework is accompanied by an essential group of specialised bodies in sports justice, both nationally and internationally. The abundant case law on sports matters is a consequence of the judicialisation of the sports phenomenon, which has put an end to many years of insulation of the world of sports and the trend of internal conflict settlement.

Professional sports and conflict go hand in hand. The economic interests at stake inform the decisions and actions of all stakeholders involved. In sports, the immediacy and dynamism of competitions require quick and effective solutions. One can discuss the validity of a decision made in past years, whereas the answer one needs before a match to be held a few days after a claim. Therefore, associations and clubs must have internal, specialised conflict settlement bodies whose decisions are effective.

The specificity of sport is mirrored in situations such as:

- Autonomy and diversity of sports organisations.
- Pyramid structure of competitions.
- Federative monopoly (1 sport/1 association).
- Limited participants (number of licenses and equipment) in competitions.
- Preserving competitive balance.
- Discrimination by sex and age.
- Provision of services related to health.

Therefore, one can conclude that the specificity of sport has enhanced the reality of a true sports law as a juridical discipline in its own right.

The legal and sporting order

The legal sporting order is the set of standards and principles that regulate the sports phenomenon in a particular territorial scope and for a specific moment.

The common sources inform sports Law of Law with some singularities. In addition, it has its peculiar sources of Law that emanate from sports organisations and bodies that settle specific conflicts that arise.

In the case of Spain, the sources of the Spanish legal system and the legal and sporting system conform with the first section of article 1 of the Civil Code, the law, custom, and the general principles of Law. The standards contained in international treaties (section 5 of the article 1) also become part of the domestic legal system. Moreover, there is case law, which complements this legal system, according to section 6.

As for the case of the Portuguese legal system, sources of Law, also applicable to sports, are, from the outset, the Constitution of the Portuguese Republic, the standards and principles emerging from general or common International Law, standards of International Conventions regularly ratified or approved, standards emanating from competent bodies of international organisations that Portugal is a member of, the provisions of the Treaties that govern the European Union and the standards emanating from its institutions, in the exercise of their powers. But so are Ordinary Laws, Government Decree-Laws, regional Legislative Decrees (Azores and Madeira), specific Constitutional Court rulings, Collective Labor Conventions and other Collective Labor Regulation instruments and Regulations. Other sources of Law in the Portuguese legal order are Custom, Case-law, Fairness, Use and Doctrine.

In its origin, the sport was governed by an autonomous private regulatory framework, which emanated from private sports organisations independent from public authorities. In that initial moment of regulation of the different sports and the creation of international organisations, there was talk of the so-called 'Island Complex', as these private sports entities carried out self-regulation of their internal organisation and the competitions they held. Therefore, international sports associations have a high degree of autonomy and are governed by their own rules, principles, and means of conflict settlement. But the constitutional enshrinement and judicialisation of sport supported and justified the intervention of public powers. Hence, a legal framework for sports has been established, in which general standards stemming from States coexist with the private standards of sporting organisations.

The rulings of ordinary courts have been decisive for the legislator to take measures and cover certain situations such as the work of professional sportspeople and their acknowledgement as workers. This was also the case in Portugal, but through legislation, through the approval of Law no. 2104, of 20 May, which lasted until 1990, in which professional sport is recognised, admitting the existence of experienced and non-amateur practitioners of sports in football, cycling and boxing. Therefore, the following rules will apply to any sporting entity or person of the 'family of sport':

- General Public Standards: provisions applicable to all citizens (including those who organise, manage or practice sport) in civil, penal, labor or tax matters, among others.
- Specific Public Standards: provisions applicable to sports and intervening subjects, such as sports laws, violence in sports, health protection of sportspeople and fight against doping, sports discipline, or those that govern sports professions.
- Private Standards: provisions stemming from sports entities themselves, such as statutes and regulations of associations and clubs.

As a basic idea, one must consider that application and compliance with the legal provisions of public authorities cannot be conditioned by the privacy regulations approved by sports organisations. Nevertheless, many conflicts are generated by the 'clash' between public and private standards.

In Spain, the Constitutional Court, in its judgment of May 24, 1985, declared that, together with the administrative organisation (Superior Council on Sport or Autonomous Communities), the legislation in force attributes delegated public functions to sports associations, meaning tutelage and control over its statutes and regulations, which require the power of legality and approval of Public Administration.

In Portugal, in 1990, the Basic Law of the Sports System (LBSD) was published, containing the basic principles of the then-new structure of the professional sport. But it is through the acknowledgement of Public Sports Utility that a sports association was granted competence to exercise, exclusively, by a mark or set of sports, regulatory, disciplinary and other powers of a public nature, as well as ownership of the rights and powers expressly provided for by law.

The statutes and regulations of international associations and national associations are binding standards due to voluntary membership or affiliation acts. The integration of sportspeople, coaches, clubs, associations and other persons and entities in international sports organisations obliges them to abide by their rules and federative principles, albeit aware that they are, in any case, subject to their national legal order, which they cannot infringe.

Given this scenario, one must answer in the affirmative to questions such as:

- Is it a crime to attack an opponent during a match?
- Can an ordinary judge decide which teams take part in a competition?
- Can an ordinary judge suppress a sporting sanction for doping?

Lex sportiva

The term 'lex sportiva' means rules and standards stemming from sports organisations to govern sports activity. Sports activity is transnational and governed by regulations that traditionally emanate from sports authorities. In the international arena, these authorities are the International Olympic Committee, the international associations, the Court of Arbitration for Sport (CAS), headquartered in Lausanne, and the World Anti-Doping Agency (WADA).

Sport must be equipped with a series of standard rules that observe the fundamental principles of the legal-public system and are, at the same time, capable of harmonising the needs of good development of sports competitions and the individual interests of stakeholders, especially sportspeople. In this sense, the metaphysical role played by CAS in articulating these rules and specific principles of sport in the manner of lex sportiva must be highlighted. Even though there is no principle of binding precedent in the CAS arbitration, each panel (court) can issue a ruling with different criteria. This homogeneous line in its orders can be seen above all in topics such as objective responsibility in doping matters.

The CAS rulings have provided a series of principles recognised by sports organisations, such as the principle of inalterability of sports results to guarantee the normal development of competitions (principle of competition) and the principle of no intervention by judicial bodies in the review of arbitral errors, the principle of sports parity or the principle of objective responsibility in matters of doping.

Principles of sport

It has been said that sport, like any other manifestation of society, is governed by the public legal system. The rules issued by private sporting organisations must accommodate such a general legal framework.

However, that is compatible with the existence of competing principles and particularities in the industry of sports, which should not be understood as unlimited autonomy of sports, the exclusive auto-normative capacity of private organisations or lack of subjection to the legal principles and rules that prevail in society. Instead, it allows responding to the specificity and needs of the sport.

Some of these principles are:

Pro competitione *principle*

Both the bodies of what is known as 'sports justice', federative and administrative, and the ordinary courts of justice have adopted this principle as a form of sport's uniqueness to safeguard the necessary immediacy of competitions and their correct development.

One of the 'pro competition' principle expressions is found in the notification of disciplinary resolutions. The disciplinary regulations of sports associations establish that notices to players, coaches, technicians, deputies, and managers can be served in the SAD or club that they belong to at any given time. Therefore, for purposes of personal notification, the club's headquarters has deemed the domicile of the player or coach. If this were not the case, competitions could be easily tampered with simply by not acknowledging the notification of a disciplinary sanction or by not reporting the address of the new domicile every time one changes clubs.

Principle of parity (par conditio) *and fairness in sports*

This principle derives from the need to defend competitive balance in all sports competitions, to maintain the maximum uncertainty of results in sports. In this sense, the *par conditio* means the condition of equality between two or more competitors. When greater equality exists between the competitors and more significant uncertainty exists in the result of the parties or sports competitions, the greater the interest to fans.

This principle of equality has numerous manifestations in sports regulations: same rules for all; an equal number of participants in each team; matches swapping sides in each half; similar limits to replacements or age and weight limits.

Principle of preservation of the purity of competition

It is aimed at the need to protect fair play in sport and this ethical dimension. Regulations on prevention, control, and repression of doping are precisely about preserving the purity of competitions. Nowadays, the Good Governance of the organisations is mirrored, namely, in the protection of competitions and the fight against corruption, the purchase of parties, or illegal contests.

Principle of immediate enforcement of sports sanctions

Sanctions imposed through the corresponding disciplinary procedure are immediately enforceable, and claims against them do not stop or suspend enforcement. This is without prejudice to the possibility of taking cautionary measures to ensure the subsequent settlement.

Principle of non-revisability of technical decisions of referees

Based on the principle of non-revisability of technical decisions, it is only permissible for disciplinary and competitive bodies to review the disciplinary effects of decisions by referees. Still, they cannot modify their technical decisions. Decisions by referees that entail a new subjective valuation of the facts cannot be reviewed; one cannot re-referee.

Principle of sportspeople taking risks

In the context of sports competitions or recreational sports, it provides a particular risk for the practitioners themselves. Sportspeople know such risks and voluntarily take responsibility for any damage or loss with respect for the rules of the game of each sport. This acknowledgement of awareness of risk does not extend to damage caused by spectators, organisers of sporting events, or owners of sporting venues.

Dispute settlement in sport

Conflict is a situation that generates confrontation between two or more people, which makes them challenging to function and causes a feeling of malaise and emotional tension.

The conflict map in sports is extensive. In summary, we can point out:

- Civil conflicts between sporting organisations or between them and their members. For example, those generated by shared use of sports facilities, transfers of players in lower categories, compensation for training rights, associative disciplinary schemes, electoral processes, civil liability for damages and losses to third parties, etc.
- Administrative conflicts of a 'public' nature may involve management or disputes of a public nature. Examples: disciplinary sanctions, request for cancellation of sports licenses, lack of permission to organise an event, violent acts in the stadium or surroundings, data protection, etc.
- Economic-mercantile and tax conflicts arising from economic rights in player transfers, image rights, financial fair play, sponsorship agreements, ambush marketing, or the commercialisation of television rights.
- Labor disputes between sporting entities and professionals working for them. For example, the dismissal of the coach mid-season, early termination of the contract by players, or negotiation of collective agreements.
- Criminal disputes, such as aggressions, interferences in the honour of persons, author's rights and intellectual property, use of substances or prohibited methods (doping), purchase of matches or illegal betting.
- Ethical conflicts related to the good governance of organisations and the behaviour of people. For example, conflicts of interest or lack of transparency.

The Universal Declaration of Human Rights establishes the equality of all citizens under the law and the right to a practical appeal before an independent and impartial court. Article 6 (1) of the European Convention on Human Rights is of similar scope: 'everyone is entitled to a fair and public hearing within a reasonable time by an independent and impartial tribunal established by law.'

Nevertheless, there are sufficient reasons to recommend having specialised bodies to settle sports disputes. Among them, we can highlight the need to have quick and effective solutions, the expertise of professionals in charge of settling, the increase in volume and complexity of conflicts or the saturation of ordinary courts.

This is why associations have sought internal solutions to respond to these needs. As an example, the FIFA statutes state in article 15 that:

> Member associations' statutes must comply with the principles of good governance, and shall, in particular, contain, at a minimum, provisions relating to the following matters: all relevant stakeholders must agree to recognise the jurisdiction and authority of CAS and give priority to arbitration as a means of dispute resolution.

FIFA recognises the jurisdiction of the CAS to settle disputes between FIFA and member associations, confederations, leagues, clubs, players, officials, intermediaries, and agents organising matches under a license. The arbitration procedure is governed by the provisions of the code of arbitration in sporting matters of the CAS. To solve this, the CAS applies the different FIFA regulations and, as a complement, Swiss law. An appeal can only be filed before the CAS when all other internal judicial channels have been exhausted. To strengthen this arbitration jurisdiction, FIFA prohibits recourse to ordinary courts.

The FIFA statutes also protect the execution of rulings, binding confederations, associations, leagues, players, officials or intermediaries to fully comply with the rulings of competent authorities. And we are applying the Disciplinary Code to take the necessary disciplinary measures. CAS has confirmed that FIFA has a general competence to enforce its rulings within the Football family.

Nevertheless, the Litigation-Administrative Bench of the Audiencia Nacional, in its judgment of June 19, 2017 (Marta Domínguez case), established that a doping sanction originating from a Swiss arbitral body must follow the procedure legally provided for enforcement of foreign arbitral awards in Spain (exequatur), with no possibility to grant direct and immediate effectiveness.

The European Court of Human Rights has confirmed that the CAS is an independent and impartial arbitral tribunal compatible with the fundamental rights, in accordance with the ruling of the Bundesgerichtshof on June 7, 2016, in the Pechstein case and the ruling of the Swiss Federal Court (4A_260/2017).

Enforcement in Spain of a CAS award, assuming that submission to arbitration has been obligatory, as in the case of the adhesion clauses of the federative statutes, could entail its nullity, and the award would not be valid. Consequently, the possible coercive executive measures in the event of non-compliance or non-payment, for example, the threat by FIFA to impose sanctions in national competitions (loss of points and even relegation), would be entirely null and void under Spanish law.

The Sentence of the Supreme Court, Litigation-Administrative Bench no. 708/2017, of April 25, 2017 (Case Roberto Heras) ruled that mandatory arbitration is unconstitutional in Spain for breaching the right to adequate judicial protection provided for in article 24 of the Constitution, where one of the parties has not freely given consent, as they have not voluntarily signed any arbitration commitment, but as a *sine qua non-requirement* to perform their profession. Furthermore, Spanish legislation prohibits subjecting disciplinary matters to arbitration, so article 35 of the Royal Decree on Sports associations establishes that 'issues may not be the object of arbitration or conciliation . . . b) that are related to the control of substances and methods prohibited in sports and security in sports practice'. The Court confirmed the compensation of 724,000 euros by the State to the former cyclist for damages and losses arising from the fine for doping in the Vuelta 2005, which was finally annulled by justice in 2012.

In Portugal, the difficulty and delay in the definitive settlement of legal sports disputes and the production of sentences in different jurisdictional orders, combined with the growing need for the claimed speciality, led to the creation of a Court of Arbitration for Sport (TAD) as an appeal body for most rulings issued within the scope of the Portuguese sport system.

We are faced with competence built from a generic perspective to a specific view, as only sports disputes or disputes related to sports practice in which there is an express excluding legal norm, namely, due to identity of one or both parties or due to a specific matter, will be removed from the scope of the TAD.

The generic competence of the TAD as advanced is recognised not only in the domain of Necessary Arbitration but also in the domain of Voluntary Arbitration, in the matters expressly provided for in the TAD Law.

In other words, the starting point for constructing a specialised body to settle sports disputes was based on the internal jurisdictional means of sports associations.

Now, the organic structure of sports associations includes two bodies assigned to settle conflicts arising from the practice of sports, the Disciplinary Council and the Council of Justice, so when it comes to exhausting the internal means of sports justice, it is no more than irrevocably relying on those jurisdictional remedies.

This does not bar, albeit involved in huge historical controversy in Portugal, access to administrative litigation when it comes to 'disputes arising from the acts and omissions of the bodies of sports associations, within the scope of the exercise of public powers', safeguarding *'the sporting effects since validly produced under the last ruling of the competent authority in the sporting order'*, this being the concept, in general terms, of a sports *res judicata*, enshrined in the Basic Law on Physical Activity and Sport; thus, the rights of access to courts and adequate jurisdictional protection are guaranteed, as values with constitutional dignity.

Conclusions

The conclusion of this Chapter is the necessary and constant search for balance between Sport and the Law. Such compensation can only be achieved assuming the recognition of the specificity of sport, which will materialise, among other things, in the establishment of a proper sporting legal order. That legal order is based on principles such as *pro competitione*, *par conditio*, the principle of preservation of the purity of competition and immediate enforcement of sports sanctions. And to achieve this goal, it is essential to adopt a specific dispute resolution system for sport, mainly based on Arbitration, despite the emergence of conflict situations with constitutional and supra-state norms and the enforcement of such decisions in the different legal orders.

Although the differences in terms of form, Portugal and Spain comply with this specificity of sport, both countries share a standard reference that allows looking at these two legal systems under the same framing prism.

Reference

Cazorla-Prieto, L. M. (2013). *Deporte y Estado*. Pamplona: Editorial Aranzad.

Chapter 6

Public policies and sport participation in Spain and Portugal

Fernando Lera-López, Antonio G. Gómez-Plana, and António de Araújo Barros Maia

Introduction

The Portugal-Spain border referred to as 'La Raya' in Spanish and 'A Raia' in Portuguese and Galician, is the longest border within the European Union (EU), with a length of 1,214 km. Along this border, many cultural, social, and economic relationships have been established over the course of many centuries. From an economic perspective for example, in 2019, Spain was the first trade partner for Portuguese exports and imports, and Portugal was the fourth trade partner for Spanish exports. In terms of tourism in the same year, according to their Statistics National Institutes, approximately 22% of Portuguese visited Spain, and correspondingly, Spanish people were the main nationality visiting Portugal.

Nevertheless, there is a lack of comparative studies between both countries in the sport field. Only some studies have analysed sports in both countries within the framework of the EU (Camy et al., 2004). According to the European Commission (2018a), sport activities compose 1.44% and 1.12% of gross domestic product (GDP), and 1.50% and 1.39% of total employment in Spain and Portugal, respectively. This chapter fills this gap by examining the transformation and evolution of sport participation occurred in Spain and Portugal during the last two decades and the relevance of the public policies in explaining this evolution. The main aspects covered in this chapter include an analysis of the evolution of sport participation in both countries that consider potential similarities. It also discusses the public policies developed in sports by policymakers in both countries, as well as the main laws that regulate this activity. It also examines the distribution of public expenditure in sports within the main levels of public administration in Spain and Portugal. The chapter concludes with a comparison of sports participation and public policies developed in both countries.

National sports organisation in Portugal and Spain and legislative framework

Sports organisation in Portugal and Spain: differences and similarities

Articles 79 and 43.3 of the Portuguese (1976) and Spanish Constitution (1978), respectively, recognise sport and physical activities as rights for their citizens.

DOI: 10.4324/9781003197003-6

Consequently, these activities have been promoted by both governments since its democratisation, although with some differences, acquiring a central position in the public sector regarding the development of the sport system in both countries and providing a clear example of the so-called process of governmentalisation of sports (Llopis-Goig, 2017) or the high degree of state involvement known as bureaucratic configuration (Camy et al., 2004).

In Portugal, the national government represented by the *Instituto Português do Desporto e Juventude* (IPDJ) controls sport in Portugal. The IPDJ acts on the 'definition, execution and evaluation of the sport public politics, as well as the support to regular and high-performance physical activity, through the availability of technical, human and financial resources' (IPDJ, 2020). This public national organisation's mission is to be in collaboration with private and public organisations and assures a centralised policy in the areas of sport and youth. Through IPDJ, the public sector finances nearly 600 sport institutions, including federations and the Olympic and Paralympic Committees. This public sector could be described as a centralised sport system.

The 169/99 Act (Assembly of the Portuguese Republic, 1999) establishes the competences of the Portuguese local administration for the financial support and organisation of sport activities. This law has been amended several times since its promulgation in 1999, but the local administration's sport competences remain a central element of the local activity for the public sector.

The Portuguese private sector is formed by the commercial private sector (for profit) and the associative private sector (non-profit). This latter sector largely consists of the sport federations. Sport national federations, together with the sport clubs and societies, professional leagues, athletes, professionals, judges, and referees, carry out these functions:

- Promote, regulate, and run the practice of the sport or a set of modalities associated.
- Represent before the Public Administration the interests of their affiliated.
- Represent their own modality with the international sport organisations where they are affiliated, as well as ensuring the participation of national teams.

The sport organisation in the Spanish public sector is characterised by a decentralised structure based on the decentralised system of public administration in Spain (Lera-López & Lizalde-Gil, 2013; Llopis-Goig, 2017). Sport policy is simultaneously developed by national, regional, and local authorities. With regard to the national authorities, national sport responsibility belongs to the Ministry of Culture and Sport, and particularly to the High Council for Sport (i.e., Consejo Superior de Deportes, CSD in Spanish), as an autonomous national institution with delimited sport actions since the National Sport Act (i.e., Spanish Parliament, 1990). Many of the actions of the High Council for Sport affect the national character of sport, such as organisation of and participation in international sport competitions, doping control, scientific research, and approving and regulating sport federations, as well as granting them financial support (Llopis-Goig, 2017). Other sport policies are carried out in coordination with the regional authorities, such as the promotion of sport facilities and the construction of sport facilities. The regional authorities have a wide range of sport responsibilities in their respective regions, including regulating and promoting sports at the different levels, supporting territorial federations, organising regional competitions, and providing their own sport services. Finally, local authorities promote sports and mainly manage sport facilities, providing local sport services to citizens.

As in Portugal, the Spanish private sector is formed by the commercial private sector (for profit) and the associative private sector (non-profit). This latter sector largely consists of the sport federations with similar functions as in Portugal. In both countries, the legal sport system situates sport federations as a driver force behind sports, assuming them to be public functions.

Legislative framework in both countries

The main law regulating the sport system in Portugal is the National Sport Act of 2007, which was partially modified in 2009 (i.e., Assembly of the Portuguese Republic, 2007). This law aims to promote physical activity and sport in Portugal based on the following essential points: equal and universal access to sport for any citizen, sport contribution to the social and territorial cohesion, coordination, collaboration, and decentralisation among national government, regional governments (particularly in the Madeira and Azores regions), and local authorities. In this context, the IPDJ was created to organise the sport system in the country and to boost engagement in sport. In addition, the National Council of Sport (*Conselho Nacional do Desporto*) was created to coordinate between Public Administration and private sport associations in their efforts to promote sport participation. The entire legal sport framework in the country is collected in the official website of the IPDJ (2021a).

The main law regulation sport system in Spain consists of the National Sport Acts (i.e., Spanish Parliament, 1980, 1990). In 1980, the National Sport Act was decisive for the democratisation and modernisation of the sport system in Spain. Nevertheless, the extraordinary increase of doping and violence and the increasing differences between professional and amateur sport participation suggested the necessity of a new regulation. The National Sport Act of 1990 established the public regulation of sport and the role played by the High Council for Sport, clarifying the distribution of competences in the public sector, as well as the creation of a federative model (Llopis-Goig, 2017) that remains in effect today. Different laws put in place later have mainly regulated the fight against doping, violence, racism, and xenophobia in sport, sport in the educational system, and the sport limited companies (i.e., Carretero-Lestón, 2020 for more details). Currently, the Spanish government is preparing a new National Sport Act, which could amend the preliminary disagreements of some sport agents (federations, professional, leagues, etc.). However, the new legislation is not going to significantly change the model of public and private collaboration at national, regional, and local levels, although improvements should be made to promote sport for women and people with disabilities and its relationship with health, social cohesion, tourism, etc.

Public expenditure in Portugal and Spain

This section describes the public expenditure on sports in both countries. This expenditure includes current and capital expenditures that support sport activities and events, sport infrastructures, and staff training, among other expenses. The comparative analysis has depended on the availability of data. The data published in the Anuario de Estadísticas Deportivas for Spain began in 2010 (i.e., Spanish Ministry of Culture and Sport, 2013–2020), while data for Portugal is available since 1996 (Fundação Francisco Manuel dos Santos, 2021). Thus, this chapter provides an analysis of data from the year 2010 to 2019 (last year with available data). Additionally, the data is presented at a national level, although there are differences across regions and municipalities in the per inhabitant public expenditure.

The main results are displayed in Table 6.1. The financial crisis since 2008 is the main driver for the decreasing evolution of the public expenditure in sports during

Table 6.1 Evolution and distribution of total public expenditure in sport: Spain and Portugal

Year	Total Public Expenditure Thousands of euros (1)	Base 2014 = 100 (2)	% on GDP (3)	Euros per inhabitant (4)	Central Government % on total expenditure (5)	Regional Government % on total expenditure (6)	Local Government % on total expenditure (7)
SPAIN							
2010	3,786,207	158	0.35	81.5	4.5	14.8	80.7
2011	3,232,669	135	0.29	69.3	4.7	17.9	77.4
2012	2,580,646	107	0.25	55.1	6.6	14.0	79.3
2013	2,391,302	100	0.23	51.2	6.4	14.1	79.6
2014	2,400,865	100	0.23	51.6	5.3	12.9	81.8
2015	2,553,215	106	0.24	55.0	5.4	11.7	82.8
2016	2,522,021	105	0.23	54.3	5.7	12.0	82.3
2017	2,636,395	110	0.23	56.7	5.4	13.0	81.6
2018	2,873,046	120	0.23	61.5	6.1	12.5	81.4
PORTUGAL							
2010	328,977	132	0.18	31.1	12.7		87.3
2011	310,743	125	0.18	29.4	12.3		87.7
2012	269,042	108	0.16	25.6	14.7		85.3
2013	286,380	115	0.17	27.4	10.2		89.8
2014	248,896	100	0.14	23.9	13.4		86.6
2015	282,991	114	0.16	27.3	13.0		87.0
2016	300,845	121	0.16	29.1	13.2		86.8
2017	336,888	135	0.17	32.7	12.1		87.9
2018	334,322	134	0.16	32.5	13.0		87.0
2019	366,199	147	0.17	35.6	12.5		87.5

Source: Adapted from Spanish Ministry of Culture and Sport (2020) and Fundação Francisco Manuel dos Santos

the first part of the time surveyed. Both countries confronted large cuts in their public expenditure linked to sports, larger than any other budgetary item. Consequently, as displayed in columns 1 and 2, these cuts show the initial decreasing trend, reaching the minimum expenditure in 2013 (Spain) and 2014 (Portugal).

The minima in absolute public expenditure are also reflected in relative terms. First, we check the evolution of public expenditure in sports with respect to GDP (column 3). It is always higher in Spain than in Portugal: Spain had a level of 0.23% in 2014, while Portugal reached 0.14% for the same year, confirming previous empirical evidence about the economic importance of the sport system in both countries (European Commission, 2018a). The faster post-crisis general economic recovery in Portugal was also accompanied by a larger increase in their Public Administration effort on sport expenditure. Hence, Portugal achieved a greater increase from 0.14% to 0.17% of the GDP, but this percentage has remained stable for Spain at 0.23%.

Second, the evolution of the population in both countries provides new insight with respect to the public expenditure (column 4). Spain spends more public resources per citizen than Portugal. Though the fall during the crisis was higher in Spain, the recovery has been slower. The per capita Spanish public expense in sport activities in 2013 fell to a minimum of 51.2 euros, while the level for Portugal was 23.9 euros in the same year, which was approximately half of the Spanish level. Spain increased this expenditure to 61.6 euros per inhabitant in 2018, while Portugal reached 35.6 euros in 2019.

Finally, regarding the typology of the financing Public Administrations, there are some similarities and differences between Spain and Portugal. Table 6.2 includes the percentage participation of each Public Administration on total public expenditure in sports in columns 5 to 7. The Central Administration in Portugal is represented in this table as the expenditure of the IPDJ, previously described. The regional government data shown in column 6 includes information only for Spain, given the relevant role of the regions in the decentralised Spanish political system, while Portugal is a centralised country where the equivalent regional authorities do not exist. Nevertheless, the main role in both countries is focused on the local government. In both countries, municipalities finance around 80% of the public expenditure in sports and other local administrations, with the percentage in Portugal slightly higher. Another common characteristic is that the shares among levels of Public Administration have remained relatively constant along the time considered.

Comparison of sport participation levels in Portugal and Spain

In this section, we develop a comparative analysis between both countries regarding sport participation. This comparison is made at three different levels, making a distinction, when possible, between men and women, sport *federates*[1], sport participants, and the primary sport activities practised in both countries.

Table 6.2 Evolution of sport federated by gender in Portugal and Spain, period 2009–2019

	Federated: total number			Growth rates		% women on total		
	2009	2019	Growth	Men	Women	2009	2019	Growth
	(1)	(2)	(3)	(4)	(5)	(6)	(7)	(8)
Portugal	**513,005**	**688,293**	**175,288**	**34.17**	**73.22**	**24.46**	**31.58**	**7.12**
North	149,231	197,154	47,923	32.11	58.46	24.70	29.62	4.93
Central	117,234	160,320	43,086	36.75	83.15	24.13	32.31	8.19
Lisboa	139,568	196,827	57,259	41.03	87.97	24.71	32.93	8.22
Alentejo	40,877	48,492	7,615	18.63	75.62	19.88	29.43	9.55
Algarve	27,380	38,235	10,855	39.65	81.30	24.14	31.34	7.20
Autonomous Region of Azores	21,634	19,253	-2,381	-11.01	11.89	29.24	36.76	7.52
Autonomous Region of Madeira	17,081	28,012	10,931	64.00	87.79	28.10	32.17	4.08
Statistical variance				459.05	639.92	7.92	5.18	
Spain	**3,470,659**	**3945510**	**474851**	**9.00**	**32.75**	**19.72**	**23.03**	**3.31**
Andalusia	554,784	522,529	-32,255	-3.11	-17.21	19.17	16.85	-2.32
Aragon	144,019	145,263	1,244	-8.57	60.84	13.60	21.68	8.08
Asturias	86,735	101,064	14,329	7.33	57.01	18.50	24.92	6.43
Balearic Islands	84,767	106,320	21,553	15.51	63.67	20.60	26.88	6.28
Canary Islands	145,503	176,308	30,805	9.80	72.48	18.15	25.83	7.68
Cantabria	61,613	78,181	16,568	16.53	70.04	19.37	25.95	6.59
Castile and León	188,545	193,955	5,410	0.74	11.27	20.22	21.87	1.65
Castilla-La Mancha	152,181	134,191	-17,990	-14.49	1.44	16.74	19.26	2.52
Catalonia	568,760	651,723	82,963	6.77	45.74	20.05	25.50	5.45
Ceuta	7,721	5,100	-2,621	-35.59	-25.85	16.84	18.90	2.06
Valencia	355,508	375,659	20,151	2.70	20.35	16.82	19.16	2.34
Extremadura	82,649	112,342	29,693	37.96	25.03	15.71	14.45	-1.26
Galicia	187,304	282,369	95,065	40.80	96.79	17.78	23.21	5.43
La Rioja	33,097	34,496	1,399	-1.01	24.87	20.24	24.25	4.01
Madrid	432,305	523,569	91,264	16.66	34.24	25.33	28.08	2.75
Melilla	8,849	10,020	1,171	6.25	42.20	19.41	24.38	4.97
Murcia	91,660	129,883	38,223	39.16	53.93	17.21	18.70	1.49
Navarra	67,383	78,815	11,432	7.80	47.33	23.19	29.21	6.02
Basque Country	216,194	280,930	64,736	25.95	42.44	24.20	26.53	2.33
Statistical variance				338.15	920.67	7.99	15.79	

Source: Adapted from Spanish Institute of Statistics and Statistics Portugal

Sport federates: evolution by gender and region

This epigraph describes the evolution of the federated in Spain and Portugal between 2009 and 2019. This is the maximum time available for a homogenous comparison between both countries using their Statistics National Institutes as data sources. The evolution of the total number of federated (displayed in Figure 6.1) shows a similar pattern for both countries: an initial phase until year 2014 when the number of federated remain relatively stable, and a subsequent phase of positive growth that has been stronger in Portugal. This pattern is especially driven

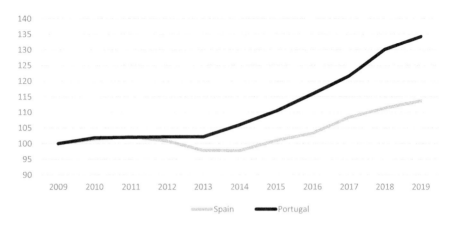

Figure 6.1 Evolution in total number of federated (base 2009 = 100)
Source: Adapted from Spanish Institute of Statistics and Statistics Portugal

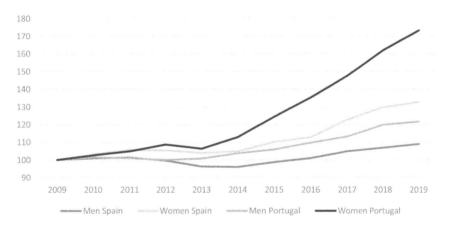

Figure 6.2 Federated by sex (base 2009 = 100)
Source: Adapted from Spanish Institute of Statistics and Statistics Portugal

by the differences between men and women. The second phase growth is driven by the number of federated women in Spain and Portugal (see Figure 6.2), given the modest growth in the number of federated men in both countries. Nevertheless, for both men and women, the Portuguese growth rates have been larger than those in Spain. The 2009–2019 Portuguese growth rate for federated men has been 34.17% (9% for Spain) and 73.22% for federated women (32.75% for Spain).

To examine the previous female bias in the federated growth rates, the national data are presented in Table 6.2 at the regional level. There are seven regions in

Portugal and nineteen in Spain, including the two autonomous cities, Ceuta and Melilla. Through this approach, we check if the female bias is present across all regions or if it has additional regional biases. The comparison is made between the two extreme points (years 2009 and 2019).

Columns 1 and 2 include the total number of federated, with column 3 showing the change in the absolute number of federated between 2019 and 2009. The positive change at the national level is generally corroborated at the regional level, with 4 exceptions out of 26 regions: Azores in Portugal and Andalusia, Castilla-La Mancha, and Ceuta in Spain. While the decrease in Azores and Castilla-la Mancha is caused by the fall in federated men, the decrease in Andalusia and Ceuta corresponds to both men and women, as columns 4 and 5 reveal. There are other regions where the number of federated men decreases (Aragon and La Rioja in Spain), but the positive growth of federated women provides an aggregated positive growth for total federated for those regions. Consequently, two statements can be inferred from the female bias: (i) it also takes place at the regional level, with the exceptions of Andalusia and Extremadura in Spain; and (ii) the statistical variance of growth rates across regions is large, and it is larger for women than for men.

Columns 6 and 7 display the share of women on total federated, while column 8 lists the increase or decrease in percentage points (i.e., column 7 minus column 6). Women's participation in 2009 is 24.46% in Portugal, compared to 19.72% in Spain. The statistical variance across regions in 2009 is very similar for both countries. The regional maximum level in Portugal is 29.24% (Azores) and 25.33% in Spain (Madrid), while the minimum level in Portugal is 19.88% (Alentejo) and 13.60% in Spain (Aragon). However, the regional evolution of this variable diverges: while the different regional growth rates by sex (see columns 4 and 5) suffer a reduction in its statistical variance across Portuguese regions, this regional variance increases significantly across Spanish regions. Hence, women's participation in 2019 is 31.58% in Portugal, compared to 23.03% in Spain. The regional maximum level in Portugal reaches 36.76% in Azores and 29.21% for Spain in Navarra. The minimum levels are 29.43% in Alentejo (Portugal) and 14.45% in Extremadura (Spain). Note that the maximum regional level of women's participation in 2019 in Spain (29.21%) does not reach the minimum level in Portugal (29.43%).

When we complement the analysis of federated with a perspective of their share on total population (not shown in tables), we see that federated men moved from 7.65% (Portugal) and 12.18% (Spain) in 2009, to 9.69% and 13.20%, respectively, in 2019. Similarly, federated women on population augmented from 2.28% (Portugal) and 3.42% (Spain) in 2009, to 4% and 3.80%, respectively, in 2019. Although Spain initially had larger shares of federated on population than Portugal, Portugal has surpassed Spain in terms of women in 2019. Again, at the regional level, the percentage of the federated population has a more homogenous pattern in Portugal than in Spain.

In general, there is an increase in the number of federated populations, not only at the national level but also at a regional level in Portugal and Spain, albeit with some particular exceptions. Also, Portugal has experienced a larger growth bias towards women than Spain, resulting in a more homogenous country for this variable. It could be argued that this is due to the more centralised sport system in Portugal than in Spain, as well as the legal framework for sport territorial cohesion.

Sport participation

This epigraph presents the data regarding the percentage of people engaged in sport activities and their frequency, making the distinction between males and females and age intervals. This comparison is strongly limited by the availability of data. In Spain, a sport survey is developed every five years, with the latest published in 2015 (i.e., Spanish Ministry of Education, Culture and Sport, 2015). In Portugal, sport surveys are not published periodically: the last two were released in 2014 and 2019 (i.e., Statistics Portugal, 2021a). We have also considered information provided by the European Commission (2018b) about playing sport in the EU.

Following European data, Figure 6.3 shows that the percentage of the population engaged in sports is higher in Spain than in Portugal; approximately 43% of the Spanish population over 15 years of age regularly practiced any sport, while the percentage decreases to 26% in Portugal.

If we consider the percentage of people who do not practice any sport, the main differences between both countries are in terms of gender and age intervals, as shown in Table 6.3. In all cases, the number of people who are not engaged in sport

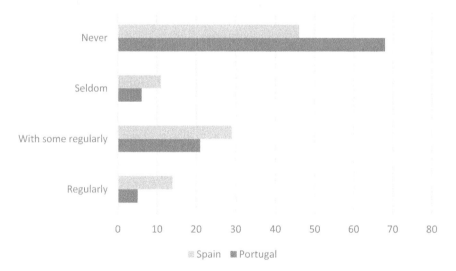

Figure 6.3 Frequency of exercise or playing sport
Source: Adapted from European Commission (2018b)

Table 6.3 Percentage of population over 15 years not engaged in sport 2017

	Portugal	Spain
Total	74	57
Men	68	51
Women	78	63
Men 15–24	38	20
Men 25–39	54	41
Men 40–54	70	56
Men 55+	89	66
Women 15–24	44	41
Women 25–39	74	61
Women 40–54	84	61
Women 55+	86	70

Source: Adapted from European Commission (2018b)

is higher in Portugal than in Spain, with the highest differences occurring among men over 55 years of age and women between 40 and 54 years of age.

Based on the national statistics provided directly by both countries, the number of people over 15 who were not engaged in sport decreased to 46.6% in Spain in 2015 and 65.6% in Portugal in 2019. This situation could be particularly dramatic among the Portuguese young population, with rates of 40.3% for those 15–24 years old and 57.5% for 25–34 years old (Statistics Portugal, 2021a), both of which are slightly higher in comparison to European data (European Commission, 2018b). The data show that an extremely high number of the young population in Portugal are not engaged in any sporting activity.

From a longitudinal perspective, national data for Portugal only collect information for 2014 and 2019 (Statistics Portugal, 2021b). The evolution shows an increase in people not engaged in sport from 64.9% to the previously mentioned 65.5%; this percentage also increased among men (59.3% to 61.7%), whereas it slightly decreased among women (69.8% to 69%). At the same time, the frequency of participation has also decreased. For example, people who practice sport at least once a week have decreased between 2014 and 2019 from 35.0% to 32.6%. Among sport participants, time devoted to sport has diminished. In 2014, 45% of Portuguese sport participants followed the World Health Organization's guidelines (WHO, 2020), with more than 150 minutes of sport activities. In 2019, the percentage abated to 42.3%.

In the case of Spain, national data are available from 1980 to 2015, showing that the population engaged in sport has doubled in thirty years, from 25% to 53.5%. In particular, from 2005 to 2015, the number rose over to 5 million people. Unlike in Portugal, the gender gap has been reduced to the middle in Spain in 15 years and has increased the frequency of participation (García-Ferrando & Llopis-Goig, 2020).

Federated sports practiced in both countries: differences by gender

Finally, in this epigraph, we compare what are the most popular federated sports in Portugal and Spain, making a distinction by gender. The set of comparative federated sports is limited by the available information for Portugal, which consists of data for 21 sports (IPDJ, 2021b). This does not include some sports that represent a not negligible number of federated, such as hunting or mountaineering.

Among men, the relative structure by type of sports from 2009 to 2019 is similar for both countries (i.e., correlation of 0.88 in 2009 and 0.86 in 2019), meaning that the changes in composition were very similar for both countries during the decade. The most played sports by men in 2019 in Spain were football (33.73% of total *federates*), hunting (10.97%), basketball (8.32%), golf (6.37%), and mountaineering (5.41%), with a relevant increase in the share of football and mountaineering during the decade. Similarly, in Portugal, football makes up 37.00% of total *federates*, followed by swimming (10.78%), handball (6.10%), volleyball (4.53), and basketball (4.16%). Between 2009 and 2009, there has been an increase in football in both countries, a relevant rise in the practice of swimming in Portugal, and a decline in basketball and golf in both countries.

Nevertheless, the structure of women federated sports is very different between Spain and Portugal: in 2009, the correlation between both countries' sports structures was 0.77 and it significantly dropped to 0.46 in 2019. This decline is mainly due to significant changes in Portugal during the decade, diverging even further for the sports played by Spanish women.

In Portugal, the majority of women played one of four sports in 2009: volleyball (16.29%), basketball (12.97%), handball (11.24%), and tennis (7.35%). This ranking changed by 2019: swimming (25.43%) was the new leader and the other sports with more than 5% were volleyball (12.94%), handball (9.40%), gymnastics (8.59%), basketball (5.49%), and athletics (5.42%). In 2009, Spain's women's sport structure was headed by basketball (18.32%), golf (15.31%), and volleyball (6.19%), whereas in 2019, the top sports were basketball (14.63%), golf (8.39%), football (7.84%), and volleyball (7.09%). Those shifts revealed the change in the practice experienced in Portugal and, to a certain point, in Spain as well.

In general, there are some common characteristics between Spain and Portugal: (i) the growth in *federates* is larger for women than for men in the sports that increase their number of federated for both sexes (i.e., football, swimming, volleyball, gymnastics, skating, cycling, rugby, motoring, or table tennis); (ii) tennis, sport fishing, and sailing experienced a decline in the number of federated men and women; (iii) there are many similarities in terms of growth rates regarding the most successful sports; for example, the sports with growth rates higher than 30% for both men and women in Portugal are swimming, gymnastics, cycling, rugby, and motoring, whereas in Spain, football, gymnastics, skating, cycling, rugby, and motoring reach those same growth rates; and (iv) basketball is facing a crisis in both countries, although with different intensities: as one of the most played sports, it suffers a clear decline in the number of federated men and women in Portugal, and a slight decline for men and small increase for women in Spain.

The main differences between federated sports in Spain and Portugal pertain to the evolution of golf (with a strong decline in Spain for men and women, while Portugal gets a slight increase) and swimming (with a huge increase in Portugal). Also, sports played more by women than men in 2019 (i.e., sports in which women's share in total federated is higher than 50%) are slightly different. In Portugal, those sports are swimming, volleyball, gymnastics, athletics, and skating, while in Spain, they are volleyball, gymnastics, and skating.

Private expenditure in both countries

The information of the private expenditure in activities related to sports is scarce, so it is not easy to compare this concept between countries. This section thus details information obtained from private expenditure surveys developed by their National Statistics Institutes: the 'Inquérito às Despesas das Famílias' in Portugal (a quinquennial inquiry for which the 2015/2016 survey is the most recent; Statistics Portugal, 2021b) and the 'Encuesta de Presupuestos Familiares' in Spain (an annual survey for which 2019 is the last available year; Spanish Institute of Statistics, 2021). Their national data can be divided into regional terms. Due to changes in their methodologies (e.g., changes in the classification of expenditures in sport goods and services), it is not possible to perform a time series analysis, and only the most recent data is presented here.

The expenditure per household in sport services presents differences across both countries and their regions. The average household in Portugal had a level of expenditure in 2015/2016 of 20,363 euros; 0.55% of this average represented expenses in sport services, with 0.50% related to participation activities and the remaining percentage to event attendance. For all the Portuguese regions, participation represents most of the expenditure in sport activities, although there is a wide regional variance in this variable: from 0.74% in the Lisbon Metropolitan region to 0.19% in Alentejo. It is possible to compare these results with Spain, where the total average expenditure by household in 2016 was 28,200 euros and the expenditure in participation and attendance to sport services accrued to 0.74%, which is above the Portuguese level. This percentage shows an increasing evolution in Spain, but due to methodological changes in the survey, it is not possible to confirm the evolution in Portugal. Hence, in Spain in 2006, the level was 0.60%, while it reached 0.79% in 2019 when there was also a high regional variance: the extreme cases correspond to Navarra (1.06%) and Asturias (0.51%). As additional information, the Spanish data also reflect that the expenditure per woman is lower than the expenditure per man since 2006. Both sexes reflect an irregular but converging trend.

Conclusions

The Spanish and Portuguese sport systems are the result of the collaboration between the public and private sectors. In both countries, the public sector is in charge of the promotion of sport (amateur and professional), the construction and management of sport facilities, and the regulation of sport in the educational system. The non-profit private agents, such as sport federations and sport clubs, play a secondary role. In the case of Portugal, the framework is based on a centralised sport policy for all the regions, whereas in the case of Spain, local and regional authorities play a more significant role in terms of the legal framework and public expenditure in sport. The IPDJ and CSD, respectively, are the national organisations in charge of the national sport policy.

Although the share of sport-related GDP and employment are very similar in both countries, (European Commission, 2018a), there are significant differences in terms of public sport expenditure based on national data. In Spain, public expenditure achieved 61.6 euros per inhabitant in 2018, while Portugal's public expenditure reached 35.6 euros in 2019. These differences are less significant in terms of private expenditure on sport, with 0.55% of this expenditure in Portugal and 0.74% in Spain, respectively, in 2016. In Portugal, the public expenditure is mainly made by local authorities (from the IPDJ resources), but in Spain, it is principally developed by local and regional authorities.

In both countries, formal participation, measured through sport federated participation, and general participation have evolved in different manners. During the 2009 to 2019 period, sport *federates* have increased significantly in both countries, particularly among Portuguese women (growth rate of 73.22% vs. 32.74% in Spain, as compared to 34.17% among men vs. 9% for Spain). Also, the importance of sport *federates* is more homogeneously distributed among Portuguese regions than in Spanish ones. From a qualitative perspective, the structure of men's sport *federates* are very similar in both countries, with football as the most important sport. However, for women's participation, both structures have been diverging in the last ten years. Nevertheless, in terms of general engagement in sport, participation rates in Portugal are clearly below the Spanish rates, particularly among young populations. Also, from a longitudinal perspective, sport rates in Spain have gradually increased, but the opposite trend has occurred in Portugal. For further research, it could be interesting to analyse the impact of COVID-19 on sports in both countries.

Note

1 Professional and semiprofessional athletes affiliated with a given Sport Federation.

References

Assembly of the Portuguese Republic. (1999). Law Nº 169/99. Diário Da República Nº 219. Retrieved May 25, 2021, from www.pgdlisboa.pt/leis/lei_mostra_articulado.php?nid=592&tabela=leis&ficha=1&pagina=1

Assembly of the Portuguese Republic. (2007). *National sport act* (Lei nº 5/2007). Diário Da República Electrónico. Retrieved May 27, 2021, from https://data.dre.pt/eli/lei/5/2007/01/16/p/dre/pt/html

Camy, J., Clijsen, L., Madella, A., & Pilkington, A. (2004). *Vocasport. Improving employment in the field of sport in Europe through vocational training*. European Commission.

Carretero-Lestón, J. L. (2020). El marco legal estatal como reflejo de los processos de cambio en el deporte. In N. Puig-Barata & A. Camps-Povill (Eds.), *Diálogos sobre el deporte* (pp. 64–74). Generalitat de Catalunya.

European Commission. (2018a). *Study on the economic impact of sport through sport satellite accounts*. European Commission.

European Commission. (2018b). *Sport and physical activity*. Special Eurobarometer 472. European Commission.

Fundação Francisco Manuel dos Santos. (2021). *Pordata database. Base de datos Portugal contemporáneo*. Retrieved April 26, 2021, from www.pordata.pt/

García-Ferrando, M., & Llopis-Goig, R. (2020). La participación deportiva em España pautas de estratificación y princiales características. In N. Puig-Barata & A. Camps-Povill (Eds.), *Diálogos sobre el deporte* (pp. 173–188). Generalitat de Catalunya.

Instituto Português do Desporto e Juventude. (2020). *Missão e atribuições*. https://ipdj.gov.pt/missão-e-atribuições

Instituto Português do Desporto e Juventude. (2021a). *Legal sport framework in Portugal (legislaçao desporto)*. Retrieved May 27, 2021, from https://ipdj.gov.pt/legislacao_desporto

Instituto Português do Desporto e Juventude. (2021b). *Sport federated rates*. Retrieved March 15, 2021, from https://ipdj.gov.pt/estatísticas

Lera-López, F., & Lizalde-Gil, E. (2013). Spain. In K. Hallmann & K. Petry (Eds.), *Comparative sport development: Systems, participation and public policy* (pp. 149–166). Springer.

Llopis-Goig, R. (2017). Spain: Putting the pieces of the sport system in place—The role of the sport federations. In J. Scheerder, A. Willem, & E. Claes (Eds.), *Sport policy systems and sport federations* (pp. 243–262). Palgrave Macmillan.

Spanish Institute of Statistics (Instituto Nacional de Estadística). (2021). *Encuesta de presupuestos familiares*. Retrieved March 17, 2021, from www.ine.es/

Spanish Ministry of Culture and Sport. (2013–2020). *Yearly sport statistics*. Spanish Ministry of Culture and Sport.

Spanish Ministry of Culture and Sport. (2020). *DEPORTE database*. Retrieved April 15, 2021, from www.culturaydeporte.gob.es/servicios-al-ciudadano/estadisticas/cultura/mc/deportedata/portada.html

Spanish Ministry of Education, Culture and Sport. (2015). *Encuesta de hábitos deportivos en España*. Consejo Superior de Deportes. Retrieved April 20, 2021, from www.culturaydeporte.gob.es/servicios-al-ciudadano/estadisticas/deportes/encuesta-habitos-deportivos-en-espana.html

Spanish Parliament. (1980). *Sports act 10/1980 of 12 April*. Retrieved May 25, 2021, from www.boe.es/eli/es/l/1980/03/31/13

Spanish Parliament. (1990). *Sports act 10/1990 of 15 October*. Retrieved May 25, 2021, from www.boe.es/eli/es/l/1990/10/15/10/con

Statistics Portugal (2021a). *Desporto em números—2020*. www.ine.pt/xurl/pub/6358545

Statistics Portugal (Instituto Nacional de Estatística). (2021b). *Inquérito às despesas das famílias*. Lisboa. Retrieved March 20, 2021, from www.ine.pt/xportal/xmain?xpid=INE&xpgid=ine_publicacoes&PUBLICACOESpub_boui=277098526&PUBLICACOESmodo=2

World Health Organization. (2020). *WHO guidelines on physical activity and sedentary behavior*. Retrieved March 11, 2021, from www.who.int/publications/i/item/9789240015128

Chapter 7

From buildings and equipment to 'spaces' for sports in Spain

Juan Manuel Murua

Planning and growth of the sports facilities network

To fully appreciate the development of the network of sports facilities and services in Spain, there are two fundamental regulatory frameworks that need to be understood: sport and spatial planning. The characteristics of these two areas and the way in which they have been applied, have given rise to an extensive network of facilities. A network that is as extensive as it is unbalanced.

The regulatory framework of sport

Spain's current extensive network of sports facilities reflects the regulatory framework that has facilitated rapid growth that is not entirely balanced. In the last 40 years, sports infrastructure has almost quadrupled in number. How has such growth been possible?

Local administrations have played a crucial role in the rise of sport in Spain, and the construction of sports infrastructure has been an essential part of this growth. This role has been driven by the regulatory framework and the distribution of power model, both in sport and in spatial planning.

The [Spanish] Law 7/1985 regulating the bases of Local Government developed municipalities' responsibilities, including those related to sports (Gallardo & Jiménez, 2004; Martínez Aguado, 2012, p. 142) and determined which of the sectoral laws (in this case in the field of sport) would be given specific powers (Viñas, 2011). In the context of sport, the [Spanish] Law 10/1990 of 15 October on Sport, along with the development of other laws at an autonomous community level, defined the powers of local corporations in sporting matters.

The Municipal Sports Services were committed to the provision of sports as a driving or generating factor for what was merely a potential demand. Municipal sport did not arise out of a logic leading town councils to meet the common needs of their residents. In this case, the municipalities endeavoured to generate that need by creating supply (Solar, 2011). In short, this regulatory drive enabled town

DOI: 10.4324/9781003197003-7

councils to become the parties responsible for providing the majority of sports infrastructure and physical and sporting activities programmes, thus playing a key role in promoting sport in Spain (Benito et al., 2012; Rodríguez-Fernández et al., 2016)

The administrations' interventionism has characterised the growth of the Spanish sports system, resulting in a high level of dependence on public funding of sport and a majority of facilities being publicly owned.

Another fundamental characteristic is the high degree of decentralisation when it comes to sport. As we will see in the next section, this characteristic is also found in spatial planning, resulting in a legal framework that makes it hard to achieve a balanced development of the network of sports services.

Spatial planning

In Spain, powers over spatial planning were handed over to the Autonomous Communities in 1978. Since then, each Autonomous Community has been entrusted with developing their own regulations (Aldrey & Rodríguez, 2010).

The spatial planning laws establish the spatial planning instruments that must be developed in each Autonomous Community (regional, sub-regional and sectoral instruments). Among the variety of options available, we should identify four main instruments which are common to all Communities: the Spatial Planning Regulations (Spatial Planning Laws), the Spatial Planning Schemes, the Partial Land Use Schemes, and the Sectoral Schemes. These Sectoral Schemes are of an operational planning nature that, within the framework of Spatial Planning Schemes for each Autonomous Community, specify the objectives, guidelines, and actions for certain sectoral areas in particular.

Another key instrument in understanding spatial planning are the Town Planning Schemes. A town planning scheme operates in a municipality and defines the land uses in that municipality, and it must conform to the land use schemes that are above them in the hierarchy. In this way, the Autonomous Communities establish a general planning framework, and the local administrations develop the town planning scheme that will operate in their particular area, in accordance with the guidelines set in that general framework . . . or at least that's how it is supposed to work.

Sports infrastructure planning

The different schemes for sports infrastructure planning come under this regulatory structure. So we can find two levels of schemes: the Sports Facilities Schemes for each Autonomous Community or smaller-scale territories and the Local Schemes for Sports Facilities and Services (Figure 7.1).

The Sports Facilities Schemes for the Autonomous Communities are of a sectoral nature as they specify the planning for the sports sector, endeavouring to

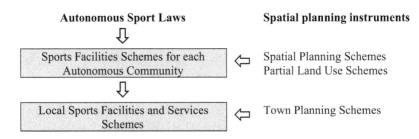

Figure 7.1 Sports infrastructure planning

achieve a balance in the distribution of services across the territory. Some of the usual criteria in these schemes are:

- To meet the population's needs.
- To adapt investments to available resources.
- To ensure respect for the environment and protection of nature.
- To establish the coordination and cooperation mechanisms of the different Administrations in the planning and execution of the different actions in the area of sports facilities.
- To safeguard social integration as regards accessibility.

The Local Facilities Schemes are also of a sectoral nature, but they operate within the framework of the Town Planning Schemes, thus maintaining the hierarchical levels. These schemes specify the actions to be taken as regards refurbishments, improvements, maintenance, and expansion of current facilities, as well as investments in new infrastructure. Furthermore, they include the necessary guidelines in the municipality's town planning to ensure the land is available and equipped appropriately, and the sports services are suitably located.

Lack of planning and its limited effectiveness

In the first section, we already mentioned the result of all those years of investment in sports infrastructure. The network of sports services has practically quadrupled in 40 years. As we have said, in the early post-dictatorship years, town councils threw themselves into investing in sports activities and facilities, in an attempt to boost the non-existent habit of practising sports in a large proportion of the population. Those early years of democratic town halls brought heavy investments and a significant growth in the network of sports infrastructure. Between 1976 and 1995, the number of services went from 48,723 to 66,352.

Although it looked like it might be a risky venture, the result was very satisfactory, and the amount of sport currently practised in Spain has reached similar levels to those of our European neighbours.

However, after that initial wave of investment in sports infrastructure, there have been a series of political, economic, social and sports dynamics that have led to the situation in which Spain has the extensive network of sports facilities that it has today. We will explain some of these dynamics later.

In general, we have noticed that the production of spatial planning schemes has been scarce. From a qualitative point of view, we can see that the execution and fulfilment of these schemes has left a great deal to be desired.

At a sporting level, this shortage of planning is even greater, and most Autonomous Communities have not drawn up their land use schemes for facilities. Local schemes for sports facilities, however, have been more commonplace. Nevertheless, this lack of spatial planning has led to many of these local schemes only looking at their own needs and interests, ignoring how they fit into a wider territorial scale and generating significant territorial imbalances or localised surpluses of certain types of facilities.

In addition to this, these sports facilities schemes have been given little consideration, and have been contingent upon other town planning interests. These schemes, whether local or territorial, have had limited coercive capacity, which has led to them not being fulfilled by the councils over and over again. Numerous facilities schemes that were approved by their town councils have not been fulfilled, and the municipalities have shown little interest in ensuring they are complied with. Town councils themselves have promoted economic and town planning development projects that go completely against the basic criteria of environmental, social or economic sustainability. There has been a plethora of golf courses with residential complexes, large stadiums, huge sports centres and, in general, sports facilities whose size and utility were not justified on exclusively technical grounds. They have ignored any land use criteria and even their own town planning, having required subsequent modifications of the town planning schemes to be able to justify outrageous investments on pointless sports spaces with no sense of scale.

The weak relationship between regional and local planning

At the end of the day, both spatial and sectoral planning are embodied in the municipalities. They are the main recipients of spatial planning schemes. Legislation covers this hierarchical system of town/spatial planning, such that municipalities, in their town planning schemes, must respect the provisions of the spatial planning policy promoted by the regional administrations. How effective the spatial planning schemes actually are depends on their materialisation on an urban scale. Nevertheless, spatial planning is one of the municipality's most relevant powers.

Consequently, the relationships between regional and local administrations must facilitate cooperation in the planning process, as well as in the implementation of guidelines that have been set out in the schemes to make sure the spatial planning policy is genuinely effective. What has happened in reality is that the few spatial planning schemes that were approved have, on many occasions, been interpreted in a somewhat distorted way or directly ignored by local schemes. The regional administrations have not made much of an effort to ensure they are complied with either.

The building boom

This panorama of planning deficiency was accompanied by the property boom in Spain from the end of the 20th century up to the 2007 recession, and which led the country to be one of the main sources of cement demand worldwide.

Throughout those years, the rampant growth in construction generated some dreadful dynamics for territorial balance. The uncontrolled rise in construction meant that many municipalities multiplied in size, and some people thought that new sports facilities were needed to provide a service to all the new homes that were being built.

The Spanish economy was like a game of Monopoly, in which everyone believed they were playing, and the majority thought they were going to win. The large construction companies reaped huge profits. They bought up plots of land that were subsequently rezoned as urban land, and they built homes in new residential paradises. Small investors came together and searched for opportunities in plots of land on which they could build, and they saw their life savings multiply. They also wanted their piece of the pie. The banks were rubbing their hands. They did not measure their profitability in terms of the percentage of profits over capital, but rather the increase in profits on the previous year. They offered financing to those large construction companies, to the small investors and to the buyers who wanted their piece of paradise with a garden, barbecue and private pool. The town halls struck it rich: they could rezone land as urban and obtain capital gains that they could use to improve their services and build new facilities, many of which were for sport.

And what about sport itself? This entire economic feast equipped the whole country with new sports infrastructure. Although the total number did not rise as much as in the previous period, the quality and complexity of the new and renovated infrastructure did increase substantially. Small halls gave way to sports centres with football pitches, swimming pools, tennis courts and multi-purpose courts. Between 1996 and 2005, the number of sports centres rose from 66,352 to 79,059.

The new residential complexes, with their detached and semi-detached chalets, offered tennis courts, swimming pools and even golf courses. Moreover, the town halls, with their coffers overflowing, were busy building new facilities or renovating and expanding on old facilities, in many cases with no practical or aesthetic sense whatsoever.

Golf courses are a prime example of this entire maelstrom of construction activity. Loads of golf courses were built as part of real estate developments with new homes. Construction companies realised that if people could not have the much-desired property on the coast, a golf course offered similar advantages. Homes overlooking the green sold for 25% more than those in the second row

(Navarro & Ortuño Padilla, 2010). Just like on the coast but without the land limitations, given that a dry inland plateau has no coastline. The usual limited water resources in certain areas were ignored, and lush green golf courses popped up all across the dry lands.

Facilities and services brought votes

Mayors, councillors and ministers were all aware of the political gains to be made by the construction of sports facilities and services. The electorate could see and appreciate a sports complex. It was a lot harder to value the effort and common sense established in spatial planning. There was money to build new sports facilities and services, and that brought votes. It was the perfect combination for the country's network of sports facilities to grow in leaps and bounds.

Did anyone even think about future maintenance and the running costs of those facilities and services? Of course they did. Many sports technicians observed the variable costs data for the facilities with some concern, but their opinion fell on deaf ears. Nobody wanted to hear the opinion of a killjoy.

The recession and the windfall

However, that party eventually came to an end. In Spain, the sub-prime mortgage crisis in 2007 and the bankruptcy of Lehman Brothers barely a year later were the last straw for an economy that, in the previous decade, had grown on the shoulders of a speculative property bubble.

Towards the end of 2008, the Spanish Government, following the example of other governments who implemented expansive economic policies, launched their Plan E. This plan aimed to provide a Keynesian response to the recession, implementing a range of public spending programmes (Bellod Redondo, 2015).

One important component of the Plan E was the 'Local Investment State Fund' (FEIL), which gave 8,000 million euros to finance investment projects to be executed by town halls. Over 30,000 projects had access to these funds, which meant an absolute windfall for local administrations. However, the rush to set them up led to town councils having to plan their projects in a short period of time, which resulted in many of the investments carried out by the municipalities being fairly unproductive.

A large sum of that money was allocated to sports facilities. It is estimated that 17.5% of those 8,000 million euros were allocated to funding investments in cultural, educational or sports facilities and buildings. In the years 2009 and 2010 over 1,000 million euros were spent on new construction work and refurbishments in sports facilities. Spain found itself with an extensive network of infrastructure that had encouraged a large proportion of the population to practise sports, but it also had considerable imbalances due to the public's lack of deep-rooted commitment and to certain political, economic, and social processes that had promoted the development of projects, whose justification is questionable.

Change of habits and model

Today, 40 years after the first Municipal Sports Services were created, we could say that Spanish society has reached a certain degree of sports maturity. The initial objectives with which they began, that is to democratise sport and promote sporting habits among the population, have reached stagnation point. The public sector management models have been adapting to general trends and the private sport sector has become consolidated. At this point, increasingly more reputable people in the field of local sports management are discussing the need to review the municipal sports model.

Taking the relational management model as a starting point, which is gradually being implemented in many local administrations, and considering a fresh approach to citizens' needs and problems as regards sporting habits and engaging in physical exercise, new sports planning processes are being drawn up that redirect the model of sport and its relationship with the city and with the territory.

In a regional/local context, there is evidence (Sport England, 1999) that sport contributes to:

- The regeneration of communities
- Safety in those communities
- The involvement of volunteers
- Health
- Young people's development and education
- Local economies
- The environment

To incorporate all these dimensions and maximise their contributions, it is necessary to change the way we understand sport and its impact on society. To do so, the new models of sports planning are working on adapting the policies, strategies, structures and management methods from public institutions.

The object of action: towards sports services and physical activity

Participation in the field of sport has not stopped growing in recent decades, as surveys analysing this practise show. The Survey of Sporting Habits in Spain (The Sports Council [*Consejo Superior de Deportes*], 2015) is carried out every five years and shows constant growth since 1975. As we have mentioned, the Municipal Sports Services have been largely responsible for this growth, as the main increase has come about in the practise of sport for all, which is the main purpose of local public action.

However, this positive reality should not take us away from another reality, and that is that the rates of sedentary behaviour among the Spanish population have reached worrying levels, to the point that it is considered a major public health problem. The National Health Survey in Spain in 2011/12 highlights that:

> In Spain, four out of ten people claim to be sedentary in their free time. 44.4% of the population aged 15 years and over claim that they do not engage in any exercise and spend their leisure time almost entirely sedentary.
> (Spanish Ministry of Health, Social Services and Equality, 2014)

Concern for this apparent anomaly, in which the number of people practising a sport increase at the same time as the levels of sedentary behaviour increase, has led many cities to consider the need to broaden their Municipal Sports Services' object of action to the treatment of sport and physical activity, in the understanding that it is the area of Sports, along with the areas of Health and Education, that have the greatest technical capacity to act on this problem.

Up until a few years ago, the promotion of healthy habits, including practising physical activity, focused on individual factors, placing the responsibility almost exclusively on the people affected. With this approach in mind, providing sports infrastructure and services was enough to enable people to choose to practise physical activity.

However, the Public Health department has since advised that healthy living habits are also linked to social, economic, educational and structural factors. In keeping with this approach, it is inferred that practising physical activity is subject to a complex network of influencing factors that determine whether or not a person, group, or community are more physically active (Sallis et al., 2006).

From this socio-ecological perspective (Dahlgren & Whitehead, 1992), the World Health Organisation (WHO) recognises the importance of the local level when it comes to creating environments that make it easier for people to engage in physical activity and that back the concept of Active Cities. The WHO defines a healthy, active city as one that is continually creating and improving opportunities in the built and social environments and expanding community resources to enable all its citizens to be physically active in day-to-day life. 'It recognises the value of active living, physical activity and sport. It provides opportunities for physical activity and active living for all' (Edwards & Tsouros, 2008).

There is a growing number of Spanish municipalities that are focusing on the model of a physically active city, and the Sports Service is a key area for launching this type of project. In many cases, following the guidelines set by the WHO, they start with a planning process that expands the traditional strategic plan for local sport, and is renamed a plan for physical activity and sport. In this way, the new position of the municipality and local administration in this regard is acknowledged.

The application of this new approach, which is broader with regard to the Municipal Sports Services' object of action, entails a change in their usual role. The administration becomes a facilitator, a dynamising agent in the community, focusing on all its citizens and working in a more comprehensive and holistic manner, endeavouring to act from different areas to generate multi-component strategies. Its actions go beyond managing the facilities from previous decades, and they now work mainly on the physical environment of cities and municipalities.

Strengthening sports policy

The idea of 'separating sports and politics', the origins of which are tied to the use of sport as propaganda for state socio-economic models, has also reached the local level. The poor use of sport in many municipalities, using it as a tool for almost clientelistic and populist promotion, the establishment of facilities that could not be justified from a technical point of view, the awarding of inexcusable subsidies or the funding of sports events and professional sports that are more akin to the Roman 'bread and circuses' than to the management of a common good, have generated a great deal of scepticism regarding the relationship between local sport and politics.

Nevertheless, the fact that sport has been used for propaganda purposes on many occasions should not be cause to repudiate sports policy. An ideological use for the purposes of propaganda should not be confused with Policy as an activity aimed at solving the problems that come with collective living, leaving sport without ideology and without the capacity to position itself before society in one way or another.

In other cases there is a biased vision that claims that by backing the idea of 'separating sport and politics', what they are actually supporting is the absence of a political discourse for sport, its organisation and management according to technocratic and market-based criteria. Technocracy without political ideology to guide it ends up being guided by the market. Municipal sport, as with other areas in which public administrations allocate resources, requires a political position for decision-making. The resources that are allocated to one or another use are limited, which requires political decisions to be made to establish which uses are a priority and which are less so. Public actions are mutually exclusive, with some that win and others that lose (or win less, so to speak). These decisions require political decision-making that establishes the general lines for sport in the municipality.

Despite this use of sport for political purposes, the political discourse of sport has always been secondary within the general political discourse (Iberm, 2002). Although there was a sports policy from the late 70s up until the early 90s that clearly backed the provision of sports for all, with the objective that such an offer would generate demand, since the 90s these sports policies have faded; it appears that they have not found a clear objective to orient themselves. The adoption of the New Public Management model has oriented the management of municipal sport, applying principles of economy, efficiency and efficacy both in the political instruments and in programmes (Leeuw, 1996), often ignoring the need for a policy that sets the tone for that management.

Sport, as a cultural, educational and social area, and with the vast array of tools available, is recovering its ideological position. The criteria for supporting associations and clubs, investment in facilities, the location of those facilities, the quality of public services, their prices, the objectives and contents of school-age sports programmes ... in all these issues and in many more, the political stance is increasingly more present.

Citizens have a right to understand the logic behind the political proposals as regards sport, what they can expect from each party according to their ideology.

> We believe that citizens should have the option to distinguish between a left-wing policy and a right-wing policy, between a conservative approach and a progressive approach. To distinguish between nuances that advocate for expansion, for improving self-management or for backing new social sectors.
> (Solar, 2011)

The consequences of a lack of political discourse around sport are damaging for sport in general, and particularly for the public sports service. Sport's capacity to transform society, to balance it, to bring it together and improve it, is overlooked. Local administrations' action could not merely limit itself to managing according to purely technical criteria that is more focused on economic sustainability than on its social capacities. It was oriented towards clients (real or potential) of sports services and it moved away from the interests of citizens, from their opinions and their capacities. 'Could apoliticality be in any way related to the defence of the privileges and comforts of national or socially dominant groups?' (Meynaud, 1972). Sport has regained that political conscience.

Citizen orientation and new challenges for the sports policy agenda

Accepting the different contributions that sport can offer to quality of life, to social structures and to the economic development of cities, will enable us to understand that all citizens are affected by decisions made in sporting issues, whether or not they practise sport.

The creation of infrastructures brings costs and benefits for everyone in a city. The promotion of local social capital through sport projects may help to create new relationships, boost a sense of community, improve coexistence and encourage the launch of new businesses, apart from the benefits for the people who directly practise sport.

Local sports policy has begun to orient itself more towards the people, and to support the city project in general. Sports planning includes social responsibility; it endeavours to bring some order to coexistence and activities according to the common good; and to respond to any contradictions and inequalities that city development may have generated.

Sport's potential for a region or city's economic and social development is the main attribute of a public sports policy. Thinking of sport in integral and cross-cutting terms and aimed at all citizens, positions local sports policy to face new objectives. We are breaking away from the former municipal sports policies, which were almost exclusively focused on managing the facilities and services, in the awarding of subsidies and in the organisation or 'purchase' of events without clear selection criteria.

Taking into consideration all the possible contributions sport can make, and with the target being all citizens, the array of challenges that are now forming part of the sports policy agenda is being considerably broadened.

The social responsibility of sport in the city and territory

Any city project must include social responsibility, attempt to bring some order to coexistence and activities according to the common good, and respond to any contradictions and inequalities that city development may have generated.

The inclusion of social criteria in municipal sports management is nothing new with regard to how responsible city management aimed at the general benefit of all citizens should be. The new local sports model is presented as a social policy, taken as a discipline that contributes to increasing or decreasing the well-being of individuals or groups (Adelantado, 2000). Furthermore, sport is habitually considered as an ideal tool for social cohesion.

Social cohesion is linked to the socio-cultural integration processes of those people who suffer exclusion, and to the use of the principle of equity, which will orient the redistributive socio-economic public policies (Borja, 2013).

There are many forms of social exclusion, which do not just come down to economic aspects, with socio-demographic and cultural issues also at play.

On one hand, a person's economic level tends to be inversely proportional to the practise of physical activity in their free time. This fact can be explained as people with low incomes tend to have longer working days, less free time and fewer options to access facilities or other places that promote a healthy lifestyle, such as safe streets, parks, walkways and communal gardens (Mcneill et al., 2006).

Changes in family models and structures have diversified and the number of single-parent families has increased. These situations, combined with a rise in the number of women who have elderly people dependant on them, entail a risk of exclusion. This risk, combined with the fact that women take on most of the housework, leads to lower levels of physical activity and makes the equality between men and women a key aspect when it comes to considering a civic model of sport.

Elderly people, particularly those who live alone, and people with functional diversity, are also among the groups at risk of exclusion. The Council of Europe promotes a social cohesion approach based on equal rights. One such basic right is access to optimum health: physical activity is an essential element for health. Although governments play a key role, all sectors of society are responsible for maintaining society's capacity for ensuring social cohesion and the well-being of all (Council of Europe, 2004).

On another point, the increase in migration and the growth of populations with wide-ranging ethnic and cultural origins, pose a major challenge for the new sports model and their integration is of the utmost importance for social cohesion. The latent opportunity is that physical activity and sport have a special impact on the training and development of social capital through the relations and agreements that arise among them and which strengthen the relationship between the children of foreign immigrants and the locals (Maza, 2004).

It is not reasonable to expect the municipal department of sports to try to directly reduce the factors that lead to social exclusion, an objective that vastly exceeds its capacity of action. However, sports institutions are working to make it easier for everyone to be able to practise sport, and to make it a vehicle for equality.

Accepting the assumption that not all people have the same possibilities to practise sport and to live an active life, whether for economic reasons, or due to gender, age, race or religion, some degree of positive discrimination is necessary to favour those demographic groups, aiming for equality of outcome, i.e. oriented towards reaching sufficient levels in all groups.

This positive discrimination is materialising in the pricing policies for sports services, in the organisation of specific activities for different groups, or in mapping resources and facilities for practising physical activity and in the accessibility to those resources and facilities. In all cases, the aim is to make it easier for people with fewer possibilities to access sports services and facilities.

Mainstreaming and networks

Along with the new objectives, different actors come into play with new needs, resources and capacity for action. This expansion of the framework within which the new local sports policy will develop requires a different management model that is adapted to a complex reality. Organisations and agents that are usually not involved in sports promotion now include sports activities among their actions as they see their potential for achieving their particular goals. Institutions at different administrative levels find themselves working on the same population group and each one has a different objective. For their part, people have become a powerful force as both consumer and producer of sports activities, developing into authentic sports prosumers (Solar, 2011).

This pluralistic approach aims to reflect the diversity of actors and the need for governments to achieve consensus and find points of agreement so that their policies can be accepted. Moreover, administrations attempt to boost the necessary resources to prepare and implement those policies, and many of them are in the hands of other actors.

We find ourselves in a situation in which the municipal policy agenda is much more complex than it was years ago. The local administration must face a complicated interplay of economic, social, cultural, environmental, and town planning issues that affect the quality of life of their citizens, and for whom the local administration is the first institutional door on which they will knock to express their needs and concerns. Furthermore, the administrations, somewhat unsurprisingly, have modified their ways of working, whether of their own accord or due to internal and external pressure, and moved towards models that are more open and collaborative with other administrations, social agents and citizens, to what is known as the local governance model.

The dilemma is an important one: there is a series of global pressures and problems, political trends based on a neoliberal narrative that favours the privatisation of public services (Brenner & Theodore, 2002), and globalised trends that are constantly changing. However, these trends generate local and personal problems that are both real and close to home, and a series of specific demands that local governments are asked to meet.

As the complexity has increased and the available resources have decreased, the shortcomings of the previous model of local sports policy have been laid bare. In this model, the municipalities have acquired a series of responsibilities that had not been taken into consideration and for which they do not have sufficient funding. Until the crisis began, they had managed to maintain this system thanks to revenue from the economic-town planning model; however, once this model had run its course, they have found themselves with a highly challenging reality and with few resources available to deal with it. There is clearly a mismatch between the needs and the resources available.

Strictly institutional policy does not stretch enough to cover all these needs, so a new model is necessary that is based on collaboration, both with other institutions and with private companies, social agents and citizens, to strive to achieve the objectives that may be set in the area of sports policy and promotion of physical activity.

In this sense, it is inexcusable to leave the developmental paradigm of past decades in which many local entities are still operating, and for which the basic orientation continues to be construction and/or expansion of facilities and the production of services. It is necessary to understand that a new local sports policy based on governance must rest on relational management: with other municipal areas, as the citizens' needs and problems are complex and intertwined; with other spheres of territorial, autonomous or state government; with private businesses; with social agents; and with citizens, with whom new channels of participation will need to be opened, beyond the minimum considered by current legislation.

Under this governance model, the Municipal Sports Service thus goes from having a role as resource provider or manager to having a relational role as facilitator and dynamising agent for local support, basing itself on:

- Mainstreaming. The citizens' problems are complex, and the reasons why they practise sport or not, why sport at school does or does not work, or why sports events have positive or deficient effects, depend on numerous factors and affect different areas. To this effect, sports administrations work to promote relationships between departments that, on many occasions, work according

to sectoral logic. This is why it is essential to construct a coherent, flexible and open network organisation that promotes continuous interaction and trust-based relationships between the different areas.
- Multi-level. With collaboration between the different levels of government and in which every participant contributes their different resources and capacities in pursuit of the common objectives. The majority of sports policies are influenced by the fact that there are different levels of government working from rationale according to their own individual powers, without associating with the rest. This new model of sports governance is aimed at generating collaboration relationships between them, in pursuit of shared objectives and common projects.
- Participation. Understood in a deep-rooted sense, not just as a consulting process but as a transfer of decision-making power and empowerment in matters that affect their own well-being. This change entails modifying how administrations operate, their ways of working and even their professional profiles, which will be aimed more at managing relations than resources.

Conclusions

The network of sport facilities and spaces in Spain is extensive and varied. However, this network is not balanced and presents both deficiencies and excesses. The peculiarity of Spanish sport development, together with political and economic dynamics that are very prone to construction, have facilitated this growth of the network.

However, in recent years, many public administrations are changing their sport policy model, which is driving a rebalancing of this network of sport spaces. Placing the citizen at the centre of sport policy has led to a change in the activities and spaces to be promoted and managed. The focus is beginning to be placed on inactive people and population groups that were not previously the target of sports policies.

As a result, we find in Spain the coexistence of two models: the developmentalist model followed for decades, which continues to grow a network without much planning; and the reformist model, which is trying to reorient itself, incorporating a different way of making sports policy and adapting its management to the needs of citizens and the environments where they carry out physical activity.

References

Adelantado, J. (2000). *Cambios en el Estado del Bienestar*. Icaria. 28.
Aldrey, J. A., y Rodríguez, R. (2010). Instrumentos de ordenación del territorio en España. En R. Rodríguez (Ed.), *Territorio. Ordenar para competir*. Netbiblio, A Coruña.
Bellod Redondo, J. F. (2015). Plan E: la estrategia keynesiana frente a la crisis en España. *Revista de Economía Crítica, Asociación de Economía Crítica*, 20, 4–22.
Benito, B., Solana, J., & Moreno, M. R. (2012). Assessing the efficiency of local entities in the provision of public sports facilities. *International Journal of Sport Finance*, 7(1), 46–72.

Borja, J. (2013). *Revolución urbana y derechos ciudadanos*. Alianza Editorial.
Brenner, N., & Theodore, N. (2002). *Spaces of neoliberalism. Urban restructuring in North America and Western Europe*. Blackwell Publishers.
Consejo Superior de Deportes. (2015). *Encuesta de hábitos deportivos 2015*. Consejo Superior de Deportes.
Council of Europe. (2004). *Revised strategy for social cohesion*. Strasbourg.
Dahlgren, G., & Whitehead, M. (1992). *Policies and strategies to promote social equity in health*. WHO Regional Office for Europe (document number: EUR/ICP/RPD 414(2).
Edwards, P., & Tsouros, A. (2008). *A healthy city is an active city*. World Health Organization.
Gallardo, L., & Jiménez, A. (2004). *La gestión de los servicios municipales deportivos*. Inde.
Iberm, M. (2002). *La transformación del deporte en una mercancía, consecuencias*, en Libro de Actas del 2º Congreso de gestión deportiva de Cataluña: nuevos retos frente a la transformación del deporte. Editorial Inde.
Leeuw, F. L. (1996). Performance auditing, new public management and performance improvement: Question and answers. *Accounting, Auditing & Accountability Journal, 9*(2), 92–102.
Martínez Aguado, D. (2012). *Nueva gestión deportiva municipal con la educación como perspectiva*. Editorial Círculo rojo.
Maza, G. (2004). Capital social del deporte. In T. Lleixà & S. Soler (Eds.), *Actividad física y deporte en sociedades multiculturales: ¿Integración o Segregación?* (pp. 43–56). Horsori.
Mcneill, L., Kreuter, M., & Subramanian, S. (2006). Social environment and physical activity: A review of concepts and evidence. *Social Science and Medicine, 63*, 1011–1022.
Meynaud, J. (1972). *El deporte y la política*. Editorial Hispano Europea.
Ministerio de Sanidad, Servicios Sociales e Igualdad. (2014). *Encuesta Nacional de Salud. España 2011/12. Actividad física, descanso y ocio*. Serie Informes monográficos nº 4. Ministerio de Sanidad, Servicios Sociales e Igualdad.
Navarro Vera, J. R., & Ortuño Padilla, A. (2010). Impacto de los campos de golf en Levante. *Ciudad y Territorio. Estudios Territoriales, 163*, 35–48.
Rodríguez-Fernández, E., Pazos, J. M., & Palacio, J. (2016). La promoción de juegos y deportes populares y tradicionales: de los centros educativos al servicio municipal de deportes. El caso de Boiro. *Revista Española de Educación Física y Deportes, 412*, 79–92.
Sallis, J., Cervero, R., Ascher, W., Henderson, K., Kraft, M., & Kerr, J. (2006). An ecological approach to creating active living communities. *Annual Review of Public Health, 27*, 297–322.
Solar, L. (2011). *El deporte como servicio local ante la 'era wiki'*. Libro de actas del I Congreso FAGDE.
Sport England. (1999). *Best value through sport: The value of sport to local authorities*. Sport England.
Viñas, J. (2011). *Els Ajuntaments i l'esport a Catalunya*. Diputación de Barcelona. Retrieved April 6, 2021, from www.observatoridelesport.cat/docus/estudis_publicats/OCE_7_estudis_publicats_ca.pdf

Chapter 8

Sports gambling in Spain

Plácido Rodríguez and Levi Pérez

Introduction

Sports gambling events have become popular leisure activities among consumers that also raise some social concerns. One of these concerns is the regressivity of gambling taxation, meaning that gambling revenues are disproportionately levied from low-income people (Gandullia & Leporatti, 2018; Pérez & Humphreys, 2011). Other concerns include moral considerations (Basham & White, 2002) and gambling-related harms beyond the loss of money (e.g., addiction, crime, work performance, social life issues) (Delfabbro & King, 2019). All these issues cause governments to hold divergent positions on sports betting (Humphreys & Perez, 2012). As Pérez (2017) discussed, sports gambling availability worldwide is determined by cultural background and regulation differences that lead to diverse market structures and legislation. Notwithstanding, a global expansion of sports gambling opportunities is observed partly because recent technological advancements and regulatory changes ease access to this type of gambling. The forms of sports gambling differ in terms of access, growth potential, and regulations.

In Spain, legal sports gambling was largely and for a long time limited to people gambling on the outcome of professional football matches through football pools, accounting for approximately one-half of the sales of the football pools market in Europe (Forrest & Pérez, 2013). Since its introduction in the 1946/47 season, football pools in Spain have long occupied an important place in the Spanish gambling market. The exceptional importance of this gambling industry in Spain lies in the scope of its economic and social benefits (Forrest & Pérez, 2013).

In 2008, just over half a century later, several bookmakers were awarded the first licences to operate sports betting in Basque Country and Madrid. Following this practice, other Spanish regions have also allowed bookmakers to operate, thereby setting up a completely new sports gambling market.

Recently, the 2011 Spanish gambling law (Law 13/2011, of 27 May) came into force, which addressed online gambling for the first time. Until then, online gambling was not strictly forbidden, but it lacked a specific regulation that would provide legal certainty to both operators and consumers. Consequently, the Spanish government began moving towards regulating and legalising sports betting in all

DOI: 10.4324/9781003197003-8

its forms (football pools, fixed-odds sports betting, sports betting exchanges, etc.) and internet gambling. Other legal forms of sports gambling in Spain include horse and dog racetrack betting and gambling on the Basque ball-game jai-alai.

Currently, the Spanish sports gambling industry consists of privately owned operators offering fixed-odds betting products (even on the Internet). The SELAE (*Sociedad Estatal Loterías y Apuestas del Estado*), assigned to the Ministry of Finance and Civil Service, was created through Law 13/2010, of 3 December. It reorganised the activity of the public entity *Loterías y Apuestas del Estado* and is a state-owned entity in charge of providing pari-mutuel sports betting. The Directorate-General supervises the Regulation of Gambling (DGOJ) market, and operators are subject to an authorisation process. It is illegal for Spanish citizens to bet with operators who do not hold a Spanish licence.

According to the 2020 Annual Gaming Report (Gómez & Lalanda, 2020), the size of the offline market was estimated at more than €2,200 million in sales revenue in 2019 (approximately 6% of the whole land-based gambling industry in Spain). This amounts to a significant increase of 65% over the 2015 figures. Fixed-odds sports betting accounts for more than 90% of offline sports gambling activity, while pari-mutuel betting has suffered a huge reduction in recent years, with its market share reduced to just 9.3% (Figure 8.1).

For the online channel, in 2019, sports gambling through state-regulated websites accounted for €748.2 million, while betting through regional government-regulated websites accounted for €30.5 million, essentially limited to sports betting. Figure 8.2 outlines the main figures of state-regulated online sports betting between 2015 and 2019, distinguishing between Gross Gaming Revenue (GGR)—also called game yield. GGR is a key metric used in gambling; it reflects

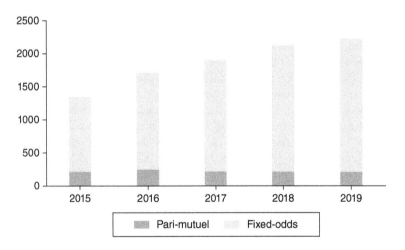

Figure 8.1 Offline sports betting in Spain (2015–2019) (million euros)
Source: Based on data from Gómez and Lalanda (2020)

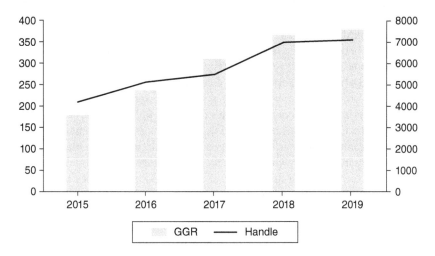

Figure 8.2 On-line state-regulated sports betting in Spain (2015–2019) (million euros)

Source: Based on data from Gómez and Lalanda (2020)

the difference between the amount of money waged and the pay out in prizes and handles the amount of money in wagers accepted over a specific period of time.

It is estimated that the whole gambling industry in Spain accounts for approximately 0.9% of GDP, which shows its relative importance within the Spanish economy.

Pari-mutuel sports betting

The football pools

The football pools are a form of pari-mutuel betting based on predicting the outcomes of football (soccer) matches. It specifically refers to long-odds, high-prize gambling games where players are required to match their guesses or forecasts with the results of a long list of fixtures to claim for a share of the jackpot prize (Forrest & Pérez, 2013).

Several papers (García & Rodríguez, 2007; García et al., 2008, 2011; Forrest & Pérez, 2011) have analysed *La Quiniela* (the commercial name for the football pools in Spain) sales using the same framework as followed in the lotto demand literature; this framework has been typical since the model developed by David Gulley and Frank Scott (1993). It should be emphasised that football pools are not a lottery because the winning combination is not the outcome of a draw but is instead related to the final results of several football matches. *La Quiniela* sales are influenced—in addition to the conventional economic determinants—by game characteristics, such as the overall expected value, the prize structure, and the composition of the list of games in the coupon (García & Rodríguez, 2007). Thus, football pool bettors use the information on the performance of football teams to make their forecasts. In this sense, sports gambling could be considered a complementary good with many sports (García et al., 2008). It is common to play football pools as part of a syndicate, where large groups of bettors (*peñas*) combine funds and knowledge to bet on football matches (Humphreys & Perez, 2012).

In Spain, *La Quiniela* was introduced in the 1940 s as a government-operated pari-mutuel game (*La Quiniela* is managed by SELAE, which also manages most of the lotteries in Spain) in which prizes are a percentage of the total revenue and players have to predict the final results of a list of football matches from among three alternatives. The alternatives include home win (1), draw (X), and away win (2). The first coupon asked players to forecast results for just 7 matches, but the list was later increased to 14 (Pujol, 2009). The format remained at 14 matches until the 1987/88 season, but a 15th match was added in 1988/89 (it reverted to 14 in 2003/04 but only for two seasons).

For the game design, changes in rules have included roll-over of the top prize to the next game edition (since the 1988/89 season, the addition of a new lower-prize tier for those correctly guessing 11 (1991/92) or 10 (2003/04) matches, and frequent increase of the entry—from 2 *pesetas* at the beginning to €0.50 from 2003/04 (it should be noted that there is a two-column minimum entry fee of €1 for a single bet).

As discussed in García et al. (2008), the exceptional importance of the football pools industry in Spain lies in the scope of its economic and social benefits. Spanish charities were the first beneficiaries of the funds obtained from sports gambling through *La Quiniela*, which later also reached sports organisations.

Additionally, special events such as the 1982 Football World Cup or the 1992 Barcelona Olympic Games benefited from the pools, as did the ADO programme (the Spanish Olympic Sports Association). At the end of the 1990s, the Spanish Royal Decree of 20 February 1998 established the current distribution of *La Quiniela* revenues. The National Professional Football League (LFP) receives 10% (in 2005, it amounted to approximately 50 million euros), the High Council of Sports (CSD) keeps 1%, and 10.98% goes to provincial councils to promote social activities and sports facilities. The Public Exchequer accounts for 23% of total revenues once the administration and distribution expenses have been discounted. Therefore, the share of revenues not distributed as prizes could be interpreted as an implicit tax on Spanish football pools' players.

Figure 8.3 shows football pools sales revenue in Spain on a game-by-game basis from 1977 to 2019. Although *La Quiniela* has recently experienced a significant decline in sales, it can still be considered a popular gambling activity among Spaniards. For several years, *La Quiniela*, together with the National Lottery and the National Organization of Spanish blind people (ONCE) lottery (a daily draw), were the only legal betting games available in Spain. However, the introduction of

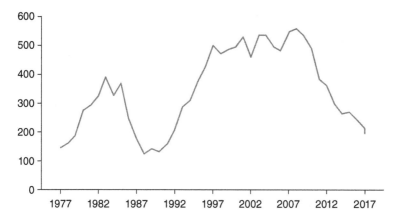

Figure 8.3 Football pools sales in Spain (1977–2019) (million euros)

lotto games to the Spanish gambling market in 1985 led to substantial cannibalisation of the pools. Still, as Forrest and Pérez (2011) analysed, there is no evidence that the products were substitutes.

Humphreys and Pérez (2010) found that 49.7% of Spanish over 18 years reported having played *La Quiniela* at some time in their lives, with 20% of these playing weekly. Therefore, it can be considered a niche product in the Spanish sports gambling market. In fact, it is the largest football pool market in Europe, accounting for approximately one-half of the sales on the entire continent (Forrest & Pérez, 2013). Furthermore, based on information from 2017, from *The WLA Global Lottery Data Compendium*, an annual review of the lottery industry based on data from World Lottery Association (WLA) members, Spain is clearly still the leading football pool market in Europe, with annual sales of €223 million. In any case, the ability of *La Quiniela* to somehow sustain a market suggests that basing a gambling product on football results is an attraction to a segment of the market.

Since 2019, SELAE markets have been a new product linked to football pools. *Elige 8* is a betting product with a price of €0.5 per single bet in which bettors select 8 of the matches included in a particular fixture in the *La Quiniela* coupon. The prizes are established apart from those of *La Quiniela*. In 2019, the sales of the game barely reached €2 million.

Other pari-mutuel betting products

El Quinigol

It should be noted that SELAE also manages Spanish football pools using alternative modes of gambling, including particular rules, structure and operation, i.e., predicting the exact score of some football games instead of just choosing the final result. *El Quinigol* was introduced in 1998 to coincide with the Football World Cup in France. It must be noted that the SELAE just offered this game in 1998 during the Football World Cup and the UEFA Champions League. Later, in 2000, the game was reintroduced to coincide with the UEFA European Football Championship. The game was permanently introduced in 2005 and is now used to bet on matches from the Spanish First Division League.

The name is derived from the fact that betters are required to predict the number of goals that will be scored by the teams involved. Each bet costs €1 and includes six matches, which naturally involve twelve football teams. Players have to mark the section corresponding to the number of goals they believe each team will score among four options (0; 1; 2; M—which means 3 or more goals). There is a jackpot prize that rolls over to the next fixture when there is no winner but other minor prizes. Currently, *El Quinigol* annual sales total approximately €7.7 million.

García et al. (2011) offer a comparison between *El Quinigol* and *La Quiniela* analysing the determinants of demand for football pools in Spain, focusing on the main economic determinants and dealing with the different effects of the main covariates on the demand for football pools according to the considered mode of waging. They conclude that both *La Quiniela* and *El Quinigol* are catching a different profile of gamblers: those who look for a higher jackpot (*La Quiniela*) and those who are attracted to a more difficult game just trying to make their stake profitable (*El Quinigol*).

Basketball pools

Additionally, in the 1971/72 season, there was an attempt to launch a pari-mutuel betting game linked to the results of basketball games. However, given the characteristics of the prize (due to the opposition of football stakeholders, it could not award cash prizes but instead awarded televisions), that product was neither successful nor continued.

Horse racing pools

Since 2005, with the reopening of the *Hipódromo de La Zarzuela* (a horse racetrack located in Madrid), the SELAE has operated horse racing pools for two different gambling products: *Lototurf*, which requires guessing the winning horse but also predicting the winning numbers from a lottery draw, and *Quíntuple Plus*, which involves guessing the winning horses of five races and the runner-up from the fifth race.

In any case, it is a gambling product with barely relevant figures (in 2011, it collected €10 million, and in 2016, it collected only €4 million), even with a 60% drop last year in the *Quíntuple Plus* game (from €2.9 million to €1.1 million). Moreover, the economic balance is clearly negative since the expenses include subsidies to the sport of horse racing in Spain paying €6.5 million per year. This amount is given to *Hipódromo de La Zarzuela*, a company managed by the *Sociedad Estatal de Participaciones Industriales* (SEPI). It is a Spanish state holding company characterised as a Sovereign wealth fund and controlled by the Ministry of the Treasury of Spain to distribute and invest in the equestrian sector.

Online pari-mutuel betting

In terms of GGR, only 0.2% of the total online state-regulated sports gambling market in Spain in 2019 was due to online pari-mutuel betting, or the commercialisation of *La Quiniela, Quinigol,* and *Quintuple Plus* through the Internet.

Fixed-odds sports betting

On 27 May, Law 13/2011 split the sports gambling market into different betting products: pari-mutuel betting products—basically, *La Quiniela*, whose operation was reserved for the SELAE, as discussed—and fixed-odds betting products—that were allowed to be privately operated under the regulation of regional governments (autonomous communities), except in the case of nationwide online gambling, regulated by the DGOJ. To date, only Madrid, Murcia, Navarre, the Basque Country, and La Rioja have opened regional online gambling markets (Gómez & Lalanda, 2020).

Overall, sports betting in Spain overlaps several channels, which differ depending on the region (betting shops, bingos, casinos, etc.) and are regulated either by regional governments or the DGOJ. However, it should be noted that, overall, the popularity of in-play betting (i.e., while the match is in play) has encouraged rapid growth in sports gambling activity, and it now represents a significant and growing proportion of the market (Forrest & Pérez, 2019). In particular, in Spain, data show that 67% of online sports betting volume and 57% of sports betting GGR were generated in-play rather than pre-play (Gómez & Lalanda, 2020).

The emergence of new technological procedures has led to the online channel gaining more prominence in the gambling market. This has also made in-play betting even more relevant and made it the type of betting most used by criminals to fix sporting events (Forrest & Pérez, 2019).

Bookmakers

Although there was no specific regulation for sports betting and online gambling, most principal international operators were actively present. Several bookmakers were awarded the first licences to operate sports betting in both the Basque Country and Madrid at the beginning of 2008. In Spain, the Statutes of Autonomy, a law hierarchically located under the Spanish constitution, grant state powers to the regions on gaming matters. Currently, all Spanish regions have bookmakers (Gómez & Lalanda, 2020).

Table 8.1 Fixed-odds sports betting for Spanish bookmakers 2019 (million euros)

Region	GGR	Region	GGR	Region	GGR
Andalucía	34.075	Castilla-León	9.400	País Vasco	35.281
Aragón	11.416	Cataluña	26.900	La Rioja	4.980
Asturias	3.456	Extremadura	6.650	Valencia	65.539
Baleares	6.100	Galicia	32.085	Ceuta	-
Canarias	19.449	Madrid	66.737	Melilla	0.753
Cantabria	3.287	Murcia	14.403	**TOTAL**	393.956
Castilla-La Mancha	15.087	Navarra	10.605		

Source: Based on data from Gómez and Lalanda (2020).

The absence of official and harmonised statistics as a result of the cession of competencies to regional governments in the area of privately managed gambling create certain gaps in the information on these networks that make it difficult to determine the exact number of outlets,

According to the 2020 Annual Gaming Report (Gómez & Lalanda, 2020), the land-based betting retail network comprises approximately 14,000 outlets and approximately 24,000 betting machines located in casinos, bingo halls, and gambling parlours. In addition, some regions (Galicia, Navarre, the Basque Country, La Rioja, Valencia and Ceuta) allow betting machines to be installed in bars and/or pubs. As a result, bookmakers' GGR reached €394.0 million in 2019, showing a slight increase from €382.5 million in 2018 (it should be noted that growth rates in previous years exceed 10%).

It can be said that the regional offline betting market in Spain has reached maturity. A large part of this market growth was attributed to the opening of the Andalusian market in 2019. Table 8.1 shows the GGR of autonomous communities of Spain, as well as their market share. The highest betting consumption occurs in the northern regions (the Basque Country, Navarre, La Rioja), where there is a large tradition in betting on traditional sports.

Most bettors in Spain are men under 45 years of age, of high, upper-middle, and middle social status, who play regularly. Based on Table 8.1, the annual expenditure per individual gambler is €298/year (i.e., €25/month) (Gómez & Lalanda, 2020).

Online fixed-odds sports betting

Improved technology has boosted the volume of sports betting worldwide and has popularised in-play betting to the detriment of betting before the event (pre-play betting). These betting activities imply both benefits and costs for the sport. In-play betting is strongly complementary to sport consumption and offers new opportunities for revenue generation from the sale of data. At the same time, the high liquidity in sports betting markets and the increased opportunities for profit from match-fixing during the game increase the risk of integrity (Forrest & Pérez, 2019).

In 2011, the Spanish government began moving towards the regulation and legalisation of sports betting in all its forms (football pools, fixed-odds sports betting, sports betting exchanges, etc.), including internet gambling. In accordance, the Spanish online sports betting industry consists, apart from the SELAE, of privately owned operators offering fixed-odds betting (Humphreys & Perez, 2012).

In 2020, the online gambling industry reported a GGR of €851 million and a growth rate of 13.7% from the previous year. Many other key figures (e.g., active players, deposits, marketing and advertisement expenses) were at all-time highs (DGOJ, 2021). However, beyond these figures, it should be noted that online gambling is perceived as a risky leisure activity (Díaz & Pérez, 2021). To try to partially address this social concern, Law 13/2011, of 27 May, requires online gambling operators to take preventive measures to protect children under the legal age and other potentially vulnerable groups of players, as well as to identify, prevent, and treat gambling-related disorders. Gainsbury et al. (2013) showed that online gambling could cause people to develop gambling disorders, especially those who are potentially vulnerable. The main business areas in Internet gambling in Spain are sports betting, poker, and other traditional gambling products such as casino table games and slot machines (Humphreys & Perez, 2012)

At the end of 2019, there were 79 licenced operators for the whole country, with a considerable increase given the new licences granted in the summer of 2019 (Gómez & Lalanda, 2020). Despite this wide offer, the market is concentrated in a few international operators (Bet365, William Hill, Bwin, 888poker, PokerStars, Partypoker, Winamax, etc.), national bookmakers (Codere, Kirolbet, Luckia, Reta, Sportium and Versus), and some bingo companies (e-bingo, Rank). In addition, several operators are developing niche strategies to complement their land base offer, as in the case of casinos in the large metropolitan areas of Barcelona and/or Madrid.

Figure 8.4. Online fixed-odds sports betting regulated by Spanish Autonomous Communities 2019 (million euros) (GGR- the total is 30.489)

According to Gómez and Lalanda (2020), online gambling regulated in Madrid, Murcia, Navarre, the Basque Country, and La Rioja represents 21% of the amounts gambled in these regions. The gambling websites regulated by Madrid, Murcia, Navarre, the Basque Country, and La Rioja accounted for approximately €30.5 million in GGR, with a betting volume (handle) almost ten times higher at €282.3 million. As mentioned in the section on sports betting, they have a significant weight in the Basque County, but they play a complementary role in their face-to-face markets in the other regions (Figure 8.4). In the sports betting market as a whole, it represents 7.5%.

Other minor sports gambling activities

The sports gambling market in Spain also includes other minor gambling activities, such as racetrack betting on horses, gambling on greyhound racing, and wagering in jai-alai games. However, this chapter focuses on racetrack betting on horses

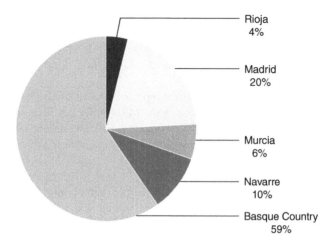

Figure 8.4 Online fixed-odds sports betting 2019

Source: Based on data from Gómez and Lalanda (2020)

Note: Figures correspond to GGR in million euros. The total GGR obtained by online fixed-odds sports betting operators, amounting to 30.489 million euros

because of the absence of data and their small relative economic importance in the overall Spanish gambling market.

Racetrack betting on horses

A portfolio of several different horse-betting products is usually offered to bettors at most international horse contests worldwide. As detailed in Muñiz et al. (2018), racetrack betting on horses is generally based on a pari-mutuel wagering system. Thus, the amount allocated to prizes constitutes a percentage of the volume of betting sales, unlike, for example, the British fixed-odds horse-betting system. Currently, horserace betting is in decline; in fact, it is just a niche product for the occasional entertainment of those attending racetracks.

Except for the trotting race, the European Trotting Union annually publishes data on the *Circuito Balear*, a horse race in the Balearic Islands. However, information on this sports gambling product is limited. Racetrack companies do not usually report betting data promptly. Since 2017, the Spanish Racetracks Association has not updated the corresponding information (Gómez & Lalanda, 2020).

According to the 2020 Annual Gaming Report (Gómez & Lalanda, 2020), approximately €5.3 million was wagered in the horse racing seasons (betting over-round—the total of all the odds on the outcome of a single event; it is what gives bookmakers their profit—almost reached €1 million). Particularly, *Hipódromo de La Zarzuela*

Table 8.2 Betting on horse racing and/or horse betting (million euros)

	2015	2015	2017	2018	2019
Horse racing betting	1.985	4.277	4.757	4.192	4.101
Circuito Balear	3.360	0.606	0.582	0.534	1.189
International horse shows	0.482	0.447	0.140	0.100	0.015
TOTAL betting at the racetrack	5.792	5.023	5.438	4.725	5.290

Source: Based on data from Gómez and Lalanda (2020)

revenues exceeded €4 million in 2018 and 2019 (its best return since 2014), and trotting races betting volume improved substantially, exceeding €1 million (Table 8.2)

Finally, it should be reminded that the SELAE offers some gambling products based on the outcome of horse racing betting (*Lotto Turf* and *Quintuple Plus*), which has been previously discussed in this chapter.

For economic insight into the racetrack betting market worldwide, see Hausch et al. (2008) and Thaler and Ziemba (1988) for a deeper analysis of betting strategies at the track, among other studies. A seminal study of betting market efficiency concerning subjective information can be found in Figlewski (1979).

Concluding remarks

The current chapter has outlined the evolution and current status of the Spanish sports gambling industry. The available information estimates the size of the market at more than €2,200 million euros, accounting for approximately 0.9% of Spanish GDP.

Currently, operating sports gambling activities in Spain requires obtaining permission from the appropriate authorities. It is the Directorate General for the Regulation of Gambling (Ministry of Consumer Affairs) that manages the regulation, licensing, supervision, coordination, control and sanctioning of gambling activities at state level, including online gambling, sports betting and football pools operated by SELAE.

However, since the regulatory and fiscal authority over privately operated gambling in Spain (casinos, bingos, slots, betting bookmaker, etc.) were transferred to the regional governments, sports gambling opportunities at regional level differ significantly and lead to a wide betting retail network including fixed-odds sports betting products and other minor sports gambling activities (e.g., racetrack betting on horses).

References

Basham, P., & White, K. (2002). *Gambling with our future? The costs and benefits of legalized gambling*. Fraser Institute Digital Publications. www.fraserinstitute.org/sites/default/files/GamblingwithOurFuture.pdf

Delfabbro, P., & King, D. L. (2019). Challenges in the conceptualisation and measurement of gambling-related harm. *Journal of Gambling Studies, 35*(3), 743–755.

DGOJ. (2021). *Mercado de juego online estatal 2020*. Retrieved May 21, 2021, from https://n9.cl/2d5rb

Díaz, A., & Pérez, L. (2021). Online gambling-related harm: Findings from the study on the prevalence, behavior and characteristics of gamblers in Spain. *Journal of Gambling Studies, 37*(2), 599–607.

Figlewski, S. (1979). Subjective information and market efficiency in a betting market. *Journal of Political Economy, 87*(1), 75–88.

Forrest, D., & Pérez, L. (2011). *Applied Economics Letters, 18*(13), 1253–1257.

Forrest, D., & Pérez, L. (2013). The football pools. In L. V. Williams & D. S. Siegel (Eds.), *The Oxford handbook of the economics of gambling* (pp. 145–160). Oxford University Press.

Forrest, D., & Pérez, L. (2019). Las apuestas: beneficios y riesgos para el deporte. *Papeles de Economía Española* (159), 131–147.

Gainsbury, S. M., Russell, A., Hing, N., Wood, R., & Blaszczynski, A. (2013). The impact of internet gambling on gambling problems: A comparison of moderate-risk and problem Internet and non-Internet gamblers. *Psychology of Addictive Behaviors, 27*(4), 1092.

Gandullia, L., & Leporatti, L. (2018). The demand for gambling in Italian regions and its distributional consequences. *Papers in Regional Science, 97*(4), 1203–1225.

García, J., Pérez, L., & Rodríguez, P. (2008). Football pools sales: How important is a football club in the top divisions. *International Journal of Sport Finance, 3*(3), 167–176.

García, J., Pérez, L., & Rodríguez, P. (2011). Guessing who wins or predicting the exact score: Does it make any difference in terms of the demand for football pools? In W. Andreff (Ed.), *Contemporary issues in sports economics: Participation and professional team sports* (pp. 114–130). Edward Elgar.

García, J., & Rodríguez, P. (2007). The demand for football pools in Spain: The role of price, prizes, and the composition of the coupon. *Journal of Sports Economics, 8*(4), 335–354.

Gómez, J., & Lalanda, C. (2020). *Anuario del juego en España 2020, Instituto de Política y Gobernanza de la Universidad Carlos III y CEJUEGO: Madrid*. Retrieved May 21, 2021, from https://n9.cl/35vbu

Gulley, O. D., & Scott Jr, F. A. (1993). The demand for wagering on state-operated lotto games. *National Tax Journal*, 13–22.

Hausch, D. B., Lo, V. S., & Ziemba, W. T. (2008). *Efficiency of racetrack betting markets* (Vol. 2). World Scientific.

Humphreys, B. R., & Pérez, L. (2010). *A microeconometric analysis of participation innsports betting markets*. Economic Discussion Paper 02/2010. Department of Economics, University of Oviedo.

Humphreys, B. R., & Perez, L. (2012). Who bets on sports? Characteristics of sports bettors and the consequences of expanding sports betting opportunities. *Estudios de Economía Aplicada, 30*(2), 579.

Law 13/2010, of 3 December—Royal Decree Law 13/2010, 3 December, approving tax and labour measures and measures to foster investment ('RDL 13/2010'). www.boe.es/buscar/act.php?id=BOE-A-2010-18651

Law 13/2011, of 27 May, on the regulation of gambling. www.ordenacionjuego.es/cmis/browser?id=workspace://SpacesStore/292cbe26-081b-44c2-8632-f5e42850ae58

Muñiz, C., Pérez, L., & Rodríguez, P. (2018). Correlation analysis of a horse-betting portfolio: The international official horse show (CSIO) of Gijón. *Journal of Physical Education and Sport, 18*, 1285–1289.

Pérez, L. (2017). Outside of the United States: The worldwide availability of sports betting. In *Dual markets* (pp. 343–352). Springer.

Pérez, L., & Humphreys, B. R. (2011). The income elasticity of lottery: New evidence from micro data. *Public Finance Review, 39*(4), 551–570.

Pujol, F. (2009). *Football betting as a cyclical learning process*. Faculty Working Paper 05/09, Department of Economics, University of Navarra.

Spanish Royal Decree of 20 February 1998 — Royal Decree 258/1998, of 20 February www.csd.gob.es/en/csd/commissions-collegiate-bodies-sporting-bodies-and-rr-ii/loteries-commission-deportivo-beneficas

Thaler, R. H., & Ziemba, W. T. (1988). Anomalies: Parimutuel betting markets: Racetracks and lotteries. *Journal of Economic Perspectives, 2*(2), 161–174.

Chapter 9

The Iberian fitness industry
Experiences from Portugal and Spain

Pablo Gálvez-Ruiz, Jerónimo García-Fernández, Celina Gonçalves, and Virginia Alcaraz-Rodríguez

Introduction

The growth of the fitness industry has been very high in recent years and it has established itself as a highly competitive market within the sports services sector. According to IHRSA (2019) this evolution translates into more than 210,000 fitness centres around the world, serving more than 184 million members. Thus, the offer of sports services is increasing at the same time as the number of people who demand services related to physical activity (León-Quismondo et al., 2020). This is giving rise to a very different typology of users due to the expansion of the offer and the variety in the typology of centres (Molina et al., 2019), but also with very changing interests and needs (De la Cámara et al., 2020).

Precisely, this increase in the number of centres and users requires better management practices, since current business models have different characteristics that affect facilities, equipment, the offer of services and activities, technology, worker profiles, etc., a situation that has been very parallel in the Iberian market as shown by studies carried out in Spain (De la Cámara et al., 2020) and Portugal (Serrano & Alves, 2019).

For its part, the European Health & Fitness Market Report 2020 (EuropeActive & Deloitte, 2020) is the last report published before the crisis produced by COVID-19. Figures from the European fitness market showed a growth of 2.3% in the number of clubs, 3.8% in the number of subscribers, reaching 64.8 million, 3.0% in revenue, and a market penetration that already exceeds 8.0%. However, the Spanish and Portuguese situations are different, and while Spain is in fourth place in terms of turnover, Portugal is not part of the top-10 worldwide. The main current lines of both markets are set out in the next section in order to analyse theirurrentt situation and future prospects.

Development and consolidation of the fitness industry in the Iberian Peninsula

Fitness industry in Portugal

The concept of fitness has varied over time. Different concepts about bodies and egos have been valued, such as character, attractiveness, happiness, strength,

DOI: 10.4324/9781003197003-9

morals, intelligence, courage, and honesty. The change in ways of thinking about the body reflects changes in social conditions. Thus, fitness is an element in constant change, its definition, criteria, and objectives being associated with social agendas, anxieties, and current problems (Maguire, 2008). Portugal also felt this evolution of fitness. It was in the 1980s that fitness was introduced in Portugal, when the commercialisation of exercise programs came from the USA (Santos & Correia, 2011).

The beginning of fitness in Portugal was used for technical aspects and aimed mainly at the male audience. Due to the massification of the fitness concept, the 1980s in Portugal were marked by the innovation of services and products, by the segmentation of the market, by the beginning of medical evaluation and individual training, and by an increase in the number of clubs. Women were attracted to aerobics practices, which revolutionised fitness, with the introduction of dances and socialisation in practice. In the 90s, there was a great evolution in fitness services, with larger spaces to receive female and male audiences. The number of activities also increased, including spinning, yoga, Pilates, weight training, personalised training, patented group classes, and step leaving its mark in this decade. It was in 1998 that the entry of the first foreign operator, Holmes Place, marked a transition phase in the fitness sector in Portugal, beginning a new period.

A new phase begins in the year 2000 with the implementation of marketing strategies, leveraging resources, maximising training in management and expanding services (Santos & Correia, 2011). The clubs operate in differentiation through the fitness brand, service innovation (personalised training), market segmentation (high class) and quality service. Some events have influenced the growth of this sector at a social and economic level. A positive event was the creation of the Association of Gymnasium Companies in Portugal (AGAP), which boosted and strengthened the market, and the negative event was the economic crisis that took place in the country (Gomes et al., 2017).

In 2005 there were 1,100 clubs for 480,000 members, with an average market penetration rate (4.8%) (IHRSA, 2005), 0.7% below the European average. The increase in knowledge of the benefits of physical activity and well-being justified the need to develop the wellness industry (health & fitness services provided in Fitness Centers and SPAs -fitness market-, preventive medicine, cosmetic and surgery services, health nutrition and natural supplementation products), and fitness organisations that wanted to position themselves as wellness included programs to quit smoking, lose weight, for nutrition, stress management, health risk prevention and health screening (Sacavém & Correia, 2008).

In 2010, there were 1,400 clubs for 600,000 members with a market penetration rate (5.66%) and a revenue of EUR 331,200,000 (IHRSA, 2010). According to the Eurobarometer (2010) this number of members corresponds to a low number (12%) of practitioners of physical activity in Portugal. However, the fall in the Gross Domestic Product (GDP) and the increase in unemployment present even more challenges for the economy in the fitness market in Portugal.

In 2010 Holmes Place was a leader among fitness clubs in Portugal, with 19 facilities. The new club openings of large operators have stagnated. However, new clubs, smaller and focused on specific target audiences, have started which kept the market stable in Portugal, at this stage, and that employed 9,000 employees. An example of this growth was the female segment that became a niche market with more than 150 clubs (IHRSA, 2010).

In the context of this evolution and, in order to guarantee a higher quality in the services provided, articles 7 and 13 of Decree-Law n. 271/2009, of 1 October, required that fitness instructors hold a professional certificate. This measure ensured the training of all those involved in order for them to have the necessary tools and skills to offer a quality service; however, it had a negative impact on the market. Bearing in mind that it was necessary to carry out a verification of the training of all professionals, going through a phase of some constraints, several institutions decided to streamline the process by implementing the Physical Exercise Technician course in order to train professionals who did not have a certificate (Gomes et al., 2017).

During the decade 2010–2020 in Portugal there was a progressive growth of fitness. Social and cultural trends in this market developed and social involvement influenced a different demand for physical activity. Different types of practice were promoted, as well as the acquisition of new products or services (personalised training, fitness magazines, related products), which helped produce the social legitimacy of fitness as a way of personal investment and social value. It was also at this stage that, in Portugal, the Fitness market gradually increased the use of the Web and social networks. This brought new tools to the market to attract and retain customers at a Low cost, due to the increase in communication and relationship skills.

Specifically, in 2013 there were approximately 1,200 Fitness Clubs for 634,446 members, of which 138,110 were new members (AGAP, 2014). In 2017, there were 1,430 clubs with 770,000 members (IHRSA, 2017). In this progressive growth at the end of the decade 2010–2020 there were five types of fitness clubs in operation in the Portuguese market: Gymnasiums/Health Clubs/Fitness & Wellness; Personalized Training Studios; Box/CrossFit; Women's Gyms; and Fitness Boutique. In this phase, it is the Women's Gyms that present a greater decline in the market and the fitness boutiques an evolution of growth. Regarding classification, low-cost clubs have an average monthly fee less than or equal to 29.90€; mid-market clubs have an average monthly fee between 29.90€ and 55.00€; and premium clubs have an average monthly fee above 55.00€ (AGAP, 2019).

In 2018, there were approximately 1,100 fitness clubs, with 21,954 workers. The spaces maintained the trend of other years with more than 1,000 m^2 (54%), while spaces up to 500 m^2 do not exceed 30% of the total (AGAP, 2019). Half of the clubs were concentrated in the big cities of Portugal, Lisbon and Porto, for a total of 593,000 members (53% women to 47% men) across the territory (AGAP, 2019), corresponding to a penetration rate of 5.8 (EuropeActive & Deloitte, 2019) and representing a 10.8% increase in the number of members compared to 2017 (EuropeActive & Deloitte, 2018).

In 2019 there was a slight increase in the number of members (16%: women 57% and men 43%), although there continued to be a high attrition rate (60%). The results of the AGAP Barometer also show that 93% of clubs have average monthly fees in the mid-market and low-cost segment, with 66% of individual clubs belonging to the mid-market segment, and 50% of chains belonging to the low-cost segment. Although in 2019 the average monthly fee has decreased slightly, this observation alone does not contradict the growth trend registered since 2016. However, with the expected economic crisis brought about by COVID-19, 2020 is likely to mark a turning point in the trend of recent years.

Fitness industry in Spain

The Spanish market in the fitness sector is highly consolidated with more than 60 operators managing nearly 4,000 centres in different formats or business models and has one of the highest penetration rates in the industry at the European level. Its growth has become so relevant that sports and fitness centres have become reference points for the promotion of sport among society and adherence to physical activity (Cheung & Woo, 2016). In fact, the operators of the different business models are aware of citizens' concern for health and consider that in a scenario of economic slowdown, this expense would be one of the last to be eliminated (BDO España, 2019).

However, the conception of current fitness centres is very recent. Just over a decade ago, the economic crisis facilitated the development of fitness centres in the Spanish market thanks to the entry of the low-cost model. This is undoubtedly the one with the greatest expansion since approximately 2010, tripling the number of centres in the last decade according to Valcarce-Torrente et al. (2020).

This business model has also been favoured by the increase made in Spain in value added tax (VAT) in 2012 with a rise of 13%, thus forcing the different organisations in the sector to carry out profound changes in their management strategy and their value proposals. It has, at the same time, backed the positioning of the low-cost as this is a business model with very tight cost management, a wide range of services, facilities with high equipment, and low prices, among its main characteristics, in addition to offering monthly services with no minimum stay time.

These novel features were very attractive in a context with significant economic and social changes. On the one hand, the offer of services and equipment made possible new ways of performing physical activity, and, on the other hand, this achieved a significant share of new users who had not used this type of centre before (bouchet et al., 2013), thus reaching a larger proportion of the population. In addition, the low-cost model entered the Spanish market with a differentiation strategy based on reduced prices that did not exceed € 20 per month. This ensured that it was within the economic capacity of a very high proportion of the population and prevented large fitness centres from being able to compete by having higher operating costs associated with them (higher worker structures, very large facilities, higher supply costs as a result of facilities such as swimming pools and spas, etc.).

The expansion of the number of fitness centres gave rise to a very competitive market, even generating a high complexity in locating attractive locations for the construction of new sports facilities with guarantees of success in terms of user volume, a fundamental pillar in this model business to secure the income account. Therefore, organisations tried to gain an advantage over their competitors to achieve a privileged position (Gálvez-Ruiz et al., 2021), with new variables appearing in management strategies such as market positioning through market segmentation, differentiation through specialised facilities and equipment, and diversification in prices. This brought about low-price (€20-€25 per month) fitness centres with a slightly higher monthly fee and that offer more services and higher quality equipment.

This new scenario facilitated the entry and expansion of the boutique model through smaller facilities (600 m^2 maximum), with an offer focused on one or two activities with a high level of specialisation, developed through expert professionals and usually in small groups (no more than ten people with a closer relationship with the client), and with technology as the protagonist (Valcarce-Torrente et al., 2017). The boutique model is booming and still has a great capacity for growth where one can find various options such as personal training studios, Pilates or yoga studios, boutique studios or CrossFit centres (García-Fernández et al., 2020a). Thus, the four sports facilities of this type that existed in Spain in 2010 have increased to 305 in 2017 (Valcarce-Torrente et al., 2017), with a total of 474 only CrossFit boxes in 2019 (Jiménez, 2019), which have been the facilities that have led this model with an activity that arrived in Spain in 2013 and that has been included by numerous sports facilities to reach a greater number and different types of users (Claudino et al., 2018). This situation is not a coincidence, the fitness sector is updated rapidly and continuously, and as a consequence new models of specialised gyms emerge (García-Fernández et al., 2020b).

Specifically, CrossFit is one of the fitness trends in Spain (Veiga et al., 2017). One of its main advantages for rapid expansion is that, as it is a registered trademark, there are great similarities between the facilities that offer this service, so that users who change centres quickly feel identified by understanding the culture and philosophy. As a result of its main characteristics, the monthly price is much higher than that of fitness centres, with fees ranging between €60–120, and they generate a feeling of belonging and loyalty much higher than that of low-cost fitness centres due to users feeling cared for individually (Aronowitz, 2018) and living out experiences with colleagues that produce the sensation of wanting to return (O'Rourke, 2015).

Finally, the fitness service built by the Spanish local administrations several decades ago has also undergone an important evolution. There is currently a high presence of organisations that manage sports facilities which offer fitness services under the formula of public-private partnership (PPP), defined by EuropeActive and Deloitte (2019) as concession operators. This allows maintaining ownership of the property by public administration while private organisations manage a sports facility and provide the service of public ownership (García-Fernández et al., 2020c). In particular, Spain is one of the European countries that has used this management formula the most and currently the four main operators have approximately 680,000 clients.

The development of this business model in recent years has made it possible to modernise sports facilities and equipment, as well as to adapt sports services to current fitness trends, offering very tight monthly prices ranging between €35 and €75 per month, allowing different subscription options, unlike previous fitness models. Thus, these are fitness centres with a focus on healthy fitness, with a range of activities and fitness equipment comparable to low-cost centres, but where there is more personalised attention and greater sports services are possible by having spaces available, sports such as those which use a swimming pool, paddle, tennis, or soccer, among others, in addition to promoting family sports.

Research as an axis for developing knowledge of the fitness sector in the Iberian Peninsula

One of the possible factors that have contributed to the fitness sector improving its professionalisation is the leadership and production of the research carried out in Portugal and Spain. In fact, different researchers from both countries have published numerous articles that have helped to understand the behaviour of these sports organisations and what are the variables that can influence the loyalty or economic performance of fitness centres (De Carvalho et al., 2013; León-Quismondo et al., 2020; Vieira & Ferreira, 2020). Although the publication topics have been different, the publications made and that respond to the problems of fitness centre managers are mostly categorised into consumer and employee perceptions, and matters. Also, they have helped to understand where the sector is heading, for example the publications made in Spain since 2017 (Veiga et al., 2017) to identify fitness trends and that so far have been met (Veiga et al., 2021).

Similarly, Portuguese and Spanish researchers have shown their interest in the publication of studies that validate questionnaires and that therefore can be used by professionals and managers in the sector, in order to collect valid and reliable information according to the variable analysed. Thus, García-Fernández et al. (2012) and Gálvez-Ruiz et al. (2015) provided to los for evaluating the quality perceived by consumers in fitness centres. Also, Rodrigues et al. (2019) and Ramos et al. (2020) identified different dimensions for a better understanding of employee satisfaction in the fitness sector. In this context, both the perceived quality and the employee satisfaction have been variables with a great repercussion in the academy and that have contributed knowledge of interest to the managers of fitness centres (Vieira & Ferreira, 2018; Grimaldi-Puyana et al., 2018; Ramos et al., 2021).

On the other hand, one of the issues that has produced the greatest concern for sports managers is consumer satisfaction and loyalty, and therefore knowledge of consumer behaviour in fitness centres. Specifically, Pedragosa and Correia (2009) influenced consumer expectations and satisfaction in Portuguese fitness centres, offering results of interest to the sector. Similarly, Pedragosa et al. (2015) also concluded that emotions in consumer satisfaction were important. For their part, Clavel et al. (2016) conducted a study in Spain which revealed a model to identify customer retention variables, which was completed with the publication prediction of customer abandonment (Clavel et al., 2019). Similarly, in Portugal, Gonçalves et al. (2016) analysed the weekly frequency and other variables to identify their relationship with loyalty, with segmentation being a technique of interest to the sector (García-Fernández et al., 2017; Rodrigues et al., 2017). Thus, this variable was analysed by García-Fernández, Gálvez-Ruiz et al. (2018) García-Fernández, Gálvez-Ruiz, Pitts et al. (2018) García-Fernández, Gálvez-Ruiz, Vélez-Colón et al. (2018), García-Fernández, Martelo-Landroguez et al. (2018), showing important findings in relation to the business model, the type of consumer, the tangible aspects, and the organisational culture. Their conclusions were of interest when finding a relationship between the loyalty and the attrition of the clients. In line with this, Rodríguez-Cañamero et al. (2018) identified the reasons why they clients withdrew from the sports service, where the consumer profile had a great explanatory capacity (García-Fernández et al., 2020a).

On the other hand, and taking into account the appearance of online sports services, Baena-Arroyo et al. (2020) concluded that the service experience and service convenience would have a positive effect on consumer loyalty, not only in face-to-face sports services as indicated by Cepeda-Carrión and Cepeda-Carrión (2018), but also in online fitness services. Thus, the new situation in the sector, derived from the global COVID-19 pandemic, not only creates a research challenge in terms of online fitness services or fitness apps, but also the leadership style of the people who run the fitness centres (Rosa-Díaz et al., 2021).

Sustainability and future perspectives

It is evident that in both countries there has been a high and continuous growth in recent years, and, in the same way, they face problems of similar characteristics. The first aspect is the VAT rate (23% in Portugal and 21% in Spain), which has not allowed the fitness market to develop along with international trends, and for this reason, there are numerous requests for reduction (to 6% in Portugal and to 10% in Spain) to enable greater accessibility and a greater adherence of the public. In this way, the different operators in the Portuguese and Spanish markets consider that such a high tax represents an obstacle to promoting a healthy lifestyle, as well as a problem for the entire population to access fitness services.

Although 2020 has been a challenge for the sector, it is expected that there will be new and better opportunities in the future, which will allow both a recovery and a new positioning. However, the sustainability of the market will depend on how demand behaves after overcoming the pandemic situation, but also on the evolution of the trends that emerged throughout this crisis period. Without a doubt, consumer behaviour is once again at the centre of the entire management strategy.

A third axis is found in the strong impact of the development of new technologies in the sector, and it is currently impossible to know what will happen in the future in the medium term. The strengthening and continuity of online training and mobile exercise apps are important business decisions for future growth and development. Emerging technologies not only pose challenges to the way fitness clubs are run, but also create opportunities to become more competitive, improving the service experience for consumers. Thus, the backing and growth of Wearable Fitness Technology (e.g., fitness trackers, smart watches, HR monitors, and GPS tracking devices) seems to be emerging in the fitness market in Portugal. However, we believe that high-intensity interval training, group training, training with free weights, PT's, and the health & wellness concept will maintain the evolution and stability of the market after the pandemic situation.

Finally, and related to the previous point, boutique centres and training centres will continue to be the growing type of fitness centres, favoured by technological development and by new trends in training in small groups. Low-cost centres will recover more slowly as a consequence of the trend towards relative overcrowding (necessary for the survival of the model), while public-private collaboration will continue to grow thanks to the high indebtedness of local administrations and the limited capacity of management in the face of the high specialisation of the operators in the sector.

References

AGAP. (2014). *Associação de empresas de ginásios e academias de Portugal: barómetro 2013*. Edições AGAP.
AGAP. (2019). *Associação de empresas de ginásios e academias de Portugal: barómetro 2018*. Edições AGAP.
Aronowitz, J. G. (2018). *Optimize your fitness, optimize your business: The balanced scorecard, analysis and application for the CrossFit affiliate*. McKenna College.
Baena-Arroyo, M. J., García-Fernández, J., Gálvez-Ruiz, P., & Grimaldi-Puyana, M. (2020). Analyzing consumer loyalty through service experience and service convenience: Differences between instructor fitness classes and virtual fitness classes. *Sustainability, 12*(3), 828.
BDO España. (2019). *El mercado del fitness en España en 2020: hacia un nuevo mapa*. www.bdo.es/es-es/publicaciones/publicaciones-tecnicas/nuestros-informes/el-mercado-de-fitness-en-espana
Bouchet, P., Hillairet, D., & Bodet, G. (2013). *Sport brands*. Routledge.
Cepeda-Carrión, I., & Cepeda-Carrión, G. (2018). How public sport centers can improve the sport consumer experience. *International Journal of Sports Marketing and Sponsorship, 19*(3), 350–367.
Cheung, R., & Woo, M. (2016). Determinants of perceived service quality: An empirical investigation of fitness and recreational facilities. *Contemporary Management Research, 12*, 363–370.

Claudino, J. G., Gabbett, T. J., Bourgeois, F., de Sá Souza, H., Miranda, R. C., Mezêncio, R., Soncin, R., et al. (2018). CrossFit overview: Systematic review and meta-analysis. *Sports Medicine-Open*, 4(11). doi:10.1186/s40798-018-0124-5

Clavel, I., García-Unanue, J., Iglesias-Soler, E., Felipe, J. L., & Gallardo, L. (2019). Prediction of abandonment in Spanish fitness centres. *European Journal of Sport Science*, 19(2), 217–224.

Clavel, I., Iglesias-Soler, E., Gallardo, L., Rodriguez-Cañamero, S., & García-Unanue, J. (2016). A prediction model of retention in a Spanish fitness centre. *Managing Sport and Leisure*, 21(5), 300–318.

De Carvalho, P. G., Nunes, P. M., & Serrasqueiro, Z. (2013). Growth determinants of small- and medium-sized fitness enterprises: Empirical evidence from Portugal. *European Sport Management Quarterly*, 13(4), 428–449.

De la Cámara, M. A., Valcarce-Torrente, M., & Veiga, O. (2020). National survey of fitness trends in Spain for 2020. *Retos. Nuevas tendencias en Educación Física, Deportes y Recreación*, 37, 427–433.

EuropeActive & Deloitte. (2018). *European health & fitness market report 2018.* https://www2.deloitte.com/content/dam/Deloitte/de/Documents/consumer-business/European%20Health%20and%20Fitness%20Report_2018_extract.pdf

EuropeActive & Deloitte. (2019). *European health & fitness market report 2019.* https://www2.deloitte.com/content/dam/Deloitte/es/Documents/acerca-de-deloitte/Deloitte-ES-TMT-European-Health-Fitness-Market-2019.pdf

EuropeActive & Deloitte. (2020). *European health & fitness market report 2020.* https://www2.deloitte.com/content/dam/Deloitte/de/Documents/consumer-business/European-Health-and-Fitness-Market-2020-Reportauszug.pdf

Gálvez-Ruiz, P., Boleto-Rosado, A. F., & Romero-Galisteo, R. P. (2015). Validación de la versión reducida del CECASDEP en usuarios de servicios deportivos. *Suma Psicológica*, 22(2), 78–85.

Gálvez-Ruiz, P., Conde-Pascual, E., Estrella-Andrade, A., García-Fernández, J., Romero-Galisteo, R. P., Vélez-Colón, L., & Pitts, B. G. (2021). Testing factorial invariance of the questionnaire of evaluation of the quality perceived in sports services in Spanish, Ecuadorian and Colombian users. *Current Psychology*, 40, 1249–1256.

García-Fernández, J., Cepeda-Carrión, G., & Martín-Ruíz, D. (2012). La satisfacción de clientes y su relación con la percepción de calidad en Centro de Fitness: utilización de la escala CALIDFIT. *Revista de Psicología del Deporte*, 21(2), 309–319.

García-Fernández, J., Gálvez-Ruiz, P., Angosto-Sánchez, S., & Grimaldi-Puyana, M. (2020c). Government and commercial alliance in sport. In A. Goslin, D. A. Kukla, R. López de d'Amico, & K. Danylchuk (Eds.), *Managing sport across borders* (pp. 147–166). Routledge.

García-Fernández, J., Gálvez-Ruiz, P., Fernández-Gavira, J., Vélez-Colón, L., Pitts, B., & Bernal-García, A. (2018). The effects of service convenience and perceived quality on perceived value, satisfaction and loyalty in low-cost fitness centers. *Sport Management Review*, 21(3), 250–262.

García-Fernández, J., Gálvez-Ruiz, P., Grimaldi-Puyana, M., Angosto, S., Fernández-Gavira, J., & Bohórquez, M. R. (2020b). The promotion of physical activity from digital services: Influence of e-lifestyles on intention to use fitness apps. *International Journal of Environmental Research and Public Health*, 17, 6839.

García-Fernández, J., Gálvez-Ruiz, P., Pitts, B. G., Vélez-Colón, L., & Bernal-García, A. (2018). Consumer behaviour and sport services: An examination of fitness centre loyalty. *International Journal of Sport Management and Marketing*, 18(1–2), 8–23.

García-Fernández, J., Gálvez-Ruiz, P., Sánchez-Oliver, A. J., Fernández-Gavira, J., Pitts, B. G., & Grimaldi-Puyana, M. (2020a). An analysis of new social fitness activities: Loyalty in female and male CrossFit users. *Sport in Society, 23*(20), 204–221.

García-Fernández, J., Gálvez-Ruiz, P., & Vélez-Colón, L. (2017). Client profile of Spanish fitness centers: Segmentation by loyalty and characteristics of the client. In M. Peris-Ortiz, J. Álvarez-García, & M. C. Del Río-Rama (Eds.), *Sports management as an emerging economic activity* (pp. 273–291). Springer.

García-Fernández, J., Gálvez-Ruiz, P., Vélez-Colón, L., Ortega-Gutiérrez, J., & Fernández-Gavira, J. (2018). Exploring fitness centre consumer loyalty: Differences of non-profit and low-cost business models in Spain. *Economic Research-Ekonomska Istraživanja, 31*(1), 1042–1058.

García-Fernández, J., Martelo-Landroguez, S., Vélez-Colón, L., & Cepeda-Carrión, G. (2018). An explanatory and predictive PLS-SEM approach to the relationship between organizational culture, organizational performance and customer loyalty: The case of health clubs. *Journal of Hospitality and Tourism Technology, 9*(3), 438–454.

Gomes, R., Gustavo, N., Melo, R., & Pedragosa, V. (2017). Portugal: A growing sport market in a dominant state model. In A. Laine & H. Vehmas (Eds.), *The private sport sector in Europe: A cross-national comparative perspective* (pp. 269–286). Springer.

Grimaldi-Puyana, M., Pérez-Villalba, M., Bernal-García, A., & Sánchez-Oliver, A. J. (2018). Comparative study of job satisfaction in workers with a degree in physical activity and sports science. *Journal of Physical Education and Sport, 18*(3), 1380–1385.

Gonçalves, C., Meireles, P., & Carvalho, M. J. (2016). Consumer behaviour in fitness club: Study of the weekly frequency of use, expectations, satisfaction and retention. *The Open Sports Sciences Journal, 9*, 1–9.

IHRSA. (2005). *The IHRSA Global Report: The state of the health club industry*. Club Business International.

IHRSA. (2010). *European health club report: The size and scope of leading markets*. International Health, Racquet & Sports Club Association (IHRSA).

IHRSA. (2017). *The 2016 IHRSA global report*. International Health, Racquet & Sports Club Association (IHRSA).

IHRSA. (2019). *The 2019 IHRSA global report*. International Health, Racquet & Sports Club Association (IHRSA).

Jiménez, E. (2019). *El número de boxes en España crece un 23%*. www.cmdsport.com/esencial/cmd-fitnessgym/el-numero-de-boxes-de-crossfit-en-espana-crece-un-23/

León-Quismondo, J., García-Unanue, J., & Burillo, P. (2020). Best practices for fitness center business sustainability: A qualitative vision. *Sustainability, 12*, 5067.

Maguire, J. S. (2008). *Fit for consumption: Sociology and the business of fitness*. Routledge.

Molina, N., Mundina, J. J., & Gómez, A. (2019). Perfil del usuario de centros deportivos privados, según género, edad y nivel de antigüedad. *Sport TK: Revista Euroamericana de Ciencias del Deporte, 8*(1), 23–28.

O'Rourke, B. K. (2015). *The rise of boutique fitness studio concepts*. www.stephens.com/globalassets/about-stephens/news-pdfs/08.05.15-the-rise-of-boutique-fitness-studio-concepts.pdf

Pedragosa, V., Biscaia, R., & Correia, A. (2015). The role of emotions on consumers' satisfaction within the fitness context. *Motriz: Revista de Educação Física, 21*(2), 116–124.

Pedragosa, V., & Correia, A. (2009). Expectations, satisfaction and loyalty in health and fitness clubs. *International Journal of Sport Management and Marketing, 5*(4), 450–464.

Ramos, L., Esteves, D., Vieira, I., Franco, S., & Simões, V. (2020). Translation, reliability and validity of the job satisfaction scale in a sample of Portuguese fitness professionals. *Current Psychology*. doi:10.1007/s12144-020-01116-1

Ramos, L., Esteves, D., Vieira, I., Franco, S., & Simões, V. (2021). Job satisfaction of fitness professionals in Portugal: A comparative study of gender, age, professional experience, professional title, and academic qualifications. *Frontiers in Psychology, 11*, 621526.

Rodrigues, F. F., Neiva, H. P., Marinho, D. A., Mendes, P., Teixeira, D. S., Cid, L., & Monteiro, D. (2019). Assessing need satisfaction and frustration in Portuguese exercise instructors: Scale validity, reliabity and invariance between gender. *Cuadernos de Psicología del Deporte, 19*(1), 233–240.

Rodrigues, R. G., Pinheiro, P., Gouveia, A., Brás, R. M., O'Hara, K., Duarte, P., & Esteves, M. (2017). Segmentation of Portuguese customers' expectations from fitness programs. *Journal of International Studies, 10*(3), 234–249.

Rodríguez-Cañamero, S., Gallardo, L., Ubago-Guisado, E., García-Unanue, J., & Felipe, J. L. (2018). Causes of customer dropouts in fitness and wellness centres: A qualitative analysis. *South African Journal for Research in Sport, Physical Education & Recreation, 40*(1), 111–124.

Rosa-Díaz, I., Martín-Ruiz, D., & Cepeda-Carrión, G. (2021). The effect of servant leadership on employee outcomes: Does endogeneity matter? *Quality & Quantity*, 1–19.

Sacavém, A., & Correia, A. (2008). A Indústria do *wellness*. In A. Correia & C. Colaço (Eds.), *Manual de Fitness & Marketing: Para a competitividade dos Ginásios e Health Clubs*. Visão e Contextos.

Santos, E., & Correia, A. (2011). *Evolução do fitness em Portugal: Mudanças e desafios*. Visão e Contextos.

Serrano, J., & Alves, R. (2019). Fitness—Concepto, evolución y motivaciones para la práctica. In J. Petrica, H. Mesquita, M. Batista, & P. Mendes (Eds.), *Psicología del deporte y el ejercicio: enfoques de investigación académica* (pp. 169–183). Edición Ayuntamiento de Idanha a Nova.

Valcarce-Torrente, M., Cordeiro, C., & García-Fernández, J. (2017). *Informe Centros Boutique España. Marzo 2017*. Valgo Investment.

Valcarce-Torrente, M., López, F., & García-Fernández, J. (2020). *8º Informe Gimnasios Low Cost en España*. Valgo Investment.

Veiga, O. L., Valcarce-Torrente, M., & de la Cámara, M. Á. (2021). National survey of fitness trends in Spain for 2021. *Retos. Nuevas tendencias en Educación Física, Deportes y Recreación, 39*, 780–789.

Veiga, O. L., Valcarce-Torrente, M., & Rey-Clavero, A. (2017). Encuesta nacional de tendencias de fitness en España para 2017. *Apunts, 128*(abril-junio), 108–125.

Vieira, E., & Ferreira, J. (2018). Strategic framework of fitness clubs based on quality dimensions: The blue ocean strategy approach. *Total Quality Management & Business Excellence, 29*(13–14), 1648–1667.

Vieira, E., & Ferreira, J. (2020). What generic strategies do private fitness centres implement and what are their impacts on financial performance? *Sport, Business and Management, 10*(3), 317–333.

Chapter 10

Economic and social effects of sporting events and organisations in Spain and the Iberian Peninsula

Ferran Calabuig Moreno, David Parra-Camacho, and Josep Crespo-Hervás

Introduction

Sporting events can be important catalysts for the communities that host them, having an impact on the host community both socially and economically. On the Iberian Peninsula, sporting events have grown considerably in recent decades. If we focus on major sporting events—excluding the Olympic Games and the World Cup (which could be considered mega-events)—Spain has hosted (and continues to host) many of the world's major sporting events. Portugal and Andorra have also played a key role in this field, hosting for years several regular or one-off sporting events (for example, the 2004 UEFA European Football Championships in Portugal, or the 2019 Ski World Cup in Andorra).

The popularity of sport, its media attention, and the high expenditure in the hospitality sector in a short period of time make major sporting events a favourite option for destinations and chief tourist attractions.

This chapter aims to provide a conceptual approach to the effects of sporting events, offering a classification of the same. On the other hand, it highlights the main contributions made in recent years on the social and economic effects of events in the context of the Iberian Peninsula.

The social and economic impact of sporting events and organisations: conceptualisation and classification

Sporting events clearly generate impacts on the communities in which they are held. In this sense, numerous studies have established classifications of the effects of sporting events (e.g. Ma & Kaplanidou, 2017; Mair et al., 2021; Preuss & Solberg, 2006). However, events of an economic and social nature have been the most researched in this area. For this reason, we will focus on explaining and determining the social and economic outcomes of sporting events.

First, we should take a conceptual approach to the social impact of sporting events. According to Taks et al. (2020), Mathieson and Wall's (1982) definition of the social impact of tourism can be applied to sporting events if we understand

DOI: 10.4324/9781003197003-10

them as phenomena that contribute to generating 'changes in value systems, individual behaviour, family relationships, collective lifestyles, safety levels, moral conduct, creative expressions, traditional ceremonies and community organisations' (Mathieson & Wall, 1982, p. 133). The social impacts of sporting events have been defined as 'any impacts that potentially have an impact on the quality of life for local residents' (Fredline et al., 2003, p. 3).

To classify the social impacts of sporting events, we can distinguish between positive and negative impacts, as well as between short-term (during the event) and long-term (after the event) social impact (Holmes et al., 2015). Examples include prestige for the host community (positive, short-term), increased traffic (negative, short-term), building community pride and community cohesion (positive, long-term), and community alienation (negative, long-term) (Taks et al., 2020). Other authors differentiate between social effects that influence the individual level (e.g. civil liberties, participation), the community level (e.g. gentrification), the host city level (e.g. pride), and the national level (destination image/accessibility) (Ritchie et al., 2020; Smith et al., 2018). Mair et al. (2021) established four categories of impact that directly affect residents: (1) volunteering, education and skills; (2) social cohesion, civic pride, and social capital; (3) inclusion and diversity; and (4) sport participation, infrastructure, and health.

Table 10.1 presents the main positive and negative social impacts of sporting events. In this compilation, socio-cultural and psychosocial impacts are also considered, since these categories have generally been included in some works under the category of the social impact of events.

Economic impact can be defined according to Crompton (1995, p. 15, as cited in Turco & Kelsey, 1992) as 'the net economic change in a host community that results from spending attributed to a sports event or facility'. Unlike social impacts, which are more difficult to discern and measure objectively, economic effects are clearly quantifiable (e.g. direct and indirect economic outcomes, investment creation, job creation) (Ritchie et al., 2009).

Within this category, various authors include those referred to in tourism (e.g. Ma & Kaplanidou, 2017) or the image of the region or community in which events take place. In this sense, large sporting events can develop the tourism industry at a destination by increasing the affluence of tourists, the duration of their stay, and their expenditure (Barker et al., 2002). Table 10.2 shows a compilation of the main economic impacts of sporting events.

Main studies on the social and economic impact of sporting events in Spain and the Iberian Peninsula

Studies on the social and economic impact in the context of Spain and the Iberian Peninsula have focused on small- and medium-scale events since no megasporting event (i.e., the Olympic Games or the World Cup) has been organised in this region since the Barcelona Olympic Games in 1992. However, although the

Table 10.1 Positive and negative social impacts of sporting events

Social impacts of sporting events

Positives	Compilations or reference studies	Negatives	Compilations or reference studies
People gain new skills and knowledge of a sporting event	Mair et al. (2021)	Changes in community structure	Preuss and Solberg (2006)
Reduction of social exclusion	Ritchie, Shipway and Cleeve (2009)	Social dislocation	Preuss and Solberg (2006)
Community and civic pride	Mair et al. (2021)	Relocation of local communities	Ma et al. (2011)
Social inclusion and diversity	Gibson et al. (2014); Mair et al. (2021)	Traffic congestion	Mao and Huang (2016)
Improvement of residents' quality of life	Ma and Kaplanidou (2017)	Excess police forces and increased crime	Kim and Petrick (2005)
Enhanced community attachment	Kim and Walker (2012)	Social conflict	Liu (2016)
Event excitement	Ma and Rotherham (2016)	Dissatisfaction with planning processes	Cashman (2006)
Symbology, brand, and national identity	Kim and Petrick (2005)	Marginalised groups	Cashman (2006); Chen and Tian (2015)
Encouragement of cultural exchange	Shipway and Brown (2007)	Disruption of daily schedules	Chen y Tian (2015)
Social capital/cohesion	Gibson et al. (2014); Mair et al. (2021)	Tendency towards defensive attitudes concerning the host region	Preuss and Solberg (2006)
Sport participation and health promotion	Mair et al. (2021)	Culture shock	Preuss and Solberg (2006)
People gain new skills and knowledge about a sporting event	Mair et al. (2021)	Misunderstandings leading to varying degrees of host/visitor hostility	Preuss and Solberg (2006); Chen and Tian (2015)

Source: Developed from Ribeiro et al. (2020), Mair et al. (2021) and Preuss and Solberg (2006)

Table 10.2 Positive and negative economic impacts of sporting events

Economic impacts of sporting events

Positives	Compilations or reference studies	Negatives	Compilations or reference studies
Increased business opportunities	Preuss and Solberg (2006); Prayag et al. (2013)	Price inflation	Preuss and Solberg (2006); Lorde et al. (2011)
Tax revenue and additional income	Chen and Tian (2015)	Increased real estate prices	Chen and Tian (2015)
Increased job opportunities	Preuss and Solberg (2006); Ma et al. (2011)	Failure to attract tourists and tourism displacement	Preuss and Solberg (2006)
Opportunity to find a better job	Preuss and Solberg (2006); Ma et al. (2011)	Better alternative investments	Preuss and Solberg (2006); Prayag et al. (2013)
Increased standard of living	Preuss and Solberg (2006)	Inadequate capital and inadequate estimation of the costs of an event	Preuss and Solberg (2006); Prayag et al. (2013)
Sustainable consumption habits	Ma et al. (2011)	Expensive security	Preuss and Solberg (2006)
Increased tourism	Preuss and Solberg (2006); Ma et al. (2011)	Over indebtedness	Preuss and Solberg (2006)
Opportunities for career development	Preuss and Solberg (2006); Ma et al. (2011)	Increased taxes	Prayag et al. (2013)
Improvement in community image	Preuss and Solberg (2006); Ma et al. (2011)	Poor sustainability of job opportunities	Ma et al. (2011)

Source: Developed from Ribeiro et al. (2020), Ma and Kaplanidou (2017) and Preuss and Solberg (2006)

Iberian Peninsula has not hosted a mega-sporting event for the last 30 years, it has hosted major sporting events. For example, regular events with a fixed location (e.g. Grand Prix motorcycle racing, Formula 1, Masters 1000 of the Association of Tennis Professionals, cycling tours of Spain, etc.). Sporadic events with itinerant locations (e.g. world championships in basketball, handball, athletics, skiing, America's Cup for sailing, the Davis Cup for tennis, or regional games such as the Mediterranean Games).

Economic impact is generally used when assessing sporting events to discern a particular relevance and wide territorial scope (Bosch et al., 2019). The chief methods have been input-output studies, computable general equilibrium, cost-benefit analysis (CBA), and contingent valuation methodology (Barajas et al., 2012). However, the most widely used methods in the context of studies in Spain and the Iberian Peninsula have been input-output studies and CBA.

First, the input-output approach involves the use of tables that adopt a macroeconomic approach at the national or regional level, enabling the development of complex economic models to simulate impact under various scenarios (Pedrosa & Salvador, 2003). Among the studies that have used this technique are those carried out by the Valencian Institute of Economic Research (IVIE), which has periodically conducted studies on the main sporting events held in the Valencian Community over the last two decades: the 32nd edition of America's Cup (Maudos, 2007), the European Formula 1 Grand Prix, the Valencia Marathon (Maudos et al., 2020), the Davis Cup, and the Volvo Ocean Race. IVIE has also estimated the economic impact of sports facilities such as L'Alqueria del Basket or the future Casal Arena stadium in Valencia. Other works that have made contributions in this sense are those carried out on soccer clubs (Aza et al., 2007), the Davis Cup in Gijón (Rodríguez & Baños-Pino, 2013), the World Roller Speed Skating Championships (Rodríguez, 2011) and Artistic Skating (Murillo et al., 2016), the Climbing World Championships in Gijón (Baños & Rodríguez, 2016), and the Moto GP World Championship event (Martí Selva & Puertas Medina, 2012).

To make a correct estimate, the expenditure made by the so-called *time switchers* (people who planned to visit a locality anyway and change the date to coincide with an event) should not be taken into account. Additionally, we should not consider the spending of those who were already visiting the host town and attended the event instead of doing another activity in the area (casuals) (Barajas et al., 2012). This type of work provides three central indicators: (1) direct expenditures; (2) total effects or gross value added (GVA); and (3) jobs generated. Table 10.3 shows the results of the data from several studies carried out on

Table 10.3 Studies using the input-output method on the Iberian Peninsula

	Direct effects	Total effects (GVA)	Total jobs
Davis Cup—Gijón (2012)	823.767	1.349.042	19
World Roller Speed Skating Championships—Gijón (2008)	1.998.000	3.542.000	53
World Artistic Skating Championships—Reus (2014)	2.089.400	5.586.960	-
Climbing World Championships—Gijón (2014)	280.726	434.856	-
Moto GP World Championship—Valencia	19.603.828	27.077.000	575
Valencia Marathon (2019)	28.209.856	15.877.835	524
31st edition of America's Cup—Valencia (2004–2007)	2.767.942.413	2.723.550.225	73.859

sporting events held in Spain and the Iberian Peninsula that have employed this method.

Second, the CBA technique, although employed less frequently, has also been used in economic impact studies in the context of the Iberian Peninsula. CBA aims to compare the benefit of sporting events for a region or country (which is the increase in the value of consumption by the local population) with the costs of the factors of production that are necessary to organise the event (Késenne, 2005). This allows for a rational decision to be made in accordance with normative criteria (allocation efficiency) and the opportunity cost principle (Barajas et al., 2012). The main problem lies in the difficulties in expressing all the relevant effects of an action, such as holding a sporting event, to a monetary magnitude (Bosch et al., 2019).

Some works that have utilised this approach in the context of the Iberian Peninsula include: the Women's Tennis Championship in Sevilla (Ramírez Hurtado et al., 2007), the XV Spanish National Championship of Beach-Volley 2005 (Rueda-Cantuche & Ramirez-Hurtado, 2007), the 2013 'Cáceres International Open' World Padel Tour in 2013 (Jiménez-Naranjo et al., 2016), the 2011 and 2015 Spanish 'Open' Winter Masters Swimming Championship of Pontevedra (Méndez et al., 2012; Sánchez et al., 2016), the 2017 XVIII Spanish Spring Open Absolute Swimming Championship (Salgado et al., 2018), and the 2015 Winter Universiade in Granada (Roca-Cruz et al., 2019). Table 10.4 presents the two chief indicators that are usually employed when applying this type of method.

Finally, in terms of economic impact, the contingent valuation method has been less frequently used in the context of sporting events and sport organisations on the Iberian Peninsula, highlighting the work on the Women's Tennis Championship in Sevilla by Ramírez Hurtado et al. (2007) or that of Barros (2002) on the UEFA European Championship 2004 in Portugal. This approach consists of valuing goods that lack a market through the creation of a hypothetical market by observing an individual's behaviour in the event of hypothetical (contingent)

Table 10.4 Studies carried out using the CBA method in the Iberian Peninsula

	Benefits	Costs
XV Spanish National Championship of Beach-Volley (2005)	350.811	140.450
Women's Tennis Championship ITF—Sevilla (2006)	331.429	33.181
World Paddle Tour Caceres (2013)	973.975	70.350
XXI Spanish 'Open' Winter Masters Swimming Championship—Pontevedra (2015)	401.154	24.012
XVIII Spanish Spring Open Absolute Swimming Championship—Pontevedra (2017)	234.348	42.891

changes in the prices or quantities of goods or services (Barajas et al., 2012; Bosch et al., 2019).

On the other hand, the works that have analysed the social impact of sporting events have been mainly quantitative in nature through the analysis of the host community's perception of the effects of sporting events for the community in which they are hosted (Liu, 2016). Tools such as closed surveys are often employed in which various indicators are consulted regarding the socio-cultural outcomes that sporting events can generate (e.g. Fredline et al., 2003; Kim et al., 2015).

These studies have carried out consultations before, during, and after sporting events. In the context of the Iberian Peninsula, the main contributions have focused on case studies of small- and medium-scale events. These studies have adapted and validated scales for measuring social impact, identified groups of residents with different perceptions, and examined the influence of socio-demographic variables.

Most of these studies are characterised by the identification of positive and negative impact factors or dimensions into which the indicators of the scales proposed are grouped. The most frequent dimensions are usually grouped into the following areas: socioeconomic impact; impacts on image; impacts on urban development and infrastructure; socio-cultural impacts the impact on sport; and negative social, economic and environmental costs or impacts.

Table 10.5 displays the list of sporting events analysed according to the dimensions of impact identified by the studies that have made contributions to the discipline from the perspective of the host community's perceptions. These studies offer different results depending on the event examined, since the host community's perceptions can vary according to the socioeconomic context in which an event takes place (Añó et al., 2012). A positive trend is observed in most of the works on the impacts generated regarding the image and international recognition of the municipalities that host them. However, in terms of aspects related to the impact on sport or at the socio-cultural level, the opposite trend is usually seen, especially at events in which the possibility of local residents participating is more limited (e.g. Formula 1 European Grand Prix or America's Cup).

Other studies include in their results the identification of groups with different perceptions of sporting events by means of cluster analysis. Most of these studies identify three clearly differentiated groups of residents according to their perceptions of an event.

In general, the majority of the studies identify two groups with clearly opposing trends in the evaluation of impact: one group that evaluates the effects of sporting events positively (favourable, optimistic, or positive), and another group that has a negative impression of the impacts (pessimistic, unfavourable, or detractors). Between these two groups, an intermediate group is usually identified, which broadly indicates diversity in the trends of impact evaluations (indifferent, realist, or moderate). Table 10.6 portrays studies carried out on the social impact of sporting events on the Iberian Peninsula that have identified different clusters of residents.

Table 10.5 Impact dimensions of the studies conducted on residents' perceptions of sporting events on the Iberian Peninsula

	Sporting event	Positive impacts	Negative impacts
Ramírez-Hurtado, Ordaz and Rueda-Cantuche (2007)	Women's Tennis Championship ITF—Sevilla	Economic effects Social effects	–
Llopis and Gil (2011)	32ª America's Cup, Valencia	Image and consolidation of Valencia social benefits Development of tourism resources and infrastructure Economic development	Negative attitudes and inconveniences Negative socioeconomic impact Negative outlook on real estate Products/services and security Negative image of the city
Añó et al. (2012)	Formula 1 European Grand Prix of Valencia	Economic impact Social impact Infrastructure impact Sport impact	–
Parra-Camacho et al. (2014)	Open ATP 500 Tenis de Valencia	Socioeconomic impact Impact on image and promotion Impact on urban development and infrastructure Socio-cultural and sport impact	–
Parra-Camacho et al. (2015)	Open ATP 500 Tenis de Valencia	–	Social costs Environmental costs Economic costs
Parra-Camacho et al. (2016)	Barcelona World Race	Socioeconomic benefits Benefits in image and international recognition Socio-cultural benefits	Costs
Ferreira et al. (2018)	European Rally Championship— the Azores Rally	Image promotion Residents' self-esteem Cultural self-development Economic development of the destination Entertainment	Pollution and environment spillover Car traffic troubles Social problems Price level increases

	Formula 1 European Grand Prix of Valencia	Socioeconomic development Urban development and infrastructure International image and recognition Sport development Socio-cultural development
Vegara-Ferri et al. (2020)	III Murcia Sport Festival	Socioeconomic benefits Socio-cultural benefits Sport benefits	Social costs
Parra-Camacho et al. (2021)	Valencia Marathon	Economic benefits and city image Social benefits Pride and identification with the community Sport impact	Socioeconomic problems

Note: Indicates that the study does not include impact dimensions in this category

Table 10.6 Clusters of residents identified in the studies conducted on residents' perceptions of sporting events on the Iberian Peninsula

	Sport event	Clusters		
Parra-Camacho et al. (2014)	Open ATP 500 Tenis of Valencia	Favourable	Moderate	Unfavourable
Calabuig et al. (2014)	Formula 1 European Grand Prix of Valencia	Moderately favourable	Moderately unfavourable	Detractors
Vegara-Ferri et al. (2020)	La Vuelta España	Positives	Moderate	Haters
Parra-Camacho and Duclos (2013)	Formula 1 European Grand Prix of Valencia	Favourables	Realists	Detractors
Parra-Camacho et al. (2016)	America's Cup, Valencia	Optimists	Indifferent	Pessimists

Conclusions

The social and economic effects of sporting events and organisations are increasingly in demand by event organisers and the public administrations that support them. While economic impacts can be clearly quantified (for example, by estimating the direct and indirect effects on the economy, quantifying jobs created, or foreign investments made), social effects are more difficult to quantify and measure objectively (Ritchie et al., 2009). These types of impacts include intangible aspects such as improved destination image, increased pride, or social capital (Mair & Duffy, 2018).

Studies on the economic impact of sporting events on the Iberian Peninsula are not very abundant, and most have focused on certain events held in geographic regions that have research institutes dedicated to this area (e.g. IVIE in the Valencian Community, the Observatory of Sport Economics in Asturias). The same trend can be seen in the case of social impact studies, since most of them have centred on regions where there are research groups dedicated to this subject matter. Similarly, most studies focus on small- and medium-scale events, which are the most frequent on the Iberian Peninsula. However, further research in this area is needed, especially in other regions of Spain, Portugal, and Andorra. Finally, the focus on analysing the influence of mega-sporting events will be conditioned by the opportunities that the countries of this region will have in the coming decades to bid for them.

References

Añó, V., Calabuig, F., & Parra, D. (2012). Social impact of a major athletic event: The Formula 1 Grand Prix of Europe. *Cultura, Ciencia y Deporte*, 7(19), 53–65. https://doi.org/10.12800/ccd.v7i19.23

Aza, R., Baños-Pino, J., Canal Domínguez, J. F., & Rodríguez, P. (2007). The economic impact of football on the regional economy. *International Journal of Sport Management and Marketing, 2*(5–6), 459–474. https://doi.org/10.1504/IJSMM.2007.013961

Baños, J., & Rodríguez, P. (2016). Economic impact of the climbing world championships. Gijón, 8–14 September 2014. *Intangible Capital, 12*(3), 822–839. https://doi.org/10.3926/ic.787

Barajas, Á., Salgado, J., & Sánchez, P. (2012). Problems to face in the economic impact of sports events studies. *Estudios de Economía Aplicada, 30*, 441–462.

Barker, M., Page, S. J., & Meyer, D. (2002). Modeling tourism crime: The 2000 America's Cup. *Annals of Tourism Research, 29*(3), 762–782. https://doi.org/10.1016/S0160-7383(01)00079-2

Barros, C. (2002). Evaluating the regulatory procedure of host-country selections for the UEFA European championship: A case study of Euro 2004. *European Sport Management Quarterly, 2*(4), 321–349. https://doi.org/10.1080/16184740208721932

Bosch, J., Murillo, C., & Raya, J. M. (2019). The economic importance of the sports sector and the economic impact of sporting events. *Papeles de economía española, 159*, 261–274.

Calabuig, F., Parra, D., Añó, V., & Ayora, D. (2014). Analysis of resident's perception on the cultural and sport impact of a formula 1 grand prix. *Movimento: revista da Escola de Educação Física, 20*(1), 261–280.

Cashman, R. I. (2006). *The bitter-sweet awakening: The legacy of the Sydney 2000 Olympic Games.* Walla Walla Press.

Chen, F., & Tian, L. (2015). Comparative study on residents' perceptions of follow-up impacts of the 2008 Olympics. *Tourism Management, 51*, 263–281. https://doi.org/10.1016/j.tourman.2015.05.029

Crompton, J. L. (1995). Economic impact analysis of sports facilities and events: Eleven sources of misapplication. *Journal of Sport Management, 9*(1), 14–35. https://doi.org/10.1123/jsm.9.1.14

Ferreira, M. J., Azevedo, A., & Pereira, F. (2018). Sport events and local communities: A partnership for placemaking. *Journal of Place Management and Development, 11*(1), 6–25. https://doi.org/10.1108/JPMD-02-2017-0019

Fredline, E., Jago, L., & Deery, M. (2003). The development of a generic scale to measure the social impacts of events. *Event Management, 8*(1), 22–37. https://doi.org/10.3727/152599503108751676

Gibson, H. J., Walker, M., Thapa, B., Kaplanidou, K., Geldenhuys, S., & Coetzee, W. (2014). Psychic income and social capital among host nation residents: A pre—post analysis of the 2010 FIFA world cup in South Africa. *Tourism Management, 44*, 113–122. https://doi.org/10.1016/j.tourman.2013.12.013

Holmes, K., Hughes, M., Mair, J., & Carlsen, J. (2015). *Events and sustainability.* Routledge.

Jiménez-Naranjo, H. V., Coca-Pérez, J. L., Gutiérrez-Fernández, M., & Fernández-Portillo, A. (2016). Determinants of the expenditure done by attendees at a sporting event: The case of World Padel Tour. *European Journal of Management and Business Economics, 25*(3), 133–141. https://doi.org/10.1016/j.redeen.2016.05.002

Késenne, S. (2005). Do we need an economic impact study or a cost-benefit analysis of a sports event? *European Sport Management Quarterly, 5*(2), 133–142. https://doi.org/10.1080/16184740500188789

Kim, S. S., & Petrick, J. F. (2005). Residents' perceptions on impacts of the FIFA 2002 world cup: The case of Seoul as a host city. *Tourism Management, 26*(1), 25–38. https://doi.org/10.1016/j.tourman.2003.09.013

Kim, W., Jun, H. M., Walker, M., & Drane, D. (2015). Evaluating the perceived social impacts of hosting large-scale sport tourism events: Scale development and validation. *Tourism Management*, 48, 21–32. https://doi.org/10.1016/j.tourman.2014.10.015

Kim, W., & Walker, M. (2012). Measuring the social impacts associated with super bowl XLIII: Preliminary development of a psychic income scale. *Sport Management Review*, 15(1), 91–108. https://doi.org/10.1016/j.smr.2011.05.007

Liu, D. (2016). Social impact of major sports events perceived by host community. *International Journal of Sports Marketing and Sponsorship*, 17(1), 78–91. https://doi.org/10.1108/IJSMS-02-2016-005

Llopis, M. P., & Gil, I. (2011). A major sporting event: Perspective of host-city residents. *Gran Tour*, 4, 32–61.

Lorde, T., Greenidge, D., & Devonish, D. (2011). Local residents' perceptions of the impacts of the ICC cricket world cup 2007 on Barbados: Comparisons of pre- and post-games. *Tourism Management*, 32(2), 349–356. https://doi.org/10.1016/j.tourman.2010.03.004

Ma, S. C., Egan, D., Rotherham, I., & Ma, S.-M. (2011). A framework for monitoring during the planning stage for a sports mega-event. *Journal of Sustainable Tourism*, 19(1), 79–96. https://doi.org/10.1080/09669582.2010.502576

Ma, S. C., & Kaplanidou, K. (Kiki). (2017). Legacy perceptions among host Tour de Taiwan residents: The mediating effect of quality of life. *Leisure Studies*, 36(3), 423–437. https://doi.org/10.1080/02614367.2015.1128475

Ma, S. C., & Rotherham, I. D. (2016). Residents' changed perceptions of sport event impacts: The case of the 2012 Tour de Taiwan. *Leisure Studies*, 35(5), 616–637. https://doi.org/10.1080/02614367.2015.1035313

Mair, J., Chien, P. M., Kelly, S. J., & Derrington, S. (2021). Social impacts of mega-events: A systematic narrative review and research agenda. *Journal of Sustainable Tourism*, 1–22. https://doi.org/10.1080/09669582.2020.1870989

Mair, J., & Duffy, M. (2018). The role of festivals in strengthening social capital in rural communities. *Event Management*, 22(6), 875–889. https://doi.org/10.3727/152599518X15346132863229

Mao, L. L., & Huang, H. (2016). Social impact of formula one Chinese Grand Prix: A comparison of local residents' perceptions based on the intrinsic dimension. *Sport Management Review*, 19(3), 306–318. https://doi.org/10.1016/j.smr.2015.08.007

Martí Selva, M. L., & Puertas Medina, R. (2012). Economic impact of a sporting event: MotoGP world championship in Valencia. *Estudios de Economía Aplicada*, 30(2), 683–702.

Mathieson, A., & Wall, G. (1982). *Tourism, economic, physical and social impacts*. Longman.

Maudos, J. (2007). *Economic impact of the 32nd edition of the America's Cup in Valencia*. Instituto Valenciano de Investigaciones Económicas.

Maudos, J., Aldás, J., Benages, E., & Zaera, I. (2020). *39 Trinidad Alfonso de València Marathon. Economic impact and evaluation of the runners*. Instituto Valenciano de Investigaciones Económicas.

Méndez, B., Sánchez-Fernández, P., & Barajas, Á. (2012). Impact of sport events: The case of the swimming championship in Spain Pontevedra 2011. *International Journal of Sports Law & Management*, 18, 72–91.

Murillo, C., Carles, M., Llop, M., Moya, X., & Planas, D. (2016). 2014 world figure skating championships in Reus: Feedback from participants and economic legacy. *Sport TK: revista euroamericana de ciencias del deporte*, 5(1), 107–118.

Parra-Camacho, D., Aguado-Berenguer, S., & Alguacil, M. (2021). The social impact of a medium-size recurring sporting event: The case of the Valencia Marathon. *Cultura, Ciencia y Deporte*. http://dx.doi.org/10.12800/ccd.v16i49.1719

Parra-Camacho, D., Aguado-Berenguer, S., & Núñez-Pomar, J. M. (2015). Costs of holding a sporting event: The host community perception. *Journal of Sports Economics & Management*, 5(1), 17–36.

Parra-Camacho, D., Añó, V., Calabuig, F., & Ayora, D. (2016). Residents perceptions about the legacy of America's Cup. *Cuadernos de Psicología del Deporte*, 16(1), 325–338.

Parra-Camacho, D., Calabuig, F., Añó, V., Ayora, D., & Núñez-Pomar, J. M. (2014). The impact of a medium-size sporting event: The host community perceptions. *Retos: nuevas tendencias en educación física, deporte y recreación*, 26, 88–93.

Parra-Camacho, D., & Duclos, D. (2013). Resident's perceptions on socioeconomic impact of a sporting event: Segmentation analysis and residents profile. *Journal of Sports Economics & Management*, 3, 4–32.

Parra-Camacho, D., Elasri-Ejjaberi, A., Triadó, X. M., & Aparicio, P. (2016). Analysis of the relationship between benefits and perceived costs and resident satisfaction with holdindg a sporting event: Mediating effect of perceived value. *Revista de psicología del deporte*, 25(1), 59–63.

Pedrosa, R., & Salvador, J. A. (2003). The impact of sport on the economy: Measurement problems. *RAE: Revista Asturiana de Economía*, 26, 61–84.

Prayag, G., Hosany, S., Nunkoo, R., & Alders, T. (2013). London residents' support for the 2012 Olympic Games: The mediating effect of overall attitude. *Tourism Management*, 36, 629–640. https://doi.org/10.1016/j.tourman.2012.08.003

Preuss, H., & Solberg, H. A. (2006). Attracting major sporting events: The role of local residents. *European Sport Management Quarterly*, 6(4), 391–411. https://doi.org/10.1080/16184740601154524

Ramírez Hurtado, J. M., Ordaz Sanz, J. Á., & Rueda Cantuche, J. M. (2007). Social and economic impact assessment of relevant sporting events in local communities: The case of the ITF female tennis championship held in Seville in 2006. *Revista de Métodos Cuantitativos para la Economía y la Empresa*, 3(1), 20–39.

Ribeiro, T., Correia, A., & Biscaia, R. (2020). The social impact of the 2016 Rio Olympic Games: Comparison of residents' pre- and post-event perceptions. *Sport, Business and Management: An International Journal*, 11(2), 201–221. https://doi.org/10.1108/SBM-02-2020-0014

Ritchie, B. W., Chien, P. M., & Shipway, R. (2020). A Leg(acy) to stand on? A non-host resident perspective of the London 2012 Olympic legacies. *Tourism Management*, 77, 104031. https://doi.org/10.1016/j.tourman.2019.104031

Ritchie, B. W., Shipway, R., & Cleeve, B. (2009). Resident perceptions of mega-sporting events: A non-host city perspective of the 2012 London Olympic Games. *Journal of Sport & Tourism*, 14(2–3), 143–167. https://doi.org/10.1080/14775080902965108

Roca-Cruz, A., González-Ruiz, J., Porcel-Rodríguez, P., & Cabello-Manrique, D. (2019). Economic impact of the attendees to the Winter Universiade 2015 in the city of Granada. *SPORT TK-Revista EuroAmericana de Ciencias del Deporte*, 8(1), 7–12. https://doi.org/10.6018/sportk.362001

Rodríguez, P. (2011). *Analysis of the economic impact of the World Speed Skating Championships (CMPV) held in Gijón. September 4–12, 2008*. Fundación Observatorio Económico del Deporte.

Rodríguez, P., & Baños-Pino, J. F. (2013). Economic impact analysis of the Davis cup semifinal Spain vs United States. *Journal of Sports Economics & Management*, 3(1), 47–63.

Rueda-Cantuche, J. M., & Ramirez-Hurtado, J. M. (2007). A simple-to-use procedure to evaluate the social and economic impacts of sporting events on local communities. *International Journal of Sport Management and Marketing*, 2(5), 510–525. http://inderscience.metapress.com/content/G0PM824191800251

Salgado, J., Sánchez, P., Pérez, M., & Barajas, Á. (2018). Economic valuation of a medium-sized sporting event: Impact of the Spanish Swimming Championship. *Journal of Physical Education and Sport, 18*(3), 1349–1355. https://doi.org/10.7752/jpes.2018.s3200

Sánchez, P., Salgado, J., Rodríguez, A., & Barajas, Á. (2016). Economic impact of the XXI Winter masters Spanish 'open' swimming championship in Pontevedra 2015. *SPORT TK-Revista EuroAmericana de Ciencias del Deporte, 5*, 169–180. https://doi.org/10.6018/254191

Shipway, R., & Brown, L. (2007). Challenges for a regional cultural programme of the London 2012 Games. *Culture@ the Olympics, 9*(5), 21–35.

Smith, A., Ritchie, B. W., & Chien, P. M. (2018). Citizens' attitudes towards mega-events: A new framework. *Annals of Tourism Research, 74*, 208–210. https://doi.org/10.1016/j.annals.2018.07.006

Taks, M., Oshimi, D., & Agha, N. (2020). Other- versus self-referenced social impacts of events: Validating a new scale. *Sustainability, 12*(24), 10281. https://doi.org/10.3390/su122410281

Turco, D., & Kelsey, C. W. (1992). *Conducting economic impact studies of Recreation and parks special events*. National Recreation and Park Association.

Vegara-Ferri, J. M., Angosto, S., & Parra-Camacho, D. (2020). Effect of residents' satisfaction between perceived impacts and future intentions regarding holding a small-scale event. *Revista iberoamericana de psicología del ejercicio y el deporte, 15*(1), 81–91.

Vegara-Ferri, J. M., López-Gullón, J. M., Ibanez-Pérez, R. J., Carboneros, M., & Angosto, S. (2020). Segmenting the older resident's perception of a major cycling event. *Sustainability, 12*(10), 4010. https://doi.org/10.3390/su12104010

Chapter 11

Sports entrepreneurship and intrapreneurship in the Iberian Peninsula

A bibliometric analysis

Alejandro Lara-Bocanegra, Paloma Escamilla-Fajardo, María Huertas González-Serrano, María del Rocío Bohórquez, and Moisés Grimaldi-Puyana

Introduction

The economic, political and social scenario has awakened interest in entrepreneurship and its stimulation as a fundamental way for the development of countries, self-employment and wealth creation (Sánchez-Oliver et al., 2019). However, the data from the latest Eurobarometer on entrepreneurship (Eurostat, 2018) show that European citizens would rather be employed by an organisation than start their own business (45.1%). At the other extreme, in countries such as the United States, citizens would rather be entrepreneurs than employees (54.8%). There are also differences within the European Union (EU): Cyprus and Greece (66% and 60.3%, respectively) occupy the top positions in terms of entrepreneurial tendencies, while Slovakia (25.6%), Belgium (30%) and Spain (40.4%) are the countries with the lowest percentage of entrepreneurs. Thus, the European challenge is to promote entrepreneurship in all EU member states, for which it launched the Entrepreneurship and Innovation Programme 2014–2020. This is a European Commission strategy that aims to provide economic, political and administrative support as an instrument to achieve economic and social growth through entrepreneurship. (European Commission, 2014).

Specifically, in the Iberian Peninsula the last economic crisis changed the social and economic paradigm, with Spain and Portugal leading the EU youth unemployment rate (Eurostat, 2018; Ubierna-Gómez, 2015). Unemployment is a problem of structural imbalance, and one of the main challenges is the generation of youth employment and the improvement of their integration into the labour market. This is considered a priority in terms of public policies (Moreno-Mínguez, 2015). Thus, based on EU recommendations and with the aim of promoting entrepreneurship, the Spanish and Portuguese governments began to implement measures to stimulate growth and job creation, such as the 2020 Entrepreneurship Action Plan (Grimaldi-Puyana, 2017).

DOI: 10.4324/9781003197003-11

As a result of these policies, the number of people wishing to set up their own businesses increased in Spain up to 2018 (Moreno, 2018). As regards Portugal, there was a rise of 6.4% in this intention up to 2019, compared to the previous year. This growth dynamic has been constant since 2012, mainly encompassing tourism and catering (Teixeira & Forte, 2017).

The fitness and sports activity sector have become a very diverse business context, manifesting itself as a growing economic sector worldwide. The study and analysis of entrepreneurship within this sector is therefore an essential element. (Sánchez-Oliver et al., 2019). According to the Yearbook of Sports Statistics 2020 (MCD, 2020), in recent years in Spain, there has been an increase in the number of companies in the sports sector dedicated to the management of facilities and/or activities of sports clubs or gyms (Sánchez-Oliver & Grimaldi-Puyana, 2017). This suggests that the number of entrepreneurs related to physical activity and sport has increased and that they in turn can play an important role in the economy and the creation of social value in addition to personal wealth (Ratten, 2012). It is in this sense that the concepts of entrepreneurship and intra-entrepreneurship in sport emerge. Both concepts have similar characteristics, such as the generation of creative and innovative projects/businesses/ideas. In the case of entrepreneurship, the subjects carry out these projects/businesses/ideas on their own, seeking their own employment and establishing themselves as their own boss (e.g. subjects who decide to create their own business by setting up their own personal training centre, specifically in Spain, franchisees of the Sano Center). However, intrapreneurship is based on the generation of creative and innovative projects/businesses/ideas by employees of a given organisation, with the aim of its growth (e.g.: an employee of a sports centre detects the need for customers to be able to book group classes in advance from their homes, so he proposes to the organisation's management the creation and implementation of an App that presents different services, including the booking of group classes).

Faced with this economic and social challenge, science has a responsibility to respond to the knowledge and training needs of society, facilitating innovation and good practice (General Secretariat for Research, MICINN, 2021). Thus, determining the state of the art and the drivers of scientific knowledge in the different areas of entrepreneurship and intrapreneurship will be key to boosting knowledge and transfer in this area. It is not yet possible to determine this despite the interest in sport entrepreneurship having been reflected in some bibliometric studies (González-Serrano et al., 2020a; González-Serrano et al., 2014; Pellegrini et al., 2020). No studies have been found that analyse how the scientific production of researchers from Spanish and Portuguese institutions has evolved, nor what their scientific contribution has been in this field of study. This information can contribute to understanding what factors stimulate sport entrepreneurship and intrapreneurship, and what policies are most appropriate to develop for its promotion. The aim of this chapter is to show the situation of research on entrepreneurship and intrapreneurship in sport in the Iberian Peninsula through a bibliometric study.

Method Data collection

An advanced search was carried out in the Web of Sciences (WoS) using the topic (TS) as a search field. The TS field searches for terms in the title, abstract and keywords: (((entrepreneur*) OR (intrapreneur*)) AND ((fitness) OR (sport*) OR (physical activity))). The search was conducted on April 29, 2021. It is important to report the date of the search as the database is constantly changing and being updated (Liu et al., 2015).

The study was limited to research articles in the strict sense, including only original papers and reviews. The following types of documents were excluded: conference proceedings, editorial letters, book reviews, news, and articles. The initial search retrieved a total of 562 documents. Subsequently, these documents were filtered by country (Spain and Portugal, as Gibraltar and Andorra yielded no results), resulting in 73 articles. These 73 articles were reviewed by the authors of the chapter, guiding their analysis. Articles that were eliminated were the result of the consensus of all the authors (triangulation). The PRISMA (Preferred Reporting Items for Systematic Reviews and Meta-Analyses) approach of Mother et al. (2009) was adopted. In the second step (screening), it was not necessary to eliminate any article, as the full text of all the articles identified was accessible. In the third step (eligibility), articles that did not meet the inclusion criteria ($n = 22$) mentioned in Figure 11.1 were removed, resulting in a total of 51 articles. Finally, the selected articles were downloaded in plain text with data on the year of publication, authors, author affiliation, title, abstract, journal, subject area, references, and the number of citations.

Bibliometric analysis

After downloading the plain text data, duplicate records were checked and homogenised. One of the problems encountered was the existence of authors identifying themselves with different signatures. The total number of articles was reviewed to avoid duplications and errors, and to find missing data for some records (institutions, countries and year of publication). Subsequently, bibliometric analysis was carried out in two different stages. First, it was the basic bibliometric indices (number of articles published per year, per author, per institution, and per journal) was calculated using HistCite statistical software (version 2010.12.6; HistCite Software LLC, New York). HistCite does not only show quantitative indicators but also presents qualitative indicators: Total Global Citation Score (TGCS) which refers to the total number of citations that the selected articles have received in the entire WoS, and Local Global Citation Scores (TLGCS) which represents the number of citations that these articles have received in the WoS only for the

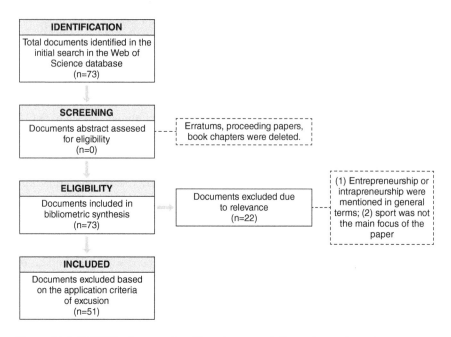

Figure 11.1 PRISMA diagram detailing the steps followed to select documents

articles selected in the specific analysis performed. Second, bibliographic coupling was performed to identify the different topics using the VOS viewer software. Bibliographic coupling measures the similarity between the two articles by identifying the number of references that they have in common. It is a suitable technique to do so since the number of references cited in the articles does not change over time, an aspect that would not be possible to control with co-occurrence analysis (Bartolacci et al., 2020). Therefore, it is useful for conducting systematic literature reviews (Caputo et al., 2018). For the correct interpretation of these network maps, it is necessary to take into account that each cluster is related to a colour. The darker the colour of the cluster, the higher the cluster density. In addition, the distance of the articles should be considered as an indication of the relationship between the other cited references. With regard to the size of the vertices, these represent the number of citations received, the more citations, the larger the size. In this case, the three most cited articles in each cluster (larger vertices) were analysed in more detail.

Main findings

Basic indicators. The 51 articles analysed were published by 86 authors from 19 institutions. Table 11.1 shows the authors with the highest number of publications, the number of citations received within the search performed (LCS), the

Table 11.1 Authors with the highest number of publications in the search (≥ 4)

Authors	Affiliation	No	LCS	GCS	GCS/No
Calabuig F	Universitat de València	16	1	78	4.88
González-Serrano MH	Universitat de València	15	1	58	3.87
Crespo J	Universitat de València	11	0	73	6.64
Escamilla-Fajardo P	Universidad Católica de Valencia	11	0	19	1.80
Núñez-Pomar JM	Universitat de València	10	0	49	4.90
Prado-Gasco VJ	Universitat de València	5	0	42	8.40
Ratten V	La Trobe University	5	9	34	6.80
Gomez-Tafalla AM	Universitat de València	4	1	5	1.25
Grimaldi-Puyana M	Universidad de Sevilla	4	0	4	1.00
Sánchez-Oliver AJ	Universidad de Sevilla	4	1	5	1.25
Valantine I	Lithuanian Sports University	4	0	16	4.00

Note: No: number of articles; LCS: local citations score; GCS: global citations score

number of total citations received (GCS) and the result between the total number of citations and the total number of articles published (GCS/No). The author with the most published articles on sport entrepreneurship and intrapreneurship is Calabuig with 16 articles, followed by González-Serrano, with 15 articles, and Crespo and Escamilla-Fajardo with 11 articles (Table 11.1). On the other hand, considering the number of citations received, the range oscillates between 4.88 and 0. Taking this into account, the authors who have received the highest number of citations (GCS) in WoS are Calabuig (GCS = 78), Crespo (GCS = 73) and Ferreira (GCS = 69) (Table 11.1).

Chronological evolution of published articles. Looking at the chronological evolution of the articles selected (see Figure 11.2), scientific production begins in 2013 with only one article. Between 2014 and 2017, a maximum of four articles per year was not exceeded, while between 2018 and 2020, there was an increase in scientific production, reaching its highest peak in 2020 with twelve publications. With regard to 2021, due to the periods of information collection, the data collected are incomplete, with eight publications in this regard. If we look at the total number of citations received by these papers, we can see that the highest number of citations was obtained between 2015 and 2018.

Institutions of the authors. With regard to the origin of the institutions and taking into account those that present at least two papers, we can indicate that Spain has six institutions involved in entrepreneurship and intrapreneurship research (Univ. Valencia, Univ. Seville, Univ. Católica Valencia, Univ. Castilla La Mancha, Univ. Granada and Univ. Internacional Valencia), while Portugal has two (Universidade de Beira Interior and UTAD University). Similarly, if we look at the institutions with the highest number of published articles, we should highlight the University of Valencia, with thirty published articles; the University of Seville,

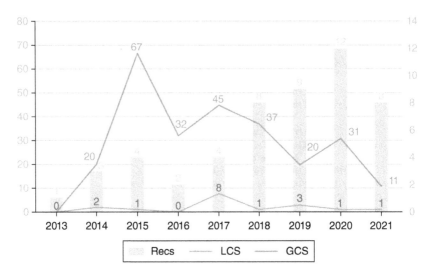

Figure 11.2 Chronological evolution of the number of publications and citations received

with ten published articles; the University of Beira Interior, with seven published articles; and the Catholic University of Valencia, with six published works. The remaining institutions contribute one to two published articles (see Figure 11.3).

Countries. As can be seen in Figure 11.4, both countries of the Iberian Peninsula are highly collaborative. The networks of collaborations with other countries are diverse, which shows that researchers from Spanish and Portuguese institutions tend to collaborate with academics from other countries to develop their research. In addition, it is worth noting that the most consolidated collaboration networks are between Portugal and Australia, and between Spain and Chile, Australia and Lithuania.

Journals. Considering the journals with the highest number of published articles, Sustainability stands out with 7 published articles and a total of 6 citations in the WoS, and the International Entrepreneurship and Management Journal with 5 articles and a total of 56 citations in the WoS (Table 11.2). However, if the number of citations, rather than the total number of published articles, is taken into account, the International Entrepreneurship and Management Journal is in first place with 56 citations in the WoS and 21.29% of the GCS (56/263), then comes the Journal of Business Research with 31 GCS, and the International Journal of Sport Policy and Politics with 30 citations in WoS.

Bibliographic coupling: A thematic analysis. The bibliographic coupling technique is used to group the search documents by topic or area within the research field. A total of 51 papers were identified for this analysis, with no minimum citation limit. However, only 49 articles were related to each other. These articles

Sports entre- and intrapreneurship in the Iberian Peninsula 129

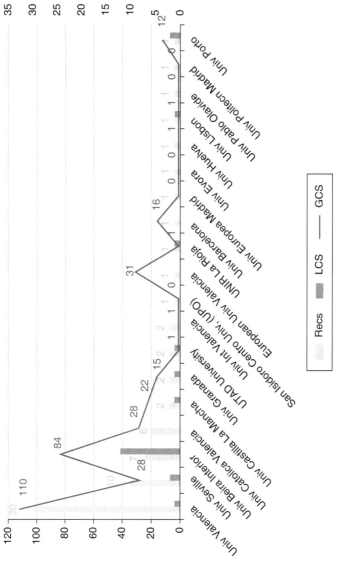

Figure 11.3 Articles published by institutions in Spain and Portugal

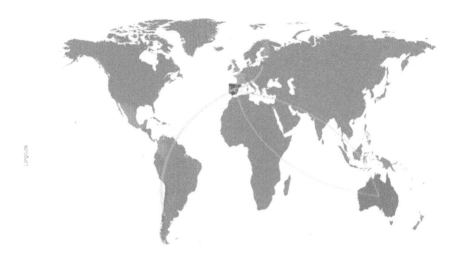

Figure 11.4 Collaboration networks between researchers in the countries of the Iberian Peninsula

Table 11.2 Main journals (≥ 2 articles)

Journal	No.	LCS	GCS
Sustainability	7	0	6
International Entrepreneurship and Management Journal	5	0	56
Journal of Entrepreneurship and Public Policy	5	3	13
Materiales para la Historia del Deporte	5	0	2
Sport in Society	4	0	18
Education and Training	2	1	18
EEuropean Journal of International Management	2	0	0
International Journal of Sport Policy and Politics	2	6	30
Technological and Economic Development of Economy	2	0	16

Note: No.: number of articles; LCS: local citations score; GCS: global citations score; SJR: Scimago Journal Rank: IF: Impact Factor; HI: h-index

were grouped into five clusters that were identified as Red, Green, Blue, Yellow, and Purple

Red cluster: entrepreneurship education and entrepreneurial intentions in sport science students

This cluster is the largest of the five clusters and is composed of 17 articles. These articles have so far received a total of 108 citations. The subject matter of these

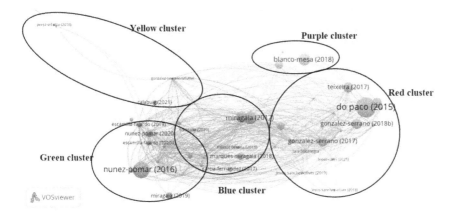

Figure 11.5 Bibliographic coupling documents

Source: Red cluster: (108 citations, 17 articles): Entrepreneurship education and entrepreneurial intentions in students from the sport field

articles relates to entrepreneurial education and entrepreneurial intentions (cognitive approach), in most cases using sport science students at the university level. However, only one article on intrapreneurship has been identified within the cluster.

One of the most relevant articles in this cluster is from Do Paço et al. (2015) with a total of 45 citations. These authors compared the psychological and behavioural factors related to the entrepreneurship of girls attending a business school and boys attending a sports school. The results showed that boys in the sports school, despite not receiving an entrepreneurial education, had higher entrepreneurial intentions. Along the same lines, another of the most cited articles in this cluster (12 citations) also highlights the hidden potential of sport science students compared to students in other fields of study. (Teixeira & Forte, 2017).

On the other hand, focusing specifically on the predictor variables of the entrepreneurial intentions of university students of sports science, González-Serrano et al. (2017) analysed the internal and external factors that affect the entrepreneurial intentions of these students in Spain. They concluded that both perceived entrepreneurial capacities to create an enterprise and perceived entrepreneurial capacity to become an entrepreneur are important for entrepreneurial intentions and that entrepreneurial education positively affects these variables. A few years later, González-Serrano et al. (2018) analysed the predictor variables of entrepreneurial intentions, but from a multicultural approach, with university students of sport sciences from Spain and Lithuania. The results showed differences in entrepreneurial variables and predictors of entrepreneurial intentions, highlighting that Lithuanian sports science students have a greater predisposition towards entrepreneurship.

Green cluster: entrepreneurial orientation and innovation as an antecedent or consequence in sports organisations

This cluster, consisting of 15 articles, is the second largest of the five clusters. These articles have until now received a total of 58 citations. This cluster is related to entrepreneurial orientation and innovation as an antecedent of the final performance of sport organisations, in most cases sport clubs, and also as a consequence of organisational variables studied in the academic literature.

The most cited article is Núñez-Pomar et al. (2016) with a total of 31 citations. The authors analysed the relationship of entrepreneurial orientation (EO), organisational size and economic performance of private Spanish sports companies through the use of fsQCA. The results showed that EO is not a sufficient condition for high performance in large sports companies, but it is in small sports companies. In this case, EO is analysed as an antecedent of financial performance. Along the same lines, another of the articles in this cluster with the highest number of citations (6), analyses the relationship between EO and social performance in Spanish sports clubs. In addition, they considered the effect of management variables such as type of financing and level of competition on this relationship. According to the results obtained, there is a positive direct effect between EO (in a multidimensional way) and social performance. Clubs with a higher level of competition and public funding obtained higher levels of prediction of social performance (Núñez-Pomar et al., 2020).

In the same cluster there is also an article that analyses innovation as a consequence of organisational climate depending on the maximum level of competition of the sports club. According to the results obtained, the dimensions of training and motivation are those that show a greater prediction of innovation both for sports clubs at the international-national level of competition and for sports clubs at the regional-local level of competition (Escamilla-Fajardo et al., 2019). On the other hand, another of the most cited articles in the cluster is that of Miragaia et al. (2019), who analyse the relationship between the financial stability of European professional football teams and their final performance from an entrepreneurial perspective. The results show that only 10 of the 15 teams analysed were efficient, proposing practical implications based on innovation and proactivity in order to improve their situation.

Blue cluster: social entrepreneurship, education entrepreneurship and bibliometric analysis

This cluster is composed of eight articles, being the third largest of the five, and having received a total of 48 citations so far. This cluster presents a double topic. On the one hand, it focuses on social entrepreneurship in sport and its repercussions in the educational field, and on the other hand, it presents different bibliometric reviews that try to shed light on the current situation of entrepreneurship in sport. On this occasion, no articles related to intrapreneurship in sport are presented.

The article with the highest number of citations in this cluster is Miragaia et al.'s (2017), with a total of 18 citations. Social entrepreneurship and actions linked to corporate social responsibility (hereafter CSR) policies are booming, so much so that Miragaia et al. (2017) find that sponsorship of a social cause and participation in social sporting events influence the motivational development and increased productivity of employees in these organisations. The main drivers for sponsorship of sport events are: customer loyalty and employee motivation, reputation and social networks, innovation and opportunity, and CSR. In this same line of work on sporting events in the community, Miragaia et al. (2018) present a study linked to the motivation presented by both teachers and students, from university studies in Sports Sciences, when it comes to getting involved voluntarily in the development of an event of these characteristics. These authors indicate that students seek to gain experience for future jobs, while teachers try to help others and contribute to the good of society (Miragaia et al., 2018).

Closely linked to the field of education and the promotion of entrepreneurship from the university are the works of Miragaia et al. (2018) and García-Fernández et al. (2017), as the latter presents an educational innovation through which entrepreneurship strategies that promote physical activity and that have the use of gamification through the creation of mobile applications in common are linked.

On the other hand, focusing all the attention on the global state of entrepreneurship in sport in the scientific literature, the work of González-Serrano et al. (2020b) is presented, with a total of 15 citations for now. This article presents the specific situation of entrepreneurship in sport in the Web of Science and its different underlying themes, carrying out an analysis of coincidence between authors, citations, and keywords, as well as a thematic analysis.

Yellow cluster: sustainable sport entrepreneurship

This cluster, composed of four articles, has received a total of three citations so far. The topic of this cluster is linked to sustainable entrepreneurship in sport, addressing it from different perspectives. On this occasion, all the citations in this cluster are attributed to the same article, of Calabuig et al. (2021).

In this sense, the authors present the current situation of entrepreneurial ecosystems, both at a generic level and linked to the world of sport, through a bibliometric analysis of WoS publications. This construct is presented as a novel, current, and growing topic, but which is not very well developed in the field of sport.

Another underdeveloped but booming field is sustainable entrepreneurship in sport (González-Serrano et al., 2020b). These authors identified mega sport events and sustainability as the sub-area of greatest development or research, followed by sport innovation oriented towards inclusion. Furthermore, it is important to note that although sustainable entrepreneurship and innovation in sport is an underdeveloped field, it has a promising future in the industry. Linked to this thematic line could adhere the article by Pérez-Villalba et al. (2018), where the main legal forms used by sport entrepreneurs are presented. This work indicates that although the legal form of cooperatives is the one that could have the greatest transfer of democratic values from sports clubs, it is not widespread among Spanish entrepreneurs.

Purple cluster: economics and entrepreneurship in sport

This cluster, consisting of three articles, is the smallest of the five, but has received a total of 24 citations. The subject matter of these articles is linked to economics and its relation to entrepreneurship in sport. No articles on intrapreneurship have been identified within the cluster.

The most cited article in this cluster is Blanco-Mesa et al.'s (2018), with a total of 16 citations. This article aims to explain how the economic environment and logical reasoning guide the decision-making process for the start-up of a new business by potential entrepreneurs through a case study demonstrating transfer from theory to practice. This could help potential investors and entrepreneurs to make a decision based on their preferences.

The second article with the most citations in this cluster is Franco and Pessoa (2014), with eight in total. This work points out that university sports alliances can be understood as collaborative entrepreneurship, in that they unite the interests of different institutions in the realisation of common projects of value and social intervention, helping universities to integrate and open up to society.

The last article in this cluster outlines the determinants of investment by fitness small and medium-sized enterprises (SMEs) in Portugal (Nunes et al., 2013). In this regard, growth opportunities and government subsidies are positive determinants of investment in Portuguese fitness SMEs, while the 2008 financial crisis had a negative influence on investment.

Discussion and conclusions

The results of this study provide a holistic view of the current state, evolution, and trends of the research in sport entrepreneurship and intrapreneurship conducted by researchers from Spanish and Portuguese universities. In addition to the identification of the number of publications, relevant authors, institutions, types of journals and collaborations by country, the most interesting finding of this study is the identification and analysis of five thematic areas. The findings of this study contribute to providing new insights about the areas of entrepreneurship that attract the interest of researchers in Spain and Portugal. It also identifies how these researchers have contributed to the development of the field of study. In addition, these findings contribute to identifying research niches and possible collaborations that can be established with researchers in other countries.

Considering the results obtained in terms of basic bibliometric indicators, regarding authorship, nine of the 11 authors with the highest number of related publications are from Spain. In the same line, looking at the institutions with more than two published papers, six of them are Spanish and two Portuguese. These data are in line with some previous bibliometric studies on sport entrepreneurship (González-Serrano et al., 2020a; Pellegrini et al., 2020). However, although researchers from Spain and Portugal typically collaborate, no collaborations have been found between them in this particular area of study. Most of these collaborations are with researchers outside Europe. Australian universities are the one that shows the largest number of scientific productions on this subject. Australia is also the place where one of the leading authors in this field of study works (González-Serrano et al., 2014).

As for the thematic areas obtained, while other previous studies identified three (González-Serrano et al., 2020a) and four thematic areas (Pellegrini et al., 2020), the current study reveals five, highlighting how the growth of this field of study is generating a diversification of them. Firstly, great importance has been given to the analysis of entrepreneurial intentions and the entrepreneurial attitude of university students related to physical activity and sport from a cognitive perspective, focusing the study on the factors that explain the entrepreneurial intentions of these students (e.g., Do Paço et al., 2015; González-Serrano et al., 2018). In fact, this has been the thematic cluster with the highest scientific production by these authors, as well as the one most cited. Therefore, researchers from Spanish and Portuguese institutions are making a great visible contribution within this thematic area of study. However, analysing the field of sport entrepreneurship at a global level, this is the topic on which the least amount of research, and therefore citations, has been generated (Pellegrini et al., 2020).

On the other hand, entrepreneurial orientation and innovation have been approached from the organisational sphere as both antecedents and consequences. This is the second thematic area where these researchers from the Iberian Peninsula have contributed the most, and it is also the second with the greatest impact in terms of the number of citations received. This line of study has highlighted the variables that can condition an organisation's entrepreneurship (Escamilla-Fajardo et al., 2019), and to what extent an organisation's entrepreneurship predicts its final performance. The latter has been addressed from economic (Núñez-Pomar et al., 2016) and social (Núñez-Pomar et al., 2020) perspectives. Compared to the field of sport entrepreneurship globally, this area could be framed as a sub-area of the third or fourth cluster with the highest number of publications and citations of the article by Pellegrini et al. (2020), related to the environmental conditions and factors that promote sport entrepreneurship or the social role of sport entrepreneurship. However, it could already be considered a specific and independent area of study.

On the other hand, the social aspect that characterises sport has also generated growing interest in recent years from an entrepreneurial perspective. So important has this boom been that it has given rise to a specific thematic area in the results of this bibliometric analysis, becoming the third cluster to which peninsular researchers have contributed the most, with a high number of citations. This cluster analyses the motivation felt by employees of an organisation or sports science students to participate and collaborate in sporting events that develop actions linked to Corporate Social Responsibility policies (Miragaia et al., 2017, 2018). In this sense, the drivers of the sport marketing and sponsorship of events of these characteristics, and the strategies to encourage intentions to voluntarily participate in the planning and development of this type of events by teachers are analysed in more detail. This cluster may constitute a sub-cluster within the second most developed cluster in terms of number of publications—but not number of citations—of Pellegrini et al.'s (2020) article, related to the social role of entrepreneurship and its implications. However, it seems to be a topic more related to intra-sport entrepreneurship, a field of study that is still in its infancy in the area of sport and on which more research is needed.

Another thematic area is more broadly related to sport economics and entrepreneurship, assessing its context. Although there are few studies in this cluster, its impact in terms of number of citations is quite high. It is therefore a field of study yet to be developed. Within it, the analysis of the influence of the external and internal environment on the decision-making mechanism when creating an organisation or company stands out (Blanco-Mesa et al., 2018). Along the same lines, it analyses the factors of the external and internal environment that intervene in investment in small and medium-sized organisations in the fitness sector (Nunes et al., 2013). The changing and dynamic environment and its perception can often have a broad impact on decisions and thus on the final performance of the organisation. This topic corresponds to the second most cited theme of Pellegrini et al.'s (2020) article, related to environmental factors and conditions influencing sport entrepreneurship. As the findings of the present study show, although it is composed of fewer articles, the impact of this topic is quite high in terms of number of citations.

Finally, another area that is attracting the interest of researchers and is currently of relevance is sustainability in sport entrepreneurship. This may be due to the development of the Sustainable Development Goals for the 2030 agenda. This field of study can be considered an underdeveloped field as only 3 papers have been published and they have received few citations. However, in the Spanish and Portuguese context, bibliometric studies have been developed that offer a broad overview of the state of knowledge (González-Serrano et al., 2020b), and which can serve as a reference to lay the foundations for future studies within this field.

Finally, there are also studies within the search that focus on the legal figure of the cooperative as a type of organisation that is not very popular among Spanish entrepreneurs (Pérez-Villalba et al., 2018). The number of citations is quite limited, but its relevance is expected to increase in the coming years. Unlike previous bibliometric studies on sport entrepreneurship (González-Serrano et al., 2020a; Pellegrini et al., 2020), this is a new subject of study.

To conclude the analysis of the contribution of researchers in the Iberian Peninsula to the development of the sport entrepreneurship field, it is necessary to mention that most of the studies in this search are empirical, and therefore there are few studies that discuss theory or conceptual matters. This is a positive aspect, as previous studies had pointed out the need for more empirical studies on sport entrepreneurship to contribute to the development of this field of study (González-Serrano et al., 2020a, 2020b). Furthermore, entrepreneurship and intrapreneurship in the sport sector from a Spanish and Portuguese perspective are still booming, with an increase in scientific production only in recent years. These findings are in line with previous bibliometric studies (González-Serrano et al., 2014; Pellegrini et al., 2020). Therefore, it can be considered that researchers in Spain and Portugal are contributing greatly to the field of study of sport entrepreneurship and intrapreneurship, one that is still in an incipient state, but which presents ample possibilities for study, analysis and research. Specifically, the development of studies on intrapreneurship in sport and the generation of collaborative networks between researchers from these two countries are two of the future challenges of this scientific community.

One of the main limitations of the present study is related to the exclusive use of the WoS as a source of information, despite the fact that it is considered in previous studies as the most reliable source (Skute, 2019). Important articles may have been omitted. On the other hand, the results of this search have been analysed qualitatively (basic bibliometric data) and quantitatively (thematic cluster analysis). However, a more comprehensive analysis such as a systematic review can be carried out in order to extend the information provided.

A future line of research could be to focus on broadening the theoretical implications of the empirical studies, as most of them only have practical and managerial implications. Furthermore, it might be interesting to extend the theoretical scientific production, including the conceptual development and relationships between entrepreneurial and intra-entrepreneurial constructs in the field of sport.

References

Bartolacci, F., Caputo, A., & Soverchia, M. (2020). Sustainability and financial performance of small and medium sized enterprises: A bibliometric and systematic literature review. *Business Strategy and the Environment, 29*(3), 1297–1309.

Blanco-Mesa, F., Gil-Lafuente, A. M., & Merigó, J. M. (2018). New aggregation operators for decision-making under uncertainty: An applications in selection of entrepreneurial opportunities. *Technological and Economic Development of Economy, 24*(2), 335–357.

Calabuig, F., González-Serrano, M., Alonso-Dos-Santos, M., & Gómez-Tafalla, A. (2021). Entrepreneurial ecosystems, knowledge spillovers, and their embeddedness in the sport field: A bibliometric and content analysis. *Knowledge Management Research & Practice, 19*(1), 65–83. doi:10.1080/14778238.2020.1752120

Caputo, A., Marzi, G., Pellegrini, M. M., & Rialti, R. (2018). Conflict management in family businesses. *International Journal of Conflict Management, 29*, 519–542.

Do Paço, A., Ferreira, J., Raposo, M., Rodrigues, R., & Dinis, A. (2015). Entrepreneurial intentions: Is education enough? *International Entrepreneurship and Management Journal, 11*(1), 57–75. https://doi.org/10.1007/s11365-013-0280-5

Escamilla-Fajardo, P., Núñez-Pomar, J., & Parra-Camacho, D. (2019). Does the organizational climate predict the innovation in sports clubs? *Journal of Entrepreneurship and Public Policy, 8*(1), 103–121.

European Commission. (2014). *Entrepreneurship and Innovation Programme (EIP)*. https://ec.europa.eu/cip/eip/index_en.htm

Eurostat. (2018). *General and regional statistics*. http://ec.europa.eu/eurostat

Franco, M., & Pessoa, N. (2014). University sports partnerships as collaborative entrepreneurship: An exploratory case study. *Administration & Society*, 46(8), 885–907. https://doi.org/10.1177/0095399713481597

García-Fernández, J., Fernández-Gavira, J., Sánchez-Oliver, A. J., & Grimaldi-Puyana, M. (2017). Gamificación y aplicaciones móviles para emprender: una propuesta educativa en la enseñanza superior. *IJERI: International Journal of Educational Research and Innovation*, 8, 233–259.

González-Serrano, M. H., Añó, V., & González-García, R. (2020a). Sustainable sport entrepreneurship and innovation: A bibliometric analysis of this emerging field of research. *Sustainability*, 12(12), 5209. http://dx.doi.org/10.3390/su12125209

González-Serrano, M. H., Crespo-Hervás, J., Pérez-Campos, C., & Calabuig-Moreno, F. (2017). The importance of developing the entrepreneurial capacities in sport sciences university students. *International Journal of Sport Policy and Politics*, 9(4), 625–640.

González-Serrano, M. H., Jones, P., & Llanos, O. (2020b). An overview of sport entrepreneurship field: A bibliometric analysis of the articles published in the web of science. *Sport in Society*, 23(2), 296–314. https://doi.org/10.1080/17430437.2019.1607307

González-Serrano, M. H., Valentine, I., & Crespo-Hervás, J. C. (2014). La investigación sobre emprendimiento en el ámbito deportivo. Revisión de los documentos publicados en la WOS. *Journal of Sports Economics & Management*, 4(1), 55–66.

González-Serrano, M. H., Valantine, I., Crespo-Hervás, J. C., Pérez-Campos, C., & Moreno, F. C. (2018). Sports university education and entrepreneurial intentions: A comparison between Spain and Lithuania. *Education + Training*, 60(5), 389–405.

Grimaldi-Puyana, M. (2017). Aplicaciones móviles para la actividad física, ocio y recreación deportiva. una aproximación a la normativa. In J. García-Fernández (Ed.), *Busca tu futuro: emprende en deporte* (pp. 105–114). Aranzadi Thomson Reuters.

Liu, W., Tang, L., Gu, M., & Hu, G. (2015). Feature report on China: A bibliometric analysis of China-related articles. *Scientometrics*, 102(1), 503–517.

Ministerio de Cultura y Deporte. (2020). *Anuario de Estadísticas Deportivas*. www.culturaydeporte.gob.es/servicios-al-ciudadano/estadisticas/deportes/anuario-de-estadisticas-deportivas.html

Miragaia, D., da Costa, C., & Ratten, V. (2018). Sport events at the community level: A pedagogical tool to improve skills for students and teachers. *Education + Training*, 60(5), 431–442. https://doi.org/10.1108/ET-12-2017-0206

Miragaia, D., Ferreira, J., Carvalho, A., & Ratten, V. (2019). Interactions between financial efficiency and sports performance. *Journal of Entrepreneurship and Public Policy*, 8(1), 84–102.

Miragaia, D., Ferreira, J., & Ratten, V. (2017). Corporate social responsibility and social entrepreneurship: Drivers of sports sponsorship policy. *International Journal of Sport Policy and Politics*, 9(4), 613–623. https://doi.org/10.1080/19406940.2017.1374297

Moreno, M. (2018). *Radiografía del emprendimiento en España*. www.computerworld.es/tendencias/radiografia-del-emprendimiento-en-espana

Moreno-Mínguez, A. (2015). La empleabilidad de los jóvenes en España: Explicando el elevado desempleo juvenil durante la recesión económica. *Revista Internacional de Investigación En Ciencias Sociales*, 11(1), 3–20.

Mother, D., Liberati, A., Tetzlaff, J., & Altman, D. G. (2009). Preferred reporting items for systematic reviews and meta-analyses: The PRISMA statement for reporting systematic reviews and meta-analyses of studies that evaluate health care interventions: Explanation and elaboration. *Journal of Clinical Epidemiology*, 62, 1006–1012.

Nunes, P. M., Serrasqueiro, Z., & Guedes de Carvalho, P. (2013). Investment determinants of fitness SMEs in Portugal. *Technological and Economic Development of Economy*, 19(1), 496–523.

Núñez-Pomar, J. M., Escamilla-Fajardo, P., & Prado-Gascó, V. (2020). Relationship between entrepreneurial orientation and social performance in Spanish sports clubs. The effect of the type of funding and the level of competition. *International Entrepreneurship and Management Journal*, 16(1), 1–19.

Núñez-Pomar, J. M., Prado-Gascó, V., Sanz, V. A., Hervás, J. C., & Moreno, F. C. (2016). Does size matter? Entrepreneurial orientation and performance in Spanish sports firms. *Journal of Business Research*, 69(11), 5336–5341.

Pellegrini, M. M., Rialti, R., Marzi, G., & Caputo, A. (2020). Sport entrepreneurship: A synthesis of existing literature and future perspectives. *International Entrepreneurship and Management Journal*, 16, 795–826.

Pérez-Villalba, M., Fernández-Gavira, J., & Caballero-Blanco, P. (2018). La economía social en el emprendimiento deportivo en España. *Materiales Para La Historia Del Deporte* (16), 36–42.

Ratten, V. (2012). Sport entrepreneurship: Challenges and directions for future research. *International Journal of Entrepreneurial Venturing*, 4(1), 65–76.

Sánchez-Oliver, A. J., Gálvez-Ruiz, P., Grimaldi-Puyana, M., Fernández-Gavira, J., & García-Fernández, J. (2019). New ways of sports entrepreneuring in the university. *Journal of Entrepreneurship and Public Policy*, 8(1), 5–21.

Sánchez-Oliver, A. J., & Grimaldi-Puyana, M. (2017). Oportunidad para emprender en ciencias de la actividad física y el deporte: tendencias en entrenamiento. In J. García-Fernández (Ed.), *Busca tu futuro: emprende en deporte* (pp. 37–44). Aranzadi Thomson Reuters.

Secretaría General de Investigación, Ministerio de Ciencia e Innovación. (2021). *Estrategia Española de Ciencia, Tecnología e Innovación 2021–2027*. www.ciencia.gob.es/stfls/MICINN/Ministerio/FICHEROS/EECTI-2021-2027.pdf

Skute, I. (2019). Opening the black box of academic entrepreneurship: A bibliometric analysis. *Scientometrics*, 120(1), 237–265.

Teixeira, A. A., & Forte, R. P. (2017). Prior education and entrepreneurial intentions: The differential impact of a wide range of fields of study. *Review of Managerial Science*, 11(2), 353–394.

Ubierna-Gómez, F. (2015). Entrepreneurial intention and the university student of tourism: A comparative analysis of bachelor and master students. *International Journal of Scientific Management and Tourism*, 1(1), 235–273.

Chapter 12

The Spanish football league and the foreign players

Gabriel Chaves, Jaume García, Daniel Ortín, and Federico Todeschini

Introduction

The Spanish football league (*La Liga*) attracts international talent from all over the world. Some of the greatest football players in history, like Ladislao Kubala, Alfredo di Stefano, Johan Cruyff, Diego Maradona, Leo Messi, or Cristiano Ronaldo, have played in *La Liga*. There is some empirical evidence supportive of a positive effect of the presence of foreign players in terms of better rankings of the clubs (Royuela & Gásquez, 2019). Although the empirical literature analysing Spanish football is growing (Barajas & Rodríguez, 2010; Carreras & García, 2018; García & Rodríguez, 2002, 2006; García et al., 2020; García del Barrio & Szymanski, 2009), empirical studies on the phenomenon of migration in the Spanish first division are still scarce. The article by Ortega (2016) is an exception.

In this paper, we analyse the phenomena of migration in the Spanish *La Liga*, with a particular focus on players from Latin America. By constructing a novel data set covering most of the foreign-born players that ever participated in a *La Liga* First Division match, we provide a detailed description of the migration phenomena by looking at the evolution and the characteristics of the players who came to Spain. We complement this descriptive exercise with an econometric investigation including starting their participation in their respective national teams after arriving in Spain.

The results allow us to provide some preliminary results about the relationship of the frequency of arrival of foreign players and the institutional setting, and the evolution of the composition (characteristics) of these flows. The estimation of some basic econometric models complements the descriptive information of this novel data set.

Institutional framework

Since its inception, professional football in Spain has been intermittently welcoming foreign players. Three periods can be identified. The first one, from the beginning of the last century until 1973, was influenced by events such as World War I and II, Spanish Civil War and Franco dictatorship, and entailed a fluctuating

DOI: 10.4324/9781003197003-12

framework regarding the possibility of signing foreign players. The second one, from 1973 to 1995, represented a stable era for incoming foreign players where regulations allowed only a limited number of foreign players in the lineup. Finally, the period after the Bosman ruling, from 1996 until nowadays, is marked by a surge in the number of foreign players all over Europe.

The first period was characterised by continuous shutting and reopening of the possibility of having foreign players. The first season of the Spanish La Liga, 1927–1928, included only three foreign players: Saprissa, from El Salvador, and Walter and Platko from Germany. While in 1933 pressures from football teams allowed the first opening of La Liga to foreign players, the Spanish Civil War closed football borders from 1936 until 1947. After that year, several historic players joined the Spanish league, like Kubala, Ben Barek, and Di Stefano. From 1953 to 1956 the border closed again, to reopen afterwards until 1962, and then shut down again until 1973. During the 1956–1962 period an important flow of international talent arrived, such as Puskas, Kocsis, Evaristo, Czibor, Vavá, or Didí. The last years of the shutdown, from 1962 to 1973, were characterised by the extremely dubious nationalisation of Latin American players with Spanish ancestors, the so-called 'oriundos', which ended up in a scandal that propelled a regulatory change.

From 1973 to 1995 the influx of foreign players was limited by the regulatory limits on the number of foreign players in the starting line-up and/or the team. A limit of two foreign players per squad was implemented, which was later relaxed to three in 1990. During that period, European football clubs had complete discretion about players' future. After a failed negotiation with his club, Belgian football player Jean-Marc Bosman sued R. C. Liège, who prevented him from moving to USL Dunkerque. The case arrived to the Court of Justice of the European Union. The verdict (December 15 1995) forbade quotas on European Union players amongst EU teams and forbade transfer fees once contracts were expired.

Bosman ruling introduced a new era of football in which European Union teams could have unlimited amounts of players from other EU's countries. La Liga, however, introduced a limit of at most three non-EU players, which is still in place nowadays. There is a vast literature analysing the effect of the Bosman ruling on different aspects of the professional football industry in Europe: international mobility (Kesenne, 2006), performance of national and club teams in Europe (Binder & Findlay, 2012), competitive balance (Dejonghe & Van Opstal, 2010), incentives to invest in football academies for young people and develop players (Norback et al., 2021), productivity and career duration of the players (Radoman, 2017), among others.

Characteristics of the foreign players in the Spanish football

The type of analysis mentioned in the introduction, requires a dataset that represented as close as possible the population of foreign players that participated at any time in the Spanish first division, as well as their careers.

As a first step, then, we needed to define the scope of players to include in our dataset. Here, we focused our attention on male players who had been born outside Spain and had been, at least once, in the squad of the football teams that played in the first division of Spain. To get this information, we scraped data for each team/season from *BDFutbol* website (BDFutbol, n.d.), and created a list of all players who fulfilled the requisite.

Using that list of players, we obtained their football career from *FootballDatabase* (Footballdatabase, n.d.). The match from the players identified in the first step with respect to this step was not completely perfect, as some players could not be traced back or did not have enough information. However, despite the lack of information of some matches for some players, this should not affect our results. Regarding the career, for each player we collected information on the club/season where he played during his career, as well as some performance, career and sociodemographic variables.

The final data set contains 2559 foreign players who were in the list of players called-up to play an official game in the Spanish First Division at some stage in his career since 1920 until 2019. In Table 12.1 we report some descriptive statistics which provide some initial information about the profile of these players.

As expected, most of these players (73.4%) arrived after the Bosman ruling, and most of them were born in Latin America (45.56%). In particular, the presence of Latin American players was more important in relative terms in the period previous to 1973. The legal and illegal double nationalities in that period explain

Table 12.1 Distribution of the relative frequencies (%) of players arriving at Spanish football

	Europe (Big 5)	Rest of Europe	Latin America	Rest of the world	TOTAL
Period					
Before 1973	3.68	2.60	7.80	1.48	4.96
1973–1996	13.80	33.01	28.82	17.80	26.65
After 1996	82.52	64.38	63.38	80.71	68.39
Position					
Goalkeeper	7.36	8.49	6.52	4.75	6.96
Defender	33.13	24.79	27.02	19.88	26.22
Midfielder	38.96	37.81	32.50	38.87	35.68
Forward	20.55	28.90	33.96	36.50	31.14
Age at arrival	25.51	25.07	23.79	23.12	24.28
Capped before arrival	44.79	58.08	40.05	60.53	48.50
First cap after arrival[1]	28.59	28.76	24.89	54.14	29.29
TOTAL[2]	12.74	28.53	45.56	13.17	100.00

1 Proportions calculated among those who arrived at Spanish football not having played for their national team
2 Relative frequencies (%) of players arriving at Spanish football by continent

this particular feature. Bosman's ruling was one of the driving forces behind the increase of European players in the Spanish league in the nineties those coming from countries associated with the Big 5 leagues. This feature is also relevant from players born mainly in Africa and Asia, as most of them were playing first for a European team before joining the Spanish football.

There is some heterogeneity in terms of the type of players (position on the field) depending on the continent they were born. Midfielders and forwards are the two most important positions but midfielders and defenders are the two relevant positions when considering players from the countries of the Big 5 leagues. At the same time, Latin American and other continents forwards seem to be preferred by Spanish teams.

With respect to the age at arrival, Latin American players and those from other continents seem to arrive about two years younger to Spanish football than European players. This could be explained by some of these transfers being understood as investments in players who could have a potential brilliant future and not being as expensive as European football players, in particular, those from the Big 5 leagues.

Additionally, whether the player was capped before arriving in Spain could be a valid proxy of the quality of the players at arrival. Although this variable is associated with the age at arrival, the proportion of Latin American players who have already played for their national team before arriving in Spain is significantly smaller than those corresponding to players coming from other continents. On the other hand, playing in the Spanish football has resulted in some players becoming capped afterwards. This is particularly significant for players from countries not in Europe or in Latin America.

In the subsample of players who were born in Latin America, some countries are overrepresented. In Table 12.2 we report the proportion of the Latin American players arrived at Spain corresponding to those countries which represented more than 2% in the whole period, with specific detail for the three subperiods

Table 12.2 Distribution of relative frequencies (%) of Latin American players by country

	Before 1973	1973–1996	After 1996	Total
Argentina	35.16	38.99	39.65	39.11
Brazil	16.48	22.32	26.93	24.79
Chile	1.10	3.87	3.79	3.60
Colombia	0.00	2.98	5.95	4.63
Paraguay	26.37	8.04	2.71	6.09
Uruguay	16.48	16.67	13.80	14.84
Other countries	5.41	7.13	7.17	6.98
TOTAL[1]	4.96	26.65	68.39	100.00

1 Relative frequencies (%) of players arriving at Spanish football by continent

which can be defined in terms of the regulations in practice. Argentina and Brazil represent almost two thirds of the Latin American players arrived at the Spanish league, Argentina representing almost 40% of the total, and Uruguay being the other country with a relevant contribution (14.8%).

There are some features worth to mention. While Argentina's contribution is quite stable since 1973, Brazil's is clearly increasing over time. Finally, even though Paraguay was the second Latin American country before the 1973 authorisation representing one fourth of the players arriving at Spanish football in that period, the presence of players from Paraguay is very small since then. Among other things, this is related to the earlier-mentioned affair of the 'oriundos', which included several Paraguayan players.

Evolution of the arrival of foreign players at Spanish football

The presence of foreign players before the seventies was quite marginal, with the exception of a period in the fifties in which signing foreign players was allowed. The introduction of televised games, particularly the broadcasting of the 1970 Mexico's World Cup, and the authorisation approved by the Spanish Sports Council in 1973, increased radically the arrivals of foreign players. Figure 12.1 highlights perfectly this change. There is a significant jump in 1973 and figures were more or less stable until 1995 (the Bosman ruling). This event generated a very significant jump in the series, being the evolution quite stable since then.

All in all, on average 28 foreign players arrived per year at the Spanish football between 1973 and 1995. This number increased up to 78 in the last period. But there have been also a change in the distribution of these players in terms of the continent of birth. While before 1973, the proportion of Latin American players was almost 72% among those arriving, it decreased substantially afterwards (52% between 1973 and 1995 and 42% since 1996). The openness of the Spanish football market after 1973 increased the presence of European players (24% before 1973 and 42% afterwards), in particular, that of players from the countries of the Big 5 leagues since 1996 (15.3% after 1995 compared to 6.6% between 1973 and 1995). At the same time, the presence of players from other continents apart from Europe and Latin America has increased substantially (almost 16% after 1995, 6.5% between 1973 and 1995 and 4% before 1973).

When looking at the characteristics of the Latin American players, Figure 12.2 highlights that after 1995 there has been significant change in the distribution of the players in terms of their position in the field. Between 1973 and 1995 the proportion of players was increasing when moving to forward position. More than three quarters of the players were either midfielders or forwards, the latter having the largest proportion (45.9%). But since 1996 the proportion of defenders have increased significantly (from 16.6% to 32.0%) and the proportion of forwards has decreased (from 45.9% to 28.4%)

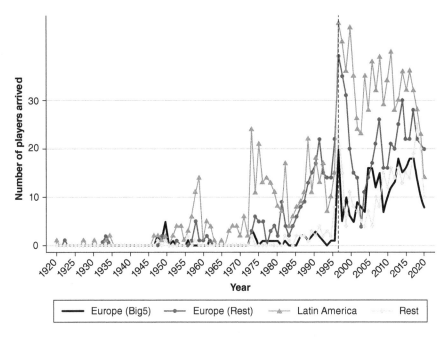

Figure 12.1 Number of foreign players arriving at Spanish football by continent of birth (1920–2019)

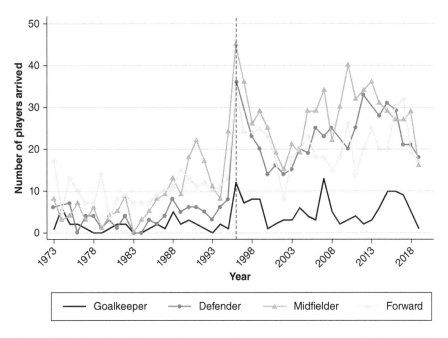

Figure 12.2 Number of Latin American players arriving at Spanish football by position on the field (1973–2019)

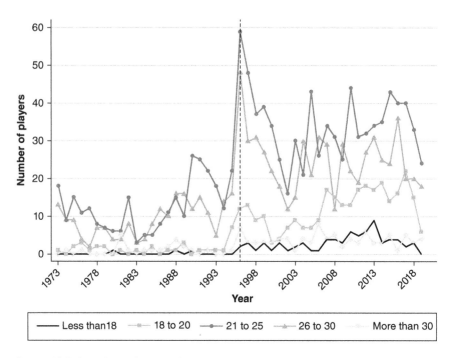

Figure 12.3 Number of Latin American players arriving at Spanish football by group of age (1973–2019)

On the other hand, Latin American players arriving at Spanish football are younger in recent periods as shown in Figure 12.3. Between 1973 and 1995 6.2% of the players were younger than 21 and after 1995 this percentage increased up to 17.7%. Still the largest proportion of players arrived is in the interval of 21–25 years of age (48.3% after 1995 and 60.0% between 1973 and 1996). This is the range of age in which players have shown their abilities and still have a long career ahead to be considered their hiring as a good investment in the short run (immediate performance with new club) and in the long run (including the benefits from a potential future transfer). This age effect translates into the proportion of capped players arriving at Spanish football. Before 1996 that proportion followed a positive trend but after 1996, just when younger players were arriving this proportion is clearly decreasing as shown in Figure 12.4.

Econometric models

As shown in the previous section the number of foreign players who arrived at the Spanish football have been increasing, in particular since the authorisation to hire foreign players in 1973. On the other hand, we also highlighted the fact that

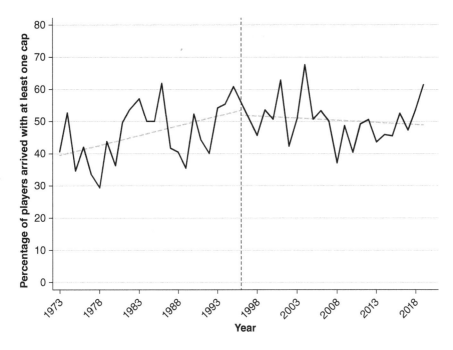

Figure 12.4 Proportion (%) of Latin American capped players among those arriving at Spanish football (1973–2019)

playing in the Spanish football could be a step to have the possibility of playing for the national team since the level of competition in Spain (Europe, in general) was higher than in the corresponding domestic leagues. In this section we pay special attention to these two issues by using simple econometric models.

The arrival of foreign players

There are several factors that could explain the profile followed by the absolute frequency of arrivals of foreign players. From the institutional point of view there are two crucial moments: the 1973 authorisation for signing foreign players and the Bosman ruling. Apart from that we could think on other factors affecting this pattern: the attractiveness of the Spanish league in terms of the level of competition, in comparison with the player's domestic league, the economic situation of Spain and of the countries of origin, and some specific events which could have an influence on the international exposure of players, like the World Cup or the corresponding continental cups. In this subsection we discuss some preliminary results corresponding to the econometric analysis of the frequency of arrival based on a very simple model in which some specific factors, but not all, are taken into account.

The dependent variable (*Arrivals*) is the absolute frequency of arrivals per year of foreign players at the Spanish league since 1926 until 2019, paying specific attention to the origin in terms of the continent of birth, in particular Latin America and Europe. We distinguish four blocks of explanatory variables: the trend, the impact of the 1973 authorisation, the impact of the Bosman ruling, and some specific international events associated with Spanish football.

When describing the evolution of the arrival of foreign players we observed a significant change in the trend followed by these arrivals since 1973. To capture this change in the trend (change in the slope in 1973), we have specified a spline by including an interaction equal to the difference between the linear trend (*Year*) and 1973, times a dummy equal to 1 for the period after 1973 (*DPOST1973*): Interaction73 = (Year—1973) * DPOST1973. In an extension of this model, we included the lagged value of the arrivals to complete the dynamic specification.

As we observed in the descriptive analysis of the previous section, the institutional changes of 1973 and 1996 represented a substantial and immediate jump in the frequency of arrivals, which declined smoothly afterwards because of the limited capacity to sign foreign players, particularly for the 1973 authorisation. We capture the jump associated with both institutional changes by including a dummy for the corresponding year (*D1973 and D1996*, respectively). The decline converges to the overall trend after five years, allowing for an unrestricted decline in the year after by including a dummy corresponding to that year (*D1974 and D1997*) and a constant decline per year in the four next years ($DD_{1974-1978}$ and $DD_{1997-2001}$).

We only included variables associated with national teams' international football competitions in which the role played by Spain was relevant. That was the case of the 1982 World Cup organised by Spain and the 2010 World Cup won by Spain. Two dummies were introduced to capture these specific competitions effect (*D1982 and D2010*).

In Table 12.3 we report the estimates of four regression models for the frequency of arrivals of foreign players based on two different specifications: a basic linear model (*Basic model*) and a model expanded by including the lagged endogenous variable (*AR(1)*). Two versions of the basic linear model for the frequency of arrivals from Latin America and Europe are also reported.

First, we estimate a significant change in the slope of the linear trend after 1973, as indicated by the significance of the coefficient of the interaction term (*Interaction73*). This happens for both the basic model and when the lagged endogenous variable is included. The estimated slope for the period previous to 1973 is not significantly different from zero.

With respect to the effect of the institutional changes in 1973 and 1996, we estimate a positive significant 'jump' (immediate change) in both 1973 and 1996. The jump is very much the same whether we include the lagged endogenous variable or not. As expected, the change associated with the Bosman ruling is much more important, and statistically significant, because there were restrictions less binding in terms of the number of foreigners compared to the 1973 authorisation which

Table 12.3 Estimates of different models for the frequency of arrivals of foreign players

	Basic model	AR(1)	Basic model	Basic model
	Full sample	Full sample	Latin America	Europe
Deterministic trend				
Year	0.015	0.025	0.083**	-0.011
Interaction73	1.855**	0.848*	0.581**	0.879**
Authorisation 1973				
D1973	29.749**	29.267**	20.225**	5.836**
D1974	18.049**	4.449	10.562**	6.169**
$DD_{1974-1978}$	-3.400**	-0.592	-0.963	-2.068**
Bosman law				
D1996	82.047**	82.130**	26.966**	37.878**
D1997	48.347**	11.110	24.103**	20.011**
$DD_{1997-2001}$	-12.300**	-3.677	-4.364**	-6.368**
World Cup				
D1982	4.649**	6.073**	7.254**	-2.973**
D2010	16.446**	17.283**	11.678**	0.730
Y_{t-1}		0.524**		
Constant	-28.216	-47.480	-150.208**	22.172
Sample size	94	94	94	94
R^2	0.949	0.960	0.884	0.929
Σ	7.930	7.016	4.927	4.180

Notes
* Significant at 5%
** Significant at 1%

initially only allowed hiring two foreign players. Instead, the declining profile after the institutional changes depends very much on the specification, in particular, whether the lagged endogenous variable is included as a regressor. In this case the lagged variable is capturing this dependence profile and none of the coefficients of the institutional change specifications, except those of *D1973* and *D1996*, are significantly different from zero. For the basic model, we can see that the decline is more accelerated from 1973 to 1974 (or 1996 to 1997) than afterwards.

With respect to the last block of regressors associated with international events relevant for Spain (the 1982 World Cup celebrated in Spain and the 2010 World Cup which was won by the Spanish team) significant and positive coefficients are estimated for both dummies (*D1982* and *D2010*) for the two models. These international events are good opportunities for promoting players and they could have an influence on the arrival frequencies of foreign players to the Spanish league. Since the basic model with a linear functional form and without the lagged endogenous variable facilitates the description of the evolution of the arrival frequencies, we re-estimated this model for the frequencies associated with players who were born in Latin America and Europe.

Most of the features commented on earlier for the total frequencies are replicated for the arrival of Latin American players and that of European players but with some differences. The impact of the institutional changes in 1973 and 1996 are affecting in the same way the arrival of players from Latin America and Europe. The impact of the 1973 authorisation is much more important in terms of the arrival of Latin American players compared to European players. There is a significant difference between the estimates of the coefficients of the dummies *D1973* and *D9174*. But the impact of the approval of the Bosman ruling has just the opposite effect, the estimated jump in 1996 is much more important for the arrivals of European players. The Bosman ruling facilitated the free movement of European players. On the other hand, the international events seem to be more relevant in terms of the frequency of Latin American players arriving at Spain.

The probability of playing for the national team for the first time once arrived at Spain

A bit more than a half (51.5%) of the players who arrived at the Spanish football in our data had not played for their national team before moving to Spain and almost 3 out of 10 (29.3%) of them played at least one game for the national team afterwards. In this subsection we make a preliminary analysis of some of the characteristics associated with football players which affects the probability of playing for the national team. To do this we estimate Probit models for the probability of playing for the first time for the national once the player has arrived at Spain.

As explanatory variables, we include four groups of variables: those associated with the *age* and *year of the arrival*, with a quadratic profile for the effect of the latter; the usual position in the tactical scheme of the team (*Position*) distinguishing four categories (goalkeeper, defender, midfielder and forward); the *continent of birth* (Latin America, a European country of one of the Big-5 leagues in Europe, rest of Europe and rest of the world), and the *club of arrival* (FC Barcelona, Real Madrid, Atlético de Madrid, a second (young) team and any other club). The estimates are reported in Table 12.4, for three different samples: the whole sample, for those born in Latin America and for those born in Europe.

As expected, the age of arrival has a negative effect on the probability of playing for the national team for the first time. This is effect is reproduced both for the subsample of Latin-American and European players, although the negative age effect is more important in the case of players born in Latin America. Additionally, there is an annual trend in this probability captured by the quadratic profile for this variable (not in the case of Europe which is linear). The effect is an inverted U profile for the whole sample and the Latin-American subsample (with a maximum at 2003 and 2000, respectively) and positive for the subsample of Europe (the more recent the arrival the higher the probability of playing for the national team). The profile for Latin American players could reflect that the frequency of recent arrivals is higher compared to the past and that most of these arrivals have not the same quality on average than the previous ones because there are less institutional constraints. This could be also associated with the results that this probability is lower for those born in Latin America than for those born in any other continent.

Table 12.4 Estimates of count data models of the number of caps after arriving at Spanish football

	Probit first cap after arrival		
	Full sample	Latin America	Europa
Age at arrival	-0.096**	-0.106**	-0.085*
Year arrival	3.887**	3.555**	0.018**
Year arrival squared	-0.001**	-0.001**	
Position (Ref.: Goalkeeper)			
Defender	-0.140	0.249	0.019
Midfielder	-0.062	-0.199	0.170
Forward	-0.148	-0.300	0.005
Continent of birth (Ref.: Latin America)			
Big-5 Europe	0.167		
Rest of Europe	0.167		
Rest of the world	0.551**		
Club of arrival (Ref.: Other clubs)			
Second team	-0.341**	-0.210	-0.590**
Real Madrid	0.746**	0.874*	0.711
FC Barcelona	-0.041	0.048	0.406
Atlético de Madrid	0.459**	0.660*	0.143
Constant	-1.904**	-3.598	-15.512**
Sample size	1231	630	472
log L	-651.93	-336.38	-266.11
Wald test (d.f.)	124.10 (12)	57.94 (10)	41.70 (9)

Notes
* Significant at 5%
** Significant at 1%

This effect is significant a 10% level for Europe and at a 1% level for the rest of the world.

In the three estimated models, the position in the field of the player, even for the goalkeepers, does not seem to affect the probability of playing for the national team. This could be a consequence of some measurement error in the definition of this variable (*Position*), except for goalkeepers.

We find some significant effects for the clubs of arrival, particularly in the model estimated with the whole sample. Playing for Real Madrid and/or Atlético de Madrid seems to increase the probability of playing for the national team compared to playing in any other team. Surprisingly, this is not the case for FC Barcelona. When the arrival team is the second (youth) team of one of the top clubs the probability is reduced. This variable is capturing (potential) quality and exposure to the media and this positive effect for the big clubs seem to be according to these features. The results are reproduced in the Latin-American players subsample, but only in terms of the point estimates and not in terms of significance. This could be reflecting the smaller sample size in this subsample and also the fact mentioned earlier that because the American market is the largest foreign market for the Spanish football, the elimination of institutional constraints translates also in an average decrease of the quality of the players who arrive to the Spanish football.

Conclusions

In this paper we have analysed how the presence of foreign players, in particular Latin American players, in the Spanish football has evolved through time by using a new data set which has been constructed specifically for this empirical exercise. A descriptive analysis which has been complemented with the estimation of an econometric model allows us to capture the influence of the institutional setting on the size of the inflows of foreign players, including the dynamics of its impact, and to show how the heterogeneity of the composition of these flows is also changing through time

Additionally we devoted specific attention to the analysis of the career of those foreign players once they have arrived in Spain. In particular, how the probability of playing for the national team afterwards is associated with some characteristics of those players. Age, year of arrival and the club they were playing in Spain have a significant effect on the probability of being capped for the first time after playing in Spain.

This is preliminary analysis of this topic using this data set. There are some limitations associated with the estimation of econometric models we use. In the case of the model for the frequency of arrivals we are not considering the macroeconomic conditions in the country of origin and Spain and the economic relevance of the football industry through time. With respect to the microeconometric model for the probability of being capped for the first time, some performance variables should be included and the analysis could be extended by looking the number of caps after arriving in Spain using count data models.

Overcoming these limitations is part of the future agenda of research in this topic, which includes also the analysis of the transfer fees paid which are included in this data set for the most recent period. Apart from that, this information can be used to help to analyse some relevant economic questions, not specific of sports economics, as it has been done by Kleven et al. (2013) when analysing the effect of tax rates on international migration by using data on European football players.

References

Barajas, A., & Rodríguez, P. (2010). Spanish football club finances: Crisis and player salaries. *International Journal of Sport Finance*, 5(1), 52–62.
BDFutbol. (n.d.). *Data set of Spanish football*. www.bdfutbol.com/en/t/t.html
Binder, J. J., & Findlay, M. (2012). The effects of Bosman ruling on national and club teams in Europe. *Journal of Sports Economics*, 13(2), 107–129.
Carreras, M., & García, J. (2018). TV rights, financial inequality and competitive balance in European football: Evidence from the English Premier League and the Spanish LaLiga. *International Journal of Sport Finance*, 13, 201–224.

Dejonghe, T., & Van Opstal, W. (2010). Competitive balance between national leagues in European football after the Bosman case. *Rivista de Diritto Ed Economia Dello Sport*, 6(2), 41–61.

Footballdatabase.eu. (n.d.). www.footballdatabase.eu/en/

García, J., & Rodríguez, P. (2002). The determinants of football match attendance revisited. Empirical evidence from the Spanish football league'. *Journal of Sports Economics*, 3, 18–38.

García, J., & Rodríguez, P. (2006). The economics of Soccer in Spain. In W. Andreff & S. Szymanski (Eds.), *Handbook on the economics of sport* (pp. 474–485). Edward Elgar Publisher.

García, J., Rodríguez, P., & Todeschini, F. (2020). The demand for the characteristics of football matches: A hedonic price approach'. *Journal of Sports Economics*, 21, 688–704.

García del Barrio, P., & Szymanski, S. (2009). Goal! profit maximization versus win maximization in soccer. *Review of Industrial Organization*, 34, 45–68.

Kesenne, S. (2006). The Bosman case and European football. In W. Andreff & S. Szymanski (Eds.), *Handbook on the economics of sport* (pp. 636–642). Edward Elgar Publisher.

Kleven, H. J., Landais, C., & Saez, E. (2013). Taxation and international migration of superstars: Evidence from the European football market. *American Economic Review*, 103(5), 1892–1924.

Norback, P-J., Olsson, M., & Persson, L. (2021). Talent development and labour market integration in European football. *The World Economy*, 44(2), 367–408.

Ortega, J. A. (2016). Jugadores extranjeros, en constante expansión. *Cuadernos de Fútbol*, 72. www.cihefe.es/cuadernosdefutbol/2016/01/jugadores-extranjeros-en-constante-expansion/

Radoman, M. (2017). Labor market implications of institutional changes in European football: The Bosman ruling and its effect on productivity and career duration of players. *Journal of Sports Economics*, 18(7), 651–672.

Royuela, V., & Gásquez, R. (2019). On the influence of foreign players on the success of football clubs. *Journal of Sports Economics*, 20(5), 718–741.

Chapter 13

The Portuguese football league 'Liga Portugal'

Thiago Santos, Pedro Fatela, Luís Vilar, and Bernardo Gonçalves

Introduction

Portuguese football has been increasingly recognised around the world. There is no doubt that players such as Cristiano Ronaldo, Figo, or Rui Costa have played an important role in the achievement of this level of notoriety. In addition, hosting the UEFA EURO in 2004 and having won this competition in 2016 has consolidated the country as one of the great representatives of European football. In 2021, Portugal was ranked in 5th place among FIFA men's football clubs, and in fourth place in the ranking of National Teams in UEFA. In terms of team management, names such as coach José Mourinho (FC Internazionale Milano, Real Madrid FC, Associazione Sportiva Roma), André Villas-Boas (Chelsea FC, Tottenham Hotspur FC), or Paulo Fonseca (Shakhtar Donetsk FC, Associazione Sportiva Roma) have also been responsible for leveraging Portugal as one of the powerful 'hubs' for exporting coaches to the other leagues in Europe.

Although some of the past and current performances of coaches and players from Portugal show a promising scenario, these outcomes do not reflect the standard or level of competition that other football leagues have in Europe, such as the 'big five' (Premier League in England, Bundesliga in Germany, La Liga in Spain, Serie A in Italy, and Ligue 1 in France). For example, one of the issues that separate the Portuguese Football League from other leagues in Europe is the sources of funding of the league which over the years have shown great disparity between historical successful teams with other less successful teams in the League. During the 2018–2019 season approximately 32% of the Portuguese clubs' total revenue came from broadcasting and media rights, followed by sponsorship or commercial agreements with 24%, UEFA awards with 20%, and revenues from away games with 15%. A large portion of this revenue has been the work of the three major national clubs, Futebol Clube do Porto, S. L. é Benfica, and Sporting Clube de Portugal (Gouveia & Pereira, 2021). The ratio between the earnings of the highest television rights received by the most important clubs in Portugal is more than 15 times that of the median club in Portugal (Gouveia & Pereira, 2021). Furthermore, according to Gouveia and Pereira (2021), although the Portuguese championship in the 2018–2019 season had the seventh-largest market for television

DOI: 10.4324/9781003197003-13

rights in European (a total of €143 million) these numbers are significantly much lower than those of the Premier League in England (€2.9 billion) or the La Liga in Spain (€1.3 billion).

Founded in 1978 with the name of the Portuguese Professional Football League (LPFP, n.d.-a), the present-day Liga Portugal is responsible for managing the professional football competitions with 18 professional clubs in the 'First' League, and 20 professional clubs in the 'Second' League. The mission of such an organisation is to ensure excellence in the organisation of the football competitions in Portugal (LPFP, 2017). In its statutes, the organisation's vision aims to become one of the most important football leagues in Europe. It is the role of Liga Portugal to organise and regulate football competitions of a professional nature; ensure and defend the interests of the stakeholders associated with the league, and exercise disciplinary control and the supervision of its members. In addition, the league thrives to develop best practices and conduct regular training in matters of organisation, management, and integrity to improve the level of competition and the overall organisation of the league's activities. In its strategy for the development of football, Liga Portugal aims to increase the league notoriety, its transparency, the valorisation of Portuguese football, as well as to accelerate the digitalisation and internationalisation of Liga Portugal and its related products.

The past of 'Liga Portugal'

The political revolution that took place in Portugal in 1974 and the changes that this revolution brought to Portuguese society contributed to fostering the professionalisation of football clubs and professional athletes in Portugal (Marie, 2021). To respond to the creation of the Players Union (founded in 1972), managers of football clubs participating in the main national competition felt the need to develop an association capable of reconciling their interests and aspirations, as well as increasing clubs' capability to participate in the direction of the league to leverage government's intervention. Thus, on February 3, 1978, the Portuguese League of Football Clubs was founded (LPFP, n.d.-a).

As seen, the emergence of Liga Portugal is directly related to the progressive professionalisation of football, which resulted in football clubs and other stakeholders facing new challenges, particularly in terms of contracts between club management and players. However, during the mid-1980s, a group of club leaders, also known as the 'Presidents' Movement', emerged and began to tackle and find solutions to common problems such as players transfer that affected the operations of the League. This movement first included all the Presidents of the 'first' National Division, which represented the original group of leaders of the National Association of Clubs. Later, the Portuguese Confederation of Football Clubs joined the movement, consisting of some dissidents' clubs from the first National Division as well as clubs from other divisions.

In the 1980s, a meeting of these two associations was held at the Buçaco Palace Hotel (later known as the 'Buçaco meeting'). In that meeting, leaders of both associations decided to strengthen the League of Clubs and end both existing associations. As a result, one employer's association was created (LPFP, n.d.). Then, in 1991 the association changed its name from the Portuguese League of Football Clubs to the Portuguese Professional Football League or LPFP (LPFP, 2017). After this change, Liga Portugal started to promote and protect the interests of the clubs as well as the organisation of the competitions that were under its patronage. Thus, during that time, the autonomy of professional competitions became officially recognised for the first time with the entry into force of the Basic Law of the Sports System (currently the Basic Law of Physical Activity and Sport), a law that defines the policies for the development of physical activity and sports in Portugal.

In 1995, when Jorge Nuno Pinto da Costa, President of Futebol Clube do Porto presided over Liga Portugal, the professional championships in Portugal was organised for the first time (LPFP, n.d.-a). At that time, the League played a dual role: on the one hand, it acted as an employer association, and, on the other hand, it was the governing body for professional football in Portugal responsible for the regulation, organisation, and management of professional competitions of the Portuguese League I (highest level of professional football); Portuguese League II (second tier of professional football) and League Cup (event created in 2008 and disputed by group stage and qualifiers of all professional football clubs).

Although the professionalisation of the management of Portuguese football had a important role in the development process of football in Portugal, the league still lacks competitive balance. Interestingly, from 1934 to 2021, the only clubs to win the Portuguese League were S.L. é Benfica (holder of 37 national championships), Futebol Clube do Porto (29-time winner), Sporting Clube de Portugal (19 championship titles), and, finally, Boavista Futebol Clube and Clube de Futebol 'Os Belenenses' (each with one national championship title). In other words, in 88 seasons of the Portuguese Football League only five clubs (from the districts of Lisbon and Porto) have won the national title. However, it is expected that once the centralisation of the broadcasting rights for the professional championships of the 2028–2029 season is implemented, this might change as other clubs, besides the 'Big Three', will also compete for the title of national champion.

Liga Portugal began with eight clubs, and since its first edition in 1934 it has grown to 20 clubs in 1987. Currently, Liga Portugal consists of 18 clubs, while many clubs claim that 16 clubs would provide greater competitive equality in the championship. Every season the top scorer award in Liga Portugal is awarded to the player who score the most goals during the competition. From the beginning, several players have received this award more than once. Some of the best goal-scorer players include names such as Peyroteo, Yazalde, Eusébio da Silva Ferreira, Fernando Gomes and Mário Jardel. Eusébio won this award seven times, and Sporting's player Yazalde scored the most number of goals in a single season, 46 goals during the 1973–1974 season.

Currently, Liga Portugal exercises its powers as an autonomous body of the Portuguese Football Federation, within the framework of the Basic Law of the Sport System. It promotes and defends the common interests of its members, manages the affairs related to the organisation and practice of professional football and its competitions. In addition, it organises and regulates the professional competitions that are disputed within the scope of the Portuguese Football Federation (LPFP, 2017). Under its Statutes, Liga Portugal is today an association of private law. Accordingly, it is governed by the respective statutes and regulations of the League.

Liga Portugal and the impact on the development of football

According to Coelho and Tiesler (2007), Portuguese football manages to attract public attention largely due to media coverage and an unusual connection between football and the political environment that takes place within the national and local representations, state institutions, and political leaders. In Portugal, football is undoubtedly the most important and popular sport and the only truly professional one (Magueta et al., 2015). No other sport even approaches football in several key indicators such as attendance, television rights, players' wages, sponsorships, etc. But despite Liga Portugal's vision to establish the Portuguese league as one of the most powerful football leagues in Europe by ensuring the excellence of the sport and its economic and financial sustainability, there is still a long way to go in terms of growth and development.

As Magueta et al. (2015) put it, when a league lacks competitive balance and winners and losers are known early on in the tournament, that league tends to lose the attention of the fans (lower attendance, lower television rates, etc.). In this sense, it has been suggested that one of the most important features that attract supporters to attend the stadium is the level of competitiveness of the match and the show provided by the clubs that play in that match. Data published in 2018 by the CIES Football Observatory (Gouveia & Pereira, 2021) analysing the competitive balance in 24 European competitions over ten seasons (2008 to 2018) places the professional football championship in Portugal as 'the least competitive' when comparing the ratio between the number of points earned by the winner of the national champion with the number of points played. For example, from 2009 to 2018, the champion of Portugal won 84.4% of the points. One plausible explanation for this phenomenon is the distribution of revenues arising from television broadcasting rights as well as other sources (Gouveia & Pereira, 2021). In Portugal, this distribution tends to favour teams that do well in the previous season as opposed to conducting an equal distribution of resources among all teams.

Despite the lack of competitiveness of the League, over the last two decades, Liga Portugal has fluctuated between sixth and seventh place in the UEFA club rankings. This means, Portuguese teams still benefit from the financial return of participating in the UEFA competitions. Every year the winner and the runner-up of the league are guaranteed their presence in the UEFA Champions League group stage, which can also be accessed by the club that ranks third in the league if it gets through the third qualifying round and the play-offs. The fourth-ranked team qualifies for the Europa League group stage and so does the winner of the Portuguese Football Federation (FPF) cup. It is important to note that the circumstances in which Portuguese teams have accessed UEFA competitions have been very inconsistent. As a result, this has had direct consequences on the financial return as well as the level of competitiveness of some of the teams that participate in Liga Portugal. First, the economic gains of the UEFA Champions League are quite uncertain and limited in most seasons to one or two clubs. Second, and regardless of the recognised talent hub within Liga Portugal, clubs are often forced to sell some of their best players, to achieve financial balance.

When comparing the market value (as of July 2021) players in Liga Portugal with the top five leagues in the UEFA rankings, Ligue 1 in France, which ranks fifth and represents the immediate competitor of Liga Portugal, has a market value three times higher of Liga Portugal (€3.59 bn versus €1.22 bn). In the case of the English Premier League, which ranks 1st, its market value is almost 8 times the value of Liga Portugal (€8.7 bn versus €1.22 bn) (LPFP, 2021). These differences determine a structural set of economic and financial challenges for many clubs in Liga Portugal which seem to limit the league's growth. Nowadays, and despite Liga Portugal showing important efforts in boosting their financial and economic growth with positive results of +€1,26 mm for the fifth season in a row (2019–2020), these efforts have shown to be insufficient for the League to achieve a more competitive league.

Despite Liga Portugal being a league that is not among the top five in Europe, it significantly contributes to the export of talent to European football (e.g. João Felix player of S.L. é Benfica sold to Club Atlético Madrid in 2020 for €127 M). The League also serves as a gateway to the European football market. For example, the number of foreign players who competed in the 2020–2021 edition of Liga Portugal reached 305, representing 57.3% of the total number of players who played in the tournament. In recent seasons (i.e., 2018–2019, 2019–2020, and 2020–2021), Brazil is the country that exported the most numbers of footballers to Liga Portugal representing 43% of the total foreign players who competed during these editions (Transfermarkt, 2021).

According to a 2019–2020 report produced by Liga Portugal, the 'Advertising Value Equivalent' (AVE) showed consistent growth throughout those years. In 2021, the AVE represented €1,322 bn, which is a 13,1% increase from 2020 (LPFP, 2021). This growth was achieved without considering the loss of attendance in the stadiums due to the COVID 19 pandemic. In 2021, the last 10 matchdays took place without fans in the stadiums, and the average attendance per match decreased by 32,7% (i.e., 7,864 people per match). Match attendance is certainly an important handicap for Liga Portugal. In 2017–2018, the average attendance to football matches was 11.945 people, quite lower when compared to Ligue 1 in France (i.e., 22,575), La Liga in Spain (i.e., 26,771), or the English Premier League (i.e., 38,495). Moreover, these differences can be even more pronounced when attendance is presented in terms of percentages of the maximum attendance in each league, where Liga Portugal reached only 31%, La Liga in Spain 70%, Ligue 1 in France 71%, and the English Premier League 96%.

As for revenue, according to the 2019 Annual Review of Football Finance (Deloitte, 2019), Liga Portugal had revenues of €431 million, which that year ranked 9th in the European Leagues. In comparative terms, the difference between the revenues of Liga Portugal and Ligue 1 is almost one-fifth (€1,692 bn). Moreover, these differences are even larger when compared to La Liga (i.e. €3,073 bn), or the Premier League (i.e., €5,440 bn). Importantly, the same report noted that despite a revenue increase of 18% in Liga Portugal, there was a growing polarisation in revenues that affected the competitive balance. Clubs that are part of Liga Portugal are not among the most valuable football clubs in world football. In 2021, none of the 'big three' clubs in la Liga Portugal reached the top twenty. S.L. é Benfica reached the 31st position with a value of €314.00 M, Football Clube do Porto reached the 35th position with a value of €281.60 M, and Sporting Clube de Portugal reached the 43rd position with a value of €225.90 M (Transfermarkt, 2021).

On the other hand, from 2019 to 2020, Liga Portugal and its member clubs contributed to the overall economy of the country by generating a volume of direct (e.g. merchandising sales) and indirect (e.g. spending on food at the match) businesses with revenues of more than €750 million, or about 0.26% of the national wealth (LPFP, 2021). Additionally, according to the LPFP report (2021), Liga Portugal employs 2,433 people. Of this number, 1,129 are players, 217 coaches, and 1,087 are employees in the areas of football support and management. During the 2019–2020 season, footballers were the stakeholders in the League with the highest remuneration, earning a total aggregate value in salaries of €244 million.

In terms of the impact of Liga Portugal in the media, some clubs have seen a significant increase in the number of followers on social media, due to a phenomenon linked to the hiring of renowned foreign players who already have celebrity status. An example of this phenomenon was the hiring in 2015 of Iker Casillas, former goalie of the Spanish National football team and Real Madrid, by Futebol Clube do Porto (Goalpoint, 2015). Similarly, the representation of Portuguese brands through well-known players in online platforms is Portuguese footballer Cristiano Ronaldo, arguably one of the most popular footballers portrayed in traditional media and one of the most featured brands on social media (Hylton & Lawrence, 2015). In this regard, the Liga Portugal, Portuguese clubs, commercial brands, and sponsors have all tried to use the online context as an ally in an increasingly dynamic and competitive market. Thus, in recent years, investment in online platforms has been one of Liga Portugal's primary strategies. Examples of this are the 'e-league' (i.e., an e-sport football league with the main Liga Portugal clubs competing in the 'First' league) and the enhancement of interaction with online fans, inside and outside the stadium. The development and promotion of the 'e-fan' concept is proof of Liga Portugal's strife to be associated with the latest developments in the digital entertainment world. As such, there is a local and global trend towards associating modern football with online consumption (Dixon, 2013).

In 2017, *Bleacher Report* (bleacherreport.com) published a ranking of the most popular football leagues in the world (Matchett, 2017). Criteria for this ranking included the newsworthiness of each league and its reputation for producing young and exciting players, total amount related to transfer rates, average goals per match in the league, the top 'eleven most valuable players', and fan attendance. As a result of this analysis, the *Bleacher Report* website ranked Liga Portugal as the seventh most entertaining European football championship, due to the reputation of the young players in the league as well as the high ranking achieved in the eleven most valuable players' category. However, when the impact of the international market is considered, particularly Liga Portugal's television revenue, this category was ranked well below the most important football leagues in Europe. In other words, outside Portugal, most people are not interested in watching the Portuguese football league. As a result of this, Liga Portugal's strategic plan for the 2019–2023 quadrennium (LPFP, n.d.-b) has focused on developing strategies and actions that contribute to boosting the brand and competition at an international level as a top priority. The title of this plan has been labelled 'Pathway to Evolution' or Caminho da (R)Evolução.

The future of 'Liga Portugal'

Liga Portugal's future and success are inherently connected with the growth and success of professional football in Portugal. Thereby, the ability to forecast and prepare the development of Portuguese professional football is a fundamental task of Liga Portugal, which must be continuously assessed and improved. In this regard, Liga Portugal's strategic plans for the 2015–2019 and 2019–2023 quadrennium, represent a global and assertive view of what must be achieved, and what tools can be used or conceived to that effect.

The more recent Liga Portugal's strategic plan (i.e. 2019–2023), projected the future of Portuguese professional football based on the performance of the previous quadrennium (i.e. 2015–2019). During that period, Liga Portugal developed a strategy that intended to create value by guaranteeing the Liga's sustainability, adopting successful practices of foreign leagues, aiming for the profitability of the show, and attracting fans and sponsors due to the credibility of the business (LPFP, n.d.-b). Furthermore, this action plan was founded on four pillars: rigor, talent, aggregation, and professionalism.

During this period of consolidation and development, Liga Portugal prepared for the quadrennium of 2019–2023, by strongly reaffirming and embracing their mission and vision, and Liga Portugal's determining values: credibility, talent, spectacle, and aggregation. Through these values, competition, business, and management are to be developed in a symbiotic manner, supporting all strategic purposes (i.e. competitiveness, internationalisation, sustainability, innovation, integrity, strategy, valorisation, dialog, business, governance, and reflection).

Hence, according to Liga Portugal's official strategic plan (LPFP, n.d.), the future of Liga Portugal will involve five strategic axes: (1) Liga Portugal's affirmation, (2) valorisation of competitions, (3) Portuguese football industrialisation, (4) digital enhancement, and (5) Liga Portugal's internationalisation. Therefore, the first step to developing Portuguese professional football is to build an environment where transparency, responsible management, professionalism, and monitoring are encouraged and duly appreciated. Apart from this, and following the logic of the strategic axis for Liga Portugal's affirmation, the reinforcement of communication on various traditional and digital platforms also seeks to place the league on a prominent level within the European football scenario. This means, betting on increasing its awareness and brand equity. In the second axis, competitions must be improved, and for that, regulation and monitoring should be constant, particularly regarding critical aspects such as financial control and fair play, licensing, sports bets, and game technologies. Third, Portuguese professional football must create a strong and fruitful relationship with the consumers (i.e. fans). Only by engaging the fans will it be possible to create value and boost the business of football. This means the successful adoption of several measures becomes critical to achieve fan engagement. Some of these measures include the reduction of violence in sport; modernisation of sport facilities particularly in the areas of security, comfort, and easy access to stadiums; the control of ticket pricing; and the enhancement in the quality of football broadcasting on TV. The fourth step is to improve Liga Portugal's digital department, seeing that this is crucial for communication, marketing and branding. To do so, Liga Portugal will need to develop synergies with big players in the digital field, who will enable the development of an e-commerce platform, to reinforce e-sports and gaming, to increase the international value of the e-league, and to create and bring to the fore the concept of the e-fan. Equally important, and once professional competitions have become more attractive to the masses, the concept of internationalisation is considered to be the main process whereby income sources may be diversified and enhanced. The internationalisation axis includes the implementation of several actions and strategies that will be all launched by 2023. These actions and strategies include the creation of an Internationalisation Department, the establishment of Liga Portugal's stores in Portugal's main airports, the use of ambassadors to promote Professional Football, the creation of fan zones within Portuguese communities, the promotion of the League Cup internationalisation (e.g. final-four abroad), and, the creation of international friendly competitions (e.g. Iberic Cup). Importantly, throughout this internationalisation process, Liga Portugal intends to adopt La Liga as their strategic benchmark.

More recently, both the Liga Portugal and the Portuguese Football Federation have been trying to find solutions to bring the attractiveness of its competitive model closer to that of the main leagues in Europe and the rest of the world. The most prominent theme in this scenario has been the centralisation of broadcasting rights.

This model has shown itself to be very promising within the sports industry if we consider, for example, the revenue obtained from the broadcasting centralisation rights that are common not only in the North American leagues (NFL 2014–2021,

€7 billion; NBA 2016–2025, €2.4 billion; and MLB 2014–2021, €1.7 billion) (EY, 2021) but also in the European context (Premier League 2019–2022, €2.8 billion; Ligue 1 2016–2020, €900 million, La Liga 2019–2022, €1.9 billion; Bundesliga 2017–2021, €1.5 billion; and Serie A 2018–2021, €1.4 billion (EY, 2021).

This scenario has allowed these leagues to achieve greater equity in the process of distributing revenue arising from contracts and broadcasting rights negotiations. In the Portuguese context, it is expected that a centralised distribution will allow, for example, the increase in the competitiveness of Liga Portugal based on the greater capacity of teams to improve their operations (i.e. sport facilities, equipment, technologies, etc.) as a result of these revenues.

Another likely significant impact of this initiative may be seen in the interaction with consumers of sport as a product and in the way the bundles are sold by the leagues that adopt the centralisation of broadcasting rights. Thus, the creation of exclusive experiences through different channels of broadcasting tends to be a differentiating factor for the product. For example, trading with specialised streaming platform services could generate different and exclusive experiences if compared with more traditional media. This form of brand management could strategically enhance the interaction with different stakeholders of the sport of football in Portugal, thus enhancing the awareness, transparency, and, brand equity of the league and Portuguese football in the world.

Conclusions and implications

Although promising, football in Portugal is still far from the major football leagues in Europe. The three main sources of revenue for clubs are television rights, commercial, and ticketing, which are heavily influenced by the quality of the product (i.e. of football).

Portuguese football nurtures a culture of low quality focused on the logic that when the club wins, the merit is in the training process; when it loses, it's the fault of others. In this scenario, there is a need for a greater competitive balance in the matches and a more equal distribution of revenue obtained from television rights, which will give smaller clubs a greater chance of competing with the bigger ones.

Continuing to focus on results means continuing to rely on revenue from player sales. This strategy is not only a high-risk management decision in absolute misalignment with UEFA's recommendations but also an impediment to high performance. It is impossible to keep the team's performance at high levels by selling (and not retaining) talent from one's squad.

According to Vilar (2021), in the 1990s Portuguese football was able to create a Portuguese player model, and in the 2000s it was able to create a Portuguese coach model. It is critical that today, a Portuguese football model may also emerge. In a globalisation era, it has become increasingly necessary for the business model of leagues and clubs to possess strategies of internationalisation, interaction with fans, and, above all, competitiveness and a healthy financial balance. In this way, when clubs' operating revenues increase they are bound to have a greater capacity to recruit better players, build more competitive squads and obtain better results.

The Liga Portugal is seen to play a fundamental role in this scenario as the foremost promoter of professional football competitions in Portugal. Any future strategy that aims to develop and improve Portuguese football, must focus on maximising the economic and sporting value, increasing its social impact to acquire greater notoriety and prominence not only in Portugal but also should aim to reach a global audience.

References

CIES. (2018). *Competitive balance: A spatio-temporal comparison*. CIES Football Observatory. https://football-observatory.com/IMG/sites/mr/mr40/en/

Coelho, J. N., & Tiesler, N. C. (2007). The paradox of the Portuguese game: The omnipresence of football and the absence of spectators at matches. *Soccer & Society, 8*(4), 578–600.

Deloitte. (2019). *Annual review of football finance of 2019*. https://www2.deloitte.com/global/en/pages/about-deloitte/articles/annual-review-of-football-finance.html

Dixon, K. (2013). *Consuming football in late modern life*. Ashgate Publishing Company.

EY. (2021). *Estudo internacional sobre direitos audiovisuais desportivos*. www.ligaportugal.pt/pt/epocas/20212022/publicacoes/estudo-internacional-sobre-direitos-audiovisuais-desportivos/

Goalpoint. (2015). *Casillas lança Porto na liderança das redes sociais*. http://goalpoint.pt/blog/futebolnacional/casillas-lanca-porto-na-lideranca-das-redes-social_22107

Gouveia, C., & Pereira, R. (2021). Professional football in Portugal: Preparing to resume after the COVID-19 pandemic. *Soccer & Society, 22*(1–2), 103–114.

Hylton, K., & Lawrence, S. (2015). Reading Ronaldo: Contingent whiteness in the football media. *Soccer & Society, 16*(5–6), 765–782.

LPFP. (2017). *Statutes of the Portuguese professional football league*. www.ligaportugal.pt/media/7979/estatutos.pdf

LPFP. (2021). *Portuguese professional football yearbook 2019–20*. www.ligaportugal.pt/pt/epocas/20202021/publicacoes/anuario-do-futebol-profissional-portugues-2019-20/

LPFP. (n.d.-a). *History of 'Liga Portugal'*. www.ligaportugal.pt/pt/40anos/

LPFP. (n.d.-b). *Caminho da (R)Evolução*. www.ligaportugal.pt/pt/paginas/conteudos/projectos-2019-23/

Magueta, D., Gonçalo, S., & Pego, P. (2015). Could fewer teams make a league more competitive? The Portuguese football league case. *Athens Journal of Sports, 2*(2), 99–110.

Marie, P. (2021). Revolução, sindicalismo e futebol. O sindicato dos jogadores profissionais de futebol durante o processo revolucionário português, 1974–1976. *Ler História* (78), 179–198.

Matchett, K. (2017). Ranking the most entertaining leagues in world football. *Bleacher Report*. https://bleacherreport.com/articles/2691880-ranking-the-most-entertaining-leagues-in-world-football

Transfermarkt. (2021). www.transfermarkt.pt/

Vilar, L. (2021). Queremos uma reforma urgente no futebol português. *O Observador*. https://observador.pt/opiniao/queremos-uma-reforma-urgente-no-futebol-portugues/

Chapter 14

La Roja, Real Madrid, and Barça

A Historic Perspective

Carles Murillo Fort and Francisco Puig

Introduction

Football, or soccer as it is known to Americans, is an activity that allows for different types of analysis. Perhaps the most common are those framed in the sporting and social spheres and are basically published in the press. However, studies of its institutional, political, and economic dimensions are becoming increasingly important, increasing its academic interest. This multidisciplinary and eclectic character leads us to adopt a historical-temporal perspective and a methodology based on the consultation of secondary sources to study the Spanish national football team (La Roja).

Football is a popular mass sport all over the world. That production grew exponentially in Spain when it achieved the Triple Crown (2008–2012). A multitude of articles and books have been written about the Spanish national football team and its performance. From a review of the most recent publications, we can distinguish at least three types of books: a) those that review the national team chronologically, combining sports information and anecdotes; b) those that analyse what its two most successful coaches (Luis Aragonés and Vicente Del Bosque) did and how they did it, and c) those that study the social impact of the La Roja phenomenon.

This chapter intersects between these three types of work and, in an original way, tries to shed light on the influence of the binomial competition-cooperation between R. Madrid and FC Barcelona, or what we call the Barça effect had on the achievement of the treble. For this purpose, we have structured this work into four parts. Following this introduction, we present the background and evolution of La Roja, highlighting the role of both clubs. The third section studies the irregular influence and trajectories that both institutions have had. The fourth section analyses the Barça effect in the sporting sphere and the game of La Roja. The chapter concludes with some reflections on the role that the national team coaches had in taking advantage of this situation and integrating them.

La Roja: background and evolution

According to the Real Federación Española de Futbol (RFEF) archives, the Spanish national football team was created in 1920 (RFEF, 2021). It comprises Spanish

DOI: 10.4324/9781003197003-14

nationality players representing Spain in the various competitions grouped under the Union of European Football Associations (UEFA) and the Fédération Internationale de Football Association (FIFA). They have used 822 players, mostly from teams in the Spanish Primera Division (or La Liga), and 57 coaches. According to the information gathered in that portal, that national team had played 715 matches up to Euro 2020, winning 418 (58%) and drawing 166 (23%). Its latest achievement was to reach the semifinals of the recent European Championship (July 2021) held in various venues and under pandemic conditions, after drawing two matches (Sweden and Poland), winning three (Slovakia, Croatia, and Switzerland), and losing on penalties to Italy.

The Spanish national football team has also been popularly known as 'La Furia Española' or 'La Furia Roja'. However, since 2008 it has been popularised as 'La Roja' thanks to its national coach Luis Aragonés and the television network Cuatro (Burns, 2012). That nickname corresponded to the desire of its then coach for greater fan identification with the national team, just as the national teams of Uruguay 'la celeste,' Argentina 'la Albiceleste' Italy 'la Azzurra,' Brazil 'la Canarinha' or France, 'les Bleus' were already popularly recognised.

The history of La Roja cannot be understood without considering the two leading Spanish football clubs, which are among the ten best in the world, Real Madrid and Fútbol Club Barcelona. Since the beginning of La Roja, Madrid and Barça (also known) have been the leading direct and indirect suppliers of players to the national team. According to our estimates, over the years, the 22 players called up or selected for each Championship, on average, nine have come directly from these clubs. However, if we classify the players according to their football school (quarries), on average, there have been ten.

In addition to that sporting background, as institutions, both clubs have significantly influenced the management and organisation of the RFEF since they concentrate the majority of Spanish fans (Real Madrid, 38% and FC Barcelona, 25%) (Llaneras, 2014). Moreover, Madrid and Barça are the second choices of other important fans such as Athletic Bilbao, Valencia C.F., or Betis Balompié, causing this Madrid-Barça binomial to attract almost exclusive media attention and overwhelmingly lead television audiences.

The polarisation of Spanish fans between the two clubs has different historical, political, and cultural reasons (Suarez, 2012). On the one hand, a tendency of Spanish society to identify with one side or the other, perhaps due to the Civil War (1936–1939). On the other hand, given the more significant presence of Barça fans in the periphery and the north, political-economic reasons could also be pointed out. Furthermore, there are also cultural issues, as the fans identify with different management models of these clubs (Murillo & Murillo, 2005). In any case, this rivalry has been very profitable for both clubs. As Neale (1964) and García (2019) argue, based on the Louis-Schmeling Paradox, the uncertainty of an outcome attracts spectators, while the certainty of victory drives them away.

Therefore, to compete better, both clubs have always tried to attract the most significant amount of talent in the market, but this has been in a balanced way that has materialised in 50/50 confrontations. This profitable rivalry is reflected in 'El Clasico' (the name given by fans worldwide to the football match between the two teams). This global event attracts 650 million spectators and brings both clubs large amounts of money in TV and advertising (Fitzpatrick, 2012).

Unlike other major European teams such as Germany or Italy, and similarly to England, the Netherlands, Portugal, or France, La Roja has evolved irregularly throughout its history, with three clear periods called the beginning, transition, and hegemony.

1 (1920–1999) is the period of introduction and growth of La Roja, as well as the period in which it recorded some great international successes such as winning its first European Championship in 1964 against Russia, but also the disappointment of elimination in the first round of the World Cup organised in Spain in 1982.

At the club level, this long period of 70 years has allowed Spanish football to go from being represented internationally almost exclusively by Real Madrid in the Champions League to being a benchmark to beat in all tournaments organised by UEFA. At the domestic level, Barça consolidated its position as the great rival in national competitions (Copa del Rey and La Liga), and other clubs such as Bilbao, Valencia, or At. de Madrid became established appearing from time to time as an alternative to the big two. This growing Madrid-Barça rivalry and the alternation offered by these other clubs was reflected in an increase in the international competitiveness of La Roja.

2 (1999–2006) is characterised as a stage without outstanding achievements and of transition. During this time, La Roja began to occupy important positions in the FIFA Ranking under coaches such as José Antonio Camacho and Iñaki Sáez, reaching third place (Figure 14.1). During these years, La Roja also

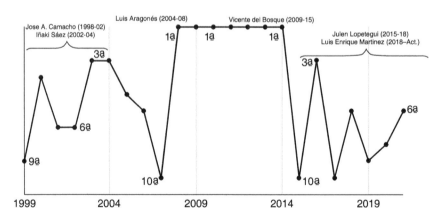

Figure 14.1 La Roja's position in the FIFA Ranking (1999–2021)
Source: Based on FIFA statistics (2021)

assimilated the critical changes in European competitions (UEFA and Champions League), the Bosman Law, the irruption of private television, the SAD Law, and the consequent professionalisation of Spanish football.

The Bosman Law established that European sportsmen and women were free to exercise their profession in any state of the European Union and did not count as foreigners. On the other hand, the arrival of private television channels in Spain allowed a technological improvement in sports broadcasting and a greater plurality of content, increasing the popularity of football. Another noteworthy aspect of this transition period was the change in the business model undergone by Spanish football. The SAD law and its revision in the sports law tried to promote the solvency of the clubs through external control, as well as their transformation from clubs to companies, inspired by the mercantilist model of the public limited companies. This transformation was carried out by all the Spanish clubs in the First and Second Divisions of La Liga, except for those that showed healthier financial balances, such as R. Madrid, F.C. Barcelona, Bilbao, and Osasuna. The first consequence of this was a change in the role of the fan, who went from being a member to a shareholder, and another was the professionalisation of football. At club level, the R. Madrid-Barcelona rivalry acquired a global character.

3) (2008–2012) a period in which something unprecedented was achieved, the Triple Crown: Euro 2008 and 2012, and the 2010 World Cup held in South Africa.

Those four years were of the hegemony of La Roja both in terms of results and play. La Roja occupied first place in the FIFA rankings, thus ratifying a resounding success in permanence and unbeaten levels. Beyond the role played by Madrid and Barça players, the success of La Roja was also due to other players from other Spanish clubs and to the two people who managed and led it, Aragonés and Del Bosque (García, 2008; Cubeiro & Gallardo, 2010; Suarez, 2012).

In short, La Roja would never have become what it has been without the support of Madrid and Barça, both for their contribution of players (half of them) and for the influence that both have exerted on the National Championship. However, the influence of both clubs has been unequal throughout this period. The following section is dedicated to their analysis.

Real Madrid and Barça: institutional and management differences

Real Madrid is one of the founders of the Spanish League. Together with FC Barcelona and Athletic Club de Bilbao, they make up the trio of teams that have always participated in the top division of that competition. The first sporting achievements date back to the seasons before the Spanish Civil War. Real Madrid CF managed to win the League (1932–1933 and 1934–1935 seasons) and the direct elimination tournament (cup tournament in 1934 and 1936). In its beginnings, the figure of Santiago Bernabéu (player and later president of the club) marked a memorable milestone in the annals of this institution.

As we noted earlier, the Franco dictatorship period was crucial in awakening an eternal rivalry between Real Madrid CF and FC Barcelona (Burns, 2012). Barça identified itself throughout this period, with the city and with Catalonia, without undermining its cosmopolitan, stately, and representative of the democratic, Europeanist and also nationalist tendencies of many of its members: 'at certain times, especially in the last twenty years of Francoism, this football club had acquired a symbolic value for the democratic aspirations, for the anti-centralist demands of the Catalans and also of many Spaniards. That is why there were thousands of Culés without a membership card, both in Barcelona and in the rest of Spain' (Murillo & Murillo, 2005).

Since 1943, Santiago Bernabéu led the Club Blanco uninterruptedly for 35 years, until it became a reference in world football, especially for its achievements in the first five editions of the recently created European Club Cup current UEFA Champions League in the 1950s. Under Bernabéu's presidency, the club built a new stadium that would later be named Santiago Bernabéu. In the meantime, Real Madrid CF won most of the Spanish League titles, some victories in the Cup tournament, and the European Cup, a situation repeated in the 1990s.

Another notable figure in this history is José Luis Núñez, who presided over Barça from 1978 to 2000. Núñez's management was impeccable in terms of cost containment and the club's asset value. At the same time, he was a timid president in terms of investment decisions in the sports field and, above all, in managing the change in the business model of professional football that was decisively taking shape on the international scene. From the social point of view, especially in his last period as the club's top manager, Núñez was determined to make two of the club's icons disappear: the figure of Johan Cruyff and the team that won the first European Cup in 1992 and, no less important, to make any vestige of care for the youth academy and local players disappear (Badía, 2003).

Figures 14.2 and Figure 14.3 illustrate the sporting results of the professional football teams of both institutions and those of their respective sports sections. The fluctuations observed in the number of official titles achieved (adding those obtained at national and international level) can be explained by a comprehensive and diverse set of factors of different types: institutional successes and crises (including the death by firing squad of FC Barcelona's president, Josep Suñol, in the summer of 1936 and the subsequent exile of the first-team squad), economic (derived from the miraculous requalification and sale of the land of Real Madrid's Ciudad Deportiva on Paseo de la Castellana in 2001, or the cost overrun in the construction of the Camp Nou inaugurated in 1957) and sporting.

In line with the transition stage of La Roja, both clubs have undergone substantial changes in their business models. On the one hand, there is the Real Madrid of the 'galacticos' era, whose architect was Florentino Pérez during his first period as president of the club. On the other hand, there is a period of decline suffered by Barça between 1998–2003 under the mandate of Joan Gaspar, which led to the election of Joan Laporta as president of the club.

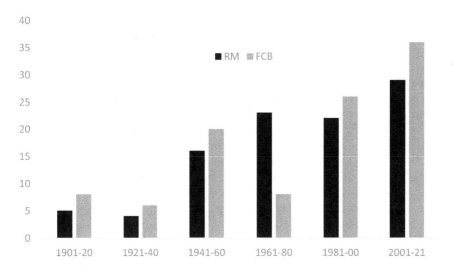

Figure 14.2 Official titles of the professional football team
Source: Based on the data reflected in the webpages of both clubs

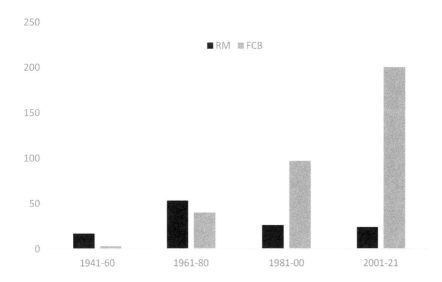

Figure 14.3 Official titles of the sports sections
Source: Based on the data reflected in the webpages of both clubs

Florentino Pérez's strategy was based on attracting the best talent on the international scene (Zinedine Zidane, Luis Figo, David Beckham, Ronaldo, and Roberto Carlos, among others) as well as retaining the best local talents who later also achieved sporting fame, such as Iker Casillas and Raúl González (Elberse & Quelch, 2008). Barça adopted a reactive and aimless strategy marked by a deep sporting, economic, and social crisis (Minguella, 2008).

The media and economic success of R. Madrid were not always accompanied in recent years by sporting results. This fact began to generate a certain opposition to the team model based on the stars of the moment and led to a change in the presidency of Madrid by Ramón Calderón in 2006–07. With the arrival of Ramón Calderón as president, there was a change in strategy to focus the composition of the Madrid squad on the idea of a team with greater attention to young talent and youth. Under Calderón, the priorities were reversed, with the desire to have a more technically balanced team gaining weight to the detriment of a formation led by a few elite players, which was Florentino Pérez's dream. On the other hand, together with the lack of titles that accompanied Gaspar's management, economic losses and the fracture in the social mass were utterly divided in their opinion about the institution's leadership. At this time, a new opposition current arose, grouped under the 'Blaugrana elephant' reference. This group promoted, shortly after, the formation of the candidacy for the presidency that won, under the leadership of Joan Laporta, the June 2003 elections. Laporta's project began with cleaning up the financial accounts, rational spending, and investment in managerial talent and institutional and sporting credibility (Soriano, 2013).

This turbulent period that both clubs experienced simultaneously was taken advantage of by clubs such as Valencia CF, which won the League in the 2001–2002 and 2003–2004 seasons. The Copa del Rey was also won by teams such as RCD Espanyol, Real Zaragoza, Deportivo de la Coruña and Real Betis. At the sporting level, these changes favoured a greater diversity among those selected in La Roja.

The globalisation of football, regulatory changes, and TVs brought about essential changes in the world of football, which both clubs faced unequally. Florentino Pérez returned to the presidency of R. Madrid in 2009. True to his strategy, he opted for big signings and the consolidation of the Real Madrid brand at a global level. According to Interbrand's ranking of the value of the best brands (several years), in its 2003 report, the Real Madrid brand was ranked seventh in its particular classification in Europe and Africa, ahead of other sports brands such as Adidas, Puma, or Ferrari. In 2010, it ranked first (and Barça second).

For their part, Barça and Joan Laporta consolidated a sports model in which the quarry played an important role and a game based on passing, combination, and teamwork that, in addition to spectacle, produced great triumphs (Murillo & Murillo, 2005). The victory in the classic of the first round of the 2004–2005 championship, with record attendance and ending with a historic 5–0 thrashing of Madrid, served to stage the 'transfer of power' (Segurola, 2004) and the beginning of what would be Barça's most glorious era.

In short, beyond the institutional and managerial differences that have been present over the years between the two clubs, what seems certain is that they have led to the Spanish football championship being positioned as the best in the world. According to the classification of the International Federation of Football History and Statistics (IFFHS, 2021), among the 19 League championships held from the years 2000 to 2018, the Spanish League was ranked as the Best League in the world in 13 of them. It uninterruptedly led that ranking from 2010 to 2018. Other leagues that in that period were also at the top and close to the Spanish League were the Italian (*Calcio*), English (*Premier*), and Brazilian (*Brasileirão*).

The Barça effect on La Roja's game (2006–2014)

The review of the history of La Roja up to this point has allowed us to understand how the rivalry between R. Madrid and Barça has favoured their level of international competitiveness, also that both clubs have benefited from this rivalry to the extent that it has positioned them as the undisputed references at a global level and, cause-effect, this has favoured the development of Spanish football. However, it is not clear what has been the contribution of each of these clubs during La Roja's most successful period. To this end, we will carry out two analyses, one of a sporting nature and focused on the results achieved by both clubs, and the other on the game, which analyses its players. The argument that underlies this analysis is based on the principle of feedback. Suppose during those years La Roja has been nourished mainly by Spanish players belonging to Spanish clubs. In that case, it is to be expected that those clubs that have been more successful and have provided a more significant number of players will be those that will have had a more outstanding contribution.

UEFA (Estadísticas UEFA, 2021) periodically compiles statistics at the club level that serve to order and assign rankings or privileged positions in draws to the teams participating in the Champions League and Europa League. According to the data collected (Table 14.1), during the period analysed from 2005–2016, the Spanish and English League were the most competitive. The only Spanish teams that appear there in that ranking regularly are Barça and Madrid. Both clubs have occupied the top positions on average during that period (R. Madrid on average fourth and Barça first).

At the players' contribution to the national team or players called up for international championships, it is also possible to observe exciting conclusions. Figure 14.4 shows the number of players and teams of origin during the periods (1990–2005) and (2006–2014). We have distinguished next to Barça and Madrid the Basque-Navarre schools (groups Basque and Navarre football, mainly Bilbao, Real Sociedad, and Osasuna), the Valencian (formed mainly by Valencia CF and Vila-Real), and At. De Madrid. A first reading shows that, on average, in the first of the periods analysed, the two leading suppliers are R. Madrid and Barça, which provide about five players. And that, in the second or more recent period, Barça is the team that on average provides more players (about six), followed by

Table 14.1 UEFA club coefficients (2005–2015)

Club	País	2005/ 2006	2006/ 2007	2007/ 2008	2008/ 2009	2009/ 2010	2010/ 2011	2011/ 2012	2012/ 2013	2013/ 2014	2014/ 2015	Posición Media
FC Barcelona	ESP	2	2	4	1	1	2	1	1	2	2	1,8
Chelsea FC	ENG	14	7	1	2	3	3	3	3	4	4	4,4
Manchester United	ENG	8	8	6	4	2	1	2	5	6	10	5,2
Real Madrid CF	ESP	3	6	10	13	13	7	5	4	1	1	6,3
Arsenal FC	ENG	7	5	5	6	4	6	6	6	9	9	6,3
FC Bayern München	GER	13	18	11	8	6	4	4	2	3	3	7,2
AC Milan	ITA	1	1	2	5	9	10	12	14	11	22	8,7
FC Internazi Milano	ITA	4	4	9	11	8	9	7	7	13	24	9,6
FC Porto	POR	11	13	17	19	15	8	9	9	10	8	11,9
Liverpool FC	ENG	6	3	3	3	5	5	11	17	32	42	12,7

Source: Based on FIFA statistics (2021)

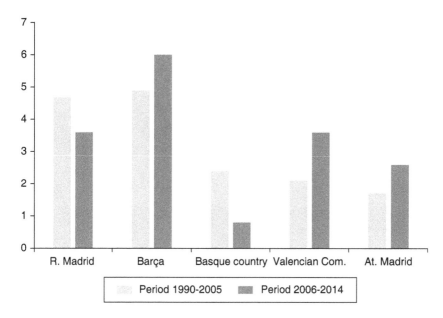

Figure 14.4 Average number of players summoned to the National Team according to their club of origin

Source: Based on data from RFEF (2021)

Madrid and the Valencian clubs with three players on average each. Some of the reasons that would explain these results would have to do with the business model implemented by Florentino Perez and Joan Laporta regarding the transfer policy and templates.

If instead of analysing the player's club of origin when being called up to the national team, we consider the club's youth academy where the player was trained (the quarry). That is to say, the lower divisions and youth teams of the professional teams through which the player has passed in his beginnings as a footballer, the results reinforce the previous conclusions. According to Figure 14.5, in the previous period (1990–2005), the two teams whose youth teams reported the most players were Madrid and Basque-Navarre (on average between four and five players each). Whereas, in the most recent period (2006–2014), the youth academy or players trained in the barça's quarry have had the most remarkable presence in La Roja (an average contribution of eight players).

One aspect that could explain this last result is that Barça has had in La Masía a place where great players such as Messi, Puyol, Piqué, Xavi, Busquets, Iniesta, and Valdés, among others, have resided and trained, together with internationally renowned stars (Ronaldinho, Eto'o, Deco, Márquez, Edmilson and, later, Henry, Yaya Touré, Keita, Alves, Mascherano, Abidal, Vidal). This training center had

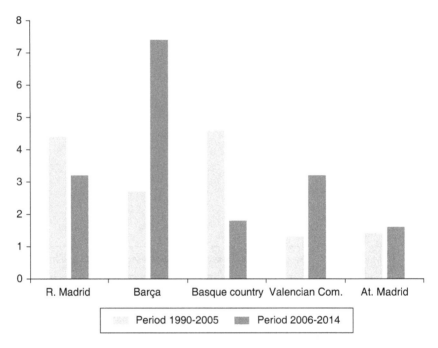

Figure 14.5 Average number of players summoned to the national team according to their quarry of origin

Source: Based on data from RFEF (2021)

its most significant relevance when the Champions League won in May 2006 by Barça, with Pep Guardiola as a coach, had in its starting line-up seven homegrown players, five of whom were Catalans. Moreover, with this base of footballers and play, the team managed to win all six official competitions (national and international) throughout 2009. The recognition and success of Barça's business model have led to the fact that the three finalists of the 2010 edition are three players from this dream team: Lionel Messi, Andrés Iniesta, and Xavi Hernández. That success undoubtedly also spread to La Roja.

Beyond Madrid and Barça

It would not be fair to conclude the historical review set out in this chapter without taking a closer look at other factors that have also influenced the success of La Roja. For this purpose, the leadership of their coaches will be analysed for their relevance in the final result (Schyns et al., 2016).

As we have noted, the two most successful coaches have been Luis Aragonés and Vicente del Bosque. Both were at different moments in time at the helm of La Roja in achieving the Triple Crown. As Burns (2012) or Frick and Simmons (2008) point out, the sporting careers of both, first as players and then as coaches, were different. They both seem to agree that they both lead La Roja at the end of their careers and, therefore, possess a great deal of experience.

In football, there is no clear and direct relationship between the coach's strategy and leadership and the results of a football team (Schyns et al., 2016). Many examples of players have failed or succeeded by changing teams and changing the coach (Soriano, 2013). Also, the effect of the change of coach depends on other variables such as the competition, the players selected, and the complementarity between them (Tena & Forrest, 2007).

Despite this background, what seems clear is that the arrival of Luis Aragonés and Vicente del Bosque in La Roja represented a new model in the sporting management of the team about the previous (Camacho and Sáez) and subsequent and current (Lopetegui and Luis Enrique) stages. Concerning Luis Aragonés, in addition to the experience and talent accumulated by his squad, one of the keys to Aragonés' success is the fact that he gave them a winning character. Aspects such as 'we have a sixth gear,' 'the best is yet to come,' 'we can,' 'win, win and win,' or 'go out and play and above all don't forget to have fun' was a psychological revolution that materialised with magnificent results.

Concerning the Championships won by del Bosque, Cubeiro and Gallardo (2010) suggest that his triumph in the World Cup in South Africa (2010) had a lot to do with the talent and experience accumulated by his predecessor since more than half of the squad repeated the 2008 and 2010 finals. Another aspect was the strong commitment between R. Madrid and Barça, who acted in unison.

Suárez (Suarez, 2012) points out that, beyond ideologies and territories or the Madrid-Barça binomial, it was the style and system of play (popularly known as tiki-taka), a coach Vicente Del Bosque faithful to his style and philosophy, and the coincidence in time and space of talented players never like before in the national team (Iniesta best player, Torres Golden Shoe, etc.) that made such a success of such magnitude possible.

Finally, it is worth highlighting another critical change that both the clubs and the national team have recently implemented: a well-defined strategic orientation and professionalisation of their staff. To be competitive in environments characterised by intense rivalry, business organisations need to be managed accordingly (Aragón-Sánchez & Sánchez-Marín, 2005). When this vision and philosophy happen, the strategy is accompanied by economic resources and talent in leadership and management; the sporting objectives begin to reach the showcases of both. For example, in the case of the RFEF, this reorientation is evident in preparing and implementing the 2020/2024 strategic plan. This strategic plan is designed with the participation of the territorial federations (which have designed their respective regional plans) and the federation's workers and employees, under the supervision of UEFA (2021).

References

Aragón-Sánchez, A., & Sánchez-Marín, G. (2005). Strategic orientation, management characteristics, and performance: A study of Spanish SMEs. *Journal of Small Business Management, 43*(3), 287–308.

Badía, J. (2003). *Crònica del nuñisme*. Ed. Pòrtic.

Burns, J. (2012). *La Roja: How soccer conquered Spain and how Spanish soccer conquered the world*. Bold Type Books.

Cubeiro, J. C., & Gallardo. (2010). *El mundial de La Roja. Lecciones prácticas del mejor equipo del mundo*. Editorial Alienta.

Elberse, A., & Quelch, J. (2008). *Real Madrid Club de Fútbol en 2007: Después de los galácticos* (pp. S10–S07). Harvard Business School.

Estadísticas FIFA. (2021). https://es.wikipedia.org/wiki/Selecci%C3%B3n_de_f%C3%BAtbol_de_Espa%C3%B1a

Estadísticas UEFA. (2021). https://es.uefa.com/memberassociations/uefarankings/club/#/yr/2021

Fitzpatrick, R. (2012). *El Clasico: Barcelona vs. Real Madrid: Football's Greatest Rivalry*. Bloomsbury Publishing.

Frick, B., & Simmons, R. (2008). The impact of managerial quality on organizational performance: Evidence from German soccer. *Managerial and Decision Economics, 29*(7), 593–600.

García, J. (2008). *Júrame que no fue un sueño*. Ed. La Esfera de los Libros.

García, J. (2019). Sport and economy: A peculiar, creative and beneficial relationship for both parties, in Sport (and) Economics. *Papeles de Economía Española*, Ed. FUNCAS, 1–24.

IFFHS. (2021). www.iffhs.com/

Interbrand. www.interbrand.com

Llaneras, K. (2014). *Mapa de las aficiones del fútbol español*. www.jotdown.es/2014/09/mapa-de-las-aficiones-del-futbol-espanol/

Minguella, J. M. (2008). *Casi toda la verdad*. Editorial Base.

Murillo, E., & Murillo, C. (2005). *El Nuevo Barça*. Editorial Península.

Neale, W. C. (1964). The peculiar economics of professional sports. *Quarterly Journal of Economics, 78*, 1–14.

RFEF. (2021). https://sefutbol.com/

Schyns, B., Gilmore, S., & Dietz, G. (2016). What lessons can we learn from football about leadership and management? In *Leadership lessons from compelling contexts*. (Monographs in leadership and management, Vol. 8, pp. 95–127). Emerald Group Publishing Limited.

Segurola, S. (2004). *Traspaso de poderes*. https://elpais.com/diario/2004/11/21/deportes/1100991617_850215.html

Soriano, F. (2013). *La pelota no entra por azar: Ideas de Management desde el mundo del fútbol*. Ediciones Granica.

Suarez, O. (2012). *Yo soy español*. Roca Editorial de libros.

Tena, J. D., & Forrest, D. (2007). Within-season dismissal of football coaches: Statistical analysis of causes and consequences. *European Journal of Operational Research, 181*, 362–373.

UEFA. (2021). *Union of European football associations*. https://es.uefa.com/

Chapter 15

Spanish women's leagues and the push towards professionalisation

José Manuel Sánchez-Santos and Mary Elena Sánchez-Gabarre

Introduction

Women's professional and semi-professional sports leagues have recently experienced a period of substantial growth around the world (Nielsen Women's Sports Research, 2018). In the case of Spain, the development of women's team sports is reflected in the sharp increase of the number of federative sports licenses that exist in a wide range of sports disciplines. A federative sport license is an identification document that certifies an athlete is registered into a given sport federation. A license allows the athlete to take part in the activities organised by the federation of his or her sport. The growth of women's team sports in Spain is closely associated with the success achieved by national teams in various sports. Several national teams have signed historic performances in the World Cup competitions as well as European Championships

As observed in Table 15.1, in Spain, women's basketball is the sport with the most numbers of federative sports licenses. The women's basketball league was the first to sign professional contracts and to establish a collective bargaining agreement. From 2008 to 2011 there was no employers' association with which to negotiate a collective bargaining agreement, so during that time, the league did not operate with a labour framework.

Football is the second sport with most women's licenses and the one that has grown the most over the past few years. In 2018 and 2019 the number of licenses reached 71,276. Women's Football is also a sport with the best potential to become a professional sport. But despite the unprecedented growth and public interest shown in women's football, it is not comparable to men's football, not only in terms of fan support but also in terms of players' contractual conditions.

Overall, women's sports in Spain are still far from reaching the level of professionalisation comparable to those of men's sports. This situation is partially a direct result of the Sport Law of 1990 (Ley 10/1990) the legal instrument that defined the requirements and conditions of professional leagues. According to this law, only two professional leagues are currently recognised as such, which are men's football and men's basketball. Therefore, only three competitions in Spain are considered professional: *LaLiga Santander* and *LaLiga Smartbank* in football,

DOI: 10.4324/9781003197003-15

Table 15.1 Number of women's team sport licenses in Spain

Sport	2010	2018	2019
Basketball	132.400	138.007	132.927
Football	33.744	65.091	71.276
Volleyball	38.868	61.906	40.607
Handball	36.174	33.923	28.795
Hockey	3.474	6.662	6.968
Total women's licenses	706.053	888.617	908.647

Source: Based on data from Consejo Superior de Deportes (2021)

organised and managed by *LaLiga*; and *Liga Endesa* in basketball, managed by the *Asociación de Clubs de Baloncesto* (Association of Basketball Clubs). Any other type of sport league that includes professional athletes (male and female) is called 'assimilated'. An assimilated league is a sport competition that in many aspects is comparable to a professional league (i.e., in terms of organisation, players' salaries, etc.), but it is not formally recognised as a professional league in Spanish law.

Moreover, according to the Sport Law of 1990, only one professional league is allowed in each sport. For this reason, the top competitions in women's football and basketball are not considered professional leagues. Therefore, it is unfortunate that despite women's and men's football or women's and men's basketball being the same sport, only the professional men's leagues are recognised and not the women's leagues.

In Spain, official state-level competitions are classified by the corresponding Spanish Sport Federation, but the decision to recognise a league as professional rests with the Higher Sport Council or *Consejo Superior de Deportes* (CSD). Some of the conditions required to become a professional league represent barriers to many women's leagues. For example, the existence of labour links between clubs and athletes and the economic dimensions of the competition. For the first requirement, and according to the Royal Decree 1006 of 1985 (Real Decreto 1006/1985), a professional athlete is someone who by virtue of a regular and established relationship, voluntarily commits to the practice of a sport in a sport entity in exchange for remuneration. Excluded from this rule are individuals who engage in the practice of sport in a club, and only receive compensation for the costs derived from the practice of their sport (e.g. transportation to training sessions, sport equipment, etc.).

Regarding the potential to generate revenues, in Spain, only a few sports generate sufficient interest to turn into a spectacle. For most women's sports, sponsorship and public subsidies represent the main sources of funding. However, considering that sponsorship and private funding are closely linked to the visibility and media exposure each sport can generate, the interest of private companies to support women's sport, although growing, is still relatively low. To sum up, the progress of women's sport towards professionalisation is mainly conditioned by two types of factors. First is the regulatory framework, and, second, is the potential for revenue generation.

In this context, in Spain, only the women's football league is on the verge of officially turning into a professional league. The *Real Federación Española de Fútbol* RFEF (Royal Spanish Football Federation) accept that due to the socio-labour characteristics of the players, the economic volume of the league, the existence of employment contracts and the minimum income of the participating clubs, the official state-level first and second division of women's football, and the first division of women's indoor football should all be professional competitions. Undoubtedly, this represents a step in the right direction towards advancing the development of women's football in Spain. More recently, as a response to a request made by the *Asociación de Clubs de Fútbol Femenino* (Association of Women's Football Clubs—ACFF), which acts as the employers' association, the Higher Council of Sport (CSD) announced its commitment towards making the competition professional by 2021–22 season onwards.

The following section provides a brief description of the professionalisation of women's sports in Spain. Then, we focus on the labour relations, particularly on the collective bargaining agreement, and finally, we focus on the economic sustainability of professional women's leagues.

The professionalisation of Spanish women's football

The Spanish first division of women's football, commercially known as *Primera Iberdrola* for sponsorship reasons and officially *Primera División PRO* or *Primera División Femenina RFEF*, is the top women's division within the Spanish football league system and the main club-level competition in the country. It began during the 1988–1989 season and since then it has been held without interruption, although it has undergone several changes in format and name. First Division and Second Division are the only two categories with semi-professional status, both under the jurisdiction of the RFEF. The other divisions depend on their corresponding regional federations. According to the Union of European Football Associations (UEFA), the *Primera Iberdrola* is considered among the most important leagues in Europe.

Although a significant number of players are now under professional contracts, the women's football league still does not have the status of a professional league because, as previously mentioned, the Sport Law of 1990 (Ley 10/1990) does not explicitly recognise it as such.

In May of 2020, the Association of Women's Football Clubs (ACFF) applied to the CSD for the league to be considered professional. These clubs (all except Barcelona, Athletic de Bilbao, and Real Madrid) represent 15 of the 18 teams that are part of *Primera Iberdrola*. According to the Royal Decree (Real Decreto 1006/1985) that regulates employment relationships of professional athletes, for a sport league to be considered professional, it must be approved by the CSD, which is a body of the Ministry of Culture and Sport. As previously mentioned, the law establishes that a professional competition must demonstrate labour links between clubs and players as well as show significant importance in economic terms. Moreover, the latest reform of the Royal Spanish Football Federation (RFEF) statutes, approved in June of 2020, includes a new category: 'professionalised competitions'. This category is intended to give greater importance to those competitions that while are not yet professional, meet the economic, professional, and labour conditions to qualify as such. The qualification of professionalised competition implies that based on the competition there will be a series of requirements for the professionalisation of players and coaches. These rules also establish the minimum working conditions to be met by those who directly participate in the league. Some of these conditions are the budget of the clubs, including a minimum budget for the staff of the first team who hold an employment contract, a minimum number of professional licenses, minimum salaries, etc. All these requirements strengthen the employment relationship between clubs and players. Moreover, these requirements are now protected after the signing in February of 2020 of the first collective bargaining agreement for women's football in Spain. The RFEF has assigned this new qualification to the *Primera Iberdrola* (1st Women's Division) and *Reto Iberdrola* (2nd Women's Division), as well as to the First Division of Women's Indoor Football. This has been a significant step towards the advancement of professional women's football in Spain.

At present, all the conditions are in place for *Primera Iberdrola* to become a professional league because the league meets all the requirements. Players have their collective bargaining agreement, there are professional contracts, the structures of the clubs are professionals, teams have the backing of the media and television and now fans start following the league. Because of the significant progress shown by the league, the Spanish government, through the CSD, announced its commitment to the professionalisation of the top two divisions. The players' football union, also known as the *Asociación de Futbolistas* Españoles AFE (Spanish Footballers' Association), has welcomed the CSD's announcement indicating that it represents an important advancement in the development of women's sport.

It is expected that in the 2022–2023 season, the Women's First Division will definitely become a professional league. The *Primera Iberdrola* will be replaced by the *Liga Ellas*, a competition in which 16 teams will participate. This league will be the first women's league in Spain to be classified as professional. The new women's first division league will no longer be organised by the RFEF but instead, it will be a new entity that will be made up of the participating clubs of the league. This new entity will be responsible to exploit the audio-visual and commercial rights and manage the revenues derived from the tournament (i.e., sponsorship, naming rights, official suppliers, etc.). To successfully advance the process of professionalisation of the league, a coordination agreement will be signed between the RFEF and the professional league. Currently, some clubs have their own audio-visual and broadcasting rights while others have negotiated in a centralised way. It is hoped that, with the professionalisation of the competition, the league's governing entity will reach collaboration agreements to maximise the benefits of the negotiations. To accomplish this, the clubs must sign an agreement with the RFEF, as is currently the case with men's football.

For the clubs, participating in the new professional league will also entail a series of obligations and responsibilities. In particular, the clubs will have to guarantee financial commitments to ensure the economic viability of the competition and be prepared to generate revenues to make the league sustainable.

The process of transformation of the league will be led by the CSD and it is hoped that, with the professionalisation, women's football will improve its visibility and impact, from fans' support to the interest of sponsoring companies. Regarding this point, a few aspects favour the visibility of Spanish women's football. First, players' skills continue to improve, particularly when clubs sign *superstars*. Second, sponsors are becoming increasingly committed to women's football. Third, there is an increased interest in media exposure.

Although with the creation of the new league, the RFEF will no longer be the organiser of the competition, its role in the success of the transformation process of the league remains critical. If the RFEF would not want to make significant changes to the existing rules that regulate professional leagues, they still could do some adjustments by relaxing some of the conditions required for the women's league to meet the requirements to become a professional league. For instance, the RFEF could allow the participation of semi-professional or non-professional players to compete in professional leagues. Semi-professional players are not amateurs because they receive regular payments from their club, but at a much lower rate than full-time professional players. In addition, the RFEF would also oversee all divisions in order to ensure that other standards are upheld.

Beyond these considerations, one of the main implications of the professionalisation of women's football in Spain is that it will open the door for other sports and women's leagues to become professional.

Women's football collective bargaining agreement: the first step towards professionalisation

For years, the lack of a collective bargaining agreement (CBA) in women's sports in Spain (i.e., football, basketball, handball, or volleyball), left these athletes without labour rights, outside the professional leagues, and with fewer possibilities of advancing their athletic careers. However, this situation started to change in 2020 with the signing of the first collective bargaining agreement for women's football. The agreement was signed by the Association of Women's Football Clubs (ACFF) representing the clubs participating in the league, and by several trade unions, including the Spanish Footballers' Association (AFE), in the representation of the players. This is not only the first collective bargaining agreement for women's football in Spain but also the first of a women's football league in Europe. This agreement has set the foundation to improve the working conditions of female footballers after decades of being neglected as a result of obsolete legislation that did not recognise women's football as professional. The CBA establishes the rules that govern the working conditions of professional women footballers who are hired by clubs or SADs, participating in the National League Championship of the Spanish Women's First Division. With this agreement, women's footballers obtain a legal framework that regulates their working hours, salaries, vacations, and sick and maternity leave.

Labour contracts between professional football players and clubs or SADs must comply with the regulations established in the Royal Decree 1006 of 1985, which regulates the special labour relationship of professional athletes. Regarding the economic conditions, the remuneration received by a professional football player is considered a salary, except payments that are excluded from such consideration by the law.

In Spain, many women's leagues provide marginal salaries and/or partial year semi-professional employment. As a result, for many female athletes making a living from playing professional sports is limited (Sherry & Taylor, 2019). From now on, players with a full-time contract receive an annual minimum salary of €16,000. Players with part-time contracts receive 75% of a full-time salary. This amount will be increased taking into consideration the Consumer Price Index (CPI) plus an additional 2% at each annual renewal. Although the establishment of a minimum wage for female players is an important step forward, the minimum wage and the average salary of female footballers is significantly lower than the minimum salary stipulated in the men's first and second divisions. In the first division, a footballer earns a minimum of €155,000 a year, while in the second division the minimum salary is €77,500 a year.

Regarding the working conditions, the regulations establish that players work 35 hours per week, have 30 days of paid vacation, and their salary must be guaranteed in the event of injuries. Moreover, professional football players who, during the term of the contract, are on sick leave due to temporary incapacity, will receive 100% of their remuneration from social security. Concerning trade union rights, professional football players have the right to become members of the union and receive all the benefits of the agreements that exist in the clubs or SADs to which they belong.

Given the part-time nature of this employment, it is important to anticipate how players will balance their playing obligations alongside other work, family, and study commitments (Taylor et al., 2020). In this regard, it is expected that both parties agree to adopt appropriate measures to balance the professional and family life of the player. In the event of pregnancy, during the last season of the player's contract, the player will have the right to opt for either the renewal of the contract for an additional season under the same conditions as she had in the previous season or opt for non-renewal of the contract.

The collective bargaining agreement of women's football is not the first CBA in Spanish women's sports. As previously mentioned, basketball players had their labour rights recognised in 2008. Among other aspects, the CBA of women's basketball established a base salary of €600 per month; set the maximum number of hours in a working day and week; regulated remunerations during vacations; and, establish indemnities as a consequence of accidents and/or occupational disability. Clubs, sport entities, and sports corporations also sought to improve the training conditions of players. Clubs also provided financial support, even if only in part, to defray the costs of childcare or the costs of caring for players' elderly parents. Currently, this CBA for women's basketball is not in longer in place. At the time it had to be renewed, one of the clubs no longer existed as an association. Finally, it is worth noting that despite the significant progress brought by the signing of the women's football CBA, the Spanish Footballers' Association (AFE) has criticised the CBA and has called for a renegotiation.

Economic sustainability of women's professional leagues

Beyond the possibility of the creation of a women's professional league, the key question is the future economic viability and sustainability of such a league. This will rest on the league's ability to generate revenues through gate receipts, stadium attendances,[1] TV audiences,[2] and the capacity to add value to sponsors. As is the case with many new competitions, some of the Spanish women's leagues are in the early phase of their product lifecycle. Therefore, they are still building their brand and fan base and still have far to go to achieve commercial viability (Mumcu, 2019). In this regard, the new league must focus its efforts on securing different sources of revenue, namely, ticket sales, television rights, and sponsorship.

The ability of women's sports to draw fans to a sport event has been demonstrated on multiple occasions over the past decade. In the case of the Spanish women's football, it proved that in the last season previous to COVID-19 (2018–2019) was capable of filling a stadium with more than 60,739 spectators (i.e., the match between Atletico de Madrid vs. Barcelona). This historic event, which broke the world record for attendance at a women's club match, was also followed by other large match attendances in other first division teams. Among these were the contests between Sevilla F.C. and Betis with 23,000 spectators and Real Sociedad and Athletic de Bilbao with 21,234 spectators.

Although in the 2018–2019 season some teams reached large attendances at their stadiums, which showed the growth of fans in Spain, the reality of many *Primera Iberdrola* stadiums was very different. During the same season, the average general attendance at matches was about 700 spectators (Table 15.2).

Focusing on teams, only Barcelona, Atlético de Madrid, and Deportivo have more than a thousand spectators. Apart from these clubs, only three teams (Madrid CFF, Valencia, and Real Sociedad) exceed 700 spectators on average in the overall season. The remaining ten clubs are well below, with Sevilla, Levante, Tacon or Rayo Vallecano, having average attendance of 300 spectators.

But despite the low attendance at the stadiums, one of the main assets to be commercialised in professional football is the broadcasting rights. An example is

Table 15.2 Primera Iberdrola Attendances (2018–2019 season)

Team	Stadium Capacity	Average Attendance	Attendance/Capacity (%)
Barcelona	6.000	2.787	46,5
Atlético de Madrid	3.000	1.345	44,8
Deportivo	2.000	1.134	56,7
Madrid CFF	3.000	848	28.3
Valencia	3.000	810	27,0
Real Sociedad	1.500	800	53,3
Betis	3.000	542	18,1
Sp. Huelva	2.000	506	25,3
Athletic de Bilbao	1.000	462	46,2
Espanyol	6.000	457	7,6
Granadilla	2.700	454	16,8
Logroño	16.000	441	2,8
Sevilla	7.000	382	5,5
Levante	3.000	372	12,4
Tacon	3.000	344	11,5
Rayo Vallecano	1.200	300	25,0

Source: Based on data from Jiménez (2020) and Soccerway (2020)

the Spanish broadcasting group Mediapro, which in 2019 purchased the television rights of 12 *Primera Iberdrola* clubs paying €3 million per season for the next three seasons. In the case of women's football, clubs hold the ownership of the television rights, and the RFEF can only exploit these rights after they have been transferred to them. The current sports legislation does not recognise the RFEF as the owner of the broadcasting rights of women's football competitions, nor does it impose any obligation on the clubs to transfer those rights to the RFEF.

The creation of the *Liga Ellas*, as the new organising entity of the forthcoming Spanish women's professional football league, is the first step to start commercialising the broadcasting rights. Until now, the commercialisation of the broadcasting rights has not been possible because of a regulatory impasse that existed between the clubs and the RFEF. The creation of the *Liga Ellas* means giving professional status to matches between women's clubs. It is expected that subsequent legislative development will allow the revenues from the broadcasting rights of these matches to be allocated to the newly created entity, in the same way that *LaLiga* (the professional men's football league in Spain) has been doing with the first and second division since 2015.

With Spanish women's football in search of visibility, reaching sponsorships deals become critical to achieving economic sustainability. Over the last few years, several private companies have been committed to investing not only in women's football but also in other women's sports. This corporate interest is aligned with a growing fans' interest in women's sports. The relationship between women's sports, the global sports economy, and sport fandom is shifting. Since the early

2000s, there has been an evident shift in corporate attention towards the use of female athletes as brand endorsers. Now, women are not only more visible as fans, but also, many female athletes have achieved celebrity status, and many others have become media personalities (Antunovic & Linden, 2015).

Morgan (2019) argues that the growing professionalisation of women's sport is opening opportunities for sponsoring firms as more companies realise the value of marketing the female athlete and using sport to empower women. This author also identifies new emerging trends specifically in the women's sport sponsorship industry. Commercial and Corporate Social Responsibility (CSR) are among the primary motivations for sponsoring a sport women's team. On the one hand, higher participation, greater attendance, and broadcasting demand are pushing corporate investment and changing the landscape of women's sport in a way that offers lucrative opportunities for sponsor involvement. On the other hand, CSR can play a key role in promoting the professionalisation of women's sports. Today, many companies implement CSR initiatives as it offers new sponsorship opportunities. In some instances, some types of collaborations with sports entities are no longer strictly linked to an economic return.

In 2019, more than 900,000 girls and women participated in a federated sport in Spain (source). Companies are aware of the growth of women's sports, but they are even more aware that consumers appreciate the collaboration with sports organisations. This collaboration and association become critical for the sustainability of leagues, sport organisations, and clubs. Therefore, as a result of many companies implementing corporate socially responsible practices, growing participation in women's sports can be expected. For many companies, commitment to gender equality as well investing and supporting women's sports, represent an important business goal. On the other hand, these collaborations and sponsorships represent the flow of critical resources to women's clubs so these can improve not only their training facilities, or the quality and working conditions of their athletes, but also contributes to raising their level of professionalisation.

Conclusions

In Spain, there are some women's sports leagues in which the contractual relationship of the athletes with their clubs is professional, but the leagues are not formally recognised as professional leagues. The push of Spanish women's sport towards professionalisation is closely linked not only to the changes in the regulatory framework but also to the increase in its potential for revenue generation.[3]

In Spain, the current Sport Law (Ley 10/1990) acts as a brake for the professionalisation of women's sport. Politicians must revise and update this legislation. Many articles include shortcomings that are at the origin of what causes significant inequalities among men's and women's sports. A much-needed new sports law should address some of these flaws. In the meantime, the imminent professionalisation of women's football is expected to be a big step on the long road to gender equality in sport.

Regarding advances in revenue generation, the process of professionalisation requires the involvement of federations, leagues, teams, sponsors, and regulators that should invest on a sustained basis to create more opportunities for women's sports to prove their commercial value. It will also require a professionalisation of club management, which would also contribute to maximising the revenue generation for the clubs. More revenues would eventually translate into higher contracts and salaries in women's sports. This will allow many more female athletes could fully dedicate and commit a career into sport. Indeed, women's football should represent a model to follow, so other competitions may gain professional status soon.

In this process of transition towards professionalisation, two key stakeholders play an essential role. First, is the government which provides public funding to the federations and updates existing legislations. Second, are the sports federations. They can facilitate the transition of the new leagues by making the requirements more flexible, especially the financial ones. Federations can also adjust and change some of their regulations and coordinate with the emerging leagues the actions needed when a new professional league is created.

Finally, the process of professionalisation of women's football in Spain was affected by the COVID-19 pandemic, particularly during 2020 and 2021. The interruption of competitions caused by the pandemic in 2020 impacted dramatically women's sport. Reductions in sponsorship and subsidies, salary cuts, and reduced contracts created a great deal of uncertainty for the federations, clubs, and athletes. Nevertheless, there is consensus that the impact created by the COVID-19 pandemic has driven a critical reassessment of many aspects of society. In particular, many organisations and institutions have realised that women have been particularly vulnerable to the effects of the pandemic. In these circumstances, it becomes critical for commercial companies to align their sponsorship portfolio with some of the values they promote, especially when it comes to supporting and empowering women (Taveras, 2020). As a result, a growing number of brands recognise the value of investing in women's sports and they see the post-pandemic as the right time to begin investing in them.

Notes

1 Meier et al. (2016) examined factors that influenced spectator's demand in the Frauen-Bundesliga (FBL) or German women's top division football, and Valenti et al. (2020) in the UEFA Women's Champions League.
2 Buraimo et al. (2021) provide a review of the literature on the factors influencing football television viewership.
3 Issues related to salary, type of hiring, media visibility, and the structure of the league are some of the main structural challenges that face the professionalisation of women's leagues in other countries. Martínez et al. (2019) discuss some of the required actions that need to be implemented in order to guarantee the continuity of women's professional football in Colombia.

References

Antunovic, D., & Linden, A. (2015). Disrupting dominant discourses: #HERESPROOF of Interest in women's sports. *Feminist Media Studies*, 15(1), 157–159. https://doi.org/10.1080/14680777.2015.987426

Buraimo, B., Forrest, D., McHale, I. J., & Tena, J. D. (2021). Television audience demand for football: Disaggregation by gender, age and socio-economic status. In R. H. Koning & S. Kesenne (Eds.), *A modern guide to sports economics* (pp. 126–151). Edward Elgar Publishing.

Consejo Superior de Deportes. (2021). *Anuario de Estadísticas Deportivas*. Ministerio de Cultura y Deporte.

Jiménez, M. (2020, April 7). Llenar estadios, la gran tarea pendiente del fútbol femenino. *As.com-Diario onlie deportivo*. https://as.com/futbol/2020/04/06/femenino/1586185282_679580.htm

Ley 10/1990, de 15 de Octubre, del Deporte. Boletín Oficial del Estado, 249, de 17 de octubre de 1990, 30397–30411. www.boe.es/eli/es/l/1990/10/15/10/dof/spa/pdf

Martínez, C. Y., Goellner, S., & Orozco, A. M. (2019). Soccer and women: The panorama of the Professional Women's Soccer League in Colombia. *Educación Física y Deporte*, 28(1), 53–90. https://doi.org/10.17533/udea.efyd.v38n1a03

Meier, H. E., Konjer, M., & Leinwather, M. (2016). The demand for women's league soccer in Germany. *European Sport Management Quarterly*, 16(1), 1–19. https://doi.org/10.1080/16184742.2015.1109693

Mumcu, C. (2019). Business analytics in women's professional sport. In N. Lough & A. Geurin (Eds.), *Routledge handbook of the business of women's sport* (pp. 239–251). Routledge. https://doi.org/10.4324/9780203702635-19

Morgan, A. (2019). An examination of women's sport sponsorship: A case study of female Australian Rules football. *Journal of Marketing Management*, 35(17–18), 1644–1666. https://doi.org/10.1080/0267257X.2019.1668463

Nielsen Women's Sports Research. (2018). *The rise of women's sport*. The Nielsen Company. www.nielsen.com/au/en/insights/report/2018/the-rise-of-womens-sports/

Real Decreto 1006/1985, de 26 de junio, por el que se regula la relación laboral especial de los deportistas profesionales. Boletín Oficial del Estado, 153, de 27 de junio de 1985, 20075–20077. www.boe.es/boe/dias/1985/06/27/pdfs/A20075-20077.pdf

Sherry, E., & Taylor, C. (2019). Professional women's sport in Australia. In N. Lough & A. Geurin (Eds.), *Routledge handbook of the business of women's sport* (pp. 124–133). Routledge. https://doi.org/10.4324/9780203702635-10

Soccerway. (2020). *Stadium capacities*. The Database of Soccerway. https://es.soccerway.com/national/spain/superliga/20212022/regular-season/r64628/

Taveras, V. (2020, September 16). Pandemic landscape reveals importance of investing in women's sports. *Sports Business Journal*. www.sportsbusinessjournal.com/SB-Blogs/COVID19-OpEds/2020/09/16.aspx

Taylor, T., Fujak, H., Hanlon, C., & O'Connor, D. (2020). A balancing act: Women players in a new semi Professional team sport league, *European Sport Management Quarterly*. https://doi.org/10.1080/16184742.2020.1815821

Valenti, M., Scelles, N., & Morrow, S. (2020). The determinants of stadium attendance in elite women's football: Evidence from the UEFA Women's Champions League. *Sport Management Review*, 23(3), 509–520. https://doi.org/10.1016/j.smr.2019.04.005

Chapter 16

La Vuelta

Impact on Local Communities

José Miguel Vegara-Ferri, José María López-Gullón, Arturo Díaz-Suárez, and Salvador Angosto

Introduction

This chapter examines the impact produced by the professional road cycling event *La Vuelta Ciclista a España* (hereinafter *La Vuelta*) on different local communities. To do so, it analyses the possible impacts generated by this event from socioeconomic, tourist, and media perspectives), assessing how these impacts directly or indirectly affect the local communities and the residents who live there. The hosting of sport events has become one of the most popular strategies used by local communities to attract tourists. Local communities seek to generate positive impacts resulting from the hosting of the event, as well as international recognition of the community through media coverage that helps to promote these tourist attractions, regenerating and revaluing the community (Balduck et al., 2011). La Vuelta is an example of this type of event. The municipalities have become aware of the different opportunities and benefits of hosting this distinctive sport event. Proof of this is the large number of requests the organisation receives from the different municipalities to host the start or finish of one of the stages (2playbook, 2021). These communities are willing to pay significant fees to the organisers to host the race in their territories, as it has a great social return and generates international publicity.

Road cycling sports events

The bicycle is a means of transport that has evolved from its origin in 1817, designed by the German Karl von Drais, to the great popularity it has acquired today (Kosche, 2018). Cycling is a sustainable and environmentally friendly means of transport that produces physical and psychological health benefits for those who use it (Avila-Palencia et al., 2018). Currently, European metropolitan areas are designing specific strategic plans to close historic areas to motorised vehicles, making cycling a popular mode of transport in urban areas (Bastian & Börjesson, 2018, Liu et al., 2020). Worldometers (2021) estimates that currently more than one billion bicycles worldwide are used both as a means of transport and as a vehicle for leisure and recreation.

DOI: 10.4324/9781003197003-16

In Spain, 89.6% of the population knows how to ride a bicycle according to data from the Directorate-General for Traffic (DGT, 2019). The Ministry of Culture and Sports (2020) found that 10.3% of Spaniards cycle weekly, making it the third most popular sport in the country. However, the vast majority of cyclists do so recreationally. The same report also shows that bicycles are present in 63% of Spanish households. This makes the bicycle the sports equipment most frequently found in Spanish households.

The cycling industry generates an economic impact of 1,871 million euros in Spain (2playbook, 2021), representing 24.6% of the sales of sporting goods in Spain in 2019 and being the highest percentage of sales among all sporting disciplines, above popular media sports like football (AMBE & Cofidis, 2020). However, cycling in the Iberian Peninsula is not as widespread as in other European countries such as The Netherlands or Denmark (European Parliament, 2015), although its popularity is increasing every year. It is estimated that 80 million trips were made by bicycle in Spain in 2015, far below the daily use in other European countries, such as France or Germany (Plevnik et al., 2015).

La Vuelta

La Vuelta is one of the most important annual sports events held in Spain, being the most important cycling competition on the Iberian Peninsula, as well as being one of the most important road cycling events in the world, along with the Tour de France and the Giro d'Italia, forming the Three Grand Tours. It is held between August and September and lasts three weeks. It is part of the calendar of the Union Cycliste Internationale (UCI) in the highest category of professional road cycling 'UCI WorldTour'.

The first edition of La Vuelta was held in 1935, with the participation of 50 cyclists who rode 3425 km distributed in 14 stages. So far, in its 86-year history, 75 editions of the event have been held; the event has undergone several critical moments, such as changes in the organising entity, wars and political-economic problems (Fallon & Bell, 2018; López & Kettner-Høeberg, 2017). Since 1979, the event has been managed by the company Unipublic, a subsidiary of the ASO group (Amaury Sport Organisation). ASO is a world leader in the organisation of sports events, specialising in major events such as the Tour de France and the Rally Dakar. This relationship has given La Vuelta financial stability, which over the years has evolved with a clear objective, to become a sport mega-event, with a high media impact and globalised (López & Kettner-Høeberg, 2017). In this new stage, the organisation established a stronger corporate identity through the colour of the race leader's jersey; red, and an 'official song' and innovative routes in search of excitement and showmanship (López & Kettner-Høeberg, 2017). These changes in the corporate image promote greater identification with the community and the event by the Spanish population.

La Vuelta is a distinctive and singular stage event, which is not held only in one country, as each edition has a different route. Kettner-Høeberg and López

(2015) describe this type of grand tour as 'a typically national sporting institution embodying and expressing national unity, while at the same time celebrating and showcasing the endless variety of a country's villages, cities, regions, landscapes, mountain ranges, and other geographical and political units' (p. 185). Considering these characteristics, La Vuelta can be held in small municipalities where other major sports events cannot be held due to the lack of sports infrastructures that can only be found in large communities (Vegara-Ferri et al., 2020).

Although the vast majority of the stages have taken place in Spanish, in recent years the event has expanded with stages in other territories such as Portugal, Andorra, France, and the Netherlands. The 2020 edition of La Vuelta turns out to be one of the most international editions, with a 410 km route which included three stages in the Dutch territory, in addition to two full stages in Portugal. In the end, these stages outside Spain had to be cancelled due to restrictions caused by the COVID-19 pandemic.

La Vuelta's host communities throughout its history

Professional sport is a social phenomenon in all countries, cultures, and social strata (Van Reeth, 2013). Since the 1992 Olympic Games in Barcelona, Spain has gained great prestige as an organiser of sports events. It has hosted World and European Championships in different sports such as basketball, swimming, athletics, and handball. The importance of these events and their impacts (i.e. socio-economic, tourism, political, environmental, cultural, etc.) are increasingly recognised, entailing a range of costs and benefits for host communities and their residents (Berridge, 2012).

Nowadays, La Vuelta, as a reference in the professional cycling calendar, is looking for innovative approaches through attractive, mediatic, and spectacular stages for the viewers. A clear example of this is its mountain top finishes and the official starts of different editions in recent years. For example, the start from a 'batea' (Floating structures for mussel farming) over the Rías Baixas in 2013, the start on board of the aircraft carrier Juan Carlos I in Cádiz in 2014, or the start of La Vuelta, 2021 from inside the cathedral of Burgos. In addition to the media spectacle, these stages generate a great direct impact on the communities where they are held.

After 75 editions of La Vuelta, more than 500 different communities have hosted the start and/or finish lines of the event. Madrid, the capital of Spain, has been the city that has hosted this sports event on the most occasions (98 stages), followed by Barcelona (81 stages). Coincidentally, these are the two Spanish communities with the largest population. La Vuelta has the particularity of not needing a large sports infrastructure, as the organisation itself, through a large team, carries out the assembly and disassembly of the start and finish lines. This allows small communities to host a stage without investing in infrastructure, receiving the focus of attention and coverage that the celebration of La Vuelta implies.

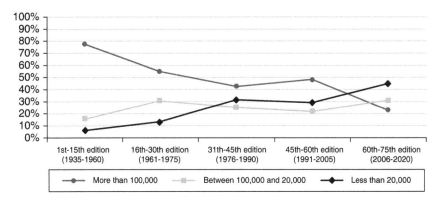

Figure 16.1 Starting or finishing location of a stage according to the number of inhabitants of the locality

Figure 16.1 shows a graphical representation of how the locations of the start or finish of the stages have evolved according to the number of inhabitants of the locality where the event took place. The locations of the start and/or finish of the stages are very varied, ranging from large communities with populations of millions of inhabitants to small municipalities with barely a hundred inhabitants. In the first editions of the event, the stages used to include the largest number of Spanish provincial capitals (Fallon & Bell, 2018). Therefore, the highest percentage of starts and finishes of the event took place in large towns that currently have more than 100,000 inhabitants (77.5%). Over the editions, the number of stages with finishes in large cities has progressively decreased to represent in recent years the lowest percentage (23.5%).

On the other hand, small towns with a population of less than 20,000 people have become more represented over time. While in the first editions they barely represented 6.4% of the starting or target localities, in recent years this percentage has reached 45% of the venues and is currently the most representative type of locality. Medium-sized towns (between 100,000 and 20,000 inhabitants) have maintained a trend with percentages ranging from 16.1% to 31.4% of the stages.

Media impact of La Vuelta and its impact on local communities

The relationship between cycling and the media has always been very present, so much so that La Vuelta was initially created and managed by a newspaper to increase its sales, as happened with the *Tour de France* and the *Giro d'Italia* (López, 2010). Therefore, during the first editions of the event, the written press was the main means of communication for the results and chronicles of the stages.

Subsequently, the event began to be broadcast on other media such as radio and television, giving greater impulse to the event and to cycling. Nowadays, professional cycling is a hugely mediatised sport, mainly thanks to television (van Reeth, 2016). Therefore, the media impact of La Vuelta is one of the most powerful assets of this event.

The event and the complementary images of the scenery and heritage along the route make it a very attractive sport for television audiences, even for non-cycling fans (van Reeth, 2013). Previous studies indicate that 61% of viewers had images of the different landscapes as their main incentive to watch the event, while the competition was an important incentive for 32% of viewers (van Reeth, 2016). Therefore, local communities hosting La Vuelta should take advantage of the passage of the event to showcase their tourist attractions.

La Vuelta is a media event broadcast in 190 countries with more than 70 hours of live broadcasts, it also has more than a thousand journalists and photographers accredited to cover the event (Unipublic, 2021). The organisation knows the importance of television and the visibility it offers, so it invests in improving the experience for the spectator, with great logistical support that includes helicopters and airplanes in charge of giving a greater diffusion of the event (Prado-Antúnez, 2020). As a consequence of this large technical deployment, the residents of the localities through which the event passes consider that La Vuelta produces a national expansion of the image of the municipality and improves the international image due to the large media impact and number of countries to which it is broadcast (Vegara-Ferri et al., 2020).

Since the entry of ASO, La Vuelta has evolved strategically through the media by adapting its stakeholder relations model. To improve the visibility and attractiveness of the race for residents, it has improved relations with the local press, maintaining permanent contact with the local media in the communities through which the race will pass each year. In this way, it manages to promote the visibility of the event in the different communities throughout the year and not only during the race (Kettner-Høeberg & López, 2015).

La Vuelta also continues to adapt to new technologies and digitalisation, with a presence on digital platforms and social networks such as YouTube, Instagram, Facebook, and Twitter. The event has more than nine million visits to its official website, more than 250,000 downloads of its APP, and one million followers of its profile on social networks. Recently, La Vuelta continues to adapt to new forms of digital communication and has become the first major tour to have an official Twitch channel with the aim of reaching new audiences, mainly younger people, and to be able to broadcast and promote the event throughout the year. In short, all this media impact around the event generates a large return in tourism advertising campaigns for the localities where it is held of a value that is difficult to calculate. Kantarmedia (2019) estimated that the advertising value equivalent to the media impact of La Vuelta 2019 was 117 million euros, analysing the cost of news in the media and social networks.

Socio-economic impact of La Vuelta on local communities

La Vuelta is an event that takes place on public roads and is completely free and open to spectators and fans who wish to watch the event live. Despite this, La Vuelta generates a great economic impact in the local communities where it is held, due to the large local spending that takes place in the short term in the hotel and restaurants sector. Only the staff managed by the event organisers, composed of approximately 2,500 people (i.e. cyclists, teams, logistics staff, communication staff, etc.), generate in just one day a direct impact of 250,000 euros for the host community of each of the stages (Unipublic, 2021). In a single edition, 400 hotel establishments are occupied by staff linked to the event and more than 800 accredited vehicles must refuel at service stations to complete the 21 stages (Unipublic, 2021). In addition, we must add the tourist expenditure generated by the spectators who attend each of the stages and the value of the media return mentioned earlier.

Despite this positive economic data, a positive economic impact on the localities is not synonymous with the success of the event. It is necessary to analyse other more intangible impacts, such as the social perception of residents. Social impact is increasingly used as a strategy to justify the organisation and funding of large-scale sports events (Leopkey & Parent, 2012). The residents of the local communities where the event is held are an important constituency and the majority of impacts (positive or negative) that occur during the hosting of an event fall on them (Bull & Lovell, 2007). Taking into account the opinion of the residents and considering their opinion and assessment of the potential benefits or detriments of holding the event is essential when allocating community resources by local governments in this type of event.

La Vuelta is a family-oriented sporting event. Spectators usually come to watch the event in groups of three or four people formed by family or friends who want to enjoy a festive atmosphere watching the passing of the peloton (Unipublic, 2021; Vegara-Ferri et al., 2020). This festive atmosphere is generated through the multiple parallel activities organised by the organisation for the population and children that help to promote the family character of the event. These activities consist of the organisation of a programme to promote cycling in local schools, the organisation of a small school competition in the finishing community before the arrival of the peloton, the publicity caravan that encourages the spectators before the passing of the peloton, or the fun zone, a space where the sponsoring and collaborating brands promote activities for all the public and promote their products. Thus, La Vuelta becomes a real cycling festival in the host community. For example, during the study carried out by Vegara-Ferri et al. (2020) on the social impact of La Vuelta, one resident commented that 'the toy factory gave us the morning off so that we could come and watch the event'.

As previously mentioned, one of the advantages of road cycling is that it is a sport that takes place on public roads, so it does not require a large sports infrastructure.

Thus, on the occasion of the event, some local communities take the opportunity to upgrade roads and road sections to increase the safety of the competing athletes. Consequently, this investment has a direct impact on the community, and the residents of these localities benefit from the improvement of local roads.

The development of large sports events in small communities or rural areas offers opportunities for participation in leisure, sport and tourism activities (Mackellar & Jamieson, 2015). Although residents also perceive the event to have negative effects (i.e. increased traffic, parking problems, increased litter, etc.), these negative impacts are often less than the positive ones, perceiving a greater overall benefit from the event (Mackellar & Jamieson, 2015). The social perception towards La Vuelta remarked that the passage of the event through the locality generated great excitement and expectation within the residents as it presented an unusual and very different experience from other events (Vegara-Ferri et al., 2020). These feelings coincide with those analysed by Berridge et al. (2019) in the Tour de France, where spectators on the road showed high values of positive feelings of interest, excitement, and enthusiasm for the event.

In turn, businesses in local communities also perceive the staging of the event in their community favourably. Vegara-Ferri et al. (2020) conducted an assessment in local businesses where a start or finish of the event took place in the 2019 edition of La Vuelta. These authors found that 94.6% of the businesses surveyed would like the event to return to their locality in future editions as they perceived an increase in sales of approximately 36.4%.

Tourist impact of La Vuelta on local communities

Spain is one of the main tourist destinations in the world, with 83.7 million tourists in 2019 (INE, 2020). La Vuelta has become a suitable tool to boost tourism in the communities that host it. Each stage generates a tourist attraction by drawing people from other areas, who come to the local community, not only to witness the stage live but also to carry out other cultural and leisure activities in the host communities.

Many cycle tourists tend to plan their holiday period to coincide with the dates of the event and follow several stages of La Vuelta. Most tourists of this profile do so in their motorhomes, taking advantage of the trip to visit different communities for the first time, while doing other socio-cultural activities. Cycling, unlike other professional sports and top-level sporting spectacles, allows fans to enjoy their idols in the front row and free of charge.

The organisation of La Vuelta estimates that in a single edition the event can have more than two million race attendees (López & Kettner-Høeberg, 2017). However, as it is an event that takes place in an open public space, it is very difficult to count spectator attendance accurately. Sports tourists attending La Vuelta travel an average of 151 km to attend a stage as spectators, spending an average of €37.7 per tourist per person (Vegara-Ferri et al., 2020). Moreover, it is not only the tourists who attend the event who spend money in the municipality; the media coverage and international broadcasting of the event means that spectators who follow the event on TV become potential tourists and may travel to these communities in the future.

As mentioned earlier, small communities are gaining presence in the event in recent years, hosting a large number of starts and finishes of La Vuelta. On many occasions, these communities are the venue for the end of key stages, as they tend to be located near high mountain passes of great difficulty. These mountain passes are very attractive for cycling fans who want to enjoy live the struggle of the best cyclists in their fight for victory. The authorities and the organisers are forced to close the town to traffic, even the day before the cyclists pass through, to avoid crowds on the day of the stage. Therefore, fans have to walk or cycle up the slopes in search of the best place to spend a great day of cycling in a festive atmosphere.

The communities near these mountain passes are often rural and remote areas that benefit greatly from the passage of the event, not only during the event but the residents are also left with many positive legacies. For example, one of the most emblematic high finishes of the event is the L'Angliru. The road leading to its summit was asphalted to allow the event to take place safely. In this way, residents who regularly use these roads have a better communication network, and the dissemination of the event worldwide has turned the mountain pass into a cycling route during the rest of the year, promoting sports tourism in the area.

Cycling tourism is booming, with increasing numbers of planned cycling trips; cyclists being attracted by the variety of natural, mountainous, and coastal landscapes (Kruger et al., 2016). The fine weather, the good condition of the roads, and the quality services in the hotels in Spain make it possible to meet the specific needs of cyclists, making it a preferred destination for many professional cycling teams to carry out their training (Rejón-Guardia et al., 2018). Javier Guillén, General Director of La Vuelta, indicates that 'when La Vuelta discovers a new mountain pass, cycling tourism in the area shoots up exponentially'. Another example is that thanks to the passage of the peloton, the only road linking the Asón and Miera valleys was built, producing a 60% increase in the number of cyclists, according to the Arredondo Town Council (2playbook, 2021).

Finally, another initiative developed by the organisation is the creation of events that recreate these stage finishes in the main mountain passes of Spain, making them accessible to amateur athletes, such as the 'Desafío Lagos de Covadonga'.

Conclusion

The La Vuelta sports event has a large budget, organisational complexity, and macroeconomic impact; and, above all, a large media coverage encompassing mass audiences and a large number of roadside attendees (Maennig & Zimbalist, 2012). These aspects allow it to achieve its objectives despite the limited time in which local communities host the event (Balduck et al., 2011). In short, La Vuelta generates a large number of benefits in the different host communities, regardless of their size, as it does not need large infrastructures to be held. The event generates a great deal of attention and media impact, which the communities can take advantage of to promote and project the community at a national and international level. Any sports fan can attend the event free of charge and enjoy an unusual experience. Like any sports event, its celebration can entail a series of negative impacts, although it seems clear that hosting a sports event such as La Vuelta nowadays entails a series of positive impacts that far outweigh the costs. The hosting of such a sports event by the local communities is currently a very profitable investment in the promotion and image of a destination and its local development.

References

2playbook. (2021). *El ciclismo, ante su mayor puerto*. Real Federación Española de Ciclismo, Telefónica & 2PlayBook. www.2playbook.com/uploads/s1/54/93/0/2p-insight-ciclismo-rfec-telefonica.pdf

AMBE & Cofidis. (2020). *El sector de la bicicleta en cifras. 2019. AMBE Asociación de Marcas de Bicicletas de España*. http://asociacionambe.com/recursos-2/

Avila-Palencia, I., Panis, L. I., Dons, E., Gaupp-Berghausen, M., Raser, E., Götschi, T., Gerike, R., Brand, C., de Nazelle, A., Orjuela, J. P., Anaya-Boig, E., Stigell, E., Kahlmeier, S., Iacorossim, F., & Nieuwenhuijsen, M. J. (2018). The effects of transport mode use on self-perceived health, mental health, and social contact measures: A cross sectional and longitudinal study. *Environment International, 120*, 199–206.

Balduck, A.-L., Maes, M., & Buelens, M. (2011). The social impact of the tour de France: Comparisons of residents' pre- and post-event perceptions. *European Sport Management Quarterly, 11*(2), 91–113.

Bastian, A., & Börjesson, M. (2018). The city as a driver of new mobility patterns, cycling and gender equality: Travel behaviour trends in Stockholm 1985–2015. *Travel Behaviour and Society, 13*, 71–87.

Berridge, G. (2012). The promotion of cycling in London: The impact of the 2007 Tour de France Grand Depart on the image and provision of cycling in the capital. *Journal of Sport & Tourism, 17*(1), 43–61.

Berridge, G., May, D., Kitchen, E., & Sullivan, G. (2019). A study of spectator emotions at the Tour de France. *Event management, 23*(6), 753 771

Bull, C., & Lovell, J. (2007). The impact of hosting major sporting events on local residents: An analysis of the views and perceptions of canterbury residents in relation to the Tour de France 2007. *Journal of Sport & Tourism, 12*(3), 229–248.

DGT. (2019). *Barómetro de la Bicicleta en España. Informe de resultados*. www.ciudadesporlabicicleta.org/wp-content/uploads/2019/12/RCxB-Bar%C3%B3metro-de-la-Bicicleta-2019.pdf

European Parliament. (2015). *Cycling mobility in the EU*. www.europarl.europa.eu/RegData/etudes/BRIE/2015/557013/EPRS_BRI(2015)557013_EN.pdf

Fallon, L., & Bell, A. (2018). *Viva la Vuelta 1935–2017*. Cultura Ciclista.

INE. (2020). *Movimientos Turísticos en Fronteras (Frontur)*. www.ine.es/dyngs/INEbase/es/operacion.htm?c=Estadistica_C&cid=1254736176996&menu=ultiDatos&idp=1254735576863

Kantarmedia. (2019). *El impacto mediático de La Vuelta 2019 supera los 115 millones de euros.* www.kantarmedia.com/es/sala-de-prensa/press-releases/la-vuelta-2019

Kettner-Høeberg, H., & López, B. (2015). The Vuelta goes glocal: Changes in the Vuelta a España's communication strategy and media relations under the new Amaury sport organization's management. *Catalan Journal of Communication & Cultural Studies, 7*(2), 181–196.

Kosche, T. (2018). A 200-year battle for position: The bicycle in urban transport. In A Becker, S. Lampe, L. Negussie, & P. Cachola. (Eds.), *Ride a bike! Reclaim the city* (pp. 16–21). Birkhäuser.

Kruger, M., Myburgh, E., & Saayman, M. (2016). A motivation-based typology of road cyclists in the Cape Town cycle tour, South Africa. *Journal of Travel & Tourism Marketing, 33*(3), 380–403.

La Vuelta. (2021). *Twitch y Podcast: las nuevas plataformas de comunicación oficiales de La Vuelta.* www.lavuelta.es/es/noticias/2021/twitch-y-podcast-las-nuevas-plataformas-de-comunicacion-oficiales-de-la-vuelta

Leopkey, B., & Parent, M. (2012). Olympic Games legacy: From general benefits to sustainable long-term legacy. *The International Journal of the History of Sport, 29*(6), 924–943.

Liu, C., Tapani, A., Kristoffersson, I., Rydergren, C., & Jonsson, D. (2020). Development of a large-scale transport model with focus on cycling. *Transportation Research Part A: Policy and Practice, 134*, 164–183.

López, B. (2010). Sport, media, politics and nationalism on the eve of the Spanish Civil War: The first Vuelta Ciclista a España (1935). *International Journal of the History of Sport, 27*(4), 635–657.

López, B., & Kettner-Høeberg, H. (2017). From Macro to Mega: Changes in the Communication Strategies of the Vuelta Ciclista a España After ASO's Takeover (2008–2015). *Communication & Sport, 5*(1), 69, 94.

Mackellar, J., & Jamieson, N. (2015). Assessing the contribution of a major cycle race to host communities in South Australia. *Leisure Studies, 34*(5), 547–565.

Maennig, W., & Zimbalist, A. (2012). *International handbook on the economics of mega sporting events.* Cheltenham, England: Edward Elgar Publishing Limited.

Ministry of Culture and Sports. (2020). *Sports Statistics Yearbook 2020; Consejo Superior de Deportes:* Madrid, Spain, 2020. www.culturaydeporte.gob.es/dam/jcr:47414879-4f95-4cae-80c4-e289b3fbced9/anuario-de-estadisticas-deportivas-2020.pdf

Plevnik, M., Retar, I., Pišot, R., & Obid, A. (2015). *Sustainable development of sports tourism.* University of Primorska, Science and Research Centre, Institute for Kinesiology Research, Annales University Press.

Prado-Antúnez, J. L. (2020). *ENAIRE con la Vuelta Ciclista a España. ENAIRE. Ministerio de Transportes, Movilidad y Agenda Urbana.* www.enaire.es/es_ES/2020_10_30/blog_vuelta_ciclista

Rejón-Guardia, F., García-Sastre, M. A., & Alemany-Hormaeche, M. (2018). Motivation-based behaviour and latent class segmentation of cycling tourists: A study of the Balearic Islands. *Tourism Economics, 24*(2), 204–217.

Unipublic. (2021). *La pasión que te toca. Libro de Ruta. La Vuelta 2021.* Madrid: Unipublic. Retrieved from https://www.lavuelta.es/es/libro-de-ruta-interactivo

Van Reeth, D. (2013). TV demand for the Tour de France: The importance of stage characteristics versus outcome uncertainty, patriotism, and doping. *International Journal of Sport Finance, 8*(1), 39–60.

Van Reeth, D. (2016). TV viewing of road cycling races. In D. van Reeth & D. J. Larson (Eds.), *The economics of professional road cycling. Sports economics, management and policy* (pp. 99–128). Springer.

Vegara-Ferri, J. M., Angosto, S., & López-Gullón, J. M. (2020). *Report 74th edition. La Vuelta 2019. Social and tourist impact.* University of Murcia. https://netstorage.lequipe.fr/ASO/cycling_vue/la-vuelta-19-informe-de-impacto-social-y-turistico-universidad-de-murcia-eng.pdf

Worldometers. (2021). *Bicycles produced.* www.worldometers.info/bicycles

Chapter 17

Traditional games and sports of the Iberian Peninsula as tourist attractions

Gonzalo Ramírez-Macías, Augusto Rembrandt Rodríguez-Sánchez, and Mª José Lasaga-Rodríguez

Introduction

The Iberian Peninsula has been endowed with a huge cultural wealth thanks to the heritage bequeathed to this Southern European territory by the Roman, Arab, Jewish and Christian cultures. No wonder, 65 places of this Peninsula have been declared by UNESCO to be World Heritage. This wealth has brought about an explosion of cultural tourism, understanding tourism as one where people travel in search of an experience associated with cultural products (Prieto, 2015).

Although cultural tourism has never been at the level of the highly sought for sun and beach tourism in the Peninsula, it does not cease to be relevant. This creates aesthetic, intellectual, emotional, even physical experiences of a very exclusive nature, being associated with the heritage of a specific region or country. In this regard, we should stress the concept of heritage, as nowadays 'there is no aspect of social life that is not given a heritage treatment' (Estévez, 1999, p. 118). Among these heritage products, architecture, archaeology, painting, and sculpture stand out but gastronomy, music, national parks, and traditional sports are just as important. The latter justifies their heritage status, as Blanchard and Cheska defended in their classic work (1986, p. 37) '[sports] they reflect the basic values of their cultural framework where they develop and therefore act as . . . a transmitter of culture'.

Based on this, in this chapter, we focus on the issue of whether traditional sports of the Iberian Peninsula have the tourist impact like other more traditional elements of cultural heritage have, such as architecture, gastronomy, painting, or archaeology. To answer this question, it is necessary to define what we consider to be a sport. For this purpose, following Jiménez-Naranjo (2019), our definition is based on Article 2 of the European Sports Charter (1992): All forms of physical activity which, through casual or organised participation, aim at expressing or improving physical fitness and mental well-being, forming social relationships, or obtaining results in competition at all levels. Regarding the concept of 'traditional', and according to Lavega and Olaso (2003, p. 13), a traditional sport would be repeated and transmitted from one generation to the next. Nevertheless, for this chapter, we have decided to include a third defining concept, that of

DOI: 10.4324/9781003197003-17

'grassroots', which, refers to those practices that belong to a group of people, and are therefore known and spread through the population (Lavega & Olaso, 2003).

Therefore, we have set ourselves the goal of analysing traditional (i.e. grassroots) sports that are common in the Iberian Peninsula and relevant for tourism. To present the information precisely, we distinguish between active tourism and passive participation in these sports. This classification criterion is based on the work of Hall (1992) who introduced the notion of a tourist taking part in a sporting activity as an observer, as well as on the work of Gamon and Robinson (1997) who discuss the possibility of active or passive tourists' participation in a sporting activity.

Traditional sports as active tourist attractions

Paths, trails and greenways

Hiking consists of walking along a marked itinerary that might be a path, a natural trail, or a greenway, depending on the type of infrastructure it has. Although walking is an action long associated with mankind, hiking as a sport started in France after World War II. It was introduced into Spain through Catalonia at the end of the 1960s, and ever since it has grown in popularity. Hiking offers its practitioners the possibility of being in contact with nature while indulging in a sporting, recreational, and tourist activity.

Infrastructure that has a historical meaning, such as railways, canals, towpaths, livestock trails, and paths, among others, receive a new lease of life thanks to hikers. They are turned into active tourist attractions and services, acting as points of interest for tourists at the same time that they emerge as an opportunity for economic development, recovery, and revitalisation of the roads and historical and cultural heritage of the area in which this infrastructure is located. Undoubtedly the *Camino de Santiago*, considered to be one of the most important pilgrimages in Europe, is the best-known road in the Iberian Peninsula: it consists of more than one road, it is a network of roads crossing not only the Peninsula but all of Europe, and their goal is to arrive at the Cathedral of Santiago de Compostela and visit the crypt of the apostle Saint James, especially for those who follow this route for religious reasons. The volume of people that travel along with it throughout the year, from different parts of the world has turned it into an activity with a strong economic impact, particularly in Galicia.

The first road was built in 842 from Oviedo by the Asturian king, Alfonso II, taking advantage of trade routes and Roman roads, making it the first official road, which came to be known as the Primitive Way. One of the routes that enable us to understand the international nature of this pilgrimage, is the *Portuguese Way* that from the 12th century enabled the flow of pilgrims towards the north of the peninsula, establishing not just spiritual but also economic and cultural connections within the Iberian Peninsula.

Via ferratas and equipped paths

The *via ferratas* have become a tourist attraction for those who seek to do outdoor sports. They are a new way of being a tourist, they allow a wide range of tourists accesses to unusual places that would otherwise be difficult to reach safely. To be specific, they consist of mostly vertical itineraries along which one travels tightly fastened to a steel cable using a system of karabiners (Forés et al., 2003).

In Spain there are more than 240 via ferratas while in neighboring Andorra there are more than ten well-kept ones, thus showing that the government of Andorra supports active tourism. These have consolidated in recent years and nowadays constitute one of the tourist attractions of the Pyrenees.

The *equipped paths* are similar to the via ferratas, although these itineraries can be both vertical and horizontal, and although they do not need a safety cable, they usually have materials or infrastructures, such as bridges or handrails, that facilitate their use and make it possible for a broader sector of the population to use them.

The origin of these types of roads is mainly historical, as most of them were created to access isolated or remote areas, although nowadays they form part of the range of active tourism activities in some areas of the Iberian Peninsula. Given the impact they have on the areas where they are located, town councils are getting involved in their construction aiming to promote tourism, thus taking advantage of the natural resources they have as a tourism wealth-creating strategy.

Of the equipped paths of the Iberian Peninsula, the *Caminito del Rey* in Malaga (King's Path) is particularly popular. It passes through the Gaitanes Ravine, between the municipalities of Álora and Ardales. It was built at the start of the 20th century since then the infrastructure of the route has been rehabilitated, the works concluding in 2015. This activity generates revenues worth millions. It has become one of the huge attractions of this southern province of the peninsula and is generating an unquestionable economic and tourist impact.

Neighbouring Portugal boasts of the Paiva Walkways (Arouca). These are 9 Kilometres of bridges, roads, and stairs beside the Paiva river, in the northeast of Portugal, between Areinho and Espiunca, where the beauty of the gorge can be observed, created by the passage of the river of over millions of years together with its natural pools and rapids, that also attract practitioners of rafting. Although the place went up in flames when it first opened, it was quickly reconstructed, thus allowing local villages to continue enjoying the success that this tour of wooden walkways entails, benefitting their economy, thanks to the effects of this tourism.

Speleological tourism

To practice speleology as a sporting activity, it is necessary to have at least some physical and mental preparation as well as being accompanied by a specialist guide. On the other hand, speleological or underground tourism, consisting of visiting tourist caves for recreational purposes, makes it possible for broad sections of the population to actively visit caves and chasms. This activity has been a practice since the end of the 18th century.

At the end of the 20th century, the Association of Spanish Tourist Caves was founded in Spain. This Association brings together caves open to the public in every corner of Spain's underground heritage. The Association has a mission to preserve these caves and show them to visitors, thus allowing the public to learn about and enjoy the caves (Durán, 2006). Visits to these spaces have become an event of interest with which they seek to promote underground tourism. The following are some examples of caves that are considered to be relevant tourist attractions in different parts of the peninsula.

To the south, we find the Grotto of the Marvels, which is the first cave to have opened to the public in the Iberian Peninsula. It is found in the town of Aracena (Huelva). This cave was discovered at the end of the 19th century. Works started in 1911 and it was opened to the public in 1914. This is a place of Tourist Interest in Andalucia and has turned into one of the most visited natural monuments in the community, with the consequent economic impact on the area. To the North, in Cantabria, the Cave of El Soplao, with geological and mining interest, not only offers tourists a visit by train or walking, but it also possesses yet another tourist attraction, full of adventure for the more daring, via an underground ferrata.

You can find a visit to the Recuenco Cave among the tour packages on offer in Andorra. This has been declared a Site of Community Interest within Natura 2000 because of the important colonies of bats that inhabit it and, more recently, has been declared a Point of Geological Interest.

Water sports

River-based sporting activities are another tourist attraction, especially at the hottest times of the year, when they become an inland alternative to coastal tourism. From activities where oars are the motor of action, such as canoeing or paddle surf, to activities that need natural elements such as the wind and the current. Many areas in the Peninsula are the perfect scenario, given their network of rivers and tributaries, for these types of activities, which in most cases end up becoming the main tourist attraction of the area.

One outstanding example is to be found in the Descent of the Sella River, from Arriondas to Ribadesella (Asturias). The origins of the feat go back to 1931 and although it started as a provincial event, it quickly became a national and international competition and is now one of the most important events in world canoeing at a level of competitive sports. But, the popularity of the descent of this river is not only apparent on the day of the Canoe Festival, declared a Festival of Interest to International Tourism, that, apart from the sporting event where tourists are welcome as spectators, it also offers other festivities such as parades, music, and food. All year round and especially during the hottest times of the year, a multitude of users go down the river by canoe, thus not just generating economic benefits for the companies directly involved in the descent of the river as an active tourism activity, but also serving as an incentive and tourist attraction to revitalise a very specific part of the Iberian Peninsula.

The *trainera* regattas, with their origins in fishing, are yet another water sport. The historic origin of these regattas lies in fishing boat (*traineras*) competitions between the autonomous communities on the Cantabrian coast (Galicia, Asturias, Cantabria, and the Basque Country). Although the first unofficial competitions date back to the mid-19th century, the first event of the national championship was not held until 1944. Its popularity and history make this a summer event of interest for anyone visiting the coast on those dates.

Traditional sports, an offer for event tourism

Ball games

Arruabarrena et al. (2014) define these games as games where a ball is passed between opposing players, the aim is to make it impossible for the opposite contender to return the ball. In the Peninsula, games of this type can be identified as sports where visitors, of said regions, can either spectate and/or practice.

Basque pelota (Basque ball) is a traditional sport played in the Basque Country, Navarra, and La Rioja, in the north of Spain. In the Basque Country, its origins date from the 16th and 17th centuries, and it was institutionalised at the start of the 20th century (González-Abrisketa, 2006). The game is played on a piece of land known as fronton, where the players ('*pelotaris*') take turns hitting a ball (preferably with their hands) against a wall called a *frontis*. There are different playing methods, depending on the size of the court. Basque pelota enjoys so much popularity that the retransmission of some of its official competitions is offered on national television. Its practice has also spread to countries on the other side of the Atlantic, which gives rise to (European and world) international competitions, where not only players but fans and spectators travel to these events.

Valencian pilota (or *pilota valenciana*) is recognised as an Asset of Cultural Interest of the region. It is played in different regional and international municipal (Alicante, Castellón, and Valencia) leagues. Traditionally a street game, it reached its maximum splendour during the 19th century with the appearance of specific playing spaces: the frontons. It evolved into a sport in 1994, with different variations in the rules of the game, both direct (without fronton) and indirect (with fronton). Today it is experiencing a period of popularity as it is played in the region's educational establishments and its games are broadcasted on regional television. This, together with the prevalence of the use of Valencian in it, emphasises its cultural identity and makes it an attractive sport for visitors to the region.

As for the ball games typically played in Gibraltar, such as netball, arriving from England at the end of the 19th century, consisting in shooting a ball through a basket without a backboard, without players running with or bouncing the ball, or leaving their restricted areas. All this makes netball a very collaborative game where physical contact is forbidden. Although it is quite insignificant in the rest of the Peninsula, it has been played a lot in Gibraltar since the start of the nineteen nineties, there are currently 30 high-level teams and 16 teams in the junior league. The participation of Gibraltarian teams in international competitions attracts teams and fans, mainly from the Commonwealth, to the Rock. In 2016 the Europe sub19 championship was organised, with teams from all over the continent and, in 2019, the Gibraltarian combined sub17 won second place in the European championship.

Cricket has also been played in Gibraltar since the 18th century, having been brought there by the British army. In 1930 the Gibraltar Cricket Club was founded, an event that represented the consolidation of this sport on the Rock. It has become progressively professionalised and now is governed by the Gibraltar Cricket Board. The participation of Gibraltarian teams in International tournaments, such as the European championships or the Twenty20 International matches, makes for an important tourist attraction, as it enables matches between local and foreign teams.

Combat sports

Combat activities and sports are common in different cultural enclaves in any society. Four have been identified in the Iberian Peninsula with the most traditional and cultural attraction, which have given rise to local and international events and competitions surrounding their practice.

The first written records of Canarian wrestling, unarmed combat between two wrestlers where no blows are permitted, date from 1420. Although it came to be forbidden as it was thought to be shameless and savage, its practice did not disappear over time and it is currently considered to be part of the historical heritage of the archipelago. It was regulated with the creation of the Federation of Canarian Wrestling in 1943, which contributed to its institutionalisation as a sport, giving rise to competitive events that continue to be held throughout the region. The different local and regional championships make this sport an important tourist attraction, a must-see when visiting the islands.

The *Juego del Palo (Game of the Stick)* of the Canary Islands consists of a stick fight between two fighters, they each try to make a mark without making any contact. Forbidden during the historical period after the Reconquista, the *juego del palo* was clandestinely transmitted within families, which kept it alive as a cultural legacy. Its public practice was once again permitted in the second half of the 19th century, and then the *Agrupación Canaria de Juego del Palo (Canarian Stick Game Group)* was founded in 1994, and the *Federación de Juego del Palo Canario (Canarian Stick Game Federation)* in 1996. Considered to be a game, not a sport (as there are no rules of competition), its practice has been passed on by word of mouth from one generation to another, making it attractive to tourists in the area who seek to have a taste of one of the most important cultural expressions of the people of the Canary Islands.

Leonese wrestling (or *aluche*) was declared an Asset of Cultural Interest in 2017. This is a sport of unarmed combat between two wrestlers, classed according to their weight, typical of the Castilla and León community. This wrestling takes place inside a circular space with a diameter of 17 meters, where the wrestlers are barefooted, wearing short trousers, a shirt, and a leather belt. The objective of the match is to grip the opponent and make them touch the ground with any part of the body or to loosen their opponents' grip on their belt. Nowadays, its practice is organised into two sections: the winter league (where they compete in teams) and the summer league (individual), with the season concluding with a traditional mass event, a tourist highlight called '*Montaña-Ribera*' *(River Bank vs Mountain)*, where teams compete based on the territorial division created by the León-Bilbao railway line.

There is yet another type of wrestling in Portugal known as the *jogo do pau (stick game)*. Considered to be a martial art, it originated in northern Portugal, from where it spread to all the other regions of the country. Used as a personal defence until the mid-20th century, the fact that only a stick is needed for its practice facilitated its transmission from one generation to another. *Jogo do pau* championships became common overtime throughout the entire territory of Portugal. It lost relevance during the second half of the 20th century and it would not be until the last decade of that century when its practice was recovered, becoming more orientated on sport-competition, and focusing on its value as a traditional practice. There are frequent exhibition tournaments in the north of Portugal, in Montalegre or Cabeceiras de Basto for example. Even around Lisbon, it is practiced as a sport in numerous gyms, apart from forming part of the physical education programme in educational establishments thanks to its anthropological and cultural roots.

Games of force and precision

Fruit of the practices that are typical of a region, people's work, and trades are often the source of opportunities to play. So, it is possible to identify some sports in the Peninsula that, through the use of force or precision throwing, have given rise to competitions that have crossed over from being spontaneity games to becoming professional sports and spectator events.

As regards games based on feats of strength, the Biscayan Federation of Basque Games and Sports has distinguished up to 17 different kinds. These rural sports were born out of the jobs of work typically and traditionally carried out in the region, that made heavy physical demands on their practitioners. It is possible to differentiate log cutting with an axe (*aizkolaritza*), lifting an iron anvil (*ingude altxatzea*) or transporting weight as far possible (*txinga erutea*), among other things. All of which can be seen in local competitions during the annual competition season, where people can attend as spectators. Likewise, there are active tourism initiatives in the area that not only give a historical tour of these rural sporting activities but also give tourists a chance to experience, if they wish, some of them.

Another of the more common competitions in traditional games is throwing objects with precision. In the Castilla and León community, traditional games have this particular feature. Formally recognised by the Federación de Deportes Autóctonos de Castilla y León since 1988, they share common features with the traditional sports of the Basque region (such as log cutting, for example), with 12 different kinds having been identified. The fact that they have local and provincial competitions and are not very physically demanding also makes these native sports a matter of high cultural interest for visitors to the region.

In Portugal we have the *jogo da malha* or *chiquilho*. This popular sport, played in both rural and urban areas, would be played after a day's work or on Sundays, being a good recreational game for the working class, for them to socialise with their family and neighbours. Known colloquially as 'the game of the poor', it is very popular among the older generation in less affluent parts of town. This is played by pairs standing apart at a certain distance and consists of throwing small metal disks to knock down a pin at the feet of the rival. Despite its working-class nature, numerous tournaments are organised throughout Portugal, with the 'Festa da Malha' in Évora, which is held every year in September, being the most notable.

Games in traditions and festivals

Anniversaries and local culture give rise to regional celebrations throughout the territory of the peninsula that sometimes include sports and games. This means that the popular attraction of the festival not only lies in its folkloric nature, but also in the physical skills displayed there, which act like a magnetism for tourists.

In the municipality of Purchena (Almería) in the southeast of the peninsula, the Morisco Games of Aben Humeya are held. Dating from 1993 and declared as being of International Tourist Interest, they are held in the main square of the town, representing the games of Moorish tradition that Aben Humeya held in the 16th century in said town. These games, where participation is free after prior registration, include not only athletic feats of speed, jumping, throwing, and shooting but also singing and dance events, and are a curious and challenging *divertimento* for local tourism.

Further up the Mediterranean coast, there is the *moixiganga*. This is a dance expression consisting of the building of human towers, typical of festivals in the communities on the Mediterranean coast of the Peninsula. The first records of these are to be found in the 15th century. Tourists can enjoy these human towers in different enclaves, with the most famous ones being the *muixeranga* (typical of the Valencian Community and of a markedly religious nature) and the *castellers* (from the Catalan community, characterised by the height of their human towers).

Now in the north of the Peninsula, the '*cremada de falles*' of Andorra takes place on the nights of the 23rd of June (the festival of San Juan) and the 28th of June (the festival of San Pedro). This consists of making a torch, traditionally from silver birchbark and nowadays from pine pulp paper, rolled up in a metal mesh and tied with a chain, which is then set alit and swung through the air, creating bright circles of fire, while walking through the streets. Just as was a historic custom in the region, there are commonly training workshops at that time of the year so that any member of the public can make and enjoy their torch in the Andorran night.

On these same summer dates, 'El Paso del Fuego' (Fire-Walking), a festival that was declared to be National Tourist Interest in 1980, is held in the town of San Pedro Manrique (Soria). This festival, which takes place at midnight on the 24th of June, consists of the local people walking across a path of burning embers in bare feet. According to tradition, the first three to cross must carry the three feminine representatives (*móndidas*) of these festivities on their backs, which guarantees a spectacle for any tourists who happen to be in the region on those dates.

In a less localised way, but also typical of popular traditions in the Peninsula, greasy poles are a feature of patron saint festivities in the summer. Thought to be an activity that came from Napoles in the 16th century, there are two types (on land and in water), where there is a greasy pole with an object on its end that the participants have to reach (food, in the olden days but usually a flag, nowadays). The version of a greased pole over water is practiced in almost every fishing port along the Cantabrian coast, spreading out to other places, such as the '*Velá de Santa Ana*' (Sevilla). While the land version is to be found throughout the Iberian Peninsula, as well as being practiced in some territories in Latin America. Owing to its amateur nature, the greasy pole is often open to anyone willing to try it, meaning that anyone who is enjoying some days off in the locality can have a go.

Conclusions

Tourism about traditional sports, in the context of cultural tourism, is becoming more and more relevant within the sports industry. Not only as part of the native cultures of the Peninsula but also as a complement to the sun and sand tourism, which is so prosperous and typical of this region of Europe.

Sports that particularly stand out among these traditional sports are the ones that relate to the natural environment, where ecotourism is combined with traditions. There, the tourist is immersed not only in the rich natural environment of the Peninsula but also finds out about the traditions, festivals, and customs of the rich cultural legacy of the Peninsula. It also important to consider that several traditional games also work as spectator sports, where people can attend as a spectator, or as a participant in those activities. Undoubtedly, this potential can and should be taken advantage of by the sports industry, as there is no reason why in Spain tourism should be confined to sun and sand. Traditional sports represent a significant part of cultural tourism.

References

Arruabarrena, O. U., i García, D. M., & Lasa, U. F. (2014). Los juegos de pelota a mano vascos y valencianos en edad escolar: una comparativa de la lógica interna y externa. *Acciónmotriz*, 12, 5–16.

Blanchard, K., & Cheska, A. (1986). *Antropología del deporte*. Bellaterra.
Council of Europe. (1992). *The council of Europe's work on sport: General works. Sport series*. https://rm.coe.int/16804c9dbb
Durán, J. J. (2006). *Guía de las cuevas turísticas en España*. Instituto Geológico y Minero de España.
Estévez, F. (1999). Descongelando cultura. Alimentación, museos y representación. In *Alimentación y Cultura. Congreso Internacional, Museo Nacional de Antropología* (pp. 117–131). La Val de Onsera.
Forés, B., Sánchez, D., & Sánchez, J. (2003). *Vías ferratas y caminos equipados*. Desnivel ediciones.
Gamon, S., & Robinson, T. (1997). Sport and tourism: A conceptual framework. *Journal of Sport Tuorism, 4*(3), 11–18.
González-Abrisketa, O. (2006). Fundación cultural en el deporte: el caso de la pelota vasca. *Revista Pueblos y fronteras digital, 1*(2), 65–82.
Hall, C. (1992). Adventure, sport and health tourism. In C. Hall y B. Weiler (Eds.), *Special interest tourism* (pp. 141–158). Pluto Press.
Jiménez-Naranjo, H. V. (2019). Modelo para la clasificación del turismo deportivo. *Eracle. Journal of Sport and Social Sciences, 2*, 5–21.
Lavega, P., & Olaso, S. (2003). *1000 juegos y deportes populares y tradicionales. La tradición jugada*. Paidotribo.
Prieto, J. J. (2015). Turismo cultural: el caso español. *International Journal of Scientific Management and Tourism, 2*, 95–114.

Chapter 18

Nautical sports in Spain

*Israel Caraballo Vidal and
José V. Gutierrez-Manzanedo*

Introduction

Nautical sports started in the 17th century in the Netherlands, where the first sailing yacht competitions began to be held (Caraballo et al., 2016). In the 19th century, the first yacht club was founded in England (The Yacht Club, London, 1815), where the first regattas were held. In Spain, nautical sports began to be practised later and linked to the royalty. The first regatta in Spain was held in Barcelona in 1900. That same year, the Federation of Yacht Clubs of the Cantabric was founded, and it consists of the following clubs: Real Club de Regatas of Santander, Real Club Náutico de San Sebastián and Real Club Deportivo de Bilbao (Caraballo et al., 2016). In Spain, there has been an expansion of nautical sports since 1960, due to the promotion carried out by the Spanish Government that encouraged tourism and real estate activities. Similarly, guidelines, legislation and technical regulation for the emergence of marinas have been established (Chapapría, 2018).

The socio-economic development of an area is highly determined by nautical sports activities, since these have a multiplier effect on the economy (Lam-González et al., 2015). This can be easily verified if we analyse the growth of tourism in some areas of the Spanish coast, such as the Balearic Islands, Andalusia, Catalonia and Valencia.

According to Ferradás-Carrasco (2001), nautical sports activities are characterised by their capacity to generate stable and qualified employment. In addition, these activities enable synergy with other types of tourism packages, have a lack of seasonality, and improve coastal infrastructures. Moreover, nautical sports activities are also characterised by their ability to adapt to changing trends in tourism demand and are attractive activities for a type of tourist with a high socio-economic level (Ferradás-Carrasco, 2002; Rivera-Mateos, 2010a).

The growth of nautical sports in Spain is associated with their ability to incorporate a greater number of services, and services related to sports and leisure time are those with better medium- and long-term prospects.

DOI: 10.4324/9781003197003-18

Littoral coast and nautical recreational infrastructures of Spain

Spain, with approximately eight thousand kilometres of coastline, has special characteristics in its orography and climate that give it a great potential to develop activities related to nautical sports and leisure (IGN, 2021). It is important to highlight that 7% of the total surface area on the Spanish coastline is occupied by port facilities (MITECO, 2021).

Among the different autonomous communities of this coastline, the Canary Islands have the longest coastline, with 1,583 km, followed by Galicia and the Balearic Islands, with 1,498 and 1,428 km, respectively (Table 18.1).

According to Rivera-Mateos (2010a), the facilities and infrastructures that support nautical activities are mainly marinas, and these can become an indicator of the level of development of coastal and river areas. The adaptation of these facilities to the required demand, as well as their quality and quantity, can help to know the level of the real and potential benefits they would be generating in the area. According to Alemany (2021), there are different types of nautical facilities in Spain, such as Marinas, which are defined as separate maritime facilities with a large offer of services for leisure sailing and users. Furthermore, marinas are considered as facilities within touristic urbanisation. Sport docks are facilities located inside a commercial or fishing port and jetties are small facilities with a limited offer of services.

However, the Spanish Federation of Associations of Marinas and Tourist Ports establishes five types of nautical facilities, specifying that not all of them are considered marinas (Rivera-Mateos, 2010b). Anchorages are characterised by the type of boat, which are located in certain places and neither docks nor piers are necessary. Sport docks are facilities inside a port where there are other types of facilities. Island ports are located in rivers or coastal estuaries, and, in these cases,

Table 18.1 Coastline of Spain in km (MITECO, 2021)

Autonomous communities	Km
Canary Islands	1,583
Galicia	1,498
Balearic Islands	1,428
Andalusia	945
Valencian Community	518
Catalonia	699
Asturias	401
Cantabria	284
Murcia	274
Basque Country	246
Ceuta	20
Melilla	9

Table 18.2 Percentage of the number of berth points by autonomous communities for a total of 131,100 berth points (DBK INFORMA, 2020)

Autonomous communities	%
Catalonia	22.4
Andalusia	16.6
Balearic Islands	15.4
Valencian Community	15.1
Galicia	8.1
Other communities	22.4

the facility invades the land area and has a breakwater to protect the mouth. The breakwater is the only element that protrudes from the coastline. Seaports are located along the coast and their mouth is protected by two breakwaters. A dry marina is an inland facility that allows the boat to dock on land and is mostly used during the seasons when the boat is not in use. They are in increasing demand, as they allow the boat to remain in good condition during the time of inactivity.

The report conducted by DBK Sector Observatory (DBK INFORMA, 2020) reflects that, in the year 2020, Spain had 292 marinas with 131,100 berth points, and 68% of these berth points were located on the Mediterranean Coast. By Autonomous communities, Catalonia is the community with the largest number of berth points (29,311; 22.4%), followed by Andalusia (21,765) and the Balearic Islands (20,170). These three communities, together with the Valencian Community and Galicia, account for 78% of the total national supply (Table 18.2).

Regarding marinas´ management, the agents or administrative formulas are as follows: Autonomous community (under direct management and indirect management based on a license), Port authorities (under direct management and indirect management based on a license), and Corporations and Nautical Club.

The development of nautical tourism

Spain has a wide coastline and potential for the development of nautical and leisure facilities, which makes it a country with great attraction for nautical tourism. Among the different types of nautical tourism, the subcategories with the largest number of studies in the academic and scientific field are cruises, nautical tourism ports (yachtsmen with or without their own boat), and boat chartering (rental of boats for recreation or diving, with or without the skipper) (Lam-González et al., 2015). These subcategories of nautical tourism have high economic profitability; thus they are considered as key elements in the tourism industry. In addition, these subcategories share the place in which they are carried out, i.e., marinas. Therefore, marinas are considered the most important facilities in the nautical tourism industry.

Some authors determine that the concepts 'Yachting tourism' and 'sailing tourism' are more current and both are linked to nautical tourism ports and charter tourism. (Besteiro, 2004).

Although nautical tourism in Spain is considered a strategic socio-economic sector, it has not been a focus of research; therefore, there are currently some gaps from a scientific point of view (Gómez-Javaloyes, 2012). This lack of scientific studies could be the reason why the development of nautical tourism has not reached its full potential. Several studies have shown that nautical products and services offered by the sector are not correctly adapted to the demands of nautical tourists (Esteban-Chapapría, 2000). This situation could be the main problem in the nautical offer design.

The concept of nautical tourism is complex, as it covers several nautical activities, and thus the points of view can be very different in the scientific literature (Luković, 2007). Nautical tourism is often associated with several tourism activities, such as marina tourism, yachting tourism, sailing tourism, and leisure boating of different scopes (Rahman et al., 2020). Some authors consider that this concept must also include other activities, such as ocean and river cruising, water sports, surfing, fishing, and squid jigging (Pavel-musteata & Simon, 2013). The most complete conception of nautical tourism is the one that defines it as the type of tourism in which the tourist are motivated by leisure, recreation, and sports undertaken at sea or intend to undertake some nautical activity in the area (Ferradás-Carrasco, 2001; Luković, 2007). Although it is not as widespread as the concept of nautical tourism, some authors have come to define this type of tourism as 'maritime tourism' (Hall, 2001; Orams & Lück, 2014).

According to Lam-González et al. (2017), marinas stimulate the development of tourism in the area where they are located, being a complement to the tourist offer and offering advantages in terms of destination valuation, tourist experience, and the added value of nautical activities. Therefore, marinas must be considered as potential facilities for the economic development of the sports and tourism sectors. However, Spanish governmental administrations have mainly focused on the study of marinas from a merchant marine and naval engineering perspective, while the sport-tourism perspective has been little studied.

The report carried out by DBK Sector Observatory (DBK INFORMA, 2020) shows that, in recent years, there has been an expansion of businesses related to nautical activities in Spain, mainly due to a context of economic development and the boom in national and international tourism. This situation has led to an increase in the number of recreational boat sales and the demand for fixed or transient boat mooring in Spanish marinas.

According to Rivera-Mateos (2010b), in addition to boat mooring, the facilities and services offered by marinas are key to the development of leisure, sport, and touristic sailing. These complementary services can be dry docks, fuel stations, mechanical services, nautical companies, nautical schools, nautical clubs, and stores.

An important characteristic of leisure nautical activities, and in which the Public Administrations and the business sector usually agree, is their capacity of adaptation to the continuous changes of the tourist demand. This tourist demand is focused on active leisure activities in direct contact with nature and is characterised by a high socio-economic status with high purchasing power (Rivera-Mateos, 2010a).

Regarding the socio-economic status and purchasing power of international tourists visiting Spain, it is observed that the total expenditure to carry out sports activities has increased since 2016, although in 2020 there was a tangible decrease (Figure 18.1). This drop is mainly due to the global pandemic of COVID-19.

Residents Travel Survey (RTS/Familitur) and Tourist Expenditure Survey (EGATUR) results show that, in the year 2020, international tourists made 400,000 trips for sporting reasons, of which 2.6% were made for leisure, recreation, or vacations (INE, 2020). It must be noted that, although the number of international tourists decreased by 72.9% with respect to 2019, the total expenditure associated with this tourism was 396,000,000 euros in 2020.

EGATUR Survey results show that, of the total trips made in 2019 by international tourists for sporting reasons, 1,947,000 were made for nautical sports and 450,000 for boating, which represented an expenditure of 2,438,000,000 and 572,000,000 euros, respectively (INE, 2020). However, in 2020, the trips made for nautical sports and boating were 644,000 and 136,000, which represented an expenditure of 736,000,000 and 163,000,000 euros, respectively. Regarding national tourism, the results of the same survey show that, in 2019, 4,283,000 trips were made for nautical sports (1,900,000,000 euros) and 4,212,000 for boating

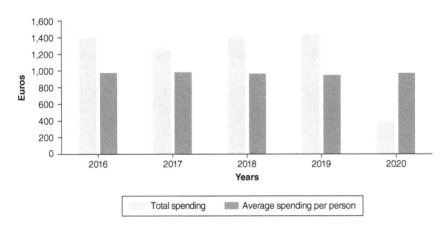

Figure 18.1 Evolution of total spending dedicated to sports activities by international tourists in Spain

Source: Based on data from INE, 2020

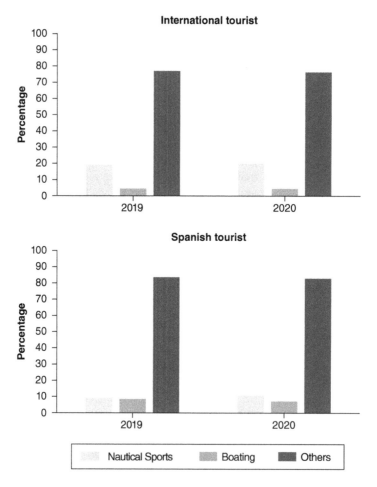

Figure 18.2 Types of trips made by Spanish and international tourists in Spain
Source: Based on data from INE, 2020

(3,284,000,000 euros). As in the case of international tourism, in 2020 there was a decrease in the number of trips for nautical sports (3,159,000,000 trips; 1,100,000,000 euros) and for boating (2,074,000,000 trips; 967,000,000 euros).

In terms of percentages and considering a total of 3,259,000,000 trips made by international tourists in 2020, trips for nautical sports was 19.8%, while only 4.2% of the trips were made for boating (Figure 18.2). For Spanish tourists, of the 30,364,000,000 trips made in 2020, 10.3% were made for nautical sports and 6.8% for boating. The results show that, compared to 2019, there was an increase in the number of trips for nautical sports. In addition, it is observed that, for this type of trip, the number of international tourists was larger than the number of national tourists in both 2019 and 2020. However, national tourists make a larger number of trips for boating compared to international tourists.

In nautical tourism, there is a modality in which a boat can be rented, with or without a skipper. This is a very interesting datum to determine the level of development of nautical tourism in an area.

Nautical sports licenses

The number of sports licenses is another indicator of the evolution of nautical tourism. Federation licenses are documents that allow the athlete to participate in official activities or competitions that are carried out in the national territory in a certain sport modality. These documents are issued by the Spanish or regional sports federations.

In 2020, the total number of federation licenses in Spain was 3,841,916, of which 153,024 were for nautical sports, representing 3.98% of the total number of licenses issued that year (Figure 18.3). The number of federation licenses increased from 2016 to 2018, reaching a total of 159,557 licenses. Between 2018 and 2019, the number of licenses decreased (144,554 licenses), although the data show an increase in 2020.

In percentage terms, regarding the total number of sports licenses, nautical sports maintain a stable representation of 4.2% for the period of 2016–2018. The values achieved in previous years were not reached between 2019 and 2020, despite its upward trend.

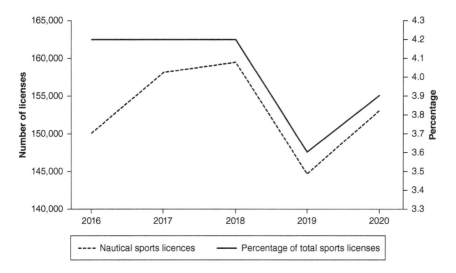

Figure 18.3 Evolution of nautical sports licenses in Spain
Source: Based on data from INE, 2020

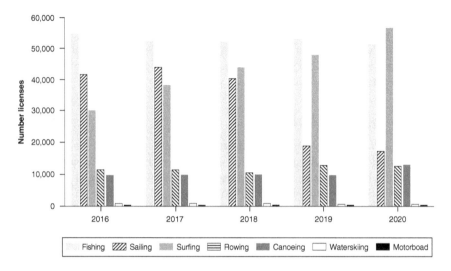

Figure 18.4 Evolution of the different types of nautical sports licenses in Spain
Source: Based on data from INE, 2020

In Spain, and based on the number of federation licenses, nautical sports with the highest representation are water skiing, jet skiing, fishing, canoeing, rowing, surfing, and sailing (Figure 18.4). It can be observed that, from the year 2018, the number of licenses decreased notably in sailing, while surfing presents an interannual growth from 2016 to 2020. In the number of federation licenses for the rest of sports, no notable changes are observed during this period of years.

By Autonomous communities, in 2020, it is observed that, in certain autonomous communities, a larger number of federation licenses are concentrated (Figure 18.5). For example, Catalonia is the region with the largest number of federation licenses in water skiing (434 licenses) and sailing (2,824 licenses), Andalusia in motorboating (94 licenses) and fishing (12,151 licenses), Castilla-La Mancha in canoeing (2,093 licenses), and the Canary Islands in surfing (11,912 licenses).

Strategies and tools to guarantee sustainability

Over the years, problems have emerged, mostly related to the number of infrastructures (nautical facilities and number of moorings) and their concentration on the Mediterranean coast of Spain (Alemany, 2021; Rivera-Mateos, 2010b). Nautical facilities are characterised by the construction of a large number of small capacities. Coastal management plans are inadequately managed. Some marinas and moorings have been built without foresight studies for their location and operation. Currently, regulations have been established to prevent uncontrolled construction and its possible impact on the coastal environment. Most of the nautical facilities

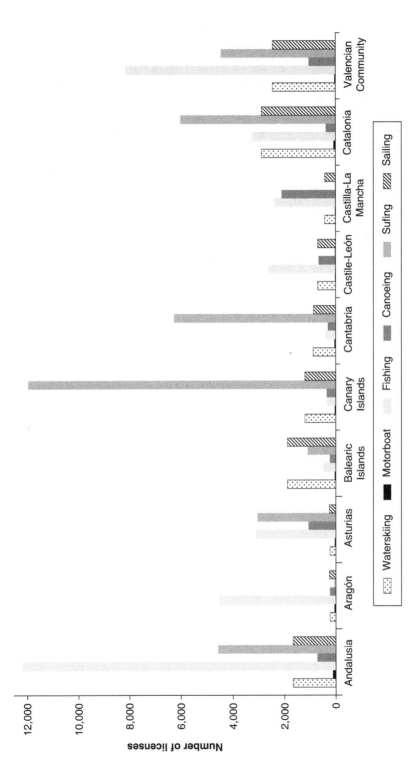

Figure 18.5 Types of nautical sports licenses in the different autonomous communities in Spain in 2020
Source: Based on data from INE, 2020

have been built without previous and independent studies of their environmental and socio-economic impact. In some cases, these nautical facilities could produce alterations of the coastal dynamics, modification of the marine environment and quality of the waters, reduction of the biological productivity, occupation of the maritime-terrestrial public domain, and covert privatisation of the management of the facilities. These circumstances could affect the image of the tourism sector and its socio-economic status. A study carried out in 2020 determined that 79% of the moorings were operated by private companies through a license, and only 21% were managed directly by autonomous entities or port entities (DBK INFORMA, 2020). The construction of some nautical facilities have been focused on tourism and leisure development and not on the services of nautical sports or recreational navigation. Nautical facilities are saturated during the summer months. This situation has led to the proliferation of illegal anchorages, for example on the Costa del Sol and the coast of Cadiz. The number of marina facilities for smaller boats has decreased, making room for port and mooring areas. Tourist exploitation of nautical activities is complex since there is no standardised regulatory framework at the national level for the planning, construction, and management of marinas. In some cases, there are incompatibilities among national, regional, and local legislation. Facilities are mainly oriented to sporting activities, and more specialised facilities designed for nautical-recreational activities are needed. Therefore, nautical-recreational activities are complementary activities, which reduces the development of nautical tourism. Services for nautical activities offered by marinas are not very diversified and have some legislative restrictions. For example, Law 21/2007 of Legal and Economic Regime of the Ports of Andalusia greatly restricts the creation of new stores, leisure spots, restaurants, and hotels in marinas. In some cases, the creation of marinas has been an excuse to carry out real estate projects, and this has increased the value of land prices. Nautical tourism companies and marinas should establish relations of integration and cooperation. Currently, there is no connection between the management of the facilities, the supply of nautical products, and the elements of the tourism system. Nautical facilities are not integrated into the urban environment to facilitate promotion and access for potential customers, including the local resident population (Ferradás, 2002). Moreover, products and services are poorly marketed and promoted. Environmental management systems are not promoted by the administrations or by companies in the sector. The nautical sector is subject to too many legal and bureaucratic hurdles, and the fiscal environment is unfavourable for the sector.

Although there are many problems and their resolution is complex, studies indicate that the solution is not the implementation of large-scale projects on the equipment and infrastructure of the ports. It is possible to implement proposals with a lower environmental impact, with great local repercussion and in synergy with the socio-cultural environment, the landscape, the territory, and the natural environment in coastal areas (Llorca & Velasco, 2002).

In addition to the problems described earlier, nautical facilities provide very important benefits and advantages for the socio-economic development of the area in which they are located. In this sense, it should be emphasised that these facilities are essential for carrying out nautical activities and for their promotion.

It should be considered that sailing is usually the first sporting activity with which one comes into contact with the sea, and with which certain values of conservation and respect for the environment are transmitted.

In an attempt to promote the nautical sports sector, Spanish administrations have developed different political actions and plans, such as the Spanish Tourism Plan Horizon 2020 (MITC, 2007). In 2020, one of the main premises of this plan was to make the Spanish tourism system the most competitive and sustainable, providing maximum social well-being.

Nautical tourism is considered a strategic and dynamic element of the tourism market, also contributing to greater sensitivity for the protection of the environment. In this sense, the main objectives proposed are to improve the legal-administrative framework for the development of nautical tourism, to improve the quality and professionalism of the services and products, and create new experiences in combination with other activities.

To adequately address the different problems mentioned earlier, it would be advisable for each facility to have a project and management in accordance with a clear and strict regulatory framework for the management of the coastline of each region or specific area.

The projects and the management of the nautical facilities must acquire new objectives and policies that are more in line with the current situation. Therefore, a revision of old policies and regulations is necessary to implement efficient and sustainable strategies. In the same way, the regulations of prohibition and/or total interruption of the facilities are not the most appropriate, since this could become an impediment for new generations to have access to nautical sports, and would only favour those who currently have boats and moorings.

Policies should be focused mainly on the preservation and progress of the coastal environment. The promotion of nautical sports such as sailing and rowing/canoeing can be very appropriate due to their low impact on the environment.

The legislation should be a tool for the various administrations (national, local, and regional) to curb attempts at speculation in the construction of new nautical infrastructure or remodelling of existing ones, in any case not associated with the real estate industry.

It would be necessary to carry out studies to determine the environmental impact that may be caused by the marina infrastructures themselves, as well as the impact derived from the use of their services and/or activities.

Nautical sports facilities must have adequate management of their use and their seasonality to avoid saturation in the months of greater affluence. One solution to this problem could be to encourage the use of dry marinas so that smaller boats that are not in use can leave their mooring to other larger boats that have greater difficulty finding a place to dock.

The companies that offer nautical services, the managers of the marinas, and the nautical tourism companies have to work together for better promotion of their sector. This greater promotion would increase the profits, and, in addition, it would allow making more efficient use of the resources and offering more affordable services to the population.

References

Alemany, J. (2021). *La náutica deportiva y los puertos de España.* http://retedigital.com/wpcontent/themes/rete/pdfs/portus/Portus_9/La_n%C3%A1utica_deportiva.pdf

Besteiro, B. (2004). El desarrollo del turismo náutico en Galicia. *Cuadernos de Turismo, 13,* 145–163.

Caraballo, I., Castro-Piñero, J., & Conde-Caveda, J. (2016). *Vela deportiva en España y Andalucía: clases Optimist y Laser.* Wanceulen.

Chapapría, V. E. (2018). Impacto económico de los puertos e instalaciones para la náutica de recreo y deportiva. *Revista de Economía Información Comercial Española, 901,* 105–114.

DBK INFORMA Observatorio Sectorial. (2020). *Puertos deportivos.* www.dbk.es/es/detalle-nota/puertos-deportivos-2020

Esteban-Chapapría, V. (2000). El planteamiento de infraestructuras para el turismo náutico. *Cuadernos de Turismo, 6,* 29–44.

Ferradás, S. (2002). El turismo náutico en el Mediterráneo. *Cuadernos de Turismo, 9,* 19–32.

Ferradás-Carrasco, S. (2001). La relevancia del turismo náutico en la oferta turística. *Cuadernos de Turismo, 7,* 67–80.

Ferradás-Carrasco, S. (2002). El turismo náutico en el Mediterráneo. *Cuadernos de Turismo, 9,* 19–32.

Gómez-Javaloyes, E. (2012). La gestión de instalaciones náuticas de recreo. *Investigaciones Turísticas, 4,* 119–131.

Hall, C. M. (2001). Trends in ocean and coastal tourism: The end of the last frontier? *Ocean & Coastal Management, 44*(9), 601–618.

Instituto Geográfico Nacional. (2021). *Relieve y costa.* www.ign.es/recursos-educativos/relievecosta/index.html#:~:text=Espa%C3%B1a%2C%208.000%20kil%C3%B3metros%20de%20costa

Instituto Nacional de Estadística. (2020). *Anuario de estadísticas deportivas 2020.* www.culturaydeporte.gob.es/dam/jcr:47414879-4f95-4cae-80c4-e289b3fbced9/anuario-de-estadisticas-deportivas-2020.pdf

Lam-González, Y. E., de León, J., & León-González, C. J. (2015). European nautical tourists: Exploring destination image perceptions. *Tourism and Hospitality Management, 21*(1), 33–49.

Lam-González, Y. E., de León, J., & León-Ledesma, C. J. (2017). Preferencias y valoración de los navegantes europeos en Canarias (España). *Cuadernos de Turismo, 39,* 311–342.

Llorca, J., & Velasco, M. (2002). Los puertos en la costa ¿un diálogo imposible? *Ingeniería y Territorio, 61,* 22–29.

Luković, T. (2007). Nautical tourism-definitions and dilemmas. *Naše more, Znanstveno-Stručni Časopis Za More i Pomorstvo, 54*(1), 22–31.

Ministerio de Industria, Turismo y Comercio (MITC). (2007). *Plan de Turismo español Horizonte 2020.* www.lamoncloa.gob.es/Paginas/archivo/081107-enlaceturismo.aspx

Ministerio para la Transición Ecológica y el Reto Demográfico (MITECO). (2021). *Perfil ambiental de España 2006.* www.miteco.gob.es/es/calidad-y-evaluacion-ambiental/temas/informacion-ambiental-indicadores-ambientales/perfilamb2006_marcogral_tcm30-185487.pdf

Orams, M. B., & Lück, M. (2014). Coastal and marine tourism. In A. A. Lew, C. M. Hall, & A. M. Williams (Eds.), *The Wiley Blackwell companion to tourism* (pp. 479–489). John Wiley & Sons, Inc.

Pavel-musteata, M., & Simon, T. (2013). Promotion nautical tourism in Romanian. *Romanian Journal of Geography, 57*(1), 63–75.

Rahman, N., Bazaruddin, N. H., Shah, S., Said, M., & Othman, M. (2020). The sustainability of nautical sports tourism in Terengganu using a cost benefit analysis. *Journal of Sustainability Science and Management, 5*, 148–161.

Rivera-Mateos, M. (2010a). Los puertos deportivos como infraestructura de soporte de las actividades náuticas de recreo en Andalucía. *Boletín de la Asociación de Geógrafos Españoles, 54*, 335–360.

Rivera-Mateos, M. (2010b). *Turismo activo en la naturaleza y espacios de ocio en Andalucía: aspectos territoriales, políticas públicas y estrategias de planificación.* Universidad de Córdoba.

Chapter 19

Global brands from the Iberian Peninsula

Nadal, Gasol, Cristiano, and Mourinho

Leonor Gallardo and Jorge García-Unanue

Introduction

Nadal, Gasol, Cristiano and Mourinho are all success stories, in both their sports careers and business. It is a known fact that sport and the economy feed off each other; these are areas that learn from each other. For this reason, many business projects should take into consideration the current activities of these athletes, which undoubtedly have an impact worldwide. In this chapter, we examine the accomplishments of these four sport figures which have transcendent the world of sport to become global brands.

Rafael Nadal is one of the most successful and recognised athletes in the world. When he was just 11 years old, he was the champion of Spain and, at 12, of Europe. When he was 17 years old, he played the Davis Cup; at 18 he won his first important tournament, and at 19, Roland Garros, became number 2 in the world ranking (Másmóvil, 2020). His victory in the Olympics Games of Beijing in 2008 should also be highlighted. His career as an athlete does not explain all his business success. In addition to the US$ 121 million he has won in prizes since 2001, he also has businesses in diverse sectors (Canal Historia, 2021).

Pau Gasol is a basketball player who has played for FC Barcelona (1999–2001), Memphis Grizzlies (2001–2008), Los Angeles Lakers (2008–2014), Chicago Bulls (2014–2016), San Antonio Spurs (2016–2019), Milwaukee Bucks (2019), Portland Trail Blazers (2019) and FC Barcelona (2021–present). As a Barcelona player (2000–2001) he received a professional player salary of 40 million pesetas, equivalent to 241,000 euros, and a termination clause of 580 million pesetas, equivalent to 3.5 million euros (Ruiza et al., 2021). Pau Gasol has earned most of his fortune by playing in the National Basketball Association (NBA), where he had accumulated more than US$ 200 million in salaries since he started in 2001 (García, 2019). The maximum salary he reached in a single season in the NBA was 19 million dollars, during the 2012–2013 season when he played in the Los Angeles Lakers, where he obtained two NBA titles (García, 2019).

Cristiano Ronaldo entered football history before the end of 2020 by breaking a financial record. He was the first football player to pass the US$1 billion mark in income, entering a select club of billionaires that includes Tiger Woods in 2009

DOI: 10.4324/9781003197003-19

and Floyd Mayweather in 2017. This placed the Portuguese footballer as one of the highest fortunes of the sport world, even in times of health and economic crisis. Cristiano Ronaldo can generate more than 100 million euros each year. No one has given Cristiano anything, his success was built from voracity, tenacity, and the ability to excel. You cannot despise his talent, physical level, technique, or intelligence, Ronaldo has achieved everything he had by his own merits.

José Mourinho is a football manager from Portugal who is considered one of the most accomplished coaches in the world. He has won 25 trophies, including four times the Best Club Coach in the World. He holds the record for winning a national title in four different countries including Portugal, England, Italy, and Spain. Mourinho is one of only three coaches to have won the UEFA Champions League twice with two different clubs, FC Porto in 2004 and Inter Milan in 2010. Mourinho's coaching career began at Benfica SL and União de Leiria, which were the first teams he managed. He continued his successful career at FC Porto, the first team with which he won the national league and the UEFA Champions League. After his first years in Portugal, he moved to England, where he won two national titles with Chelsea. He continued his career in Italy where he won his second UEFA Champions League with Inter Milan, along with two national championships with the same club. After two years, he signed with Real Madrid, where he spent three seasons winning the Spanish League, Spanish Cup, and the Super Cup. He then returned to Chelsea and won the Premier League for the third time, and then he later moved to Manchester United. He was Tottenham Hotspur's manager from November 2019 until April 2021.

Rafael Nadal

Personal brand and sponsorship

Rafael Nadal, also known as *Rafa*, is the tenth most commercially valuable athlete in the world. In 2016 this tennis player from Mallorca earned a total of 30.1 million euros in advertising and sponsorship agreements only, which makes him the tenth highest world athlete for earnings, without considering his earnings from competition. In 2020, Rafa Nadal became Santander Bank new 'long-term' ambassador. This was reported by the bank itself after signing an agreement with the tennis player, who had been linked for a long time with Sabadell Bank as his personal sponsor and the main sponsor of the Barcelona tournament, which he never fails to attend. Between June 2018 and June 2019, his accumulated earnings reached almost 32 million euros, where 24 million came from his sponsorships (Alonso, 2017).

Nadal's main financial support from the beginning of his career was from Nike. Under his hefty endorsement deal, which according to some sources was about 10 million euros a year before his last renewal in 2020, he did not include any other commercial logo on his clothing. The Oregon company also sponsors his macro sports complex, the Rafa Nadal Academy. Nadal's other main sponsors are

Telefónica, Kia, Babolat, Mapfre, Heliocare and Richard Mille. Nadal is a clear example of diversification, supporting not only personal projects but also sports facilities and sport academies (La Información, 2019).

Wealth and assets

Forbes estimates that Rafael Nadal´s total assets are worth around 300 million euros (Forbes, 2020). Since 2001, when he turned pro, he has won US$121 million in prize money. Nadal is one of the biggest attractions in world tennis and can demand appearance fees of more than US$1 million. Together with Abel Matutes Prats, former Spain's Minister of Foreign Affairs, Nadal is part of a group of investors who bought the building in the Salamanca district in Madrid for about 25 million euros. In addition, Nadal, Abel Matutes Prats, and other celebrities such as Enrique Iglesias and Pau Gasol, have opened four restaurants called Tatel located in Miami, Ibiza, Madrid, and Beverly Hills. Moreover, Rafa Nadal is an entrepreneur and advertising champion for several world-renowned brands. In Spain, he is one of the best-known images, along with Pau Gasol and Fernando Alonso. Finally, Rafa Nadal's website is also considered a gold mine, where people can buy products from the brands he wears.

Social responsibility

Since 2010, the entrepreneur's social and philanthropic activities have been concentrated on the Rafael Nadal Foundation, an entity dedicated to the social inclusion of children in vulnerable conditions, care for young people with intellectual disabilities, and the promotion of sports and academic talent. There are 23 centres throughout Spain and one in India. Also, the NETS school (Nadal Educational Tennis School), which in collaboration with the Vicente Ferrer Foundation helps an average of 250 children each year. In 2014 the Foundation opened a centre in Mallorca, where complementary school training is provided as well as socio-educational and psychotherapeutic needs for those who needed it. Moreover, Rafael Nadal joined NBA player Pau Gasol in supporting the Red Cross in efforts to raise at least US$10 million in support of those affected by COVID-19 in Spain.

Entrepreneurship

The tennis player inaugurated the famous Rafael Nadal Academy. The annual season at the Rafael Nadal Academy costs 56,000 euros per student, the monthly program 6,500 euros, and the weekly training around 2,000 euros. All of this is complemented with access to a gym, swimming pool, and other related services. As a newcomer to the world of franchises, the Rafa Nadal Academy, a tennis education centre that has grown rapidly in a period of four years, expanded to three new locations in the world, adding to the success of its flagship academy in Mallorca. This business plan brings together a series of evaluation tools and practical measures in an effort to achieve a franchise model that is ready to be used in the Singapore market (Berenstein, 2017). The project is based on the first experiences of the headquarters of the Academies established in Spain, Greece, Mexico, and Kuwait. It collects a series of good practices from the Academy and provides strength to some weak areas of the current business model. Finally, based on research and the financial model, the business plan concludes that Singapore is an ideal location for the next Rafa Nadal Academy.

In 2014 Nadal decided to enter the real estate business in style by becoming the developer of two luxury hotel complexes and buildings in large major cities. Currently, this project manages about 41 million euros, but it is not possible to talk about the real estate business without considering Mabel Capital, the investment firm in which Nadal owns a third of its capital after a successful operation that took place in 2020. The company ended 2019 with 110 million euros of equity and 6.64 million euros in benefits (Castelló et al., 2020).

Contribution to sport tourism

A recent study examined the effect Rafael Nadal's performance in the Grand Slams has on the market value of Iberia, the leading airline in Spain. The analysis shows that his victories in the matches of the Grand Slam tennis tournaments caused an increase in the market value of Iberia (Nicolau & Santa-María, 2017). The market value of Iberia was achieved via brand knowledge enhancement of Spain, which is Nadal's home country. This finding confirms not only the value of Rafa Nadal as a global brand but also his contribution to enhancing the brand of Spain. By enhancing the country's brand, Nadal is contributing to enhancing even further Spain as a tourist destination.

Pau Gasol

Wealth and assets

Pau Gasol has not only earned a great deal of money through basketball, but he has also known how to manage it well. Gasol has always led a quiet life without eccentricities, and currently, his net worth stands at 57 million euros, which includes buildings, farms, and the different homes he has both in Spain and the United States (Nieto, 2021). In the Sant Gervasi neighbourhood of Barcelona, he owns a three-story mansion where he resides when he is in Spain. It is not his only residence in the country, since he owns a 251-hectare farm near Madrid, specifically, in the town of Almoguera, in Guadalajara (Nieto, 2021). In the United States, he lives in San Francisco, after selling his Los Angeles house located in Redondo Beach for approximately three million dollars

The brand ambassador

Gasol has now become a perfect brand ambassador since he has avoided becoming an 'advertisement man' and made a few good deals. He has defeated the commercial aggressiveness that can take hold of great athletes, maintaining a great image and personal brand, and giving good publicity and fame to those brands with which he collaborates. According to Forbes magazine, all these agreements bring in about 2.5 million euros a year.

The brands of which Pau Gasol is a well-known ambassador include (Fraile, 2014) *Nike*, a historical ally of the Catalan since its early day. Gasol has done multiple advertisements for them, and *Nike* released clothes and equipment personalised by Pau Gasol himself. Another company is *Banco Popular* where Gasol has had a long-term relationship with this bank. Gasol has been key in the international expansion of the bank and has greatly helped it to gain market share in Spain, mainly in the savings market, thanks to the *Gasol Deposit*. The Pau Gasol Academy stands out among his collaborations with this bank; a summer campus for athletes with the support of many brands, which helped Banco Popular to attract and retain customers. Then is *San Miguel 0´0*, the non-alcohol pilsner-style lager. Gasol became an ambassador for this non-alcoholic beer brand several years ago. Together with his brother Marc Gasol, they have shot multiple commercials for this company with highlights that include announcements for the Spanish Men's Football team during international championships, particularly at the FIFA World Cup. Finally, is Iberia. Gasol also collaborates with the Spanish airline, for which he has carried out several campaigns, including that for the 2014 FIFA World Cup.

Entrepreneurship

Pau Gasol's most important investment is the Mabel Capital hotel group and the restaurants managed by this conglomerate, led by Abel Matutes (García, 2019). This group also has the support of other athletes mentioned in this chapter, such as Nadal and Cristiano. In 2005 Gasol he created a real estate company to manage his image rights; Futur 16. His father, Agustí Gasol, is the sole administrator of this company, which according to the last income statement had obtained 710,000 euros with a positive balance of 125,000 euros (Nieto, 2021).

Social responsibility

Pau is also known for his solidarity, highlighting the Gasol Foundation, known nationally and internationally. This foundation was started together with his brother Marc Gasol, to reduce the impact of obesity from childhood, give all children the opportunity to discover healthy habits, regardless of their physical condition (Gasol Foundation, 2021). In addition, he has been a goodwill ambassador for UNICEF since his move to the NBA, a charity with which he has worked in various humanitarian projects around the globe to help people who live in impoverished conditions.

Social media dominance

Pau Gasol has managed to handle himself well on social networks, reaching more than 10 million followers across the main social networks worldwide. On Twitter, he has 7.3 million followers, on Facebook 4.3 million, and Instagram 1.8 million. According to a study by Personality Media (2016), he is the second-best known and most valued Spaniard among Spanish athletes, only surpassed by his friend Rafa Nadal.

Cristiano Ronaldo

Wealth and assets

No one can have a real idea of what Ronaldo owns, except his management company, but most sources estimate that the figure is between 230 and 290 million euros. According to Forbes, Ronaldo earned more than any other athlete on the planet in 2016, at US$ 88 million, and was fourth on the list of the top 100 celebrities, behind musicians Taylor Swift and One Direction, and author James Patterson. These accounts were published amid controversy over his tax matters, and he revealed an income of more than 220 million euros before taxes in 2015 (Goal, 2015).

Entrepreneurship

Every step that he has taken in his career has been perfectly thought through and guided by his representative, Jorge Mendes, and his will to become the best in the world (in both sports and economics). He doesn't do anything for nothing. He acts with the knowledge of possible risks and takes advantage of his image by synchronising it with his other activities (Sánchez-Flor, 2020).

Cristiano's wealth is largely due to his self-esteem. Both discipline and effort are necessary to reach 35 years of age and have earned a billion dollars. The player has created his brand around the acronym CR7. This brand mainly focuses on its underwear line, but it has also evolved to include other clothing products, leisure, homes, shops, a shoe line, a chain of gyms, technology applications, video games, a museum, a bar, and so on. Cristiano also owns a chain of hotels, Pestana CR7 (Lisbon, Funchal, Madrid). The challenge will be to consolidate his brand after his retirement, as Michael Jordan did (Sánchez-Flor, 2020).

Cristiano participates in 19 SICAVS worth 14 million euros in Luxembourg (made up of the world's leading banks). His advisers have invested in large assets, including pharmaceutical companies such as Bayer AG and Roche (1.3 million euros each), and companies such as Apple, Zurich, Volkswagen, Carrefour, and Johnson & Johnson. We must not forget his role as an investor in fixed income, in hundreds of companies and banks: Iberdrola, Telefónica, Adidas, Coca Cola, Calsberg, McDonald's, and Pemez (Ribas, 2018).

Big data as part of his strategy

The world of football is a clear example of the expansion of Big Data in sport. There is thousand of data analysis of his attacks, shots for goals, possession of the ball, and other plays. His contribution to the success of his team is largely explained in his clear decision-making capacity and the elaboration of strategies that make him a master in the art of incorporating technology into his life and profession and thus enhancing his talent (Gallardo & Cubeiro, 2018). The numbers accompany Cristiano Ronaldo, he knows it and he makes it known to the coaches. His relationship with the data is close, which makes him an insurance for game performance purposes. In this same sense, the numbers also accompany him in business. The attraction numbers in its different business and advertising facets allow filtering the businesses to be developed and where they should be developed.

Sponsorship

Ronaldo's biggest endorsement deal is with Nike, and this is said to be the second 'lifetime contract' that the sportswear brand has awarded, after offering similar terms to three-time NBA champion LeBron James. Hookit sponsorship analysts estimate that Ronaldo's social presence alone brought Nike about 430 million $ in 2016. He also has commercial agreements with other brands, such as Armani, Tag Heuer, PokerStars and Castrol (Goal, 2020).

Social responsibility

In 2015, Cristiano Ronaldo was recognised by Dosomething as the most charitable sports star in the world. His collaborations include those with UNICEF, World Vision, and Save the Children, Ronaldo uses his fame to promote various causes including child hunger, obesity, and biodiversity. An example of this was a donation of 83,000 dollars to a 10-year-old fan who needed brain surgery, and a contribution of $165,000 to the cancer centre in Portugal that treated his mother. After the 2016 UEFA Champions League final, it was reported that the former Manchester United player asked his agent Jorge Mendes to donate his 600,000 euros premium to a charity he supports, and in 2018, he joined Enrique Iglesias to raise funds for the Portuguese Institute of Oncology (Goal, 2020).

Control of social networks

According to Hookit, Ronaldo was the first athlete to reach a total of 200 million followers on Facebook, Instagram, and Twitter. His Facebook page, in particular, is by far the most popular of any athlete. Ronaldo has more than 122 million people following him, ahead of the almost 90 million that Messi has. On Instagram, he also leads the ranking among sports stars, with 124 million followers. That puts him in fourth place, only behind Selena Gomez, Kim Kardashian, and the official Instagram account (Goal, 2020).

Jose Mourinho

Leadership

Mourinho's method is based on thorough preparation, total commitment, and challenging his players to do their best. He studies the game meticulously, and the phrase that is heard repeatedly is 'he knows what he is doing'. His knowledge gives his players confidence in themselves. This has proven to be contagious and inspiring, and players give it their all in return. He pushes people to always do their best. Players see how he gives everything for the team and they want to do the same in return. They know that their effort will be rewarded. He has turned groups of talented individuals into winning teams (Radošević et al., 2020).

One of Mourinho's players once said about his leadership style: Mourinho awakens feelings in people. When those feelings are of confidence and security, you end up winning eight league titles in 13 years. When they are scared and mistrustful, people end up looking for a new job (Kinley & Ben-Hur, 2020).

Communication management

The sports industry has developed so much that sports coaches have become as popular today as the best athletes in the world, which was not the case in the past. Today, many coaches appear more often in the media, and some are more popular than their players. A clear example of this is Mourinho. Mourinho is probably the only coach who knows the press very well and manages to use them for his own benefit. He uses the press to his advantage, and it has become a game, a pure marketing strategy. Sometimes the press is used as a channel through which coaches can motivate their players (Goal, 2015).

Personal brand

Mourinho, beyond the benches, has created an image for himself, and generates economic income external to sports. Eleven brands from different sectors trust him to be a spokesperson in their campaigns: Heineken (beer), Hublot (watches), Jaguar (cars), BT Sport (pay to watch TV), Adidas (sportswear), Atlantis Hotels (accommodation), Lipton Ice Tea (drinks), EA Sports (video games), American Express (financial services), Yahoo (telecommunications) and Paradise Co. (gambling) (As, 2019). This all meant a total of almost 11.5 million euros in commercial contracts, without counting social networks. He also collaborated with different television stations in the broadcast of matches during the 2018 World Cup in Russia, and the Asian Cup, where he obtained an income close to 2 million euros (La Vanguardia, 2019).

Special collaborations

XTB is a European broker with offices in several countries, including Spain and the United Kingdom. In 2020 Mourinho announced his collaboration with XTB as the starting point for a new global branding campaign entitled 'Be Like José'. This is a commercial strategy, which is based on the desire to do things well, and knowing how to learn from mistakes, which are factors of success for both the world of football and for finance (xtb, 2021).

Wealth and assets

José Mourinho has an annual salary of € 23 million for being a coach, which represents an income of 88,461 euros per day. (Tu Salario, 2020). Added to the different sponsorships, his income as a commentator and his investments, his assets oscillate in more than € 30 million, without adding the different investments in companies and real estate, where the official data is not known.

Conclusions

In this chapter, 'Nadal, Gasol, Cristiano and Mourinho', we have presented the beginning of a new era, in which Talent is the most valuable resource. They were born in Spain and Portugal and have become the world's most influential athletes and coaches. The Brand is a promise of value. To this day, Nadal, Gasol, Cristiano and Mourinho brands exceed billions of euros. Being the most followed athletes on social networks. In all cases, these sports figures have created a charismatic figure with clear associated values. But they all agree on something: 1) Commitment to social responsibility. Linking with social works in a public way, 2) the association of their brand with strong sponsorships that also unify in a unique way along with the rest of facets, not only sports and 3) a discreet way of managing their assets, expanding their businesses and companies without negatively affecting their image. All this thanks to taking advantage and value of talent, in a global way and not just sporting.

References

Alonso, L. (2017). *Rafa Nadal is the tenth athlete with the highest commercial value in the world*. www.rafanadalpartidoapartido.com/noticias/2017/01/12/rafa-nadal-es-el-decimo-deportista-con-mayor-valor-comercial-del-mundo.html

As. (2019). *The 'brand' Mourinho: Without bench*. https://as.com/futbol/2019/02/05/internacional/1549357849_646634.html

Berenstein, M. (2017). *Rafa Nadal, an example for young and veteran entrepreneurs*. https://emprendedoresnews.com/emprendedores/rafa-nadal-ejemplo-para-emprendedores-jovenes-y-veteranos.html

Canal Historia. (2021). *Profiles: Rafa Nadal*. https://canalhistoria.es/perfiles/rafa-nadal/

Castelló Monsech, M., Mokry, A. C. H., & Quinata Chennaux, B. J. (2020). *The Rafa Nadal academy franchise model in Singapore*. Master of Science International Business.

Forbes. (2020). *#80 Rafael Nadal*. www.forbes.com/profile/rafael-nadal/?sh=5bcbad311bb0
Fraile, C. (2014). *Pau Gasol—endorsement & brand ambassador. TV commercial: NIKE, Banco popular, San Miguel, foundation.* http://cesarfraile.es/en/anuncios-pau-gasol-popular-nike-san-miguel-iberia/
Gallardo, L., & Cubeiro, J. C. (2018). *CR007: Licencia para Ganar. Cristiano Ronaldo, el James Bond del fútbol.* Liberman.
García, J. (2019). *Pau Gasol's fortune: 200 million in salaries, mansions and Michelin-starred restaurants.* www.elmundo.es/loc/famosos/2019/11/25/5dd7c76cfc6c83ca1a8b461d.html
Gasol Foundation. (2021). *Pau Gasol and Marc Gasol foundation.* www.gasolfoundation.org/es/
Goal. (2015). *José Mourinho is dedicated to playing with the media.* www.goal.com/es/news/23/inglaterra/2015/10/05/16051572/deco-jos%C3%A9-mourinho-se-dedica-a-jugar-con-los-medios-de
Goal. (2020). *What is Cristiano Ronaldo's net worth and how much money does he make?* www.goal.com/es/noticias/cual-es-el-patrimonio-neto-de-cristiano-ronaldo-y-cuanto-gana-la-/1aou2k35wytbt1izlhy1u5xin3
Kinley, N., & Ben-Hur, S. (2020). *Leadership OS.* Springer International Publishing.
La Información. (2019). *Rafa Nadal's economic empire after the twelve Roland Garros: From hotels to yachts.* www.lainformacion.com/economia-negocios-y-finanzas/nadal-dinero-ganado-carrera-publicidad-negocios_0_1034897751.html
La Vanguardia. (2019). *The millionaire figure that Mourinho will now charge.* www.lavanguardia.com/television/20190115/454159706956/mourinho-comentarista-television-sueldo-futbol.html
Masmóvil. (2020). *Entrepreneur Rafael Nadal: The lesser-known side of the Roland Garros legend.* https://blogempresas.masmovil.es/rafael-nadal-emprendedor-faceta-menos-conocida-leyenda-roland-garros/
Nicolau, J. L., & Santa-María, M. J. (2017). Sports results creating tourism value: Rafael Nadal's tennis match points worth €12,000,000. *Tourism Economics, 23*(3), 697–701.
Nieto, J. (2021). *Pau Gasol and the example of managing a fortune as an NBA player.* www.elespanol.com/deportes/baloncesto/20210212/pau-gasol-ejemplo-gestionar-fortuna-jugador-nba/558445481_0.html
Personality Media. (2016). *Pau Gasol desbanca a Rafa Nadal.* www.personalitymedia.es/sitio/index.php/es/noticias/notas-de-prensa/item/142-pau-gasol-desbanca-a-nadal
Radošević, I., Gavrilović, A., Parčina, I., & Ahmić, D. (2020). *Coaching management in the sports industry.* University of Travnik.
Ribas, N. (2018). *Cristiano Ronaldo's business.* https://cronicaglobal.elespanol.com/deportes/cristiano-ronaldo-negocios_124100_102.html
Ruiza, M., Fernández, T., & Tamaro, E. (2021). *Pau Gasol. Biography.* www.biografiasyvidas.com/reportaje/pau_gasol/#:~:text=Pau%20Gasol%20debut%C3%B3%20en%20la,Jerry%20Stackhouse%2C%20se%20mostr%C3%B3%20imparable.
Sánchez-Flor, U. (2020). *Cristiano Ronaldo's $ 1 billion . . . and his 142 abs at 35.* www.elconfidencial.com/deportes/futbol/2020-04-07/cristiano-ronaldo-dinero-forbes-fortuna-negocios_2537756/
Tu Salario. (2020). *Salary José Mourinho.* https://tusalario.es/salario/vip/jose-mourinho
xtb. (2021). *JOSÉ MOURINHO Ambassador of XTB.* https://es.xtb.com/jose-mourinho-embajador-pr-xtb

Chapter 20

Sport governance in Portugal

Luiz Haas and Tiago Ribeiro

Introduction

Portugal is internationally recognised in sport by top-level football players and coaches such as Cristiano Ronaldo, Luís Figo, and José Mourinho and by the recent achievements of the football men's national team that won the European Championship in 2016 and the UEFA League of Nations in 2018/2019. In the context of Olympic sports, Portugal has produced several European champions such as Telma Monteiro and Jorge Fonseca in Judo along with many world-class athletes such as Fernando Pimenta and Emanuel Silva in Canoe Sprint, and Ticha Penicheiro in Basketball. However, even with some remarkable achievements at the Olympic Games such as Rosa Mota and Carlos Lopes in the marathon and Nelson Évora and Patrícia Manona in the Triple Jump, Portuguese athletes still fall below when compared to other European nations, particularly in terms of total number of Olympic medals (Fernandes et al., 2011).

The sport system in Portugal has been described as highly bureaucratic (VOCASPORT, 2014, p. 58) with a high level of government intervention that over the years has significantly shaped the governance of sport. Hoye and Cuskelly (2007) state that the relations between the government and non-profit sport organisations differ according to the type of organisations involved (i.e., national federations or local clubs) and the level of government involvement (i.e., local, regional, or national). In Portugal, the government's intervention in sport has taken on several forms. One of the most common forms of interventionism has been creating legislative instruments and allocating public funding (Carvalho & Mazzei, 2019).

This chapter discusses the transformation that has taken place inside the political governance of sport in Portugal since 1974 when the country returned to a new democratic period. The inclusion of sport into the 1976 Constitution of Portugal and the laws that regulated the sport system marked the starting point to understand the role of sport organisations and other stakeholders within the broader sport system in Portugal. Thus, in this chapter we will examine the role played by major sport organisations in Portugal and how several pieces of legislation impacted the way national governing bodies (NGBs) adopted practices of good governance in sports. The next section discusses the analytical framework

DOI: 10.4324/9781003197003-20

of sport governance, providing a theoretical support to the governance initiatives developed in Portugal.

Analytic Framework

Governance has been a topic widely debated in sport with many articles and books published on this subject (Dowling et al., 2018). Different concepts of governance exist in the scholarly literature whether they come from the public administration or management literature. Therefore, the definition of governance depends on what type of phenomenon is being studied (Geeraert & Bruyninckx, 2014).

Sport is characterised by existing in a complex environment where international federations (IFs) in partnership with national sport federations (NSFs) have the power and authority to control each sport autonomously from the State. However, many national organisations depend on governmental support to function, especially on financial resources derived from public money. Moreover, this relationship is even more complex as governments also influence the broader environment through sport-specific laws. If other interest groups such as the media, regulators, and sponsors are added into this equation, then sport governance becomes a 'complex network of stakeholders who act and respond to different agendas with little or no coordination among them' (Bravo & Haas, 2019, p. 81).

In a simple explanation, sport governance is how sport organisations and the system where they function are steered and controlled (Shilbury et al., 2013; Dowling et al., 2018). To facilitate the discussion of governance at different levels, Henry and Lee (2004) separated this concept into three approaches: systemic, organisational and political.

According to Henry and Lee (2004), systemic governance is related to the interactions between the multiple organisations within the sport system. These relations include competition, cooperation, and mutual adjustment between sport organisations acting at different levels (local, national, and international), government, transnational actors (i.e., European Union, United Nations), regulatory agencies (i.e., WADA and National Anti-Doping Organisations), sponsors, media, and representative associations (i.e., European Club Association, EU Athletes).

The second approach of sport governance refers to organisational governance, which focuses on the internal environment of sport organisations. Also known as 'good governance' or 'corporate governance', this concept emphasises the processes, norms, and standard management practices used to steer each sport organisation ethically. In recent years, many high-profile sport organisations (i.e., IOC) and governments (i.e., UK, Australia) have published governance codes to encourage and inform the importance of adopting good practices in sport organisations. Walter and Tacon (2018) examined the governance 'codification' process in the UK sport sector and they found that adopting a code of governance helps the organisation create external and internal legitimacy.

Finally, the third approach is political governance, which describes how the processes and policies used by governments and governing bodies influence the functioning of the sport system. This influence can be exerted through direct or indirect intervention strategies such as funding, legal regulations, or moral pressure.

The following sections discuss how these three approaches of sport governance proposed by Henry and Lee (2004) have been manifested in the sport system in Portugal. We begin discussing political governance since in Portugal's case it provides a basis for the other two. Also, to illustrate the high dependency of many sport organisations with the public structures a brief description of how sports are funded in Portugal is provided.

Political sport governance in Portugal

In Portugal, there is a historical background to this political dimension. A series of critical shifts regarding the political governance of sport have taken place in Portugal in the last 50 years, and it all started with the decline of the *Estado Novo*, or the New State, which was the authoritarian and nationalist regime that existed in Portugal from 1933 to 1974 that had social control of youth as one of its objectives and used sports to do so (Fernandes et al., 2011). But on April 25, 1974, Portugal's political system changed due to the 'Carnation Revolution' which overthrew the authoritarian regime and began a democratic phase in Portugal (Drumond, 2013) that viewed sports as a political resource in making progress toward a plural and participative society.

This new way to promote sports is evidenced in the first Constitution of the Republic of Portugal promulgated in 1976 where it recognises sports as a fundamental right (Meirim, 2004). Furthermore, the right to physical education and sport is enshrined in Article 79 under the umbrella of Section II dedicated to 'Rights, Freedoms, and Safeguards' under Chapter III that covers 'Cultural Rights and Duties' (Mestre, 2010). Article 79 provides an encompassing meaning for the term sports including recreational, performance, and elite levels where all three seek to promote a healthy living environment not only for professional athletes, but also for ordinary people as well (Meirim, 2004; Carvalho & Mazzei, 2019). In addition, the inclusion of physical education and sport in the Constitution shows the beginning of the legal interventionism of the State within the sport sector. However, during this time state interventionism was still weak as it was characterised by a period of dispersing and non-integrated sport policy (Mestre, 2010) where the government programs still reflected the lack of a serious commitment to sport.

The first nine years (April 1976 to November 1985) of the 'democratic phase' in Portugal were characterised by substantial disinvestment in government support for sport organisations and the practice of sport was mainly motivated by political reasons (Fernandes et al., 2011). This period is referred to as the first Portuguese constitutional government during which Portugal had nine different administrations with eleven ministers of sport. This period had the highest turnover of governmental officials and sports secretaries (Silva, 2009).

In the late 1980s, the passage of a sport policy strategy titled 'Sport in the 1990s' brought new ideas to Portuguese sport. This document included a model for sport development according to the latest trends in Western Europe (Fernandes et al., 2011). The policy focused on three main objectives: (1) promote access to sport, (2) facilitate a subsidiary model for elite sport, and (3) contribute to the development of sport clubs. Based on this strategy, sport organisations across Portugal worked to enhance their operations seeking to strengthen the relationship between sport for all and high-performance sport. As a result of these efforts, the next administrations included in their program the need to provide support for Portuguese athletes while focusing on better results at the European and World Championships and also at the Olympic Games. The results achieved by the Portuguese athletes in the 1984 Los Angeles and 1988 Seoul Olympic Games also contributed to make legitimate and strengthen the sport development process in Portugal (Pires, 2015).

Changes to these initial policies took place in the early 1990s. The Portuguese government published the Basic Sport System Law (Law No. 1/1990 of January 13th) that for the first time defined the main features and objectives of the national sports system (Fernandes et al., 2011). This legislation established a general legal framework and aimed to identify and regulate the role of the main stakeholders: the non-governmental sport organisations (i.e., national federations, regional associations, and sport clubs), the National Olympic Committee (NOC), as well as the public offices that were in charge to manage sport in Portugal (e.g., Portuguese Institute of Sports) (Silva, 2009). In this way, the entire sport system witnessed the creation of several public organisations that established guidelines towards the modernisation of their structures such as the National Institute of Sport (NIS), the Sport Studies and Training Centre (SSTC), and the Sports Activities Support Complex (SASC). Despite its significance importance, this law was never effectively monitored and took more than a decade to become a reality (Mestre, 2010). As a result, during this time a comprehensive sport system was never fully implemented, but instead these efforts were only a series of sporadic and uncoordinated public interventions.

A review of the 'Basic Sport System Law' took place during the 2000s resulting in the approval in 2007 of the 'Basic Law of Physical Activity and Sport'. Its objective is to promote and offer guidance in promoting sport activity as 'an indispensable cultural factor for the complete education of the human being and the development of society' (Law no. 5/2007 of January 16th, p. 1). This law directly touches several aspects of the Portuguese Sports System such as sport at schools and universities (curricular and extracurricular activities), sport in the armed forces, sport at the workplace, sport in prisons, etc. (Mestre, 2010). In addition, this law covers not only participatory sport, also known as 'sport for all,' but also professional and high-performance sport.

Over the last decade (2010–2020) the Portuguese government has developed a set of documents and policies aimed to reach out to the younger population and broader population of sport participants in Portugal. Some of these documents and initiatives are the national policy titled 'Strategic Options', the Public Institutes, and the legislation related to sports practitioner employment contracts. But despite these efforts, the political governance of sport in Portugal has still fallen short in many fronts and remains highly dependent on the State.

Systemic sport governance in Portugal

After 1974, the role of the Portuguese government in sport was reorganised across three levels: national, regional, and local. However, over the lasts 50 years, the decentralisation of many sport entities regarding central government control has been a characteristic in the governance of many national governing bodies (Lopes, 2017). Thus, throughout this time there was a change from a model of central control by a single entity (e.g., State General-Directorate) to a more decentralised system operating at different levels. Many sport organisations began to structure and organise their activities in alignment with the need of regional governments and local authorities such as city halls and parish councils, which have also acquired a growing role at the local level (Sousa, 2013).

Over the years, the organisational structure and line of reporting of the Portuguese sport governance system have changed to include different Cabinets and Ministries (e.g., Ministry of Education, Ministry of Culture, and Presidency). Currently, the highest public authority related to sport in Portugal is the Secretary of State for Youth and Sport who depends on the Ministry of Education (Portuguese Republic, 2021). The role of this office is to establish policies and guidelines at a national level and to foster the best technical and material conditions for sport development so all types of sports activities can be developed (Mestre, 2010). Figure 20.1 shows the most current structure of the Portuguese sport governance system.

The main public entity of the Portuguese sports system is the Portuguese Institute for Sport and Youth (IPDJ), which operates with managerial and financial autonomy (Mestre, 2010). The IPDJ role is to support the identification, implementation, and evaluation of national public policies and support regular and high-performance sport through technical, human, and financial resources (IPDJ, 2021).

In link to the IPDJ is the Portuguese Anti-Doping Authority (ADoP) that focuses on controlling and fighting doping in sport. This organisation is responsible for enforcing the rules towards doping control (Mestre, 2010). Related to this entity is a governmental initiative named the National Plan for Ethics in Sport (PNED), which aims to disseminate and promote the experience of ethical values involved during the practice of sport.

At the national level, there is also the General-Directorate of Education that oversees sport in schools (*Desporto Escolar*). This organisation provides support for the development of sport activities as well as investment in sport facilities at schools (Lopes, 2017). Furthermore, in higher education, there is the Portuguese

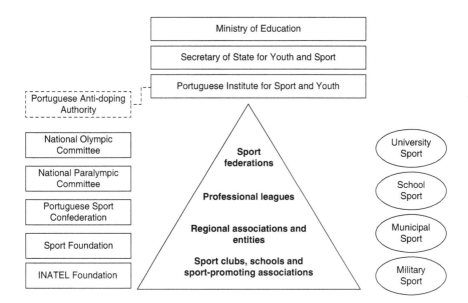

Figure 20.1 Pyramid structure of Portuguese sport governance

University Sport Federation that is an umbrella federation responsible for coordinating, promoting, and developing collegiate sports inside institutions of Higher Education (Yandjou, 2011). Meanwhile, in the structure of the Ministry of National Defence, the Committee on Physical Education and Military Sports, created in 1965, is responsible for supporting Military Sports comprising all of the sport activities and competition events of the Portuguese Armed and Security Forces (Frazão, 2015). Moreover, at the local level, sport is supported by the City Hall and parish councils to promote physical activity and sport for all (Medroa, 2018). It is important to note that some Portuguese City Halls also provide support to elite athletes, clubs, as well as sports facilities.

Regarding the voluntary, non-profit sport system in Portugal, sport clubs support is guaranteed by the Regional Associations and National Governing Bodies (NGBs or National Federations). In Portugal, there are single-sport federations, which are those that include people or National Sporting Organisations (NSOs) who play the same sport (i.e., Portuguese Basketball Federation) and there are multi-sport federations (i.e., Portuguese Winter Sport Federation), representing a range of sports for their specific areas, namely sports for the disabled or sports played within the education system. In addition, many NGBs include athletes, clubs, and regional associations in their governance structure, and also those who engage in sport competitions within a professional league.

Other non-governmental sport organisations also support and represent their members with other public and private stakeholders. The Portuguese Sport

Confederation, an umbrella organisation founded in 1993, provides support to affiliated NGBs. The Sport Foundation, a private foundation with public-interest status founded in 1995, provides support for the development of sport mainly at the elite-performance level. Similarly, the National Institute for the Use of Free Time (INATEL) created in 1935 exists to promote the conditions for leisure and recreation for workers by developing and enhancing cultural, physical, and sport activities through social inclusion and solidarity. Lastly, the Olympic Committee of Portugal and Paralympic Committee of Portugal (OCP and PCP) have the exclusive responsibility to organise and manage the Portuguese delegations that participate in the Olympic and Paralympic Games. Among other responsibilities, the Olympic Committee of Portugal holds the right to the exclusive use of the Olympic symbols within the national territory. Meanwhile, the role of the Paralympic Committee is essentially related to the Paralympic and Deaflympic Games, and it must comply with the International Paralympic Committee (IPC) rules.

The structure of the systemic sport governance in Portugal has allowed the development of a particular organisational culture (i.e., amateur, familiar, and unskilled) that has influenced the day-to-day functioning of many sport organisations with different organisational requirements. Over time, this issue has contributed to the development of strong lobbies that have sought to exert control over some of these sport organisations (Lopes, 2017). Despite this governance structure, and considering that over the last decade many NGBs have undergone significant changes in terms of becoming more democratic organisations (i.e., recognising the role of players, referees, and coaches in their organisational governance), there is still much to be done to achieve a higher level of good governance. Although these changes have contributed to create new synergies and management strategies in the Portuguese sports system (Lopes, 2017), the governance and leadership weaknesses of NGBs have remained, lacking sport strategy plans and many still depended on public subsidies (Correia, 2017). As a result, Portugal has failed to make progress at the same pace as other countries within the European Union. Portugal needs to rethink its governance structure and move closer to other developed countries and benchmark how they develop their sport system.

One of the ways to understand the relationship between political and systemic sport governance in Portugal is through sports financing. Thus, in the next section we briefly discuss how public funding is allocated throughout the sport system in Portugal and how sport organisations are influenced by the public entities that govern sport in this country.

Sports financing in Portugal

In Europe, sports financing occurs mostly at the local and regional level with variations occurring in each country. For example, in Germany, Switzerland, and also in Scandinavia, the central government budget for sport is limited in absolute values compared to other sources of sports financing (Andreff, 2006). On the other hand, countries that operate with a more centralised system such as France, Italy,

Portugal, and Hungary, the central government contributes with a more significant share of its public budget in the overall sport finance.

In Portugal, NGBs and sport events with public interest recognised by the Portuguese government may be eligible to benefit from aids or financial support from the state and local authorities (Mestre, 2010) through the program agreements for sport development that is established in the Portuguese law. The approval of this type of contract depends on the specific program.

In the last decades, many sport programs in Portugal have been operated and funded based on the Spectators-Subsidies-Sponsor-Local (SSSL) model proposed by Andreff and Staudohar (2000). This model involves collecting revenues from spectators, subsidies, sponsors, and also local authorities. However, most NSOs and amateur sport clubs still depend on public subsidies or local authorities (city hall or parish councils) to fund their operations.

In Portugal, the involvement of the state in sport is evident in regards to financing. Thus, financing of Portuguese sports is structured in a model that relies primarily on public sources. The existing legal and economic methods created to stimulate other sources of revenue are still not sufficient to mitigate the high dependency on public funds (Tenreiro, 2017). Figure 20.2 shows the funding of Portuguese elite sport in 2021, highlighting the state subsidisation.

Lotteries and legal betting are also important modes of financing in Portuguese sports given that a levy of the 'Social Games'[1] is included in the sport sector. According to Decree-law No. 23 of October 21, 2018, the revenues obtained through the lotteries are divided as follows (COP, 2020): (1) 3.6% are allocated to the Ministry of Internal Affairs (e.g., policing of sporting events), (2) 3.8% are allocated to the Presidency of the Council of Ministers (e.g., for culture and gender equality programs); (3) 32.9% go to promote the quality of life of the elderly and disabled people by the Ministry of Labour, Solidarity, and Social Security; (4)

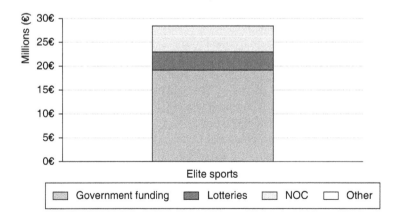

Figure 20.2 Portuguese elite sport financing

Source: De Bosscher and Shibli (2021)

15.7% are allocated to the Ministry of Health to support the National Health Plan; (5) 2.2% go to the Cultural Promotion Fund of the Ministry of Culture; (6) 4.8% are for the Regional Governments of Madeira and Azores; and finally (7) 10.2% of these funds are allocated to the Ministry of Education and used in support of school sport with 0.4% of this amount going to support underprivileged students and 8.8% being allocated to the Portuguese Institute of Sport and Youth to promote sport and youth activities and develop infrastructure. The remaining revenues are kept by Santa Casa da Misericordia of Lisbon (a non-profit organisation that oversees the 'social games'), which retains the remaining 26.5% of the funds to develop other social projects.

The breakdown of how the lottery funds is distributed provides evidence of the growing reliance of sport on lottery receipts and its direct competition with other public services that also compete for lottery funds (e.g., social security, education, or health). There is no doubt that the lottery and governmental financing have taken on a crucial role in the Portuguese sport system, being perhaps almost a non-substitutable resource, particularly for elite and non-elite sport.

Organisational sport governance in Portugal

As noted throughout this chapter, the Portuguese state intervenes in sport by legislating and financing the activities that impact the functioning of most of NGBs. This intervention directly impacts the organisational governance of most sport organisations, particularly NGBs. As noted by Hoye and Cuskelly (2007), environmental influences impact the organisational governance in non-profit sport organisations, which include the regulatory environment, the relationship between government and non-profit sector, the government sport policy, and governance guidelines from sport agencies.

The state intervenes in the Portuguese sport system mostly through financing the non-profit sport sector. The relationship that exists between the government and the sport sector is critical for NGBs to achieve their goals. This relationship is governed by a set of rules established in the Legal Regime of Sport Federations (Decree Law no. 93/2014 of June 23rd) that regulates the functioning of NGBs. Basically, this law mandates that prior to qualify to receiving public funding, an NGB must comply with all the rules that regulate their operations. According to this legislation, each NGB is responsible to organise and carry out its activities within the principles of freedom, democracy, representation, and transparency. Furthermore, NGBs must be organised independent of the State and neither be affiliated with any political party nor religious institution.

The Legal Regime of Sport Federations imposes on most NGBs a compliance burden to fulfil all legal procedures. Even though there are no official governance guidelines for sport organisations, this legislation works as a path for NGBs to adopt good organisational governance principles. Henry and Lee (2004) established seven principles for adopting good governance practices in sports organisations, namely: transparency, accountability, democracy, social responsibility, equity, efficiency, and efficacy. The concept of good governance in sport has received significant attention in the scholarly literature. In 2013, there were more than 35 publications that addressed proposals for principles of good governance in sport (Chappelet & Mrkonjic, 2013). Geeraert (2018) developed an instrument to assess the adoption of good governance practices in NGBs in different countries. The instrument involved 274 indicators divided into four dimensions: transparency, democratic process, internal accountability & control, and societal responsibility. In the following paragraph we use Geeraert's model to illustrate how the Legal Regime of Sports Federations impacts the organisational governance of Portuguese NGBs.

The transparency dimension allows the monitoring of the organisation's internal work by different stakeholders. Concerning this principle, the Legal Regime of Sport Federations require all NGBs to publish internal documents on their official websites. Mandatory documents are by-laws, regulations, decisions of disciplinary bodies, budgets and financial statements for the last three years, annual activity plans and reports, board composition, and contacts. Although most NGBs comply with this legal requirement, some critical documents such as multiannual strategic plans and minutes of board meetings are still not easily found on many NGB websites.

The dimension of democracy deals with issues such as clean and fair elections, the participation of different actors in the decision-making processes, and the existence of an internal environment that allows open debate and participation. The legislation also regulates the conditions NGBs must establish in order for these organisations to function in a democratic and open way. As result, NGBs must demonstrate that the election of representatives includes representatives from different groups of the General Assembly, including club officials, athletes, coaches, and referees.

In addition to the by-laws of the general assembly, the law also regulates the electoral processes of NGBs. Elections must occur every four years and be carried out through a secret ballot. Furthermore, there is a term limit for the president, board members, and members of other bodies to remain in power. These individuals and positions cannot be elected more than three times to the same body.

The legislation also mandates that NGBs must operate on the principles of accountability and internal control. It establishes that the General Assembly is responsible for supervising the direction of the NGB, being responsible for the election and removal of members of internal bodies, approving the accounts and the annual financial report and the activities report, and for amending the by-laws. In addition, each NGB must include in their organisational structure different bodies, including president, board, financial council, disciplinary council, justice council, and referee council. In addition, an independent external auditor must assess the NGB's annual financial reports.

The law also provides some general principles for procedures for internal disciplinary proceedings. The disciplinary and justice councils ensure a disciplinary process for applying sanctions with defence guarantees and appeals to higher levels. Concerning potential conflict of interest for members of the board, the law stipulates that member of any internal body lose their mandate if they enter a contract in which they have a direct interest for them. Even though this is part of the law, there is little information on how board members should declare a conflict of interest.

Finally, the legislation specifies some recommendations for NGBs on matters relating to the principle of social responsibility. The law states that NGBs may lose the right to formalise contracts with the State when they do not comply with legislations related to doping, violence, corruption, racism, and xenophobia. Furthermore, NGBs should also have disciplinary regulations to sanction violations both during and outside competitions and consider issues related to ethics.

Regarding the principle of democracy, there are still few initiatives being made by Portuguese NGBs especially on issues related to gender equality, the promotion of dual careers for athletes, and the promotion of environmental sustainability actions. These issues are minimally addressed by most Portuguese NGBs. It also represents areas that are already a work in progress for many NGBs in other European countries (Geeraert, 2018).

Conclusions

Sport Governance in Portugal is influenced by significant State interventionism, especially through several pieces of legislations that enforce the structure of the sport system and the functioning of many sport organisations within this system. This type of intervention is common in countries where the government exercises a great deal of power over sport (i.e., France, Greece, and Brazil). Many of the legal bodies exert their influence at the national level, shaping power dynamics between organisations that work in this network (Jonson & Thorpe, 2019).

As much as the Portuguese legislation provides a direction for the sports system to establish its network and for sport organisations to adopt good governance practices, some aspects of the legislation still need more work. Overall, the role of the State and its intervention can be considered positive as it establishes clear guidelines for those responsible for directing the sport organisations in Portugal. On the other hand, this pattern generates homogeneity in the system and limits the freedom for stakeholders to establish the structures that best fit their own needs.

In addition to the legal aspects, adopting good practices in sport organisations also depends on other factors such as the local culture and the level of professionalisation in the sport sector (Anagnostopoulos et al., 2019). Although these topics have not been covered in this chapter, they are certainly possible subjects for further study. In this regard, the challenge for developing systemic governance where actors are well adjusted and organisations adopt good governance practices is not only in increasing government control, but also in developing understanding and coordination among the various stakeholders that participate in the sport system (Bravo & Haas, 2019).

Note

1 In Portugal, Social Games refer to gambling activities related to sport (e.g., lotto games, lotteries, and football betting). Revenues from these sources support programs for disadvantaged groups or specific social programs such as funding sport programs.

References

Anagnostopoulos, C., Van Eekeren, F., & Solenes, O. (2019). Sport governance in Europe. In D. Shilbury & L. Ferkins (Eds.), *Routledge handbook of sport governance* (pp. 53–64). Routledge.

Andreff, S. (2006). Sport and financing. In W. Andreff & S. Szymanski (Eds.), *Handbook on the economics of sport* (pp. 271–281). Edward Elgar.

Andreff, W., & Staudohar, P. D. (2000). The evolving European model of professional sports finance. *Journal of Sports Economics*, 1(3), 257–276.

Bravo, G. A., & Haas, L. (2019). Government policy and principles of good governance in Latin America. In D. Shilbury & L. Ferkins (Eds.), *Routledge handbook of sport governance* (pp. 79–93). Routledge.

Carvalho, M. J., & Mazzei, L. (2019). Estado: intervenção no desporto. In A. Correia & R. Biscaia (Eds.), *Gestão do desporto: compreender para gerir* (pp. 83–99). Faculdade de Motricidade Humana.

Chappelet, J. L., & Mrkonjic, M. (2013). *Basic indicators for better governance in international sport (BIBGIS): An assessment tool for international sport governing bodies* (No. 1/2013). IDHEAP.

COP. (2020). *O Financiamento ao Desporto Jogos Sociais e Apostas. Comité Olímpico de Portugal*. https://conpaas.einzelnet.com/services/mediaservice/api/media/144fb52af79f197416d85ad1c47e9cc3f7028b8a

Correia, J. P. (2017). *Governação do Sistema Desportivo de Elite*. Jornal A Bola. www.abola.pt/nnh/2017-04-19/governacao-do-sistema-desportivo-de-elite-artigo-de-jose-pinto-correia-2/667385

De Bosscher, V., & Shibli, S. (2021). *Tokyo 2020 Evaluation of the elite sport expenditures and success of 14 nations*. https://spliss.research.vub.be/sites/default/files/atoms/files/Tokyo%202020%20Evaluation.pdf

Decree Law no. 93/2014 of December 31. *Legal regime of sport federations*. https://dre.pt/dre/detalhe/decreto-lei/93-2014-25676922

Dowling, M., Leopkey, B., & Smith, L. (2018). Governance in sport: A scoping review. *Journal of Sport Management*, 32(5), 438–451.

Drumond, M. (2013). Ao bem do desporto e da Nação: relações entre esporte e política no Estado Novo português (1933–1945). *Revista Estudos Políticos*, 7(1), 298–318.

Fernandes, A. J. S., Tenreiro, F. J. S., Felgueiras, L., Quaresma, S., & Maçãs, V. M. O. M. (2011). Sport policy in Portugal. *International Journal of Sport Policy and Politics*, 3(1), 133–141.

Frazão, P. (2015). *Desporto Militar em Portugal: Contributos para uma nova visão estratégica*. Master thesis. Evora University, Portugal.

Geeraert, A. (Ed.). (2018). *National sports governance observer. Final report*. Play the Game: Danish Institute for Sports Studies.

Geeraert, A., & Bruyninckx, H. (2014). You'll never walk alone again: The governance turn in professional sports. In J. Mittag & S. Güldenpfennig (Eds.), *Sportpolitik im*

Spannungsfeld von Autonomie und Regulierung: Grundlagen, Akteure und Konfliktfelder. Klartext Verlag.

Henry, I., & Lee, P. C. (2004). Governance and ethics in sport. In J. Beech & S. Chadwick (Eds.), *The business of sport management* (pp. 25–42). Prentice Hall.

Hoye, R., & Cuskelly, G. (2007). *Sport governance.* Routledge.

IPDJ. (2021). *Missão e Atribuições.* Instituto Português do Desporto e Juventude. https://ipdj.gov.pt/miss%C3%A3o-e-atribui%C3%A7%C3%B5es

Jonson, P. T., & Thorpe, D. (2019). Regulation context of sport governance. In D. Shilbury & L. Ferkins (Eds.), *Routledge handbook of sport governance* (pp. 35–52). Routledge.

Law no. 1/1990 of January 13. *Basic sports law of sport system.* https://dre.pt/dre/detalhe/lei/1-1990-333524

Law no. 5/2007 of January 16. *Basic sports law of physical activity and sport.* https://dre.pt/pesquisa/-/search/522787/details/maximized

Lopes, J. (2017). *Gestão do Desporto. Manual de Curso de Treinadores De Desporto.* IPDJ.

Medroa, T. (2018). *As Autarquias e a Promoção de Atividade Física no Meio Rural [City halls and the promotion of physical activity in rural areas].* Master thesis. University of Lisbon. Portugal.

Meirim, J. M. (2004). O desporto no fundamental: um valor lusófono. *Povos E Culturas, 9*(1), 249–259.

Mestre, A. M. (2010). Sport governance in Portugal. *The International Sports Law Journal, 1*(2), 32–38.

Pires, G. (2015). *A Gestão do Desporto.* www.abola.pt/nnh/2015-03-21/a-gestao-do-desporto-segundo-gustavo-pires-artigo-de-manuel-sergio-76/538158.

Portuguese Republic. (2021). *Áreas de Governo.* Governo de Portugal. www.portugal.gov.pt/pt/gc22/area-de-governo/educacao/secretarios-de-estado

Shilbury, D., Ferkins, L., & Smythe, L. (2013). Sport governance encounters: Insights from lived experiences. *Sport Management Review, 16*(3), 349–363.

Silva, A. (2009). O Estado, os governos e a administração pública desportiva. In J. Bento & J. M. Constantino (Eds.), *O Desporto e o Estado* (pp. 67–84). Porto: Afrontamento.

Sousa, V. (2013). *A gestão do desporto municipal. Análise ao desenvolvimento organizacional: estudo centrado na comunidade intermunicipal do Tâmega e Sousa.* Master thesis. Instituto Superior de Educação e Ciências. Lisboa.

Tenreiro, F. (2017). Um instrumento de financiamento do desporto. *Lusíada. Economia & Empresa, 22*(1), 145–165.

VOCASPORT Research Group. (2004). *Vocational education and training in the field of sport in the European Union: Situation, trends and outlook.* European Observatoire of Sport and Employment. http://eose.org/wp-content/uploads/2014/03/vocasport-Final-Report-English-Version.pdf

Walters, G., & Tacon, R. (2018). The 'codification' of governance in the non-profit sport sector in the UK. *European Sport Management Quarterly, 18*(4), 482–500.

Yandjou, P. (2011). *The role of university sports federations in enhancing student sports—A comparative case study between Portugal and Finland.* Master thesis. University of Jyväskylä.

Chapter 21

Evaluating the performance of Spanish sport federations

A multiple goal approach

Patricio Sánchez-Fernández, Luis Carlos Sánchez, and Angel Barajas

Introduction

The Spanish legal system recognises the Spanish sport federations as private entities and gives them legal status.[1] Spanish sport federations are made of autonomous sport federations, sports clubs, athletes, coaches, judges and referees, professional leagues (if any), and other groups of interest that promote, participate, and/or contribute to the development of sport. In addition to having their own attributes, Spanish sport federations exercise delegated public administrative functions, as, by law, they are collaborating agents of the public administration to protect and promote their respective sport disciplines. Moreover, as acting agents of the public administration, they receive public funding. Another relevant characteristic of sport federations is their alignment and association with the Olympic movement where they play a significant role.

The federative sport model, declared a public utility by law, is based on a mixed structure that combines its private nature with its role as a collaborative body of the administration. This official collaboration also commits federations to their official duties while justifying the tutelage and control of the administration over the exclusive public functions they perform. However, throughout their existence sport federations have not been exempted from challenges. Recently, many sports, particularly individual sports, have been increasingly operating and functioning outside the traditional federative model. For this reason, these types of sport have already received a response from many sport federations as well as the public entities, where their presence is recognised in regional sport laws.

Likewise, in the case of federated professional sports, some major sport clubs have also started to distance themselves from the federative jurisdiction. But despite this reality, many sport federations in Spain, as well as others in neighbouring countries in Europe and across the world, continue to be part of the federative model in which top-level sport is organised.

This chapter aims to examine the grounds the Spanish sport system is based, namely its sport federations. More specifically, in this chapter, we identify a set of indicators that will allow for the assessment to which the objectives of sport federations are met. In this process, we pay special attention to the public-private

DOI: 10.4324/9781003197003-21

arrangement in which sport federations coexist because public and private policies seldom coincide. Sport objectives may diverge or not coincide with the economic-financial objectives of a private entity. Thus, when establishing a control system, the information that will allow us to identify those indicators will reflect a wide array of contexts. Developing an appropriate set of indicators requires identifying the critical aspects of these indicators and the variables to be measured. As noted by Barajas et al. (2006), indicators must aim to evaluate factors that indicate the performance obtained according to proposed goals and objectives. Besides, it is even more important to obtain a balanced set of indicators that truly reflect the performance of the public investment, rather than having an endless set of indicators but fail to provide a clear idea of performance.

This chapter is organised as follows. First, it describes the structure of the management of sport in Spain, granting special attention to sport federations. Then, it presents the methodology and a set of indicators that allow us to assess performance. Finally, it discusses the results and presents a few general ideas that are drawn from these results.

Structure and management of sport in Spain

The federated sport model constitutes the main structure for high-level sport[2] in most developed countries. This scenario makes it very difficult for sport to operate outside of a sport federation. One of the most notable exceptions is the university sport system in the United States, which is led by the National Collegiate Athletic Association (NCAA). In this model, the role that in many countries is led by a sport federation, is supplanted (to some extent) by the work done by hundreds of university athletic programs that are part of the NCAA.

According to the Annual Report of the Higher Sports Council (CSD, 2020), since 2008, Spanish sport federations have received approximately €300 million annually from the Spanish government. This amount includes funding for the Royal Spanish Football Federation (RSFF) together with the rest of the sport federations. The distribution of these funds between the RSFF and the sport federations has changed significantly over the years. Specifically, the former represented 30% of the total received in 2005, and then increased up to 51.6% in 2017. Since 2008, the percentage of the funding for the rest of the federations have gradually. In 2017, they received 48.4% of the total funding.

Moreover, the federations' own resources increased from 58.8% of the total in 2005 to 77.1% in 2018 (CSD, 2020). This increment is explained by the increased generation of football's own resources. However, if the resources of the Football Federation are not considered in this equation, then the total amount received by the sport federations decreases by 58% in 2018. Another factor that explains the reduction in funding for the Spanish sport federations is the money they received from the ADO program,[3] which has plummeted from €12.1 million in 2008 to €1.9 million in 2018. As a result, it is possible to observe that sport federations have a strong dependence on public funding. The contribution of the CSD has become a determining factor for the financing of federated sport while other types of subsidies (especially the ADO) have decreased.

As can be seen in Figure 21.1, in 2014, federations' own revenues exceeded 60% of the total revenues. This marked the end of a growing trend that began in 2010. From that year onwards, federations' own revenues have surpassed this threshold.

Regarding sport federations' own revenues, Table 21.1 shows how the main source of income comes from two sources: licenses and fees, and organisation of competitions. Together they represent more than 50% of the revenues during the last decade. Sponsorship and advertising barely reached 20% of the average annual income from their own resources for that period.

These financial challenges are aggravated by an undefined sporting strategy that translates into a reduction in the competitive capacity of Spanish sport. However, despite the individual talent of some athletes and the success accomplished by some federations that have contributed to achieve good sporting results, there are areas in need of improvement, mostly in terms of medium, and long-term strategic planning and management.

In the case of Spain, the federative structure of sport requires organisations in different administrative territorial levels (i.e., state or regional), to focus on different strategic goals. Thus, the State is responsible for the development of high-level sport, while organisations at the regional or local level are responsible

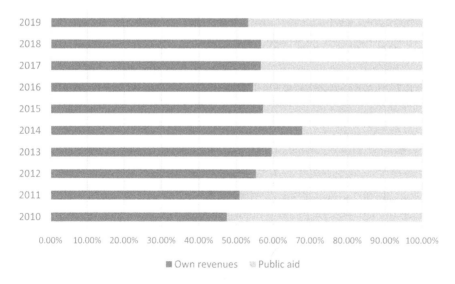

Figure 21.1 Income of the Spanish Sport Federations, percentage distribution from 2010–2019

Source: Based on CSD (2020) data

Note: Data does not include the Spanish Football Federation

Table 21.1 Own resources of the Spanish Federations, percentage distribution from 2009–2018

Year	Advertising and sponsorships	Licenses and fees	Competitions	Training activity	Other resources
2009	16.8%	37.3%	27.3%	4.3%	14.3%
2010	20.2%	34.3%	26.2%	4.7%	14.5%
2011	16.7%	34.9%	29.4%	4.7%	14.3%
2012	12.9%	31.2%	24.8%	4.6%	26.5%
2013	14.5%	26.8%	32.0%	4.2%	22.5%
2014	12.0%	23.3%	19.3%	3.4%	41.9%
2015	14.9%	38.2%	22.2%	5.6%	19.1%
2016	21.0%	34.3%	23.6%	5.5%	15.6%
2017	17.7%	33.5%	23.4%	5.8%	19.6%
2018	20.4%	28.0%	31.1%	4.6%	15.9%

Source: Based on CSD (2020) data

Note: Data does not include the Spanish Football Federation

for promoting sports. Specifically, the Central State Administration, through the Higher Sports Council (CSD) as the maximum sports authority, is responsible for reaching legal-administrative agreements with Spanish sport federations concerning objectives, sport programs (especially high-level sports), budgets, organic structures, and functional structures. Thus, the CSD signs the corresponding agreements of a legal-administrative nature with the respective sport federations and grants them financial subsidies to perform their activities.

National sport federations (NSF) are non-profit non-governmental organisations. The goal of a federation is to promote the development of its sport at the high-performance and grassroots levels. Even despite their nongovernmental nature, federations have obtained public subsidies for their work. The Spanish government has two main goals in sharing these funds among each federation[4] (1) for the development and promotion of the sport and (2) the success in sport competitions. This combination of goals including elite and grassroots development has also been reported to occur in sport organisations in the United States (Dittmore et al., 2009), Belgium (Winand et al., 2011), as well as Russian football associations (Solntsev & Osokin, 2018).

Even though securing profits is not a goal for NSFs, financial losses represent a risk for their long-term sustainability. This is why economic sustainability should be considered a goal for a NSF. In this way, our study finds three different goals to measure the performance of the Spanish NSF.

Martín et al. (2018) conducted a comparative analysis between the Spanish sport model with those countries that over the last decades have shown significant levels of sport performance. In that study, the authors focused on examining the best key practices for success, identifying challenges and opportunities, as well as identifying those countries that serve as a model to follow in the areas of sport finance, sport management, and sport development. Taking as a reference the sporting success, the shifting levers and areas of improvement of the current model were determined. Likewise, key actions were prioritised in terms of added value and impact.

Cabello et al. (2011) analysed the Spanish federated sport through the opinion of key figures in the Spanish sport and the economic figures that influence this sector. These authors identified the urgent need for change based on a review of the sources of public and private financing and of an analysis of the federative management and the structures of the system. Likewise, Cabello et al. (2009) identified the need for institutional coordination as another key element for enhancing the effectiveness of the Spanish sport model. The main conclusion is that with adequate internal and external financing, better results and greater satisfaction for all stakeholders can all be achieved (Puga-González et al., 2020).

Methodology

In this work, we examined the performance of NSFs with regards to a combination of ratios for each of the three goals: (1) *Sport Development*, (2) *Success in Competitions* and (3) *Financial Management*. To homogenise the measures of the three goals, we estimated the average of the ratios to obtain a score for each goal being 100% the maximum score achieved by each federation with the best result in all the ratios. In this way, a sport federation with a score of 50% in Sport Development would have achieved half of the punctuation with respect to the best performance federation.

Scores include different variables to measure each goal. In the case of *Sport Development*, we included three variables: number of licences, number of clubs, and NSFs' ability to generate their own non-subsidy income. Although authors such as Dolles et al. (2012) and Omondi-Ochieng (2020) used this last variable to measure NSFs financial performance, we chose to include it as a sign of grassroots development. Popular sport disciplines such as football can obtain private funds more easily than other less popular sports like pentathlon. In this way, we argue that securing private resources can represent the spread of the sport, but it makes no impact on an NSF sustainability. While public funds can make an NSF more dependent on these types of resources, the dependency on sponsors can also imply revenue volatility.

Our work used percentage values to homogenise the three variables to consider the percentage of licences and clubs with the data of the sport federation with the most licences and clubs. Additionally, we estimated the percentage of their own resources over total revenue and compared this data to the data of the most successful NSF.

The second estimated score measures *Success in Sport Competitions*. Here we included the number of Olympic medals achieved in the games of the current century and the number of medals achieved in European and World championships in the last two years. To develop the score, we estimated the percentage of the results for each NSF as compared to the most successful federation.

The third score measured was the economic performance of each sport federation, and we labelled it as *Financial Management*. Here we included the last financial report available of each NSF which included three types of ratios. Sparvero and Kent (2014) found in their study on non-profit sport organisations in the U.S. that long-term economic sustainability has no dependence on the amount of debt or revenues; but rather represents the capacity to pay debts with NSF resources. Therefore, in our study, we choose to use three financial ratios instead of absolute values. These financial ratios were (1) working capital ratio, (2) debt ratio and (3) safety margin.

The working capital ratio is calculated by taking the current assets of each NSF, subtracting the current liabilities preferred dividends, and dividing the result by total assets. This ratio is an important measure of financial health because creditors can measure a company's ability to pay off its debts in the short term. The debt ratio is also introduced to measure the relative amount of debt in relation to total assets. It gives information about the NSF assets provided from debt. Finally, the third ratio is estimated by dividing the NSF surplus by total income. It reveals the safety margin of the federation with the losses. This ratio is negative if an NSF already obtains/makes losses.

Results

Combining data for each goal, we elaborate on three rankings: Sport Development, Success in Competitions, and Financial Management to evaluate the performance of the Spanish National Sport Federations. The results of this analysis are shown in Table 21.2 and summarised in Figure 21.2.

The results reveal that NSFs scored best in financial management. Moreover, the results in this goal show less variability with only two NSFs obtaining a score below 40%: boxing and badminton. On the other hand, tennis and archery achieved a score above 80%. On the contrary, scores for sport competition show the largest dispersion. The NSF of canoeing achieved almost the maximum possible score with sailing and cycling also obtaining high scores. The scores of NSF for athletics or judo are in the middle range while several other sport federations obtained low scores. The scores on sport development showed an extreme distribution with only one NSF obtaining a score higher than 40%, which is the football federation achieving the maximum score of 100%. basketball and golf are close to 40%, while seven NSFs were below 10%.

When examining the relationship between the performance of the goals as it is showed in Figure 21.3, we can distinguish three scenarios. First, a significant group of NSFs showed low scores in sport development and sport competitions. Second, most of the NSFs obtained a combination of middle-range scores in sport development and financial management. Third, it is not possible to find a homogenous group of federations when we study simultaneously the sport competition success and the scores of financial management.

Moreover, in the case of the maximum score achieved by the football federation in sport development, Figure 21.3 also shows two other extreme cases. The first

Evaluating the performance of Spanish sport federations 251

Table 21.2 Performance rankings of National Sport Federations

National Sport Federation	Sport Development Scoring	Sport Development Ranking	Financial Management Scoring	Financial Management Ranking	Success Sport Competitions Scoring	Success Sport Competitions Ranking
Archery	25%	9	86%	1	5%	26
Athletics	18%	16	52%	20	54%	5
Badminton	19%	14	39%	29	6%	21
Basketball	39%	2	72%	5	23%	13
Boxing	12%	22	15%	30	6%	24
Canoeing	8%	26	56%	14	99%	1
Cycling	21%	12	64%	9	76%	3
Fencing	9%	24	54%	16	6%	24
Football	100%	1	48%	23	9%	17
Golf	39%	3	77%	3	5%	27
Gymnastic	25%	10	46%	25	24%	12
Handball	30%	4	41%	28	15%	15
Hockey	13%	21	52%	21	6%	21
Equestrian	28%	5	53%	19	14%	16
Ice sports[5]	8%	25	53%	18	6%	23
Judo	26%	6	70%	7	50%	6
Pentathlon	4%	30	55%	15	1%	30
Rowing	6%	29	43%	26	3%	29
Rugby	17%	18	57%	13	4%	28
Sailing	7%	27	70%	6	79%	2
Shooting	18%	17	76%	4	23%	14
Swimming	17%	19	42%	27	65%	4
Table tennis	20%	13	51%	22	9%	18
Taekwondo	19%	15	68%	8	47%	7
Tennis	26%	7	85%	2	33%	9
Triathlon	22%	11	64%	10	38%	8
Volleyball	25%	8	62%	11	8%	19
Weightlifting	6%	28	60%	12	33%	10
Winter sports[6]	10%	23	47%	24	7%	20
Wrestling	15%	20	54%	17	27%	11

case is the boxing federation which shows the lowest scores when the financial management/sport development and financial management/sport competition are analysed. The second case is the highest score achieved by the canoeing federation in sport competition with a low score in sport development.

In view of these results, we can classify the Spanish NSFs into five groups:

1. Those NSFs with a weak performance in the three rankings such as badminton, boxing, winter sports, ice sports, hockey, pentathlon, and rowing.
2. Those NSFs with a strong performance in the three rankings such as basketball, cycling, judo, taekwondo, tennis, and triathlon.
3. Those with a strong performance in some of the rankings, but weak in others. This is the case of handball which shows good scores in sport development,

	Sport Development	Sporting Competitions	Financial Management
Archery	25%	5%	86%
Athletics	18%	54%	52%
Badminton	19%	6%	39%
Basketball	39%	23%	72%
Boxing	12%	6%	15%
Canoeing	8%	99%	56%
Cycling	21%	76%	64%
Fencing	9%	6%	54%
Football	100%	9%	48%
Golf	39%	5%	77%
Gymnastic	25%	24%	46%
Handball	30%	15%	41%
Hockey	13%	6%	52%
Horse riding	28%	14%	53%
Ice sports	8%	6%	53%
Judo	26%	50%	70%
Pentathlon	4%	1%	55%
Rowing	6%	3%	43%
Rugby	17%	4%	57%
Sailing	7%	79%	70%
Shooting	18%	23%	76%
Swimming	17%	65%	42%
Table tennis	20%	9%	51%
Taekwondo	19%	47%	68%
Tennis	26%	33%	85%
Triathlon	22%	38%	64%
Volleyball	25%	8%	62%
Weightlifting	6%	33%	60%
Winter sports	10%	7%	47%
Wrestling	15%	27%	54%

Figure 21.2 Performance rankings of National Sport Federations

but a weak performance in financial management. The gymnastics federation achieved good performance in sport development, but weak performance in financial management and sport competitions. The canoeing federation obtained greater success in sport competitions. Fencing and rugby showed good performance in financial management.

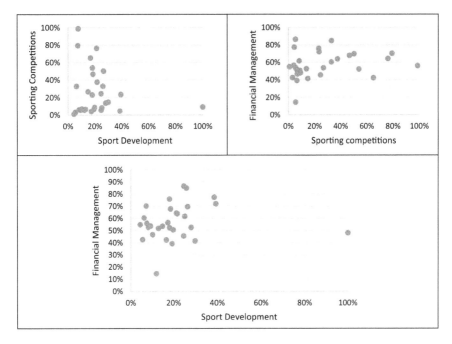

Figure 21.3 Combination of scores in each goal

4. Those with a weak performance in some of the ranking, but strong in others. Football is the NSF with the highest score in sport development. However, is weak in financial management. Golf and archery have not achieved good sport results, but they have demonstrated good performance in the other two categories. Weightlifting and sailing show a low level of sport development in regards to their performance in financial management and sport competitions. Swimming and athletics show a weak performance in financial management.
5. Those with an equilibrium in the three categories of performance are the NSFs of equestrian (horse riding), wrestling, table tennis, shooting, and volleyball.

Conclusions

Spanish sport federations show a set of weaknesses in terms of their performance, not only from a financial point of view but also in terms of sport development and sustainability, and sports performance.

Regarding the financial aspect, it is worth noting that most NSFs are strongly dependent on public subsidies, especially from the CSD. Furthermore, this has been aggravated by the decrease in funds from the ADO program, which would require a review of this important form of funding. This public dependency not

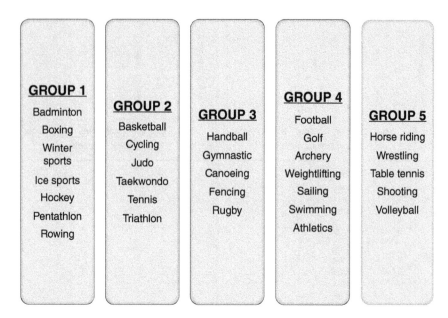

Figure 21.4 Groups of national sport federations

only represents a clear limitation for many sport federations in terms of management, but also a loss of financial autonomy. On the other hand, resources that are generated by NSFs arise from the competitions they organise and the money derived from licenses. Other sources of income such as advertising or training activities remain marginal in most of the federations. This aspect, which contrasts with other types of institutions of a similar nature, reveals a field of action that remains to be explored in short-term financial management. Hence, we concur with Martín et al. (2018) who suggest the need of implementing three initiatives to improve the financial structure of an NSF. These initiatives are:

- Review of the federation's own resource models.
- Use of big data to re-think the offer of federative services according to consumer profiles.
- Promote the regulatory development of the participation regime in the collection of Sports Bets[7]

Moreover, an improvement in strategic planning leading to a change in the sporting model should also be added to this financial component. This could be a sport strategy on a global scale to guide the initiatives and actors of the sector towards common goals and objectives. This planning exercise, so commonly present in other areas of the private and even public domain, continues to be a pending issue. In fact, something along this line appeared for the first time in the failed draft of the sports law of January 30, 2019, which centred on maximising available resources and focusing on the long term and not the short term, which has been a characteristic of Spanish NSFs.

The analysis of specific data of different sport federations allows us to combine their assortment of realities around the three axes under study. This summary and grouping work provide a result of interest from the very start given that it enables the identification of five clusters. In addition, this classification is far from any initial consideration or intuition in terms of assessing large federations vs. small, individual sports vs. collective sports, or some type of sectoral characterisation. Our result classifies NSFs by performance and development; this vision facilitates decision-making processes such as the ones indicated earlier. In general, good financial performance results of most federations disclose management focused on economic responsibility. The federations with the worst scores should follow the practices of the better scoring federations.

The low scores of most federations in sport development signal that it is not a problem of each federation's management. A common program is required to spread the popularity of a sport and improve participation.

Good results in the canoeing and sailing federations sport competitions versus their low score in sport development can be a sign of good managerial practices. It could set an example for other federations that could learn from it.

Also, it is important to highlight the six outstanding federations in the three rankings: basketball, cycling, judo, taekwondo, tennis, and triathlon. These federations serve as an example of successful managerial practices that could be benchmarked by other NSFs. It would be important to conduct more analyses to identify their key strengths. Another aspect that is important to highlight is the difficulty in optimising the development of the three axes. Good proof of this is the fact that many NSFs are outstanding in one or two categories, but they lack in a third category. This is the case for athletics, swimming, football, golf, archery, weightlifting, and sailing. Other NSFs like handball or gymnastics show room for improvement given that they only excel in one of the dimensions. It should be noted that federations' performance is not only an issue of resources or size. Although it is true that large NSFs typically achieve higher scores, at least in one of the objectives, we can also find small federations that show weak results in all of the metrics. Also, it is possible to find NSFs that achieve a balanced result in all of the three categories.

In sum, and although many challenges await sports federations in the short and medium-term, the plan developed by NSFs, as pointed by Sanchez-Fernandez (2019), must be based on a set of aspects that will determine their future viability. This includes technical excellence, adaptation to the market, and financial independence. This study raises awareness of some of these challenges; yet other challenges that also affect the performance and growth of many NSFs such as the proliferation of non-federated sports, the use of PED, or the boom in other forms of leisure should be part of the agenda that should be also examined by scholars and practitioners in the field of sport.

Notes

1 Sports Law 1990 (article 30).
2 High-level sport refers to a sport that is practiced at the highest level of performance, typically reserved for athletes that compete at World Championships, Olympic Games, etc.
3 The ADO (*Asociación Deportes Olímpicos*) program is an initiative that allows private companies to sponsor Olympic sport federations.
4 Order ECD/2681/2012
5 Ice Sports Federation includes ice hockey, curling, bobsleigh, skeleton, luge and skating.
6 Winter Sports Federation includes ski, snowboard and biathlon.
7 Collected in the additional sixth clause of Game Law (Ley 13/2011).

References

Barajas, A., Sanchez Fernandez, P., & Fraiz Brea, J. A. (2006). *Indicadores para la evaluación de la inversión en deporte en Galicia*. Editorial, Toxosoutos.
Cabello, D., Camps, A., & Puga, E. (2009). *Evaluation model of excellence in sporting organizations*. XIII Olympic Congress—Copenhagen. International Olympic Committee.
Cabello, D., Rivera, E., Trigueros, C., & Pérez, I. (2011). Análisis del modelo del deporte federado español del siglo XXI. *Revista Internacional de Medicina y Ciencias de la Actividad Física y del Deporte/International Journal of Medicine and Science of Physical Activity and Sport*, 11(44), 690–707.
CSD. (2020). *Las grandes cifras económicas de las federaciones deportivas españolas 2009–2018*. Consejo Superior de Deportes, Madrid.
Dittmore, S., Mahony, D., Andrew, D. P., & Hums, M. A. (2009). Examining fairness perceptions of financial resource allocations in US Olympic sport. *Journal of Sport Management*, 23(4), 429–456.
Dolles, H., Söderman, S., Winand, M., Zintz, T., & Scheerder, J. (2012). A financial management tool for sport federations. *Sport, Business and Management: An International Journal*, 2(3), 225–240.
Ley 13/2011, de 27 de mayo, de regulación del juego. Boletín Oficial del Estado (BOE) número. 127, de 28/05/2011
Martín, I., Vallbona, A., Valeri, X., Losada, I., Fernández, M., Benarroch, D., Martín, P., & Fernández, S. (2018). *Estudio comparativo internacional de los modelos de deporte de alto nivel*. Deloitte, Asociación del Deporte Español (ADESP), Confederación de Federaciones Deportivas Españolas (COFEDE).
Omondi-Ochieng, P. (2020). Financial performance of the United Kingdom's national nonprofit sport federations: A binary logistic regression approach. *Managerial Finance*, 47(6), 868–886. https://doi.org/10.1108/MF-03-2020-0126.
Puga-González, E., España-Estévez, E., Torres-Luque, G., & Cabello-Manrique, D. (2020). The effect of the crisis on the economic federative situation and evolution of sports results in Spain. *Journal of Human Sport & Exercise*, 17(2).
Sanchez-Fernandez, P. (2019). *Federaciones Deportivas: planificarse o morir*. Sociedad Española de Economía del Deporte, SEED. Editorial.
Solntsev, I., & Osokin, N. (2018). Designing a performance measurement framework for regional networks of national sports organizations: Evidence from Russian football. *Managing Sport and Leisure*, 23(1–2), 7–27.
Sparvero, E., & Kent, A. (2014). Sport team nonprofit organizations: Are sports doing well at' doing good'? *Journal of Applied Sport Management*, 6(4), 98–116.
Winand, M., Rihoux, B., Qualizza, D., & Zintz, T. (2011). Combinations of key determinants of performance in sport governing bodies. *Sport, Business and Management: An International Journal*, 1(3), 234–251.

Index

3 Fs (Fátima, Football, and Fado) 18–19

Abidal 173
Active Cities 77
administrative conflicts 53
ADO programme (*Asociación Deportes Olímpicos*) 20, 88, 246–247, 253, 256n3
advertising revenue 166, 192
Advertising Value Equivalent (AVE) 158
aerobics 99
Africa 2, 15, 143, 167, 170, 175
Age of Discovery 1, 12n3
Agrupación Canaria de Juego del Palo (Canarian Stick Game Group) 204
aizkolaritza 205
Alentejo 63, 67
Alfonso II (King of Asturia) 200
Alicante 203
Alonso, Fernando 2, 35
aluche (Leonese wrestling) 205
Alves 173
ambush marketing 53
America's Cup (sailing) 112, 113, 115
Andalusia/Andalucia 3, 63, 202, 209, 211, 216
Andorra 2, 109, 190, 206–207
Annual Gaming Report 86, 92, 94
Annual Review of Football Finance 159
Anti-Doping Authority of Portugal 39
Aragon 63
Aragonés, Luis 165, 175
arbitration 50, 53–55
archery 250, 253, 255
Argentina 144, 165
ASO (Amaury Sport Organisation) group 189
Asociación de Clubs de Baloncesto 178

Asociación de Clubs de Fútbol Femenino (Association of Women's Football Clubs–ACFF) 179, 181
Asociación de Futbolistas Españoles (Spanish Footballers' Association) 180
Association of Basketball Clubs (Spain) 43
Association of Gymnasium Companies in Portugal (AGAP) 99
Association of Spanish Tourist Caves 202
Association of Tennis Professionals 112
Association of Women's Football Clubs (ACFF) 179, 181
Associazione Sportiva Roma 154
Asturias 7, 67, 200, 202, 203
athletes: from Africa 2, 143; amateur 239; as ambassadors during iconic events 31; from Asia 143; as brand endorsers 159, 185; Catalan 174; collective bargaining agreements (CBAs) for 177, 179, 180, 181–183; dual careers of 25; European 144, 149–150, 152; *federates* 60–64; foreign players 140–152; foreign players (by age group) 146, *146*; foreign players (by continent of birth) *145*; foreign players (in Portugal) 159; foreign players (relative frequencies of) **142, 143**; as global brands 222–230; increase in number of in Spain 17, 19; international exposure of 147; media portrayal of 159; official definition of 178; players' unions 155; Portuguese players in Europe 158; proportion of capped players *147*; protection of young 25, 29; on the Spanish national team 165, 172–174, *173*; value promise of 11; women's salaries 182–183; youth academy of 173–174, *174*; *see also* football players; Latin American players; women

Athletic Bilbao 165, 166, 167, 179, 183
athletics 250, 253, 255; participation in 66–67; world championships 112
Atlético de Madrid (Atletico Madrid) 2, 151, 166, 183
ATP tennis tour 3
Australia 128, 135, 233
autonomous communities 71–72, 73, **210**; berth points in **211**; nautical sports licenses in 216, *217*
Autonomous Region of Madeira 39, 49, 58, 240
Autonomous Region of the Azores 39, 49, 58, 63, 240

badminton 250, 251
Balearic Islands 94, 209, 210, 211
Ballon d'Or 35
Barça 2, 165, 166, 179, 183; comparison with Real Madrid 167–168, 170–171; effect on *La Roja*'s game 171–174; official titles *169*; rivalry with Real Madrid 166–167, 168
Basic Law of Physical Activity and Sport (Portugal) 55, 156, 235
Basic Law of the Sports System (LBSD) (Portugal) 19, 50, 156, 235
basketball 16, 222, 232; basketball pools 90; competitions organised by 178; federations 66; financial management of 250, 251–253; official recognition of 177; performance ratings 255; in Spain 36; women players 177, 182–183; world championships 112
Basque Country 3, 91, 92, 93, 203; traditional games and sports in 205–206
Basque pelota (Basque ball) 10, 203
Basque-Navarre schools 171, 173
beach football 35
beach volleyball 114
Beckham, David 170
#BeInclusive sports awards 31
Belgium 123
Benfica 2
Bernabéu, Santiago 167, 168
berth points 211, **211**
Betis Balompié 165, 183
betting, legal 6, 239, 243n1; *see also* gambling
bibliometric analysis 125–126, 132–133, 135, 137
bicycling *see* cycling

Big Data 227–228
Bilbao 171
bingos 95
Biscayan Federation of Basque Games 205
Blaugrana elephant 170
Bleacher Report 160
boat chartering 211
boating 213–215, *213*, *214*
boat mooring 10, 212; *see also* marinas
Boavista Futebol Clube 156
bolos serranos 3
bookmakers 91–92, **92**, 95
Bosman ruling (Law) 25, 26, 142–143, 144, 148, 150, 167
boxing/cross fit 100, 250, 251
brand ambassador 225–226
brand equity 161, 162
branding 11, 170; of athletes 222–230; brand ambassador 225–226; of Liga Portugal 161; personal brand 223–224, 226, 229; of women's leagues 183
Brasileirão 171
Brazil 144, 158, 165; *Brasileirão* 171; sport governance in 242
broadcasting rights 180, 183–184
Bulgaria 32
Bundesliga (Germany) 154, 162
Busquets 173

Cáceres International Open World Paddle Tour 114
Cadiz 218
Calcio (Italy) 171
Calderón, Ramón 170
Camacho, José Antonio 166
Caminito del Rey 201
Camino de Santiago 10, 200
Camp Nou 168
Canarian wrestling 204
Canary Islands 204, 210, 216
Canoe Festival 202
canoeing 202, 216, 250, 251, 252, 255
canoe sprint 232
Cantabria 203, 207
Carlos, Roberto 170
Casal Arena stadium 113
Casillas, Iker 159, 170
casinos 95
castellers 206
Castellón 203
Castilian language 34
Castilla-La Mancha 63, 216

Catalan community 206
Catalonia 168, 174, 209, 211, 216
Cathedral of Santiago de Compostela 200
Cave of El Soplao 202
CEE 24
centralisation 156, 161, 162
Ceuta 63, 92
charter tourism 211–212
Chelsea FC 154
chiquilho 206
CIES Football Observatory 157
Circuito Balear 94
Citizens of the European Union and Sport 21
civil conflicts 53
Climbing World Championships 113
Club Atlético Madrid 158
Club Blanco 168
Clube de Futebol 'Os Belenenses' 156
club licenses *see* licenses
cluster analysis 115, 118, 126, 130–137, 255
coastal management 216, 219–220
coastal tourism 202
codification 233
collaboration networks 128, 130, 135
collective bargaining agreements (CBAs) 177, 179, 180, 181–183
Colombia 186n3
Columbus, Christopher 1, 12nn1–2
combat sports 204–205
commercialisation 25, 53, 91, 99, 184
Committee on Physical Education and Military Sports 237
COMPASS project 29, 33
competitions: international 12; professionalised 180; *see also individual competitions by name*
competitive balance 8, 48, 51, 141, 156, 157, 159, 162
computable general equilibrium 113
conflict: administrative 53; civil conflicts between sporting organisations 53; criminal disputes 53; dispute settlement 52–55; economic or tax 53; ethical 53; labor disputes 53
Congress of Sports Clubs (Lisbon) 15
CONI 29
Consejo Superior de Deportes see High Council for Sport/Higher Council of Sport/Higher Sports Council (CSD; Spain)

Constitutional Treaty 26
construction boom 74–75
Contador, Alberto 36
contingent valuation methodology 113, 114–115
cooperatives 134, 136
Copa del Rey 166, 170
Corporate Social Responsibility/corporate social responsibility (CSR) 133, 136, 185
corruption 27, 29, 52, 242
cosmetic and surgery services 99
Costa, Jorge Nuno Pinto da 156
Costa, Rui 154
Costa del Sol 218
cost-benefit analysis 7, 113, 114, **114**
Council of Europe 24, 26–27, 28, 80
Council of Europe, Youth, Culture and Sport 27
Council of European Sports Ministers 27
Council of Milan 25
Court of Arbitration for Sport (CAS/TAD) 50–51, 53–54, 55
COVID-19 pandemic 2, 21, 27–28, 68, 98, 101, 104, 158, 183, 186, 190, 213, 224; *Conclusions on the impact of the COVID-19 pandemic on the sports sector* 27
cremada de falles 206–207
cricket 204
criminal disputes 53
Croatia 165
CrossFit centres 100, 102
cruising 212
Cruyff, Johan 140, 168
CSD *see* High Council for Sport/Higher Council of Sport/Higher Sports Council (CSD; Spain)
Cuatro 165
Cubeiro 175
cultural diversity 25
cultural heritage 199
cultural tourism 199
Cup Winners' Cup 15
cycling 3, 36, 66, 250, 251, 255; recreational 188–189
cycling events 188–189; tours of Spain 112; *see also La Vuelta Ciclista a España*
Cyprus 123

Davis Cup (tennis) 112, 113, 222
Deaflympic Games 238
Deco 173

del Bosque, Vicente 175
democratisation 2, 14, 17, 19, 57, 58
Denmark 32, 189
Deportivo de la Coruña 170, 183
Descent of the Sella River 202–203
Desporto Escolar (sport in schools) 236
development 2, 3, 5, 7–9, 10, 12
dictatorships 14–17, 22, 168
diplomacy 31
Directorate General for Physical Education, Sport, and School Health (*Direcção-Geral de Educação Fisica, Desportos e Saúde Escolar*) 15, 18
Directorate General for Sports (DGD) 19
Directorate General for the Regulation of Gambling (Spain) 95
Discoveries 5, 34
discrimination 28, 48, 81
dispute settlement 52–55
diving 211
dog racetrack betting 86, 93
Domínguez, Marta 54
doping 25, 28, 51, 57, 58
Drais, Karl von 188

economic-mercantile conflicts 53
economics, and entrepreneurship 134
economies 34, 46; local 10, 76
Edmilson 173
education entrepreneurship 132–133
El Clasico 166
El Paso del Fuego (Fire-Walking) 207
El Quinigol 89–90, 91
Employment 21, 22, 29, 31; self- 123, 124; sport-related 24, 46, 56, 68, 179, 180, 182, 209, 236
England *see* United Kingdom
entrepreneurial orientation (EO) 132
entrepreneurship 7, 123–137; articles published in Spain and Portugal 129; by athletes 224–225, 226, 227; authors publishing research on 127–128, **127**; bibliographic coupling technique 128, 130, *131*; bibliometric analysis 125–126, 132–133, 135, 137; collaboration networks 128, *130*, 135; countries producing research on 128; data collection method 125; education and intentions of sport science students 130–131; environmental factors influencing 135, *136*; journals publishing research on 128, **130**; number of publications and articles on 126–128, *128*; orientation and innovation in sports organisations 132, 135; research on 126–137; sustainable 133–134; *see also* sport entrepreneurship
Entrepreneurship Action Plan 123
Entrepreneurship and Innovation Programme (EU) 123
entrepreneurship education 130–131
equestrian (horse riding) 253
equipped paths 201
Erasmus + program 4, 26, 27, 29–31, 33
ethical conflicts 53
Eto'o 173
EU Athletes 233
EUEFA European Football Championships, 2004 109
Eurobarometer 4, 21, 28, 31–32, 99, 123
Europa Cup, Portugal (2004) 29
Europa League 158
EuropeActive 102
European Champion Clubs' Cup 15
European Charter on Sport 6
European Club Association 233
European Club Cup 168
European Commission 28, 29, 56, 64, 123
European Convention on Human Rights 53
European Council of Niza 25
European Court of Human Rights 54
European Cultural Agreement 24
European Cultural Convention 24
European Cup 168
European Football Championship (Euro) 22
European Health & Fitness Market Report 98
European Observatory of Sport and Employment (EOSE) 28
European Solidarity Body 27
European sport certificate 24
European Sport for All Charter 10, 18, 24–25; *see also* 'sport for all'
European Trotting Union 94
European Union: Council of Education, Youth, Culture, and Sports 26; entrepreneurship in 123; financial support for sport by 30; Foundational Treaties 25; impact and actions of initiatives in sport 28–31; Ministers of Education, Culture, and Youth 25–26; Ministers of Sport 28, 31; Pierre de

Coubertin plan of action 33; Portuguese athletes in 158; promotion of sport by 4–5, 25, 33; regulatory frameworks for sport 24–28; Working Plan for Sport 27; *see also* Bosman Law/ruling
European Union Competence in the Field of Sport 29
European Week of Sport 4, 30–31, 33
European Year of Education through Sport (2004) 29
Eusebio 2
Évora, Nelson 232
exercise 64, 76; exercise apps 104, 105; *see also* physical activity
Extremadura 63

Falangism 16
family sports 103
fascism: in Portugal 15–16; in Spain 16–17; and sport 15, 16, 18–19
FC Barcelona 8, 9, 167, 222
FC Internazionale Milano 154
FC Porto 223
Federación de Deportes Autóctonos de Castilla y León 206
Federación de Juego del Palo Canario (Canarian Stick Game Federation) 204
federated sport model 246–249, *247*, **248**
federates 60–64, 66–67, 68n1; participation by gender 66–67
Fédération Internationale de Football Association (FIFA) 165
Federation of Canarian Wrestling 204
Federation of Yacht Clubs of the Cantabric 209
Felix, João 158
fencing 252
Ferreira, Eusébio da Silva 156
Festa da Malha 206
festivals 206–207
FIBA World Championships 36
FIFA 54; Disciplinary Code 54; *La Roja's* ranking in 166
Figo, Luis 2, 22, 154, 170, 232
financial ratios 250
Finland 32
Fire-Walking (*El Paso del Fuego*) 207
First European Conference on Sports (Athens 1999) 25
First European Sports Forum (1991) 25
fishing 212, 216
fishing boat competitions (*traineras*) 3, 203

fitness apps 104, 105
fitness boutiques 100, 102
fitness clubs/centres: boutique model 100, 102; business model for 101–102, 104; and consumer satisfaction 104; employees of 100, 103, 124; low-cost segment 100–101, 102, 103, 105; management of 103–104; monthly fees 100–101, 102, 103; in Portugal 100–101; studies of 103; types of 100; *see also* fitness industry
fitness industry 6–7; development of new technologies for 105; marketing strategies 99; in Portugal 98–101; professionalisation of 103; research as an axis for developing knowledge of 103–104; in Spain 101–103; sustainability and future perspectives 104–105; *see also* fitness clubs/centres
fitness instructors 100
fitness magazines 100
fitness trackers 105
FNAT (*Fundação Nacional para a Alegria no Trabalho*) 15, 19
folk games 3; *see also* traditional games and sports
Fonseca, Jorge 232
Fonseca, Paulo 154
football 8–9, 103, 113; amateur 22; broadcasting rights 161–162; European leagues 158, 162; federations 66; financial management of 250, 253; industrialisation of 161; internationalisation of 155, 160, 161, 162; as monopoly in Spain 21; North American leagues 161–162; official recognition of 177; performance ratings 255; players' unions 31; in Portugal 22, 35, 154–163; professionalisation of 156, 167, 179–181; in Spain 21, 36, 164–175; sport development ranking 253; women players 8, 179–181, 182; *see also* football clubs; football coaches; football players
Football Clube do Porto 159
football clubs 2; governing bodies 31; see also *La Liga*; *La Roja*; *other football clubs by name*
football coaches 35, 228, 229, 230, 232
football pitches 74
football players 31, 35, 140, 141, 143, 150, 152, 182, 222, 232

football pools 6, 85–89, 89
Formula 1 Grand Prix racing 35, 112, 113; European 115; of Spain 3
frameworks: administrative 219; analytical 232–242; cultural 199; of the EU 56; for football pools 87; general planning 71; institutional 140–141; labour 177; legal 5, 20, 46–55, 64, 68, 156, 182; legislative framework in 56–59; regulatory 4, 24–28, 70–71, 179, 185, 218, 219; sport as 37, 39; for sports policy 81
France 165, 166, 189; *La Vuelta* in 190; Ligue 1 154, 158–159, 162; sport governance in 242; sports financing in 238–239; Tour de France 189, 191
Franco, Francisco 17, 168
free movement 29
Fútbol Club Barcelona *see* Barça
Futebol Clube do Porto 35, 154, 156, 159
Futre, Paulo 2
futsal 35

Galicia 92, 203, 210
Gallardo 175
gambling: basketball pools 90; betting machines 92; bookmakers 91–92; *El Quinigol* 89–90, 91; fixed-odds 6, 86, 91–93, **92**; football pools 6, 85–89, 89; horse and dog racetracks 86, 93–95; horse racing pools 90–91; on jai-alai 86, 93; *La Quiniela* 87–89, 90, 91; legal betting 6, 239, 243n1; lotteries 87, 88, 89, 90, 239–240, 240, 243n1; offline 6, 86; online 6, 85–86, 91–93; online (fixed-odds) 94; online (pari-mutuel betting) 91; online (state-regulated) 87; pari-mutuel sports betting 87–91; privately operated 95; regulation of 93; in Spain 85–95
gamification 133
Gasol, Pau 11, 2, 35, 222, 224; as brand ambassador 225–226; entrepreneurship 226; social media dominance 226–227; social responsibility 226; wealth and assets 225
Gasol Foundation 226
Gaspar, Joan 168, 170
GDP, sport-related 6, 20, 46, 56, 60, 68, 87, 95, 99
gender 19, 24, 27, 31, 61, 64, 65, 66, 81, 185, 239, 242

gender equality 19, 27, 185, 239, 242
General Law of Physical Culture and Sport (Spain) 41
General-Directorate of Education 236
Germany 166, 189, 238; Bundesliga 154, 162
Gibraltar 2, 203–204
Gibraltar Cricket Board 204
Gibraltar Cricket Club 204
Giro d'Italia 189, 191
global brands 11; *see also* branding
global community 34
globalisation 5, 26, 162, 170; and sport success 34–36
golf courses 73, 74–75
golfing 250, 253, 255; federations 66–67; LPGA events 3
Gomes, Fernando 156
González, Raúl 170
good governance 11, 26–27, 52, 53, 232, 233, 238, 240–241, 242
governance: corporate 233; defined 233; organisational 233; political 234; systemic 233; *see also* good governance; sport governance
governmentalisation 57
GPS tracking devices 105
Grand Prix motorcycle racing 112
Grand Slam tennis tournaments 225
greasy pole 207
Greece 32, 123, 242
Gross Gaming Revenue (GGR) 86–87, 93
Grotto of the Marvels 202
Guardiola, Pep 174
Gulley, David 87
gymnasiums 100, 124; *see also* sport clubs; sport facilities
gymnastics 66–67, 252, 255

handball 66, 112, 251, 255
health 2, 16, 17, 24, 26–28, 29, 31, 32, 37, 47, 48, 49, 59, 76–77, 99, 101, 103, 104, 105, 110, 188, 226, 234, 240; and wellness 105
health clubs 100; *see also* fitness clubs/centres
healthy lifestyle 80
heart rate monitors 105
Henry 173
Henry the Navigator (Henrique de Portugal) 1
Heras, Roberto 54

Hernández, Xavi 173, 174
High Council for Sport/Higher Council of Sport/Higher Sports Council (CSD; Spain) 40–41, 43, 57, 58, 68, 88, 178, 179–180, 181, 248; Annual Report 246
hiking 10, 200
Hipódromo de La Zarzuela 90–91, 94
HistCite statistical software 125
hockey 251
Holmes Place 99–100
homophobia 28
horse racetrack betting 86, 93–95, **95**
horse racing pools 90–91
horse riding (equestrian) 253
human rights 53–54
Hungary 239
hunting 66

Iberian Peninsula 1–3; as tourist destination, 9–10; *see also* Portugal (Portuguese Republic); Spain
Iberic Cup 161
ice sports 251, 256n5
Iglesias, Enrique 224, 227
immigrants/immigration 4, 81; *see also* athletes; Latin American players; migration
INATEL (National Institute of Portugal for the Use of Workers' Leisure Time) 19
inclusion policies 26–27, 29, 31, 33, 110, 133, 224, 238
Induráin, Miguel 2
INEF (*Instituto Nacional de Educação Física*, National Institute of Physical Education) 15, 19
infrastructure 18, 59, 70–71, 72, 110, 115, 200, 201; coastal 209; creation/construction of 70, 74, 75, 77, 79, 240; for cycling 190, 193, 196; investment in 71–73, 190; lack of 16, 22, 190; for nautical sports 10, 209, 210, 216, 218, 219
ingude altxatzea 205
Iniesta, Andrés 173, 174, 175
innovation 7, 124, 132; *see also* intrapreneurship
input-output methods 7, 113, **113**
Instituto Portugués do Desporto e Juventude (IPDJ) 57, 58, 60, 68
integration 4
Inter Milan 223
international associations 50
international competitions 12
International Federation of Football History and Statistics (IFFHS) 171
international federations (IFs) 233
International Law 49
International Olympic Committee 43, 50
International Paralympic Committee (IPC) 238
internationalisation 155, 160, 161, 162
interval training 105
interventionism 11, 36, 37, 44, 71, 232, 234, 242
intrapreneurship 7, 124–125, 134, 137
Investment Initiatives in Response to Coronavirus 27
ISEF (Higher Institute of Physical Education) 19
Italy 165, 166; Calcio 171; Giro d'Italia 189, 191; Serie A 154, 162; sports financing in 238–239

jai-alai 86, 93
Jardel, Mário 156
jet skiing 216
jogo da malha 206
jogo do pau (stick game) 205
judo 232, 250, 251, 255
Juego del Palo (Game of the Stick) 204
Juventus 35

Keita 173
Kingdom of Spain *see* Spain
Kubala, Ladislao 140

labor disputes 53
La Buelta a España 3
La Liga 3, 8–9, 22, 36, 38, 154–163, 165, 184, 223; attendance statistics 158–159; 'Buçaco' meeting 155–156; competitions organised by 177–178; economic impact of 159; e-league 159; European players in 144; 'First' vs. 'Second' League 155; foreign players in 140–152; frequency of arrival of foreign players 147–150, *149*; future of 160–162; history of 155–157; impact on the development of football 157–160; institutional framework 140–141; media impact of 159; official strategic plan 160–161; popularity of 160; 'Presidents' Movement' 155; probability of foreign players playing

for national team 150–152, **151**; revenue 159
LaLiga Santander 177
LaLiga Smartbank 177
L'Alqueria del Basket 113
L'Angliru 195
Laporta, Joan 168, 170, 173
La Quiniela 6, 87–89, 90, 91
La Raya (A Raia) 56
La Rioja 63, 91, 92, 93
La Roja (Spanish Men's National Football Team) 8, 9, 159; background and evolution 164–167; management and leadership 174–175; players by team of origin *173*; position in FIFA ranking *166*
Latin American players: by age group 146, *146*; evolution of arrival at Spanish football 144, 146–152; frequency of arrival in La Liga 147–150, *149*; in Portuguese clubs 35; by position on field *145*; probability of playing for national team 150–152, **151**; proportion of capped players *147*; relative frequencies by country **143**; in Spanish clubs 8, 140–152
La Vuelta Ciclista a España 9–10, 188–196; economic impact of 192, 195; host communities 190–191; impact on local communities 191–192; media impact of 191–192; social perception of 193–194; socio-economic impact of 193–194; starting or finishing location of a stage according to number of inhabitants 191, *191*; tourist impact of 194–195
Law 1/90 19
Law 21/2007 of Legal and Economic Regime of the Ports of Andalusia 218
Law of Sport (Spain) 41, 42, 43
LBSD (Basic Law of the Sports System) 19, 50, 156, 235
leadership 11, 104, 170, 174–175, 229
League 1, football Portugal (Portuguese League I) 38
League 2, football Portugal (Portuguese League II) 38
League Cup (Portugal) 156
Legal Regime of Sport Federations (Portugal) 240–241
legal sporting order 48–50
legalization of sports betting 93
leisure boating 212
leisure nautical activities 211–215

Leonese wrestling *(aluche)* 205
Levante 183
Levitt, Theodore 34
lex sportiva 46, 50–51
licenses 6, 48, 53–54, 177, **178**, 180, 211, 247, 254; club 29; for nautical sports 215–216, *215–216*, 218
Liga Ellas 180, 184
Liga Endesa 178
Liga Portugal see *La Liga*
Ligue 1 (France) 154, 158–159, 162
Lisbon Agenda 29
Lisbon Treaty 24, 26, 33, 48
Lithuania 128, 131
local economies 10, 76
Local Global Citation Scores (TLGCS) 125
Local Investment State Fund (FEIL) 75
Local Schemes for Sports Facilities and Services 71–72
Lopes, Carlos 232
Lototurf 90
lotteries 87, 88, 89, 90, 239–240, 243n1
Lotto Turf 95
Louis-Schmeling Paradox 165
LPGA golf events 3

mainstreaming 82–83
malha 3, 206
management: direct 42, 211; indirect 42, 211; New Public model 78; relational model 76, 82; of stress 99; *see also* sports management
Manchester United 35, 223, 227
Manona, Patrícia 232
Maradona, Diego 140
marathon 232
marinas 10, 209, 210–211, 212, 218
marina tourism 212
maritime tourism 212
marketing strategies 20, 53, 99, 136, 229; for Liga Portugal 161
Márquez, Marc 35, 173
Mascherano 173
Masters 1000 (tennis) 112
Matutes Prats, Abel 224, 226
Mediterranean Games 112
Melilla 63
Mendes, Jorge 227
Messi, Leo 140, 173, 174
migration 81; international 152; *see also* immigrants/immigration
Military Sports (in Portugal) 237

Ministry of Culture and Sport (Spain) 40, 57, 189
MLB 162
Mocidade Portuguesa Feminina (Portuguese Female Youth Organisation) 15
Mocidade Portuguesa (Portuguese Male Youth Organisation) 15
moixiganga 206
móndidas 207
money laundering 29
Montaña-Ribera 205
Monteiro, Telma 232
Moorish tradition 206
Morisco Games of Aben Humeya 206
Moscardó, General 16
Mota, Rosa 232
MotoGP 35; World Championship 113
motorboating 216
motorcycling races 3, 35, 112
motoring 66
mountaineering 66
Mourinho, José 11, 22, 35, 154, 223, 232; communication management 229; leadership 229; personal brand 229; special collaborations 230; wealth and assets 230
muixeranga 206
Municipal Sports Services (Spain) 70, 76–77, 82
Murcia 91, 93

Nadal, Rafael 2, 11, 35, 222; contribution to sport tourism 225; entrepreneurship 224–225; personal brand and sponsorship 223–224; social responsibility 224; wealth and assets 224
National Anti-Doping Organisations 39, 233, 236
National Association of Clubs (Portugal) 155
National Basketball Association (NBA) 35, 162, 222, 226
National Census of Sports Facilities 18, 19
National Collegiate Athletic Association (NCAA) 246
National Council of Sport (Portugal) (*Conselho Nacional do Desporto*) 58
National Delegation of Physical Education and Sports (DNEFyD; *Delegación Nacional de Educación Física y Deportes*) 16; see also National Sports Delegation (Spain)
National Football League (NFL) 162
National Governing Bodies (NGBs) 237–238, 239; good governance in 240–241; internal disciplinary proceedings 241–242; and social responsibility 242; and sport governance 232–243
national governments 20, 57–58, 233
National Health Survey (Spain) 77
National Institute for the Use of Free Time (NATEL) 238
National Institute of Physical Education (INEF; *Instituto Nacional de Educación Física*) 16
National Institute of Sport (NIS; Portugal) 235
National Lottery 88
National Network of High-performance Centres 38
National Olympic Committee (NOC; Portugal) 235
National Organization of Spanish blind people (ONCE) lottery 88
National Plan for Ethics in Sport (PNED) 236
National Professional Football League (Spain) 43, 88
National Sport Act (Portugal) 58
National Sport Acts (Spain) 57–59
national sport federations (NSFs) 233
National Sporting Organisations (NSOs) 237
National Sports Charter 19
National Sports Council (Portugal) 39
National Sports Delegation (Spain) 16, 17; see also National Delegation of Physical Education and Sports (DNEFyD; *Delegación Nacional de Educación Física y Deportes*)
National sports federations (NSF) 248–250; groups of 254; initiatives for improving financial structure 254–255; performance rankings 252, 253; see also sport federations
National Sports Meeting (ENDO) 18
natural supplementation products 99
nautical clubs 212
nautical sports 10, 209–220; berth points 211; construction of nautical facilities 216, 218–219; different types of licenses for 216; licenses for 215–216, 215; licenses in autonomous communities

217; recreational infrastructures of Spain 210–211; strategies and tools to guarantee sustainability 216, 218–220; and the tourist industry 209, 211–215
nautical sports marinas *see* marinas
nautical tourism 211–215; boat chartering 211; cruises 211; nautical tourism ports 211
naval stations 10
Navarra 67
Navarre 91, 92, 93
NBA (National Basketball Association) 35, 162, 222, 226
neoliberalism 82
netball 203–204
Netherlands 166, 189, 190, 209
New Public Management 78
New World exploration 1
NFL (National Football League) 162
non-revisability of technical decisions of referees 52
Núñez, José 168
nutrition 99

ocean cruising 212
Olaso, José Antonio Elola 16
Olympic Committee of Portugal (OCP) 38, 238
Olympic Games 38; Athens (2004) 29; Barcelona (1992) 19–20, 36, 88, 110, 190; Beijing (2008) 222; Los Angeles (1984) 235; Portuguese participation in 232, 235, 238; Seoul (1988) 235
Organic Law of the Ministry of National Education (Portugal) 18
organisations: national 68; private 37–38, **40**, 42–43, **42**; public sector 38–39, 40–42, **40**, **42**
Osasuna 167, 171
outdoor sports 6, 201

paddle 103
paddle surf 202
Paiva Walkways 201
par conditio (principle of parity) 51–52, 55
Paraguay 144
Paralympic Committee of Portugal (PCP) 38, 238
Paralympic Games 38, 238
participatory sport 235
patron saint festivities 207

Pau Gasol Academy 226
Pechstein case 54
Penicheiro, Ticha 232
pentathlon 251
perception 7, 103, 115, 136; social 193, 194
Pérez, Florentino 168, 170, 173
personal brand 223–224, 226, 229; *see also* branding
personalised training 99, 100
Peyroteo 156
PGA golf events 3
physical activity 80; benefits of 99; and sport policy 82–83
physical education 18, 20
Physical Education Law (Ley de Educación Física) 16, 17–18
Physical Exercise Technicians 100
Pierre de Coubertin plan of action 29
Pilates 99, 102
pilota valenciana (Valencian pilota) 203
Pimenta, Fernando 232
Piqué 173
player transfers 29
Players Union (Portugal) 155
players' unions 155, 181–183
Poland 165
policymakers 3, 56
popular culture 4, 14, 34
Porto 2
Portugal (Portuguese Republic) 1–2; border with Spain 56; Carnation Revolution 234; Constitution of the Portuguese Republic (CRP) 37, 49, 232, 234; economic impact of sports in 46; end of dictatorship in 14–16, 37; entrepreneurship in 123–124; *Estado Novo* 234; Europa Cup (2004) 29; European Championships 35; fitness industry in 98–101; historical background of sport in 14–22; *La Vuelta* in 190; legal framework for sports industry 46–55; legislative framework in 58–59; levels of sport participation 32; official encouragement of sport in 18–19, 21–22; Portuguese Constitution 56; Portuguese legal system 49–50; professional football in 8–9; public sport expenditure 59–60, **59**; socio-cultural background of sport in 14–22; sport expenditure in 21; sport governance in 11, 22, 232–243; sport participation

levels in 21–22, 60–67, **61**, 62, 64, **65**; sport systems in 34–39, **40**, 43–44; sporting events in 109; sports disputes and arbitration in 54–55; sports organisation in 56–58; traditional games and sports 206; World Championships 35; *see also La Liga*
Portuguese Anti-Doping Authority (ADoP) 236
Portuguese Basketball Federation 237
Portuguese Confederation of Culture and Recreation Associations 38
Portuguese Confederation of Football Clubs 155
Portuguese Football Federation (FPF) 22, 156–157, 161; cup 158
Portuguese Football league 8
Portuguese Institute for Sport and Youth (IPDJ) 236, 240
Portuguese Institute of Sports 235
Portuguese language 34
Portuguese League of Football Clubs 8
Portuguese Olympic Committee 57
Portuguese Paralympic Committee 57
Portuguese Professional Football League (*Liga Portugal*) see *La Liga*
Portuguese Sport Confederation 237–238
Portuguese Way 200
Portuguese Winter Sport Federation 237
Premier League (England) 154, 155, 158, 159, 162, 171, 223
'Presidents' Movement' 155
preventive medicine 99
Primera División PRO 179
Primera División RFEF 179
Primera Iberdrola (1st Women's Division) 179, 180, 183; attendances **184**
principle of parity (*par conditio*) and fairness in sports 51–52
PRISMA diagram *126*
pro competitione principle 51, 55
professional sports 58; basketball 222; as business 46; as commodity and spectacle 19; cricket 204; cycling 188–195; football 8–9, 85, 132, 140, 141, 155–157, 160–163, 168, **169**, 173, 179–184; games of force and precision 205; promotion of 67, 234, 235; regulation/governance of 20, 22, 25, 37–38, 42–43, 48, 49, 50, 53, 58, 78, 237; Spanish leagues 43; women's 8–9, 177–186

propaganda, fascist 14
public funding 6, 11, 20, 31, 71, 132, 186, 232, 238, 240, 245, 246
Public Health department (Spain) 77
Public Sport Organisations 38
Public Sports Utility (Portugal) 50
public-private partnerships (PPPs) 27, 102–103, 105
Purchena (Almería) 206
purity of competition 52
Puyol 173

QEQ (European Qualifications Chart in the sports sector) 28
Quintuple Plus 90, 91, 95

racism 24, 26, 29, 31, 41, 58, 242
Rafael Nadal Academy 223, 224–225
Rafael Nadal Foundation 224
rafting 201
Ramos, Sergio 2
Raul 2
Rayo Vallecano 183
RCD Espanol 170
Real Betis 170
Real Club de Regatas of Santander 209
Real Club Deportivo de Bilbao 209
Real Club Náutico de San Sebastián 209
Real Federación Española de Futbol (RFEF) 164, 175, 179, 180, 181, 184
Real Madrid FC 2, 8, 9, 35, 151, 154, 159, 165, 167, 179, 223; comparison with Barça 167–168, 170–171; official titles 169; rivalry with Barça 166–167, 168
Real Sociedad 171, 183
Real Zaragoza 170
Recuenco Cave 202
referees, non-revisability of technical decisions of 52
refugees 31
regattas 203, 209
Regional Associations 237
regional base associations 38, 39
Regulation of Gambling (DGO) market 86
residents, local 70, 110, 115, 188, 190, 192–195
Reto Iberdrola (2nd Women's Division) 180
RFEF see Real Federación Española de Futbol (RFEF)
river-based sports 202–203; river cruising 212

Ronaldinho (Ronaldo de Assis Moreira) 173
Ronaldo, Cristiano 2, 11, 22, 35, 140, 154, 159, 170, 222–223, 232; big data as part of his strategy 227–228; control of social networks 228; entrepreneurship 227; social responsibility 228; sponsorship of 228; wealth and assets 227
rowing 216, 251
Royal Decree 1006 178, 182
Royal Decree on Sports associations 54
Royal Spanish Football Federation (RSFF) 246
rugby 66, 252
Russia 166

S. L. é Benfica 15, 154, 156, 158, 159
SAD Law 167
SADs 182
Sáez, Iñaki 166
sailing 66, 112, 209, 216, 250, 253, 255
sailing tourism 211–212
Salazar, António de Oliveira 15
San Pedro Manrique (Soria) 207
sanctions, immediate enforcement of 52
Santa Casa da Misericordia (Lisbon) 240
Santiago Bernabéu stadium 168
Scandinavia 238
Schools for Physical Education Instructors 19
scientific research 57
Scott, Frank 87
Secretary of State for Youth and Sport (Portugal) 38, 236
sedentarism 31, 76–77
SELAE (*Sociedad Estatal Loterías y Apuestas del Estado*) 86, 88, 89, 90, 93, 95
Sella River 202
Serie A (Italy) 154, 162
Sevilla FC 2, 183
Shakhtar Donetsk FC 154
shooting 253
Show Racism the Red Card project 31
Silva, Emanuel 232
skating 66–67, 113
Skiing: world championships 112; World Cup 109
Ski World Cup 109
slot machines 95
Slovakia 123, 165
small and medium-sized enterprises (SMEs) 134

smart watches 105
soccer *see* football
social capital 79, 81, 110, 118
social cohesion 25, 59, 80–81, 110
social entrepreneurship 132–133
social exclusion 80
Social Games 239–240, 243n1
social media: athletes' presence on 11, 226–228; and *La Vuelta* 192; and *Liga Portugal* 22, 159
social responsibility 11, 79, 80–81, 230, 240; of athletes 224, 226, 228; corporate (CSR) 133, 136, 185; of National Governing Bodies (NGBs) 242
Sociedad Estatal de Participaciones Industriales (SEPI) 91
Spain 1–2; autonomous communities in 39–42, 44, **210**; border with Portugal 56; Civil War 16; coastline of **210**; economic impact of sports in 46; end of dictatorship in 16–17; entrepreneurship in 123–124; fitness industry in 101–103; historical background of sport in 14–22; increase in number of athletes 17, 19; legal framework for sports industry 46–55; legislation regarding sport 19–20; legislative framework in 58–59; official encouragement of sport in 17–18; official support for sport in 20–21; political instrumentalisation of sport in 22; public sport expenditure 59–60, **59**; Royal Decree of 21 April (2020) 21; socio-cultural background of sport in 14–22; Spanish Constitution 17, 39, 41, 56; Spanish legal system 48–50; sport federations in 245–256; sport participation levels in 60–67, **61**, **62**, **64**, **65**; sport system in **42**; sport systems in 34–36, 39–44, 43–44; sporting events in 109; sports disputes and arbitration in 54; sports organisation in 56–58; structure and management of sport in 246–249; World and European Championships in 36, 190
Spanish Agency for the Protection of Health in Sport 41
Spanish Cup 223
Spanish Federation of Associations of Marinas and Tourist Ports 210
Spanish football league *see La Liga*
Spanish Footballers' Association (AFE) 181, 183

Spanish Global Sport Foundation
  (*Fundación España Deporte Global*) 21
Spanish Men's National Football Team see
  La Roja
Spanish Olympic Committee (*Comité
  Olympic Español*, COE) 16, 43
Spanish Olympic Sports Association
  (ADO programme) 20, 88, 246–247,
  253, 256n3
Spanish 'Open' Winter Masters Swimming
  Championship of Pontevedra 114
Spanish Paralympic Committee (*Comité
  Paralímpico Español*), 43
Spanish Racetracks Association 94
Spanish Sport Federation 178
Spanish Sports Council 144
Spanish Tourism Plan Horizon 2020 219
spatial planning 70–75, 71–74
specificity 46–48, 51, 55
spectacularization politics 15
spectator sport 14, 19, 207
Spectators-Subsidies-Sponsor-Local
  (SSSL) model 239–240
spectator violence 28
speleology 201–202
spinning 99
sponsorship 136; of athletes 53, 223–224,
  228, 230; of clubs and events 46, 133,
  136, 154, 157, 247, **248**; of women's
  sports 178–180, 183–186
sport: access to 20–21, 235; amateur 58;
  assimilated leagues 178; as business
  11–12; as cultural, educational and
  social area 78–79; cultural impact
  of 3; as culture 19; decentralisation
  of 70–71; democratisation of 14, 17,
  19–20, 57, 76; as diplomatic tool 31;
  economic dimension of 29; economic
  impact of 2, 3, 7, 24, 29, 46; educational
  functions of 25, 68; and the elderly 80;
  elite 235, 239; in the EU 27; family
  103; functions of 2; gambling on
  85–95; good governance in 240–241;
  governmentalisation of 57; Iberian
  (context), 4–5; individual vs. collective
  255; international 26; interventionism
  in 232, 234, 242; legal frameworks for 5,
  47–48; levels of participation in 32–33;
  literature on 3; municipal 70–71, 78–81;
  and national identity 2; organisation of
  29; participatory 235; political impact
  of 3; popular 20; and popular culture 4;
  principles of 51–52; private expenditure
  on 67; promotion of 20, 24–26, 31,
  40, 42, 67–68; prosumers of 81; public
  spending on 20, **59**; pyramid structure
  of 30; regulatory frameworks for 4,
  24–28, 68, 70–71; as right of citizens 18,
  25, 56–57; rural 205–206; separation
  from politics 78; social aspect of 25, 29,
  31, 47, 135–136; social impact of 3, 7,
  24, 32–33; in Spain and Portugal 2–3;
  specificity of 47–48; sport development
  goal 251–253; state support for 37–38;
  success in competitions 251–253;
  and the tourist industry 3; used for
  propaganda purposes 78–79; value for
  youth 15, 24, 25–26; as vehicle for
  equality 81; *see also* nautical sports;
  professional sports; traditional games
  and sports
sport agents 37, 44n1
sport citizenship 19–20
sport clubs 43; amateur 239
sport consumers 7, 81, 85, 103–105, 161,
  162, 185
Sport Confederation of Portugal 38
sport economics 3, 5–6
Sport England 29
sport entrepreneurship 7, 123–137;
  sustainable 133–134; *see also*
  entrepreneurship
sport equipment 178, 189
sport facilities: accessibility of 81–83;
  building boom 74–75; built under
  fascism 15; change of habits and model
  76; in the city and territory 80–81;
  construction and management of
  67–68; infrastructure planning for
  71–72, 72; investment in 79; lack of
  planning for 72–73; maintenance and
  cost of running 75; move towards sports
  services and physical activity 76–78;
  National Stadium (Lisbon) 15; network
  of 83; political benefits of 75; public
  investment in 6; recession and windfall
  75; regional vs. local planning 73–74;
  regulatory frameworks 70–71; in Spain
  16, 18, 19, 70–83; spatial planning
  for 71
sport fandom, and women's sports 184–185
sport federations 11–12, 38, 43, 246–249,
  247, **248**; comparison of participation
  levels 60–64, **61**, 62; financial

management of 249–250, **251**; financing for 246–248, 247, **248**; initiatives for improving financial structure 254–255; legal status of 245; methodology of study 249–250; performance rankings 252, 253; regulation of 57–58; results of study 250–255; Spanish 245–256; sport development goal 249, 250–251, **251**; success in competitions 249, **251**; *see also* National sports federations (NSF)
sport fishing 66
'sport for all' 17, 18, 19, 20, 24, 28, 76, 235, 237
Sport Foundation (Portugal) 38, 238
sport governance 11–12, 232–243; analytic framework 233–234; organisational (in Portugal) 233, 240–242; political (in Portugal) 234, 234–236; in Portugal (pyramid structure) 237; sports financing (in Portugal) 238–240; systemic (in Portugal) 233, 236–238
sport habits 18, 32, 72, 76–77, 226
Sporting Clube de Portugal 15, 154, 156, 159
sporting divide 20–21
sporting events 10, 26; in Andorra 109; economic effects of 109–118; environmental impacts of 115; integrity and transparency in 26–27; in Portugal 109; positive/negative impacts of 110, **111–112**, 115; residents' perceptions of **116–117**, **118**; social 133; social effects of 109–118; in Spain 109; *see also individual events by name*
Sport Institute of Portugal 38
sport law 3, 5, 46–55; general public standards 49; legal sporting order 48–50; legislative framework 58–59; in Portugal 49–50; principles of 55; private standards 49; in Spain 48–50; specific public standards 49
Sport Law of 1990 177–178, 179, 185
Sport Lisboa e Benfica 35
sport marketing 136; *see also* marketing strategies
sport participation: and public policy 6; in sport federations 60–64, **61**, 62, 64, **65**; *see also* athletes; women
sport planning 76, 79
sport policy 3; challenges of the new agenda 79–80; changes in 83; local 79; mainstreaming and networks 81–83;

municipal 81–82; and the promotion of physical activity 82; public 79–80; strengthening 78–79
sport practice 5, 34, 37
sport promotion 20, 24–26, 31, **40**, 42, 67–68
Sports Activities Support Complex (SASC) 235
sports betting *see* gambling
sports centres 73, 74; *see also* fitness clubs/centres
sport science students 130–131, 133, 135
Sports Development Fund (Portugal) 18, 19
sport services 58, 67; online 104
sports events: host communities 7, 109–110, 115, 190–191, 193, 196; with public interest 239; sponsorship of 46, 53, 133, 136, 154, 157, 247, **248**; and sport tourism 9–10
Sports Facilities Schemes 71–73; for the Autonomous Communities 71–72
sports financing: elite 239–240; in Portugal 238–240
Sports Foundation (Portugal) 238
sports heroes 4, 11
sports industry: legal framework for in Portugal 46–55; legal framework for in Spain 46–55; in Spain 21
Sports Institute 19
sports management 3; adaptation of 83, 98, 101, 102–103, 238; brand 162; club/team 154, 155, 165, 175, 186; coastal 216; communication 229; comparison of 169–171; environmental 218; financial 12, 101, 250–254; of football 38, 159, 160, 161, 162; of marinas 211, 218, 219; municipal 80; organisational 124, 233; professionalisation of 156; in Spain and Portugal 3–4, 5, 246–255; of sport facilities 7, 41, 68, 124; training in 99; variables in 132; women in 27
sports organisations: alignment with regional governments 236; entrepreneurship and innovation in 132; good governance in 240–241; non-profit 29, 37–38, 57–58, 68, 232, 237, 240, 248, 250; private sector 37–38, 57, 58, 76; public sector 57–58, 76
sportspeople taking risks 52
sports sanctions, immediate enforcement of 52

Sport Studies and Training Centre (SSTC; Portugal) 235
Sport System Act (LBSD) 19, 50, 156, 235
sport tourism: and *Basque Pelota* 10; and *Camino de Santiago* 10; and *La Vuelta España* 9–10, 194–195; Rafael Nadal and 225; and sports events 9–10; and *Valencian Pilota* 10
squid jigging 212
stadiums 73
stakeholders 5, 11, 34, 36, 44n1, 46, 48, 50, 53, 90, 155, 159, 162, 186, 232, 233, 235, 237, 241, 242, 249
State Commission against Violence, Racism, Xenophobia, and Intolerance in Sport (Spain) 41
state interventionism *see* interventionism
statistics 28, 46, 56, 61, 65, 67, 92, 124, 142, 171
Statutes of Autonomy 91
Stefano, Alfredo di 140
stress management 99
Suñol, Josep 168
Super Cup 223
Superior Council on Sport or Autonomous Communities (Spain) 50
Support Plan for Olympic Sport (ADO) 20, 88, 246–247, 253, 256n3
surfing 212, 216
Survey of Sports Habits in Spain 18, 76
sustainability, in sports entrepreneurship 133–134, 136
Sweden 32, 165
swimming 253, 255; championship events 114; federations 66–67
swimming pools 74, 103
Switzerland 165, 238

table tennis 66, 253
Tacon 183
taekwondo 251, 255
tax conflicts 53
television, and sport 15
television rights 53, 154–155, 162, 166, 184
tennis 35, 103, 250, 251, 255; ATP tennis tour 3; Davis Cup 112, 113, 222; federations 66; Grand Slam tournaments 225; Masters 112; Rafael Nadal 223–225; Women's Tennis Championship 114
tennis courts 74

Torres 175
Total Global Citation Score (TGCS) 125
Tottenham Hotspur FC 154, 223
Tour de France 189, 191
Touré, Yaya 173
Tour of Portugal (*Volta a Portugal*) 3
tourism/tourist industry: beach tourism 199; charter tourism 211–212; coastal tourism 202; cultural tourism 199; and cycling 195; international tourism 213–214, *213*, *214*; and *La Vuelta* 188, 194–195; marina tourism 212; maritime tourism 212; nautical tourism 209, 211–215; social impact of 109–110; Spanish tourists 213–214, *214*; speleological tourism 201–202; and sport 3, 26; and traditional games and sports 199–207; yachting tourism 211–212
town planning 71–73, 81, 82
traditional games and sports: ball games 203–204; combat sports 204–205; games of force and precision 205–206; paths, trails and greenways 200; speleological tourism 201–202; and the tourist industry 199–207; in traditions and festivals 10, 206–207; *via ferratas* and equipped paths 201; water sports 202–203
traditions 10, 206–207
traineras 3, 203
Treaty of Amsterdam 25
Treaty of Lisbon 24, 26, 33, 48
Treaty of Maastricht 24
Treaty of Rome 24
Treaty of Tordesillas/Tordesilhas 5, 34
Treaty on the Functioning of the European Union 26, 48
triathlon 251, 255
triple jump 232
txinga erutea 205

UCI WorldTour 189
UEFA *see* Union of European Football Associations (UEFA)
UK Sport 29
unemployment 2, 7, 99, 123
UNESCO World Heritage sites 199
Union Cycliste Internationale (UCI) 189
Union of European Football Associations (UEFA) 31, 165, 175, 179; Champions League 35, 90, 158, 162, 166, 167,

168, 171, 223; club coefficients **172**; EURO 154; Europa League 35, 171; European Football Championship 90, 114, 157–158; League of Nations 232; Super Cup 35
Unipublic 189
United Kingdom 166, 233; Manchester United 223, 227; nautical sports in 209; Premier League (England) 154, 155, 158, 159, 162, 171, 223; Tottenham Hotspur FC 223
United States 246
Universal Declaration of Human Rights 53
University Sport Federation (Portugal) 237
Uruguay 144, 165

Valdés 173
Valencia 7, 203, 206, 209, 211
Valencia CF 165, 166, 170, 171
Valencia Marathon 113
Valencian clubs 172–173
Valencian Institute of Economic Research (IVIE) 113
Valencian pilota (*pilota valenciana*) 10, 92, 203
value promise 11
Velá de Santa Ana (Sevilla) 207
via ferratas 201
Vicente Ferrer Foundation 224
Vidal 173
Vila-Real 171
Villas-Boas, André 154
Vocaesport 28
volleyball 66–67, 253
Volta a Portugal (cycling) 3
volunteers/volunteering 29, 32, 76, 110
Volvo Ocean Race 113
VOS viewer software 126

WADA 233
walking 10, 200
water skiing 216
water sports 202–203, 212
Wearable Fitness Technology 105
Web of Sciences (WoS) 125, 128, 133, 137
weightlifting 253, 255
weight training 99, 105
White Book on Sport 29
winter sports 251, 256n6
Winter Universiade 114

women: as athletes 179; basketball players 182–183; as brand endorsers 185; as fans 185; federated 62–63, 62, 66–67; and the fitness industry 99, 100; and the football industry 8, 9; levels of sport participation 32; in management and coaching posts 27; as media personalities 185; participating in sports 22, 31; and the professionalisation of sport 177–186; team sport licenses in Spain **178**; team sports for 177–186; youth organisations for 15; *see also* women's leagues
women's leagues: attendances **184**; collective bargaining agreements (CBAs) 181–183; economic sustainability of 183–185; professionalisation of 179–181, 186n3; in Spain 177–179
Women's Tennis Championship 114
World Anti-Doping Agency (WADA) 50
World Cup 110; (1966) 15; Mexico (1970) 144; Real Madrid 166; South Africa (2010) 36, 148, 149, 167, 175; Spain (1982) 88, 148, 149, 166
World Health Organization (WHO) 65, 77
World Lottery Association (WLA) 89
World Roller Speed Skating Championships 113
wrestling 253; Canarian 204; *jogo do pau* 205; Leonese 205

xenophobia 31, 41, 58, 242
XV Spanish National Championship of Beach-Volley 114
XVIII Spanish Spring Open Absolute Swimming Championship 114

yacht clubs 209
yachting tourism 211–212
Yazalde 156
Yearbook of Sports Statistics 124
yoga studios 102
youth: public policies for 2, 18, 25–28, 29, 31, 38, 57, 123, 234; and sport 24, 25, 28, 31, 236, 240; unemployed 123; youth academies 168, 173; youth teams 151, 170, 173
youth organisations 15

Zidane, Zinedine 170

Printed in the USA
CPSIA information can be obtained
at www.ICGtesting.com
LVHW021734041124
795688LV00040B/1232